The Qur'an and the

C000102291

Ramon Harvey

EDINBURGH
University Press

Edinburgh University Press is one of the leading university presses in the UK. We publish academic books and journals in our selected subject areas across the humanities and social sciences, combining cutting-edge scholarship with high editorial and production values to produce academic works of lasting importance. For more information visit our website: edinburghuniversitypress.com

Edinburgh University Press Ltd
The Tun – Holyrood Road
12 (2f) Jackson's Entry
Edinburgh EH8 8PJ

First published in hardback by Edinburgh University Press 2018

Typeset in 10.5/12.5 Times New Roman by
IDSUK (DataConnection) Ltd, and
printed and bound in Great Britain by
CPI Group (UK) Ltd, Croydon CR0 4YY

A CIP record for this book is available from the British Library

ISBN 978 1 4744 0329 0 (hardback)
ISBN 978 1 4744 5275 5 (paperback)
ISBN 978 1 4744 1719 8 (webready PDF)
ISBN 978 1 4744 1720 4 (epub)

Contents

Foreword by M. A. S. Abdel Haleem

The current volume is a very significant study of the Qur'an. It deals with one of its core themes: justice. As the Qur'an itself states, the pursuit of human justice was a main objective of the various prophets sent by God: 'We sent our messengers with clear signs, the Scripture and the Balance, so that people might uphold justice' (Q. 57:25).

The academic study of the Qur'an is a flourishing field, and numerous studies have appeared in recent years of its history, theology, law, and various historical interpretations, but the central issue of justice in the Qur'an does not seem to receive the attention it deserves, and that this book captures.

The Qur'an and the Just Society deals with basic issues such as: what is justice? How is it realised in society? This is not a mere theoretical discussion, but rather an exploration of real situations in the Qur'an. The Qur'an itself was not revealed as a book of theoretical ideas but primarily comments on actual situations involving Muslims in the societies of Mecca and Medina in the seventh century CE. The Qur'an comments on moral questions in context, setting general principles to be followed. This book treats justice in the same way, discussing politics, peace treaties and alliances, jihad and jizya, and then moving on to address distributive justice, including trade, prohibition of usury, alms, war booty, marriage, and inheritance. The final part deals with corrective justice: public and private crimes.

A distinguishing feature of this book is the author's deep and intimate knowledge of the unique Arabic language and style of the Qur'an, which is crucial for proper understanding and judgement, especially when dealing with the issue of hermeneutics in Chapter 3. Without an understanding of intra-textuality, semantics, syntax-pragmatics, textual structure, and socio-historical context, readers of and writers about the Qur'an are likely to fall into the problem of atomistic rather than holistic interpretation. For instance, the author points out distinctive nuances between the Qur'anic deployment of *'adl* and *qisṭ*, both important words for justice. He also uses the above hermeneutic principles to show that the Qur'an consistently affirms meaningful just relationships between members of the Medinan Muslim community and non-Muslim Arabians in all parts of social life: political alliances, trade, marriages, witnessing bequests, and even compensation for manslaughter.

This insightful and timely book leads the reader on an exploratory journey through the various manifestations of the objective of divine scripture, 'so that people may uphold justice'.

For God and the Messenger
li-llāhi wa-li-l-rasūl

Preface

In front of the Kaʿba, I am struck by the nature of time. The centuries that have passed since the lifetime of the Prophet Muḥammad seem flattened like the impossibly sheer silk walls of the House of God. Although the mosque complex is a flurry of construction, the Kaʿba itself stands imperiously. Worshippers move in concentric rings around it much as ever – the calm in the eye of the storm engulfing the Muslim world, perhaps.

The rituals associated with a visit to the Kaʿba have survived the ravages of time in a way that the social institutions of classical Islamic civilisation palpably have not. Likewise, the waves of people circling around and around the black cube, representing the totality of human cultures, bear powerful witness to the enduring impact of the Qur'an, the scripture that impels pilgrimage to this location.

This book is motivated by the Qur'anic pledge for perpetual relevance. In an unfair world in dispute over the nature of justice, I invite contemplation of the Qur'an's vision for the just society and its offer of principles that transcend time.

Ramon Harvey
14 Jumādā al-Ākhira 1437/23 March 2016
Mecca

Acknowledgements

This book started life as a PhD thesis submitted to the Department of the Near and Middle East in the School of Oriental and African Studies (SOAS), University of London. I would like to thank my doctoral supervisor, Professor M. A. S. Abdel Haleem, for his treasury of insight into the Qur'an and his continual encouragement and support for my scholarship. It is an honour to have him pen the foreword. I would also like to send my appreciation to Dr Ayman Shihadeh and Professor Abdul-Hakim Al-Matroudi, who read chapters of the thesis and provided positive feedback and constructive criticism, as well as Dr Mustafa Shah, who has been supportive of my related research on Qur'anic variant readings.

From SOAS, I was appointed to the Cambridge Muslim College (CMC) as a research fellow, where I spent two years substantially rethinking and rewriting this book, as well as developing other projects. I am profoundly grateful to Dr Tim Winter and the team at the CMC for their support of my work and I am happy that I have been able to remain a visiting member of the faculty.

Since September 2016, I have joined Ebrahim College (EC) as Lecturer in Islamic Studies. Within the vibrant environment of EC in the heart of East London, the book has taken its final shape. I would like to thank the director, Shaykh Shams Ad-Duha Muhammad, all the EC staff, and my students for their encouragement.

The road to publication is long and a writer craves sympathetic readers. I would like to pay particular tribute to my friend and colleague Dr Harith Bin Ramli, whose questions, provocations, detailed annotations, and coffee-fuelled conversations have provided the whetstone at which I have been forced to sharpen my thinking and assess my own theological assumptions. Likewise, my friend Dr Samer Dajani has kindly read chapters and provided useful points from his own areas of interest. My thanks is also extended to Andrew Booso for commenting on an early draft of the whole book and Saquab Ashraf for his help with the diagrams.

I am grateful to Nicola Ramsey at Edinburgh University Press (EUP) for her positivity towards this book from the outset and to her whole team for the warm, patient, and understanding way in which they have worked with me. I also thank my two anonymous reviewers who were extremely encouraging about the book's potential and provided thoughtful and constructive critique, leading to a more comprehensive and better-framed text overall.

The present work has lived with me for the last eight years and all the challenges and joys of life during that time. So many more teachers, mentors, friends, and students deserve to be recognised than I can mention here; I send thanks to all.

This book would not exist save for my parents and wonderful family. Special praise must go to my mother Barbara, who has done everything she can to support my education, from my first word to my first lectureship. Finally, it is only fair that the most gratitude should go to those who make the biggest sacrifices, and so I would like to send all my love and affection to my wife Shukri and my amazing children Safiya, Leila, and Yusuf.

Set up the weighing scale with justice and do not fall short in the Scale (*wa-aqīmū al-wazna bi-l-qisṭ wa-lā tukhsirū al-mīzān*).

The Qur'an[i]

'If we should watch a city coming into being in speech,' I said, 'would we also see its justice coming into being, and its injustice?'

Socrates in *The Republic*[ii]

Introduction

The idea of justice is compelling yet elusive. Plato, in *The Republic* (*Politeia*), arguably began the Western tradition of ethics with his reasoned attempt to elucidate the principle on which to found the just society.[1] A parallel concern is found in the world's great scriptures. Here, the discourse concerning the establishment of social justice is often more exhortatory than discursive, and is mirrored by a focus on the divine justice of the final judgement and the eternal settling of accounts.

This universal significance of the concept of justice, and the practical aspiration of striving to realise it, seems connected to the idea that it is a crystallisation of ethics as a whole. In the words of Aristotle, echoed in Islamic intellectual history by no less a figure than al-Ghazālī (d. 505/1111), 'justice is complete virtue to the highest degree because it is the complete exercise of complete virtue'.[2] It is unsurprising, therefore, that it perennially unites otherwise diverse political, social, and legal actors in relating their struggles to a higher moral ideal. Justice grounds many discourses, including politics, war and peace, the distribution and use of resources, family relationships, and punishment. Its abiding resonance within our moral lives proves its continuing relevance as a subject of intellectual enquiry and demands us to continue the timeless search for its principles.

The book in your hands frames this quest as a reading of the scripture that perhaps deals most directly with issues pertaining to justice: the Qur'an. Within its world view, the continuous human responsibility to establish justice within society is identified as one of the reasons for the descent of revelation into the world, 'We sent Our messengers with clear signs (*al-bayyināt*), the Writ (*al-kitāb*) and the Scale (*al-mīzān*), so that people could uphold justice (*al-qisṭ*)' (Q. 57:25).[3]

Despite this concept's centrality to the Qur'an, modern scholarship has paid comparatively slight concern to it as an animating principle within the scripture's ethical discourse. Partly this can be explained by the training and interests of scholars, who tend to focus instead on the history of ethical theories about the Qur'an. A prime example of this is Majid Khadduri in *The Islamic Conception of Justice*, in which he disposes of the Qur'anic question within a few pages.[4] Majid Fakhry, in his *Ethical Theories in Islam*, draws a distinction between the 'moral ethos' of the Qur'an and the later strictly ethical theories built upon it. While he devotes a short chapter to the former, he uses it almost exclusively to seek the scriptural foundations for later theological controversies.[5] Such approaches are also sometimes connected to the assumption that the Qur'an lacks an underlying ethical structure, or even basic moral consistency.[6]

Even Toshihiko Izutsu, who puts the study of the Qur'anic moral system at the heart of his *Ethico-Religious Concepts in the Qur'ān*, provides relatively little discussion of justice. The concept appears almost as an aside in his analysis of *birr* (goodness, or piety).[7] A prominent exception to this tendency is Fazlur Rahman in his *Major Themes of the Qur'ān*. Although he does not fully develop his analysis of justice, he makes it the keynote of his third chapter, 'Man in Society'.[8] More recently, Wael Hallaq has touched on the concept's significance in his investigations into Qur'anic morality.[9] One of the more obvious intentions of the present volume, then, is to begin to fill this gap in the field by providing a detailed study of societal justice in the Qur'an.

An argument can be made that the inherent difficulty of defining the idea of justice, a problem extending beyond the confines of Qur'anic studies, has contributed to this lacuna. Commentators variously regard it as a universal concept – with an essential form acknowledged by virtually all cultures[10] – and a relative one, dependent on speaker and context.[11] J. D. Gericke sums up Plato's attempt to solve this conundrum as follows, 'What Socrates promises us is a standard of justice; what we get is an elaborate metaphor. But so it has been ever since, with the great discussions of justice.'[12]

Writing a book in this rich lineage brings with it certain constraints. As previous efforts within the literature demonstrate, justice can be studied on different levels: in the relationship between God and humanity, as a virtue within an individual's ethical constitution, and as a condition characterising a particular type or arrangement of society. Although I refer to the first two of these discursive fields, especially through trying to determine the Qur'an's moral theology, my main focus is on the societal manifestation of justice. Without doubt, the Qur'an strongly emphasises the development of virtues and the perfection of character, particularly through the concepts of *taqwā* (piety, or consciousness of God), *iḥsān* (spiritual excellence) and *tazkiyat al-nafs* (purification of the self, or soul). However, this personal level of ethics deserves a volume in its own right and will only enter into the current work when required for the explication of social ethics.

In the pages that follow, I produce a thematic reading of the Qur'anic blueprint for the just society. That the Qur'an could contain such an ethical structure beneath the surface of the scripture's language, and encoded within the dynamic reshaping of the lives of its first audience, has been a fundamental assumption in writing this book. Angelika Neuwirth seems to have a similar idea in mind when she states, 'There was a vivid image in the Qur'an of the Ideal City – the City of God – long before al-Fārābī's famous reworking of Plato's *Politeia*.'[13]

I read the Qur'an as an intensely moral text, continuously and repeatedly hailing the reader, or listener, as a responsible agent who must make choices with deep spiritual implications. Despite this concern, the Qur'an proffers no formal ethical theory; rather it is the interpreter who must discern a pattern of meaning within its discourse, and build a theoretical edifice consonant with its injunctions.[14]

My effort to reconstruct the Qur'an's discourse of justice within its initial social context, therefore, despite drawing on past reports and narratives, is primarily a theological and exegetical task, rather than a historical one. This also means that I tend to pay more attention, albeit critically, to the Muslim community's own cumulative record of that origin, than to the philology of Late Antiquity.[15]

Likewise, in analysing many areas of legislation, my intention is to emphasise the scripture's moral spirit ahead of its legal details. As Hallaq has suggested, 'we must understand and appreciate its "moral" message and structure as integral to, and as enveloping, its "legal" conception and discursive practice.'[16] In practical terms, this means that, in tracing the development of the just society throughout the period of revelation, I mainly use the term 'legal' to express the embedding of moral injunctions in social institutions.[17] It also means that the book can be read as a response to Fazlur Rahman's 'double movement' theory,[18] in which he calls for 'a systematic identification of rationales or objectives of the Qur'an in terms of its principles and values, which would define the ethics of the Qur'an'.[19] In the pages that follow, I propose a definition of *qisṭ* (societal justice) within the Qur'an and a model by which the ethical principles, or *ḥikma*s, that embody it can be extracted and thematically arrayed.

Despite conceiving of the Qur'an's *ḥikma*s as universal values, the question of their practical application in times and places beyond the initial revelatory context must remain outside the scope of this study. I recognise that for many modern Muslim thinkers the purpose of trying to extract such values is precisely for contemporary interpretation of the *sharīʿa* (divine law and moral code). The risk that such scholar-activists face is that, in interpreting the Qur'an in order to service a particular reform agenda, their emphasis on activism can belie a lack of sound scholarship. I am nonetheless hopeful that in some way this book will have a beneficial impact on tangible questions of justice today. That I do not directly address such contexts reflects the limits of my knowledge and expertise, as well as the space available and my judgement that, at a time of rushed appeals to scripture, the Qur'an must be deeply understood before it is used to campaign.

In my preference to distinguish my contextualising and reconstructive hermeneutic from its potential modern-day implications, my work has similarities not only with that of Fazlur Rahman, but with the more developed four-stage model proposed by Abdullah Saeed. In it, he puts such analysis at the third stage, after initial engagement and textual study, but before the final stage of application to the contemporary context.[20]

Of course, I recognise that, despite my best efforts to understand the Qur'an in its own *Weltenschauung*, the interpretive process necessarily also takes place, to a degree, within the framework of my contemporary concerns, or 'horizon' in the terminology of Gadamer.[21] I am, therefore, not concerned with trying to reach a pure state of dispassionate objectivity – a scholarly chimera – but rather to aspire to consistency in following my own theoretical and methodological postulates.

One of the most important of these is the distinction between, in Islamic terms, the absolute and complete meaning of the Qur'an known to God and the limited and partial meanings understood by its human readers. To read is to interpret. Insofar as the application of hermeneutic principles results in coherent understandings, one is building a cognitive model purporting to correspond to a greater reality.[22] It is quite possible to make truth claims about these models – this is what occurs whenever anyone champions a theory – but the claim must be justified. Thus, the field remains open for different, even conflicting, conceptualisations of the same scriptural material within rival systems of categorisation and justification, without thereby relativising truth as such.[23]

Wilfred Cantwell Smith makes the same point when referring to the perspective of devout Muslims, although I propose that this view could be entertained by anyone interested in engaging the Qur'an on 'its own terms':

> [T]he true meaning of the Qur'an is what God means by it; the true meaning of any word or verse is the meaning in the mind of God, to which, he or she might well go on to say, the various meanings that the historian observes in the process of their earthly development constitutes an on-going and ever-varying approximation.[24]

If it is granted that ultimate cognisance of the infinite divine purpose is beyond the reach of the finite observer, is it then foolish to attempt to extract essential principles from God's communications? Perhaps we are like the Prophet Moses in Sūrat al-Kahf who is unable to stay silent when faced with the seemingly inexplicable actions of his sage travelling companion. As this figure, usually taken to be al-Khaḍir, tells him in Q. 18:68, 'And how can you be patient in matters that you cannot encompass in knowledge (*wa-kayfa taṣbiru ʿalā mā lam tuḥiṭ bihi khubra*)?'[25]

In the second chapter of this book I give an answer, of sorts, to this contention. I propose that though human beings are called upon to trust in God's wisdom when responding to the harmful events of their lives, this does not imply the unknowability of the moral principles and values upon which His *sharīʿa* is based. Hence, we can read the case of Moses and al-Khaḍir as an illustration of the mystery of God's wisdom, not His Law per se. In fact, I would argue that the reason the story works rhetorically is that Moses, a master of the Law, is exasperated by his inability to deal with a series of exceptional cases requiring knowledge of future events. My view, then, is that while our fallibility in interpreting the principles underlying the *sharīʿa* may sometimes be greater than our basic understanding of its laws and guidelines, it is not of a different order altogether.

A few words about the genesis of this book may be useful at this juncture. The genealogy of the method by which I selected and sorted scriptural material is found within the generic procedure for thematic exegesis (*tafsīr mawḍūʿī*) in Ṣalāḥ al-Khālidī's *Al-Tafsīr al-mawḍūʿī bayna al-naẓariyya wa-l-taṭbīq*.[26] Some of the principal steps included noting all of the relevant Qur'anic verses on the subject of societal justice by working linearly through the entire text, grouping these according to preliminary topic headings, placing them within the theoretical model presented at the end of Chapter 2, and then interpreting according to the hermeneutic indices described in Chapter 3.

As in any investigation of this type, the final form represents the result of a creative process taking place over a significant period; one in which theory both shapes and is shaped by the outcome of successive acts of interpretation. It thus conforms in crucial ways to the paradigm of the hermeneutic circle.[27] Nonetheless, the principles and procedures described within Part I are the basic building blocks of the study.

The terminology used to speak about the chosen theme is also important. The phrase 'social justice' can encompass the entire societal arena, subsuming political, socio-economic, and judicial matters alike.[28] However, it is commonly used in the more restricted sense of 'socio-economic justice'. For this reason, I prefer societal justice for the all-encompassing Qur'anic concept.

In terms of the relationship of this book to the corpus of classical *tafsīr*, I regard exegetical works as invaluable sources to inform my own reading by reporting context, lexical materials, grammatical possibilities, and juristic derivation, as well as compiling previous exegesis. I do not take them as normative guides to the correct meaning of the Qur'an, but as illustrative of common interpretations that may agree or conflict with my own understanding. Hence, my choice to use a particular commentary varies according to the specific interpretive needs of the situation and is rarely stated explicitly. Likewise, when reference is given to the juristic views of individual Muslim scholars, or the classical schools of jurisprudence, it is either in the interest of clarifying the likely range of meanings that a particular Qur'anic text may embody, or so the positions taken in this book can be easily compared to prevailing views. The intention is not to invoke such figures as authorities, nor to trace the later development of Islamic law.

I also recognise the importance of variant readings (*qirā'āt*) for the interpretation of the Qur'an. For the sake of convenience, I have used the dominant reading of Ḥafṣ from ʿĀṣim throughout the book with occasional reference to other canonical or attested variant readings when they are of particular interest or significance.

Translations from the Qur'an reflect my interpretive decisions, although I have derived great benefit from the excellent work of Abdel Haleem. Quotes from the Hebrew Bible are mainly taken from *Tanach: The Stone Edition* by N. Scherman, while reference to the New Testament follows the King James Version due to its status as the most widely known translation.

I note that this book contains the names of prophets and other revered figures in their familiar English versions, when such exist, except when transliterating Qur'anic verses. These figures are usually provided with honorific expressions within the Islamic tradition, which should be read as implicit. Given my focus, I have generally not provided dates of death for early Muslims and have used my discretion in providing this information for classical Muslim scholars when their names first appear in the text.

I have tried to write this book in a manner that is accessible and relevant for different types of readers: the scholar of Islamic or Religious studies; the graduate-level student, or advanced undergraduate; and the interested general reader. Depending on where one falls on that spectrum, a range of strategies are possible for those not reading cover to cover. For example, those more interested in my understanding of distinct Qur'anic themes than detailed discussions of theology and hermeneutics may want to skip Chapters 2 and 3, while others may want to select particular parts or chapters. My recommendation is that all readers first read Chapter 1, which outlines many of my core ideas about the Qur'an's moral world view.

Part I

Qur'anic Ethics

1

Moral Narrative

In God's wisdom all things begin and so shall they end. This is the idea that animates this chapter, a reflection upon the story that the Qur'an tells from the primordial beginning of human existence to its infinite future. Unlike the Bible, in which the historical unfolding of God's covenant with humanity is traced through the linear order of the text, the Qur'an's moral narrative must be reconstructed from passages dispersed throughout its pages. In one sense this reflects more general principles of Qur'anic structure; in another it accords with the attention it pays to the metaphysical patterns of the wider human condition, rather than the history of particular peoples. God's wisdom is the constant that informs His creation of the world, just as it underlies both His justice and mercy in the Hereafter.

God is named *al-ḥakīm* (or described as *ḥakīm*), an intensive active participle usually translated as the Wise, ninety-two times in the Qur'an.[1] In Arabic, this word has a number of possible meanings, including the one who judges, brings to perfection, or possesses intimate knowledge of something.[2] Aside from God, it is only used for His revelations: *al-kitāb* twice in Q. 31:2 and 10:1; *al-qur'ān* and *al-dhikr* in Q. 36:2 and 3:58, respectively; and in Q. 44:4, 'for every wise matter (*amr ḥakīm*)' distinguished therein. The Arabic root *ḥ-k-m* has the basic verbal meaning of preventing something from *fasād* (corruption),[3] or removing a barrier to *iṣlāḥ* (rectification),[4] hence it is a term with an inherently moral connotation.

In this chapter, *ḥikma* emerges as the conceptual pivot for verses relating to the moral nature and actions of God. The Qur'anic discourse is read as framing the choices made by human souls against the background of God's wisdom, which must remain – for the present purposes at least – a basic postulate rather than a demonstrated theorem. This is not to deny that there are a number of valid questions connected to the idea of God's wisdom and, by extension, His justice. The current chapter, however, is focused on analysis of the scriptural material that ultimately grounds the theological enquiry found in Chapter 2. This means that fundamental philosophical debates about the nature of God, the world, and human beings will be left for the most part bubbling under the surface. The principal focus will remain the moral narrative of humanity within a sacred history.

By turning to this wide canvas and sketching the Qur'an's story of the spiritual journey undertaken by individuals and societies, it is possible to articulate the relationship between key concepts within its world view. This chapter, then, is not just of importance for the remainder of the book, which focuses on the theme of societal justice, but for anyone interested in the Qur'anic message. The narrative to follow passes through four distinct stages and is divided into sections accordingly: primordial covenant (*mīthāq*), natural disposition (*fiṭra*), prophecy (*nubuwwa*), and eschatology (*ākhira*).

I. Primordial covenant (*mīthāq*)

In the Qur'an, human history is only ethically meaningful due to the possession of moral responsibility. This is appropriately portrayed in Q. 33:72 by a powerful vignette in which vast natural elements cower at the offer of the Trust (*al-amāna*), 'We offered the Trust (*al-amāna*) to the heavens, the earth, and the mountains, yet they refused to bear it and feared it (*fa-abayna an yaḥmilnahā wa-ashfaqna minhā*). Humanity bore it – it has always been hasty and foolish.'

The verse's impact is heightened by the personification of the heavens, earth, and mountains with the plural feminine verbs *abayna* and *ashfaqna*, usually reserved for intelligent beings. The Trust can be interpreted as symbolic of the moral responsibility accepted by humanity, enabling it to freely enter into a covenant with God. Human souls then promise their Lord (*rabb*) that they shall recognise Him and render their lives to His worship, which is the ultimate purpose of their existence. This idea is mentioned in Q. 51:56, 'I created jinn and humankind only to worship Me' – in which worship (*yaʿbudūn*) can be understood to also imply that they recognise, or intimately know (*yaʿrifūn*), God.[5]

The Qur'anic covenant has a reciprocal structure.[6] Human beings are obliged to fulfil their commitments and, in turn, it is inconceivable that God, as *al-ḥakīm*, will break His promise to them (Q. 13:31).[7] The worldly life furnishes the arena of their testing, as mentioned in Q. 67:2, 'He is the one who has created death and life to test which of you is best in deeds (*li-yabluwakum ayyukum aḥsanu ʿamalan*).' When they return to Him they are promised just recompense for the manner in which they spent their lives based both on the internal state of their hearts (Q. 26:89) and the actions of their limbs (Q. 24:24).[8]

However, as mentioned in Q. 6:54, 'Your Lord has taken it upon Himself to be merciful.'[9] Thus God's justice is balanced with His mercy (*raḥma*), a defining attribute, the documentation of which far exceeds the scope of this study.[10] The same can be said of the human level, in which a person's quality of justice (*ʿadl*) is transcended by his or her spiritual excellence (*iḥsān*).[11]

In the Christian Bible, the Old and New Testaments are named after an English archaism for a covenant, the idea being that an ancient covenant with the patriarchs, such as Abraham in Genesis 17, and renewed with the Israelites, was superseded – or strengthened – by a new one for the community of Christ.[12] The Qur'an presents instead a primordial covenant with all of humanity in Q. 7:172–3:

> [Prophet], when your Lord took out the offspring from the loins of the Children of Adam and made them bear witness about themselves (*ʿalā anfusihim*),[13] He said, 'Am I not your Lord?' and they replied, 'Yes we bear witness.' This is so you cannot say on the Day

> of Resurrection, 'We were not aware of this,' or, 'It was our forefathers who, before us, ascribed partners to God, and we are only the descendants who came after them: will you destroy us because of the deeds of those who invented falsehood?'

These verses evoke a primordial time in which humanity collectively entered into a covenantal relationship with God, thereby affirming their obligations to Him. The image of all people emerging from their parents to bear witness may imply that this scene takes place after the creation of Adam, as suggested by Wadad al-Qāḍī, who reads it as a distinct stage of human life between the heavenly and worldly realms.[14] However, as a primordial spiritual action, extracting 'the offspring from the loins of the Children of Adam' no more requires Adam to have been physically created 'in history' than it does his descendants. Furthermore, not only is Adam implicitly included within the covenant of Q. 7:172, but his paradigmatic role within the Qur'anic moral narrative is underpinned by this prior acknowledgement of God's Lordship.[15]

Stylistically, Q. 7:172 brings the reader directly into the scene in which the covenant is affirmed, making the Qur'an's audience privy to the act. The call to testify and its response can be taken as an indication that the natural disposition of the human being is to incline towards belief in God *ab initio*.[16] The rationale given for this witnessing is to establish a proof to be used on the Day of Resurrection should human beings deny their responsibilities as servants entirely, or blame their forbears for their disbelief. The covenant is thus the freely made confirmation of a pre-existing relationship between Lord and servant, in which humankind is not only made cognisant of the fundamental moral implications of its existence, but confirms accountability to its Creator.

Here enters the central concept of *dīn* (religion), the living of one's life as a transaction of the debt (*dayn*) of one's own existence, accounted for by God on *yawm al-dīn* (The Day of Reckoning).[17] In the primordial stage of history, the creation of each life-to-be is recorded as a debt owed to God. The worldly existence that follows is for humans to spend their lives in worship of their Creator, fulfilling various 'debt obligations' that are placed upon them by divine Writ. The eventual Day of Reckoning shows either a profitable or loss-making transaction to be carried into eternity.

Referring to such fundamental existential responsibilities, the word *dīn* in the Qur'an is used in both positive and negative contexts. The former includes common phrases such as *al-dīn al-qayyim* (the upright religion), *dīn al-ḥaqq* (the religion of truth), and *dīn allāh* (the religion of God), while the latter include Q. 109:6, 'For you, your *dīn*, and for me, mine' and Q. 3:85, 'The one who is pleased with other than devotion (or: Islam) as religion (*ghayra al-islāmi dīnan*), it will never be accepted from him'.

The narrative of Adam in the Qur'an prefigures that of his descendants, mapping for them the moral territory of their own lives by introducing the ideas of stewardship, obligation, transgression, and repentance. Q. 2:30 records a conversation between God and His angels, in which He is quoted as saying, 'Indeed I am placing upon the earth a steward (*innī jāʿilun fī al-arḍi khalīfa*).' The expression used highlights the personal present tense of the action and, in placing *fī al-arḍi* before *khalīfa*, draws attention to the divine plan for human beings to undertake their role of stewardship upon the earth.[18]

Like *ḥakīm*, the word *khalīfa* takes the intensive form *faʿīl*, meaning *fāʿil*, an active participle, but with an attached *tāʾ* for additional emphasis.[19] In the same verse, the angels reply, 'How can You put someone there who will cause damage (*yufsidu fīhā*) and bloodshed (*yasfiku al-dimāʾ*), when we celebrate Your praise and proclaim Your holiness?' In response, God says, 'I know what you do not.'

There is considerable discussion in both early exegetical literature and modern academic studies about the meaning of *khalīfa* in this passage, with the following main possibilities suggested: successor, deputy, substitute, cultivator, and ruler.[20] Al-Rāghib al-Iṣfahānī (d. 422/1031) provides an insightful analysis of the term *khilāfa* as representation of another, either for one who is absent, one who has died, one who is incapacitated, or to honour the representative.[21] As the first three meanings cannot be applied to God, the final meaning of an honoured representative, or steward, best fits the context of the act of creation in Q. 2:30.[22] This provokes two questions: what is the meaning of God's steward? And why would the angels attribute corruption and bloodshed to such an honoured figure?

It is evident from both the initial statement and the angelic response that the word *khalīfa* is not meant to apply only to Adam, but to include his descendants, the Adamic creation. This concision accords with Arabic usage, in which the named patriarch of a tribe, or clan group, can be used to indicate descendants.[23] As Q. 2:31–3 show, human beings are given a special status due to an ability to gain knowledge of things within creation:

> He taught Adam all of the names. Then he presented all things to the angels, saying, 'Tell me their names if you are truthful.' They said, 'Glory be to You, we know nothing save what you have taught us. You truly are the Omniscient, the Wise. He said, 'O Adam, inform them of their names.' When he had informed them of their names, He said, 'Did I not tell you that I know the hidden of the heavens and the earth, and that I know all you reveal and conceal?'

This passage is a clear echo of Genesis 2:19 (emphasis in the original):

> And out of the ground the Lord God formed every beast of the field, and every fowl of the air; and brought *them* unto Adam to see what he would call them: and whatsoever Adam called every living creature, that *was* the name thereof.

Teaching Adam names may symbolise humanity's ability to form moral evaluations, as well as authority over the creation and the power to cultivate the earth for His sake.[24] Conversely, the reference to corruption and bloodshed perhaps alludes towards the capacity of humans for free will and the potential that they will reject this role. The angels are surprised that God would entrust such responsibility to a being unable to wield power with complete justice, in contrast to their own absolute obedience.[25] The answer 'I know things you do not' could thus refer to the superiority of flawed, but nonetheless free, humanity over its perfectly obedient, yet volitionless angelic counterpart.[26] It is also possible this indicates the help that God will send by way of the prophets and their followers to bring guidance and establish justice.[27]

Both these positive and negative elements of the human being are given further resonance in the remainder of this pericope. Q. 2:34 mentions the order for the angels to prostrate in honour of Adam and the refusal of the Devil, Iblis, who was included in the command.[28] Q. 2:35 provides the initial 'debt obligation' upon the first two human beings, 'O Adam, live with your wife in the garden and eat from it in comfort as you like, but do not approach this tree, as then you will become wrongdoers.' It is the failure of the couple to abide by the prohibition that leads to their descent into the world in Q. 2:36.

In Q. 20:120, the Devil whispers, 'O Adam, shall I lead you to the Tree of Immortality (*shajarat al-khuld*) and a kingdom that will never age?' Thus, it is evident that despite the pleasant nature of the garden, Adam knew that he would eventually die and face his reckoning. The attraction of the tree is that it seemingly offers a shortcut to Paradise without death. As the Devil says in Q. 7:20, 'Your Lord only forbade you from this tree lest you become angels, or immortals.' Moreover, the fact that God previously informed the angels that he was placing a steward upon the earth points to His prior knowledge of the outcome to this test. It also provides human beings with the basic pattern of obligation, transgression, and repentence. After his mistake, Adam 'received some words from his Lord' (Q. 2:37), which are often associated with the prayer for forgiveness in Q. 7:23, 'Our Lord, we have wronged ourselves, if you do not forgive us and have mercy upon us, we will be lost.'[29] Q. 2:37 goes on to mention, 'He accepted his repentance: He is the Ever Relenting, the Most Merciful (*al-tawwāb al-raḥīm*).'

Finally, when God tells Adam and his wife to enter into the worldly realm, He gives them a divine promise of guidance, an allusion to the future dispensation of revelation. He also informs them where the human story will end, in either a permanent return to paradisial existence, or the torture of Hell (Q. 2:38–9).

II. Natural disposition (*fiṭra*)

The Adamic narrative leads to human beings entering into the world, but what is the moral status of this new home and of people born within it? The picture that the Qur'an paints appears to be one in which the natural world has an essential morality with which human beings are expected to interact.[30] As an arena designed for the testing responsibilities of *dīn* and stewardship, it is appropriate that creation itself comes with a built-in moral setting, an idea encapsulated in the Qur'an by the Scale (*al-mīzān*).[31]

In Q. 55:7–12:

> He has raised up the sky. He has set the Scale so that you may not exceed in the Scale: set up the weighing scale with justice and do not fall short in the Scale. He set down the Earth for His creatures, with its fruits, its palm trees with sheathed clusters, its husked grain, its fragrant plants.

Here, God's setting of the Scale is revealed to be for the purpose of testing the ability of humans (and jinns) to live according to it. Placing the *mīzān* between the description of the heaven, or sky (*al-samāʾ*), and the earth with its flora and fauna implies it is natural and applicable universally throughout the created order. The command 'set up the weighing scale with justice (*wa-aqīmū al-wazna bi-l-qisṭ*)' utilises a familiar metaphor for the just society, with *wazna and mīzān* both belonging to the root *w-z-n*, meaning to weigh.[32] A human level of action is envisaged that mirrors the divine with the steward to measure out earthly justice according to the standard set by God.

This description also alludes to the theme of moral freedom with the second person address in Q. 55:8–9, as the command to weigh with justice assumes the possibility that its addressees will not. This underscores a difference with animals that are placed besides vegetative life as the recipients, not the agents, of moral choices.[33]

As human beings are also part of the created order, it stands to reason that they would reflect the setting of the Scale. Within the Qur'an, this is expressed by the concept of *fiṭra* (natural disposition) in Q. 30:30:

> [Prophet] stand yourself up devoutly for the religion – the natural disposition God instilled in humanity (*fa-aqim wajhaka li-l-dīni ḥanīfan fiṭrata allāhi allatī faṭara al-nāsa ʿalayhā*); there is no altering God's creation – that is the upright religion, though most people do not realise it.

Q. 30:30 can be read as Qur'anic support for the notion that human beings inherently aim to obtain faith and morality.[34] This would be a consequence of their receipt of the Trust in Q. 33:72 and the reason that no dissension is recorded among human souls in Q. 7:172, the verse of the primordial covenant, to which it is often linked in exegetical literature.[35]

This reading of *fiṭra* as an active inclination of human beings towards recognition of God and worshipping Him is contrasted with their propensity for temptation by the Devil and beguilement by the pleasures of the world. Although this can lead to the corruption of this initially innocent state, there is no concept of original sin in the Qur'anic world view.[36] Just as the narrative of Adam's fall contains within it his forgiveness and redemption, the life of each human being starts from the same point as Adam in returning to the state of *fiṭra* and being tested as he was.[37]

If it is granted that there is an objective moral setting to the world, the epistemological question of whether this is knowable before the arrival of revelation still remains. First, it is important to distinguish what can be known from what typically is known in any given society. The Qur'an castigates a great swathe of humanity as astray from the truth, for instance in Q. 6:116, 'If you obeyed most of those on earth, they would lead you away from the path of God. They follow nothing but speculation; they are merely guessing.'

As pointed out by Hourani, the epistemological issue of the knowability of moral values according to the Qur'an is less clear than the ontological one pertaining to their basic nature, partly because of the obvious emphasis in the scripture on the importance of its own guidance.[38] This question is usually connected to enquiry into whether human beings are accountable before they are recipients of revelation, although as A. Kevin Reinhart has shown, the discussion can encompass a cluster of related issues.[39] As this book deals primarily with the just society as envisaged by the Qur'an, the question is mainly of interest in the theoretical sense of what it illuminates about the scripture's moral world.

Proceeding from the above interpretation of the primordial covenant and the Scale, it would seem most coherent to understand the Qur'an as affirming that basic norms of morality are rationally knowable to a human actor in the state of *fiṭra*. However, the question is finely balanced with interpretations possible that challenge this assumption. An illustrative contested verse is Q. 17:15, 'We never punish a people until we send a messenger (*wa-mā kunnā muʿadhdhibīna ḥattā nabʿatha rasūlan*)', which can be understood as either a radical stance that human moral obligation is predicated on the revealed messages brought by prophets, or a statement about God's practice of sending a warner before destroying a community, as commonly narrated in the Qur'an.[40]

The difficulty with the use of verses such as Q. 17:15 to uphold the voluntaristic thesis is arguably that to do so they must be dislocated from their textual context to serve an argument that originates from theological, not Qur'anic, concerns.[41] Q. 17:4–7 presents a brief history of the warnings and punishments inflicted on the Children of Israel, while the verse following on from Q. 17:15 begins, 'When we decide to destroy a town'. Thus, the meaning of the verse is seemingly descriptive not prescriptive: God's practice in dealing with the past nations has been to provide warners to each community before they are destroyed. As Q. 17:17 goes on to declare, 'How many generations We have destroyed since Noah! Your Lord knows and observes the sins of His servants well enough.'[42]

If it is overall more plausible that the state of *fiṭra* includes both ontological and epistemological dimensions of morality, then the next question to be addressed is the proper role of prophecy and revelation within the Qur'anic moral narrative. This is the subject of the next section.

III. Prophecy (*nubuwwa*)

The Qur'an presents God as intimately aware of human frailties: the heart under constant threat from the whispering of the Devil, the temptations of worldly life, and its own selfish promptings. He does not leave humanity alone to become steeped in corruption, but rather sends prophets with guidance (*hudā*). This is in harmony with the *fiṭra* that it encounters and yet is able to supplement it, so as to assist humankind in overcoming its weaknesses to confirm its covenantal agreement to believe in and worship God.

The Qur'an mentions in a number of places that humanity in general was once a single community (*umma wāḥida*). In Q. 10:19, 'Humanity was a single community, then they split'; in Q. 2:213, 'Humanity was a single community, then God sent prophets as the bearers of good tidings and warnings, revealing for them the Writ with truth, so that they could judge between the people in that which they differed.' In other verses, such as Q. 16:93, 32:8, and 5:48, which presumably refer to a later stage of history, it is said that God could have kept the people within a single community, but that divine wisdom prevailed in allowing divergence between them.

An aspect of this wisdom is explained in Q. 49:13, 'O humankind, We have created you from male and female and have made you peoples and tribes so that you may come to know one another. Certainly, the most noble of you in the sight of God is the most pious of you.' This verse can be read as a definitive rejection of any kind of ethnic supremacy. The creation of diverse nations makes possible the universal experience of encounter with those who differ greatly in culture, yet share the same fundamental humanity. Making the criterion of measure *taqwā* ensures that material circumstance plays no part in the eventual eschatological success of moral actors.

As well as a general category for all of humanity, the word *umma* can refer to a particular prophetic community, such as in Q. 7:159, 'There is a group among the community of Moses who guide with the truth, and who act justly according to it (*wa-min qawmi mūsā ummatun yahdūna bi-l-ḥaqqi wa-bihi yaʿdilūn*).'[43] *Milla* seems to be a specific term for the same idea and is especially associated with the legacy of the Prophet Abraham, as in Q. 16:123, 'Then we inspired you to follow the community (*milla*) of Abraham devotely; he was not a pagan.' The Qur'an also has an idea of brotherhood. At the level of humanity as a whole, Q. 4:1 states, 'People, be mindful of your Lord, who created you from a single soul, and from it created its mate, and from the pair of them spread countless men and women far and wide.'[44] For the community of believers specifically, it emerges in Q. 49:10, 'Truly the believers are brothers, so reconcile between your brothers. Be mindful of God; perhaps you will receive mercy.'

As a *milla* is formed around a prophet, such a community receives a particular dispensation of God's *sharīʿa*. This concept of a divine law and moral code for humanity has an implicit scriptural basis, as well as the explicit statement in Q. 45:18, 'Now We have set you [Muḥammad] on a clear religious path (*sharīʿatin min al-amr*), so follow it.'[45] The word *sharīʿa* in Arabic is derived from the path that leads to a watering hole, symbolically conveying the way to what is most vital in life.[46] It should be noted that in the Arabic lexicon of the Qur'an there is no clear distinction between the equivalents of 'law' and 'morality', the two seamlessly blending in the term *sharīʿa*.[47]

Numerous Qur'anic descriptions of the prophets and messengers highlight their role as bringers of glad tidings and warnings, referring respectively to the promise of Paradise and the threat of Hell. The general Qur'anic pattern is to describe each messenger of God as sent to his people with the repeated refrain, 'O my people (*yā-qawmī*)'. Uniquely, the Prophet Muḥammad is sent to the totality of humanity and jinn, as mentioned in Q. 21:107 and 46:29–31.

In Q. 2:151, more detail is given about the purpose of sending the Prophet Muḥammad to the inhabitants of Arabia:

> We have sent among you a messenger of your own to recite Our signs (*āyātinā*) to you, purify you (*yuzakkīkum*) and teach you the Writ (*al-kitāb*), the Wisdom (*al-ḥikma*), and [other] things you did not know.[48]

The word *āyāt* can be used for signs, revelations, proofs, or Qur'anic verses. For this discourse about the Prophet these ideas dovetail insofar as the verses of the Qur'an are presented as inimitable and therefore proof of the divine origin of the discourse.[49] The term thus connotes the means by which the Prophet establishes his authenticity as speaking for the divine and engendering faith in his community, without which he cannot proceed in his mission. Next, *tazkiya* (spiritual purification) is mentioned, as it is only on the basis of interior change, for good or ill, that one ensures success or failure in the world and Hereafter.[50] This can be associated with the higher level of spiritual excellence known as *iḥsān*, a going beyond the basic requirements of one's obligations to develop one's virtues.

The two terms encapsulated in the repeated Qur'anic phrase *al-kitāb wa-l-ḥikma* are important for understanding the scripture's moral narrative in general and the concept of *qisṭ* (societal justice) in particular. The word *kitāb* from the root *k-t-b*, meaning to write, is commonly translated as 'book'. However, Daniel Madigan in *The Qur'ān's Self-Image*, after a comprehensive semantic analysis of this root, concludes that the meaning of *kitāb* is much closer to God's authoritative address than His Book.[51] In my view, the translation of Writ is usually most appropriate, as it captures the senses of writing, scripture, authority, and prescription, which are all important aspects of the word. For numerous verses that mention the sending or giving of the *kitāb*, the general meaning of revelation, or scripture, can be suitable. In some cases the word can indicate a physical book, such as Q. 4:153, 'The Scriptuaries[52] (*ahl al-kitāb*) demand that you make a book (*kitāban*) come down from the heavens for them.'

The verb *kataba* also has a more restricted meaning within the Qur'anic lexicon of prescription and obligation. This can be seen in Q. 2:183, 'Fasting has been prescribed for you (*kutiba ʿalaykum al-ṣiyām*).'[53] The verbal noun *kitāb* can have a similar meaning.[54] For example, in Q. 2:235, a verse pertaining to the marriage of widows once their waiting period (*ʿidda*) has elapsed, 'Do not confirm the marriage tie until the obligation (*kitāb*) has reached its set time.'[55]

This usage leads to the possibility that, at least in certain contexts, *kitāb allāh*, or simply *al-kitāb*, is more plausibly understood as God's Writ, or ordinance, than

His Book, or Qur'an.[56] An example of this is Q. 33:6, 'In God's Writ (*kitāb allāh*), blood-relatives have a stronger claim than other believers and emigrants, though you may act towards your allies according to what is recognised. That is protected in the Writ (*al-kitāb*).'[57]

An alternative angle from which to approach the same idea is by looking at the Qur'anic verses that mention prophets as possessing both scriptures of some kind and *al-kitāb*, which would seem to suggest a more specific meaning for the latter. In Q. 3:184 and 35:25 there is the statement, 'They came with proofs (*al-bayyināt*), scriptures (*al-zubur*) and enlightening Writ (*al-kitāb al-munīr*).' In Q. 5:110, God addresses the Prophet Jesus, saying, 'And when I taught you the Writ (*al-kitāb*), the Wisdom (*al-ḥikma*), the Torah and the Evangel.'

Another relevant verse is Q. 4:54, which states, 'We gave the family of Abraham the Writ (*al-kitāb*) and the Wisdom (*al-ḥikma*); and we gave them a mighty kingdom.' Apart from using the same phrase, this is interesting due to the close association between descendants of Abraham and a ritual law. A reference is also made in Q. 2:231 in the context of regulations for divorce, 'Remember the blessing of God upon you and what he has sent down to you of the Writ and Wisdom (*al-kitāb wa-l-ḥikma*), so that you would be admonished with it.' The point of mentioning this in the middle of legal injunctions could be to encourage adherence to these particular obligations.

Kutub, the plural form of *kitāb*, can also refer to specific laws. Thus, Q. 98:2–3, 'A messenger from God reciting purified scriptures (*suḥufan muṭahharatan*), in them upright laws (*kutubun qayyima*)',[58] as well as one interpretation of Q. 66:12, 'Mary, daughter of ʿImrān, who guarded her womb, so We breathed into it. She confirmed the truth of the words of her Lord and His laws (*kutubihi*; or: scriptures). She was a pious supplicant.'

Madigan also raises the theological issue of how different scriptural dispensations and their associated laws and obligations relate to the nature of God and specifically His attribute of speech.[59] A full exploration of this question is beyond the proper scope of this chapter. In brief, I would suggest that the concept of God's wisdom could make sense of the idea of a multiplicity of revelation and its appropriateness in different times and places.

Exegetes often interpret *al-ḥikma* in Q. 2:151 as the Qur'anic rulings (*aḥkām*),[60] the prophetic Sunna, or even *fiqh*,[61] which should be read as understanding rather than jurisprudence in this context. Wisdom, however, is the most generally applicable rendering and, in some cases, is relatively incontestable, such as Q. 2:269, 'He gives wisdom to whom He wants and whoever receives wisdom has been given much good.' One of the most important places pointing towards a more specific meaning for *ḥikma* is found in Q. 17:39, following a significant list of moral injunctions. The verse reads, 'That is part of what your Lord has inspired in you of the Wisdom (*dhālika mimmā awḥā ilayka rabbuka min al-ḥikma*).'[62] The word *dhālika* (that) refers back to this ethical material, which begins with Q. 17:22, 'Do not take beside God another deity' and ends with Q. 17:37, 'Do not walk upon the earth ungratefully'.[63] It is particularly interesting that many of these rules are accompanied by a rationale. An example is Q. 17:26–7, 'Do not waste. Truly those who waste are the brothers of the devils and the Devil was very ungrateful to his Lord'. Another is Q. 17:31, 'Do not kill your children fearing poverty, We will provide for them and you. Truly, killing them was a grave sin.' Or, again, Q. 17:33, 'Do not take life – which God has sanctified – except by right. We have given authority to the kin of the one who is killed unjustly, so do not be excessive in (retaliatory) killing. He will be aided.'[64] It seems that, in these cases, *ḥikma* refers specifically to the wise benefits of the revealed injunctions. As Hallaq observes, '*ḥikma* is operative in a matrix of justice.'[65]

Returning to the phrase *al-kitāb wa-l-ḥikma*, I propose that a consistent reading can be developed by understanding the pair of terms, in general, as referring respectively to the revealed obligations conveyed by messengers and their wise purposes, a position that also finds support in the analysis of al-Farāhī.[66] This interpretation avoids the charge that can be levelled at the gloss of the phrase as the Qur'an and Sunna by al-Shāfiʿī (d. 204/820) that it does not account for the full range of its scriptural usage.[67] Moreover, it is a key insight for the investigation conducted later in this book and gives a Qur'anic indication that the existence of command and prohibition – a morality of the Law – can coexist with a teleology focusing on its higher purposes for the benefit of society.[68]

Of course, just as the possibility of understanding the word *kitāb* to refer to the Law does not prevent it meaning the totality of the revelation, reading *ḥikma* as the rationale of divine laws does not eliminate from the Qur'an wisdom not associated with rule-following. Such material is prominent in the many Qur'anic stories and parables. As mentioned in Q. 54:4–5, 'Truly, warning tales that should have restrained them have come down to them – far-reaching wisdom (*ḥikmatun bāligha*) – but these warnings do not help.'

If the *kitāb* and *ḥikma* brought by messengers within the Qur'anic world view are understood as the divine Writ and its wise purposes, it becomes important to relate this to the wider life of the people. The key verse that allows this broader conception is Q. 57:25, 'We sent Our messengers with proofs (*al-bayyināt*), the Writ (*al-kitāb*) and the Scale (*al-mīzān*), so that people could uphold justice (*li-yaqūma al-nāsu bi-l-qisṭ*).'

This is a particularly important verse for this book as it draws together the various threads discussed hitherto, and acts as a point of departure for the presentation of the theme of societal justice. Here the messengers are given three elements: proofs to establish their credentials, similar to the term *āyāt* discussed above; the Writ, obligations of revealed Law; and the Scale, insight into the measure of morality, or natural law, set within the creation. This mirrors Q. 42:17, 'It is God who has revealed the Writ with truth and the Scale.' These elements are provided for a very particular reason, empowering humanity to establish justice (*qisṭ*).

The term *qisṭ* is one of the two Arabic words in the Qur'anic vocabulary that most closely correspond to 'justice' in English. The other one is *ʿadl*. Based on a study of their linguistic and scriptural meaning, it can be suggested that these two terms have differing connotations beyond the general meaning of justice: *ʿadl* an internal quality of equity,[69] *qisṭ* justice established concretely within the social sphere.

ʿAdl is the verbal noun of *ʿadala*, for which the lexicographical sources give at least seven distinct shades of ethical meaning, all of which can be traced to usage in Qur'anic passages: to act justly, or equitably;[70] to be fair in judgement;[71] to be impartial in speech, or witness;[72] to straighten someone to a state of moral uprightness, or from disbelief to faith;[73] to offer a compensation in place of punishment for a sin;[74] to deviate, or turn away from the truth;[75] and to set up something as equal to something else, which can have a positive connotation approximating the first of these, or a negative one referring to the sin of *shirk*, worshipping anything else alongside God.[76]

The root concept, or etonym, that underlies these different shades of meaning is signified by the noun *ʿidl*, which refers to half the load placed on a beast of burden, counterbalanced by an equal one on the other side.[77] The essential idea, taken from observation of the physical world and applied to the moral one, is fairness or impartiality in a person's conduct, or balance within their internal state.[78]

The final two senses mentioned above are also examples of the Arabic phenomenon of *aḍdād* (opposite meanings carried by a single word). These signify, respectively, the complete upset of this balance, which leads to deviation, or the attempt to falsely equate two things that are not equal.

Qisṭ is usually defined within Arabic lexicons as effectively synonymous with the more commonly used *ʿadl*, but not vice versa, as *ʿadl* tends to be defined as the opposite of negative qualities, such as *jawr* (injustice, or oppression);[79] *ẓulm* (wrongdoing), literally putting something in the wrong place;[80] and *fasād*, corruption that causes imbalance within the moral world.[81]

Although *qisṭ* is derived from the verb *qasaṭa*, the form *aqsaṭa* is much more common.[82] This is due to *qasaṭa* usually meaning to act unjustly, or tyrannically, and *aqsaṭa* taking on a privative function – to remove injustice.[83] Therefore, the concept of *qisṭ* has a degree of transitivity that is less pronounced than for *ʿadl*. In other words, *qisṭ* is about establishing a just world, while *ʿadl* is about remaining personally just.

Qisṭ can mean a portion or share (*qism*, or *naṣīb*) with the connotation of one's rightful or just share, hence the following terse definition, *al-qisṭ huwa al-naṣīb bi-l-ʿadl* (*qisṭ* is one's portion of *ʿadl*).[84] The word can also refer to a measure of half a *ṣāʿ*, which is a small bowl varying in size according to local custom, or a balance or instrument used for the purpose of weighing.[85] This indicates a connection to physical measurement. Muḥammad Dāwūd argues, '*Al-qisṭ* is more specific than *al-ʿadl* and for that reason the scale (*al-mīzān*) is described with *al-qisṭ* and *al-qisṭās*,[86] so *al-qisṭ* is clearly manifested justice such as sharing matters into portions and calculating them materially by their perceptible weight.'[87]

A proverbial saying in Arabic is *idhā ḥakamū aʿdalū wa-idhā qasamū aqsaṭū* (when they judged they were impartial and when they shared out they were even-handed),[88] which neatly encapsulates the distinction between *ʿadl* as the internal quality from which flows *qisṭ* as the condition of social justice.

These observations are supported by a number of Qur'anic verses featuring derivatives of both roots. An example is Q. 4:135:

> You who believe, uphold justice as witnesses for God (*kūnū qawwāmīna bi-l-qisṭi shuhadā'a li-llāh*), even if it is against yourselves, your parents, or your close relatives. Whether the person is rich or poor, God can best take care of both. Refrain from following your own desire, so that you can act justly (*fa-lā tattabi'ū al-hawā an ta'dilū*)[89] – if you distort or neglect justice, God is fully aware of what you do.

This is similar to Q. 5:8:

> You who believe, be as witnesses for God upholding justice (*kūnū qawwāmīna li-llāhi shuhadā' a bi-l-qisṭ*). Do not let hatred of others lead you away from justice (*allā ta'dilū*), but adhere to justice (*i'dilū*), for that is closer to awareness of God. Be mindful of God: God is well aware of all that you do.

In both cases, there is a call to establish justice for the sake of God as witnesses. One indication of these verses is legal testifying, although the language also makes possible a wider meaning with witness given directly to God.[90] The noun *qisṭ* is used for a standard, or condition, of social justice, while *'adl* refers to personal ethics.

Another instance in which *'adl* and *qisṭ* are both present within a single verse is Q. 49:9:[91]

> If two groups of the believers fight, you [believers] should try to reconcile them (*fa-aṣliḥū baynahumā*); if one of them is [clearly] oppressing the other, fight the oppressors until they submit to God's command, then make an equitable and even-handed reconciliation between the two of them: God loves those who are even-handed (*fa-aṣlihū baynahumā bi-l-'adli wa-aqsiṭū inna allāha yuḥibbu al-muqsiṭīn*).

Here, the reconciliation is to be made with *'adl* but beyond that the believers are ordered *aqsiṭū*. The word choice makes it unlikely that the two terms are entirely synonymous, as then the imperative verb would be a superfluous addition. It is for this reason that *al-'adl* here can be understood as referring specifically to the fairness and impartiality of the reconciliation following the cessation of hostilities, as it is not appended to the earlier instance of the phrase *fa-aṣlihū baynahumā* in the verse.[92] Moreover, *aqsiṭū* can be read as an order to make just material restitution between the parties as part of the reconciliation process.

Q. 60:8 reads, 'He does not forbid you to deal kindly and justly with anyone who has not fought you for your faith or driven you out of your homes: God loves the just (*inna allāha yuḥibbu al-muqsiṭīn*).' In similar fashion, this can be interpreted as giving such people a portion (*qisṭ*) of wealth, because maintaining the quality of *'adl* is necessary whether or not the other party is belligerent.[93]

This understanding of *qisṭ*, combined with the previous discussions of *mīzān* and *ḥikma*, makes possible the following definition: societal justice is the condition of society realised by the Wisdom of God's Writ, which matches the Scale of moral value. Such a just society is the highest moral aspiration of human civilisation as a collective activity, manifesting within it all other praiseworthy values, such as mercy, goodness, and piety. For each person, their *dīn* consists of attempting to fulfil human stewardship of the earth and a successful resolution in the Hereafter. As al-Attas points out, the concept of *dīn* necessitates the establishment of a cosmopolis on the earth with certain general features.[94] These include 'the natural tendency of man to form societies and obey laws and seek just government'.[95] Implicitly, then, the Qur'anic discourse posits the just society as built upon natural law foundations.

In the Qur'an, this pattern is embodied in the person of the Prophet Muḥammad who lives at the culminating point in sacred history, receiving the final revealed code in the cycle of reform and corruption. Thus, in Q. 33:40 he is described as *khātam al-nabiyyīn* (the Seal of the Prophets), which matches the statement in Q. 3:81 that God took a pledge from the prophets confirming his authority over them. This is mirrored in several verses that state the community of believers are to act as witnesses for other communities, in both the world and the Hereafter, with the Messenger as a witness for them.[96] The Prophet Muḥammad is thus envisaged within the Qur'an as the delegate of divine authority and the final successor to all prophets – the *khalīfa* of God *par excellence*.

However, the very fact that the Qur'an is addressed to the Prophet, rather than about him, means that exegetes have often found evidence for the foregoing in subtleties of expressions, rather than unequivocal statements. Al-Alūsī (d. 1270/1854) analyses Q. 2:30, 'When your Lord said, "Indeed I am placing upon the earth a *khalīfa* (*idh qāla rabbuka innī jāʿilun fī al-arḍi khalīfatan*)"' and spots that a plural addressee in the previous verse becomes a single one with the appearance of the *kāʾ* in *rabbuka* (your Lord). He argues that turning the address directly to the Prophet highlights that he has the greatest portion of the stewardship mentioned.[97]

The Qur'an pictures the Prophet Muḥammad, like the Prophet Abraham before him, as the exemplar of conduct to be followed, 'The Messenger of God is an excellent model (*uswatun ḥasanatun*) for those of you who put your hope in God and the Last Day and remember Him often' (Q. 33:21).[98] This excellence is in the higher purposes for which human beings have been created, both proximate, establishing societal justice as God's stewards, and ultimate, making a successful return to Him in the Hereafter.

The personal narrative of the Prophet Muḥammad is also relevant here. The following phrase is repeated twice in the Qur'an in Q. 9:33 and 61:9:

> He is the one who has sent His Messenger with guidance and the religion of truth, in order to reveal to him the religion, all of it, despite the dislike of the pagans (*huwa alladhī arsala rasūlahu bi-l-hudā wa-dīni al-ḥaqqi li-yuẓhirahu ʿalā al-dīni kullihi wa-law kariha al-mushrikūn*).

A nearly identical phrase occurs in Q. 48:28, but replaces 'despite the dislike of the pagans' with 'and God suffices as a witness (*wa-kafā bi-llāhi shahīdan*)'. This verse can be read as indicating that the divine revelation will be completed despite the enmity of those who oppose the Prophet, an interpretation attributed to the Companion Ibn ʿAbbās.[99]

In contrast to this, one strand of classical exegesis, widespread in modern translations of the Qur'an, understands *li-yuẓhirahu ʿalā al-dīni kullihi* as 'to make it dominant over all other religions'.[100] However, this view does not fit well with the linguistic construction of the verse in two respects. First, the word *dīn* here is singular not plural.[101] Second, when the Qur'an uses the expression *aẓhara/yuẓhiru* x *ʿalā* y it does not refer to dominance, but rather to making something known. Examples are Q. 66:3, which refers to God revealing something secret to the Prophet connected with his wives,[102] and Q. 72:26, which states that God does not reveal the unseen to anyone (the exception of His chosen messengers is given in the next verse).

A further point is that both Q. 9:33 and 61:9 follow verses mentioning God 'perfecting His light'. This can be understood in the sense of successive revelations to the Prophet Muḥammad illuminating his knowledge of God's Writ. The process was declared complete during the Prophet's only pilgrimage in 10/632, when he recited the famous words of Q. 5:3, 'Today I have completed your religion (*dīn*) for you, perfected My favour upon you and am pleased with devotion (or: Islam) as religion for you (*raḍītu lakum al-islāma dīnan*).'

IV. Eschatology (*ākhira*)

The final stage of the spiritual journey according to the Qur'an, like the first one, takes place in a realm beyond natural human knowledge and concerns all that comes after death, including the grave itself, resurrection in bodily form, the terrifying Day of Judgement, and the final residence in Paradise or Hell. The Qur'anic eschatology accounts for a substantial portion of the text as a whole and its outline is well known. However, my main concern in this book is with justice as implemented within the world, not justice that comes hereafter. For this reason, the discussion here shall be limited to what is sufficient to complete the moral narrative.

Upon dying, the human being is confronted with the opening of a reality that was hitherto hidden from sight. With this comes an awareness of one's moral responsibility and the return to God for judgement, as mentioned in Q. 50:19, 'The trance of death will bring the Truth with it: "This is what you tried to escape."' Al-Ghazālī writes:

> Upon death there stand revealed before him certain things which were never disclosed to him in life, in the way that things may be revealed to a man who is awake which were concealed from him during his slumber, for 'people are asleep, and when they die they awake'.[103]

The logical corollary to moral obligation is the existence of corresponding consequences, either reward or sanction, and this is what the eschatological arena provides. A person's truthfulness to their covenant, the acknowledgement of God's Lordship, is the most fundamental duty and God examines it along with fidelity to His messengers, outward conduct, acts of worship, and inner purity of heart. Based on these, He sends the human being to an ultimate fate of either Paradise or Hell.

It is axiomatic within the Qur'an that God is absolutely just in carrying out His judgement. As mentioned in Q. 10:54, 'They will be judged justly and not wronged (*quḍiya baynahum bi-l-qisṭi wa-hum lā yuẓlamūn*).'[104] Despite the Qur'anic focus on the theme of justice, and God's description in the Qur'an as possessing numerous specific attributes of perfection, as well as statements, such as Q. 7:180, 'The Most Excellent Names (*al-asmā' al-ḥusnā*) belong to God', there is no mention of God as al-ʿAdl, or al-ʿĀdil (the Just), within the text. The meaning is often expressed through the negation of injustice to God, while, in positive terms, the phrase *bi-l-qisṭ*, as well as *bi-l-ḥaqq* (in truth; in justice) as a qualification to God's action, expresses the same idea.[105]

Furthermore, although the name al-Ḥakam (the Judge) does not formally feature in the Qur'an, its attribution to God is implied in Q. 6:114; and the verb *ḥakama* is used to describe God's action in Q. 40:48. Relevant too is Q. 95:8, 'Is God not the most decisive of judges (*aḥkam al-ḥākimīn*)?'[106] It is also important to consider that the word *ḥakīm* in certain moral contexts does not just connote God's wisdom, but can extend to His justice in deciding who is to be rewarded and who is to be punished.[107]

That the name *al-ḥakīm* directly relates to justice is a subtlety that has been missed by many of those writing on the Qur'anic moral system. Daud Rahbar produced a large study entitled *God of Justice*, in which he examined the contextual significance of more than twenty words and phrases used within the Qur'an as they relate to 'God's stern justice', yet failed to analyse the term *ḥakīm*, or even *ẓulm* (injustice) as the antonym of justice.[108] Toshihiko Izutsu, usually very attuned to the moral significance of words, also does not make the connection between the name *al-ḥakīm* and justice.[109] Wael Hallaq comes close to this idea with his suggestion that *ḥakīm* means 'a perfected and most consummate ability to regulate the affairs of created beings (*tadbīri khalqihi*), including meting out punishment and reward'.[110]

This concept of perfect divine justice is predicated on the idea that God establishes judgement that takes into account every piece of evidence, and does not wrong a single soul:

> We will set up scales of justice (*al-mawāzīna al-qisṭ*) for the Day of Resurrection so that no one can be wronged in the least (*fa-lā tuẓlamu nafsun shay'an*), and if there should be even the weight of a mustard seed, We shall bring it out. We take excellent account (Q. 21:47).

In this verse, the scales of justice in the Hereafter parallel the Scale set up to measure moral value within the worldly life. The description of God as one who does not wrong His servants is also an important linguistic habit of the Qur'an in discussing His justice.[111] The implication is that there are certain minimum and maximum standards to operate in the dispensation of justice in the Hereafter: neither reduction in one's good deeds, nor increase in the recompense for one's bad deeds.[112]

Furthermore, after establishing this on the basis of His wisdom, God also reserves the right to increase greatly the reward for deeds, recognised through such verses as Q. 2:261, 'God gives multiple increase to whoever He wishes: He is limitless and all knowing'; as well as to forgive transgressions. The remission of major sins is mentioned in Q. 4:48, 'God does not forgive the joining of partners with Him: anything less than that He forgives to whoever He will, but anyone who joins partners with God has committed a tremendous sin.'[113]

However, even *shirk* can be forgiven through sincere repentance before death, as mentioned in Q. 4:110, while bad deeds done in a state of disbelief can be forgiven or changed by God into good deeds following faith, as in Q. 25:70.[114]

Thus, an implicit theology can be detected in the Qur'an's dual promise regarding God's absence of injustice and presence of mercy. Rather than these two elements being arbitrary manifestations of His will, such that any punishment would be just and any reward merciful, they reflect the deeper mystery of His wisdom. God's mercy is absolute, but human beings come to it on His terms.

This chapter has shown that reading the Qur'an's story of the human condition holistically can furnish us with key aspects of its moral theology that are lost when considering verses in isolation. The leitmotif of this narrative is God's wisdom to create life as a debt owed and ultimately repaid as a test of morality. Although this notion of wisdom makes human life purposeful and intelligible, there remains an element of ineffability in its application as a quality to characterise the divine. Within the created world, it is represented by the Scale, read here as a Qur'anic analogue to the natural law. This interpretation, combined with the Qur'an's general discourse and specific notion of *fiṭra*, leads to a moral realist metaethics, corresponding to the knowability of at least basic ethical norms before the descent of revelation. The justice that the Qur'an calls upon its audience to establish, then, is predicated on realising the wisdom of God's revealed Law such that it builds upon His natural law.

2

Theology and Ethics

'Why is there something instead of nothing?' is, according to Heidegger, the fundamental question of metaphysics.[1] The Qur'an consistently answers it by affirming a unique divine Creator who is both in need of no further explanation and is the ultimate ground of explanation for everything else. This point is perhaps made most succinctly in Sūrat al-Ikhlās, 'Say "He is God, singular. God, eternally besought by all. He does not beget, nor was He begotten. And there is nothing at all like him"' (Q. 112:1–4). If the existence of the world is a brute fact, yet does not seem to be an adequate explanation for itself, the conceptual appeal of a necessary wise eternal being endowed with creative ability is obvious.[2] Human beings who come to believe that such a being exists, justifiably give themselves up in devotion.

The reading of the Qur'an in the previous chapter was centred on the divine attribute of wisdom as an ultimate basis for the human moral condition. Arguably, *ḥikma* can play this role, as unlike *ʿilm* (knowledge), it can be conceived as not only descriptive of the state of the creation, but providing some value judgement of how it ought to be. This is also clear in Arabic from the connection between the root *ḥ-k-m* and ethical action.[3] It follows that the idea of *ḥikma*, when juxtaposed with evil within the world, can be used for theodicy, in the words of Milton, 'to justify the ways of God to men'.[4] Building on this idea of wisdom, I proposed a number of characteristics of Qur'anic moral theology, including stable and knowable moral qualities inscribed within the world to which the revealed law conforms.

Although providing an exegetical framework for the Qur'anic moral world view, the discussion in Chapter 1 avoided elaboration on the attendant theological and philosophical issues: how are we to conceive of divine attributes? How do these attributes relate to the metaphysics of the world and the metaethical grounding of morality? Finally, what normative ethical and legal theory may be developed from these foundations?

The development of the Muslim tradition of *kalām* (rational theology) can in one sense be explained by the impulse to answer these kinds of questions. In the classical period of Islam, three major theological schools, the Muʿtazila, the Ashʿarīs, and Māturīdīs, entered into rich debate over the nature of God and ethics. The main themes of enquiry concerned the proper ontology of the divine attributes, including the question of which, if any, should be understood as eternal, as well as the nature of God's moral relationship to His creation. The positions taken by these schools flowed over into discussions pertaining to the foundations of ethical knowledge and even the justification of practical jurisprudence (*fiqh*) via the genre of legal theory (*uṣūl al-fiqh*).

The very existence of different theological schools, all defending their positions with reference to the Qur'an, underscores the extent to which the scripture may be interpreted to accommodate diverse intellectual systems. This chapter will assess the above themes as they emerged within their doctrinal complexes in the light of the Qur'anic criteria already derived. The argument that will be presented has three elements. First, that the Māturīdī school in general, and its eponym the Samarqandī theologian and exegete Abū Manṣūr al-Māturīdī (d. 333/944) in particular, is the best fit to the Qur'anic picture.[5] Second, that his system has interesting implications for the ethical theory grounding practical jurisprudence, as discussed in *uṣūl al-fiqh*, when compared to the dominant (and more Muʿtazilī-influenced) Ḥanafī tradition of *uṣūl* and its Ashʿarī counterpart. Finally, a constructive effort will be made to propose a neo-Māturīdism, drawing from but not limited to his thought. For this, I will refine the Qur'anic principles articulated in Chapter 1 to outline a natural law theory of ethics that will tease out the moral structure of the Qur'anic system of justice studied later in this book.

I. Theodicy

The *kalām* tradition emerged from Qur'anic foundations as well as engagement, both appreciative and critical, with pre-existing theological and philosophical ideas. Plotinus (d. 270 CE) had long since argued for the necessity of explaining the world with reference to a single first cause, seeing its creation as an inevitable, and eternal, emanation from this source of unity.[6] This view was prominently represented in Muslim lands by al-Fārābī (d. 339/950–1), who merged his philosophical output with aspects of contemporary religious discourse.[7] Meanwhile, Christian thinkers, such as the theologian Augustine (d. 430 CE) and the philosopher John Philoponus (d. 570 CE), had influentially insisted that creation appeared *ex nihilo* as the result of a distinct act of God's will, a cosmological position that, unlike emanationism, would gain the acceptance of most Muslim theologians.[8]

Like the monotheistic scriptures that preceded it, the Qur'an describes a personal God, not an abstract first principle. This means that, when entering into theological speculation, Muslim thinkers from all three major schools of thought accepted some application of observed personal characteristics to God, such as His willing and knowing. This common position was enshrined in the principle of *qiyās al-ghāʾib ʿalā al-shāhid* (the hidden is analogous to the manifest).[9]

The Muʿtazila were concerned that treating such divine attributes as co-eternal with the divine essence led to a disavowal of God's *tawḥīd* (unicity). They would thus state that God was, for instance, knowledgable through His essence not an eternal attribute of knowledge. This position contributed to the famous controversy over the status of the Qur'an, in which the Muʿtazila argued that it must be the created speech of God.[10] On this fundamental question, Ashʿarīs and Māturīdīs were united in opposition to what they saw as *ta'ṭīl* (nullification) of God's essential attributes. They generally followed the well-established formulation that, while God's eternal attributes cannot merely be identified with His essence, they also cannot be understood as entirely separate entities.

On the moral plane, the Mu'tazila strongly emphasised *qiyās al-ghā'ib 'alā al-shāhid*, applying ethical arguments drawn from human experience to the actions of God. They argued that the existence of the world mandates that God must have created it for a wise reason, which as it cannot be to benefit Him, must be for the sake of humanity.[11]

Abū al-Ḥasan al-Ash'arī (d. 324/936), himself a former member of the school, reacted to this formulation, countering with the proposal that God creates solely at the behest of His own divine will. Any benefits that God provides to His creatures are by virtue of His free and unimpeded choice and even the norms of morality could be entirely different if He so wished. In al-Ash'arī's thought, then, God's dominant characteristic is His will, which is absolutely unconstrained. Such a conception leaves no place for an attribute of wisdom that decides what ought to be, as distinguished from His perfect knowledge of what is (and is not).[12] Some modern scholars have argued that this approach of al-Ash'arī, which became dominant in later Sunnism, marginalised the idea of God's wisdom within the later Islamic theological tradition.[13]

An alternative approach to the divine nature is taken by al-Māturīdī who, allowing a circumscribed place in his theology for *qiyās al-ghā'ib 'alā al-shāhid*,[14] affirms from the observation of the world the existence of its Creator and a number of personal attributes.[15] Of these, he stresses an eternal attribute of wisdom (*ḥikma*) for God – distinct from His knowledge – that He never contravenes.[16] Pessagno comments:

> Wisdom (*al-ḥikma*) is one of the recurrent terms which al-Māturīdī uses in regard to all aspects of reality. It is not for him a vague term, not a passing Qur'ānic reference. Rather, it is almost synonymous with purpose (*al-qaṣd*) and denotes his assertion, sometimes explicit, but always present, that reality is rational and therefore subject to reasonable analysis. This position is central to his later struggle with the problem of evil.[17]

Maintaining established Ḥanafī doctrine, al-Māturīdī also affirms a further eternal attribute that expresses God's creative activity, as well as all of His actions within the world: *takwīn* (*ex-nihilo* creativity).[18] To recap the differences regarding divine personal attributes between the three schools that have been introduced: al-Māturīdī posits *ḥikma* and *takwīn* as eternal attributes, in contrast with al-Ash'arī who left them out of his theological doctrine, as well as the various schools of the Mu'tazila who denied the existence of such hypostases entirely.[19]

Al-Māturīdī puts his conception of divine attributes to work in developing his moral theology. He states that it is not conceivable that God fails to act with wisdom, because he is essentially wise (*ḥakīm bi-dhātihi*).[20] He expands this view of

God's wisdom as an eternal attribute alongside others, such as His knowledge and power,[21] by writing that, 'the interpretation (*taʾwīl*)[22] of [God's] *ḥikma* is *iṣāba*, which is putting everything in its place. That is the meaning of justice (*ʿadl*), and His action does not depart from it.'[23] In other words, it is impossible for Him to be characterised with *ẓulm*, as this means putting something in the wrong place.[24] For al-Māturīdī, God's wisdom is logically prior to both His unlimited, free giving (*faḍl*) and His justice, through which it is expressed.[25]

It should be noted that al-Māturīdī, following the Qur'an, makes the attribute of wisdom foundational and ineffable – it is his answer to why there is a world. The only attempt that can be made to understand it is to look for its traces upon the created order.[26] This implies that there is a close association between the eternal attributes of *ḥikma* and *takwīn* within his system. Thus, he mentions the equivalence of *ḥikma* to *aḥkama,* defining it as 'meeting the reality in each thing and putting it in its place'.[27] Meanwhile, *takwīn* is explained by the following formulation: 'everything is as He knows it will be, so He creates it in accordance with His knowledge in its pre-ordained time, without needing to return to it'.[28]

Although these definitions are similar, it seems that al-Māturīdī envisaged a distinct role for the two attributes. The system may be reconstructed along the following lines: His *takwīn* acts in accordance with His knowledge of what is to be, which He wills and by His power it occurs. His wisdom provides the content of what ought to be. The meaningful difference between knowledge and wisdom here may be queried and it was (see below). However, as will be shown, if they are to be treated as a single attribute, the coherence of al-Māturīdī's system is only preserved by reading it substantially in terms of God's *ḥikma*. That is, treating God's action as stemming from His wisdom, rather than His knowledge merely descriptive of the objects of His will.[29] Such a position is at the heart of al-Māturīdī's theodicy: he is able to assert that all things that happen do so in accordance with God's wisdom and conversely that certain things, while not impossibilities for God's will and power, are inconceivable by virtue of His wisdom.[30]

Ashʿarīs presented a quite different picture of what they termed the attributes of God's action (*ṣifāt fiʿlihi*). Abū Bakr al-Bāqillānī (d. 403/1013) distinguishes this class, in which he includes *khalq* (creation) and *ʿadl* (justice), from that of personal attributes (*ṣifāt dhātihi*), on the basis of their lack of eternality.[31] In this conception, as developed by al-Juwaynī (d. 478/1085), attributes of action are nothing more than the manifestation of God's creation of accidents to characterise featureless atoms moment by moment.[32]

The developed form of this argument, as presented by Fakhr al-Dīn al-Rāzī (d. 606/1210), is to put the Māturīdī position (which he calls Ḥanafī) on the horns of a dilemma: they either mean by *takwīn* the effects of God's *irāda* (will) in a given object and so it refers to a relational attribute (*ṣifa nisbīyya*) with no existence except when its object is brought into being, or they mean the attribute that causes the effect, which is merely *irāda*.[33] A similar point is made about *ḥikma*: either it means God's knowledge, or his action. In the former case, it is nothing other than his attribute of *ʿilm*, which Māturīdīs already accepted; in the latter it is merely an aspect of creation generated by His will and power.[34]

These critiques had a tangible effect on the development of Māturīdī theology as a school tradition after the lifetime of its eponym. Abū al-Yusr al-Bazdawī (d. 493/1099) takes a firm stance on the eternality of *takwīn* as one of the *ṣifāt al-fiʿl*, alongside others, such as *takhlīq* (creation from existing material) and *raḥma* (mercy).[35] He curiously omits *ḥikma* from his entire discussion of the divine attributes.[36] For Abū al-Muʿīn al-Nasafī (d. 508/1114), while *ḥikma* remains categorised as an eternal attribute, it is understood to be either *ʿilm* or *ʿamal* (action).[37] Under pressure from the Ashʿarī challenge, he retreats to affirming *ḥikma* as some variety of eternal action, although he still lists *ḥakīm* and *khāliq* (Creator) as eternal attributes.[38] Two centuries later, a pillar of the classical school, Abū al-Barakāt al-Nasafī (d. 710/1310), takes this argument to its logical conclusion. Divine wisdom, in the sense of God's perfect knowledge, is referred back to Him being *al-ʿalīm* (omniscient), while in the sense of *itqān* (perfecting) and *iḥkām* (mastering) in relation to the creation it is understood as coming under *takwīn* as His eternal action.[39] The later Māturīdīs, therefore, abandoned the conception of an independent attribute of *ḥikma*, collapsing it into *takwīn*.[40]

Thus, while both Ashʿarīs and Māturīdīs hold that God's attributes of will and power make created things possible, the latter argue that an eternal creative ability extantiates them in time. Furthermore, al-Māturīdī himself also affirms an eternal attribute of wisdom, which within his system provides a certain ethical modality to God's creation that he deems essential and irreducible.

The Muʿtazila, although rejecting the notion of eternal attributes, propose a human-centred conception of justice in their concept of divine wisdom. An early view, which was maintained by the Baghdadī school of Muʿtazila, went so far as to declare that God necessarily provides the greatest benefit for humanity, a position known as the doctrine of the 'most salutary' (*aṣlaḥ*).[41] Therefore, they saw any form of harm created by God as being a necessary evil allowing the manifestation of a greater beneficial good. In their system, the desire to bring about such goods for humanity is the factor (*ʿilla*, pl. *ʿilal*) that ultimately necessitates God's actions in the world.[42]

In presenting his refutation of this view, al-Māturīdī does not just make a general case, but argues against the teaching of specific groups, including the circle of the Muʿtazilī al-Kaʿbī (d. 319/931) who was active in Transoxania[43] as well as the Thanawiyya (Zoroastrian dualists).[44] He represents the former as claiming that anyone who acts without seeking a benefit is not wise, and the one who acts without an *ʿilla* acts futilely. Applying this understanding to God, they argue that as He is exalted above receiving benefit or harm Himself, His wisdom in acting is occasioned by His benefiting others or warding off harm from them.[45]

In his response, al-Māturīdī begins by asserting that none of God's actions can be characterised with anything other than wisdom as He is eternally wise (*ḥakīm*). This means that one cannot describe Him as acting with an *ʿilla*, which would be an indication of need or weakness.[46] Furthermore, an act may proceed from God who does not benefit with it. In this context, he quotes Q. 7:54, 'For Him is the creation and the command (*lahu al-khalqu wa-l-amr*)',[47] and remarks that as the creation is His, He can do with it what he likes.[48] Thus, He is under no requirement to benefit it, although crucially His action cannot fail to be wise.

This means that, like the Basran Muʿtazilī Abū Hudhayl (but not the Baghdadī al-Naẓẓām),[49] al-Māturīdī affirms that God retains the power to commit injustice, but that it it is inconceivable that he ever does.[50] As well as due to His eternal wisdom, this reflects His perfection.[51] On this question, al-Ashʿarī holds that it is impossible, by definition, for God to commit injustice, as the concept is solely defined with reference to His will.[52]

Al-Māturīdī approaches the problem of harm, God's creation of things harmful to human beings outside of their free decisions, by declaring that though injustice (*jawr*) and folly (*safah*) are bad, and justice and wisdom are good, particular types of created things may vary, being wise in one situation, but foolish in another.[53] As it is established that God is bountiful, generous, free of need, and omniscient, then it is necessary to describe His every action as wisdom and justice, or grace (*faḍl*) and beneficence (*iḥsān*).[54]

In any particular case, the ultimate value of a decreed thing in terms of its wisdom is hidden from both the observer's sensory and mental knowledge.[55] A human act of injustice or even cruelty will nonetheless be a benefit for someone else, whether by means of guidance, admonition, reminding of blessings, warning of affliction, recognition of God, and so on.[56] There is a need, then, for human beings to be humble and patient, for they are not fully able to grasp the providential arrangement of the universe.[57] But, while al-Māturīdī denies that the human being can know the divine wisdom of each and every particular event, this does not imply that one cannot come to an understanding of morality without the aid of revelation, or fathom the general wisdoms of revealed legislation.

The question of moral ontology and epistemology shall be returned to below when dealing directly with al-Māturīdī's metaethical moral realism. It is useful to mention at this juncture that tying the Law so closely to God's wisdom makes his system teleological in the sense of always leading humanity towards beneficial purposes. Setting out a reading of the Qur'anic moral system according to a natural law framework shall be the subject of the discussion in section III.

The problem of human evil is a specific subset of the existence of harm and one that presents a more intense moral quandary. One may grant al-Māturīdī's point that the various harms experienced within the world can be explained as beneficial from another point of view, and ultimately wise and just, without thereby conceding the specific requirement for the human being to have the capacity to do evil. In other words, one may imagine human beings that sometimes become hurt, or sick, yet live entirely free from morally wrong actions. In fact, this is how the Ashʿarīs, as voluntarists, understand the state of the world before the arrival of a revealed law (when it arrives, evil is just disobedience to God's commands). Thus, one aspect of the problem is providing an explanation on the human level of the wisdom in the capacity to do evil at all, while the theocentric issue that emerges is whether the objective existence of evil compromises God's attributes of wisdom and omnipotence.

Al-Māturīdī argues that as human beings were made for testing, they were given faculties of discernment and knowledge of praiseworthy and blameworthy actions. God encourages them to perform good actions and to develop noble virtues through choosing what is good, and leaving what is bad.[58] The key concept used in this account is that of free will, or choice (*ikhtiyār*), which has an important role in his theodicy as the central locus of human agency. For al-Māturīdī, the existence of human free will is proven by the necessary knowledge of sense experience.[59] The argument he uses against determinists (*ahl al-jabr*) is that everyone knows the reality of choice from their own experience, and can affirm that the self is a responsible agent (*fāʿil kāsib*). If it were conceivable to deny the validity of sensory experience, then it would lead to denial of all the senses and knowledge of the world as a whole, which is absurd.[60] Therefore, human beings are created for a wise purpose (*ghāya*) – in the sense of a human *telos* – which they require free will in order to fulfil; their capacity to do evil gives meaning to the choice of faith and piety.

If the creation of human responsibility and setting the conditions by which free will can be exercised purposefully and fruitfully affirms God's wisdom, what then of His omnipotence? How can human beings be truly responsible for actions that are entirely created by God? This is the line of thinking espoused by many of the Muʿtazila, which led them to the belief that God grants the power to act just before an action takes place, such that in the next moment the human being acts entirely alone.[61] Of course, the Muʿtazila did not see this as compromising God's omnipotence, as the action ultimately depends on Him.

This position was not just unacceptable to al-Māturīdī, but to a broad spectrum of Sunnī theological opinion that held that nothing within the creation was able to escape the direct power of God, even for a moment.[62] Ashʿarīs, for instance, invoke the maximally occasionalist notion of *kasb* (acquisition): human acts are created by God, yet acquired by human beings.[63] This emphasis on the ontology of divine creation leads to what one may call a psychological approach to the problem of free will; human beings experience choice, even though their actions occur with a power granted by God for a specific intended act, willed by God from eternity.[64]

With his *ikhtiyār*, al-Māturīdī presents a concurrentist alternative. God gives human beings the power to select from contrary actions, although for actualisation of an act, He must concur with the agent's choice in the moment it takes place.[65] If we put this idea into the broader frame of his system, it is possible to attempt an actual resolution, rather than a merely psychological one, to the competing claims of divine predestination and human free will. As was mentioned previously, al-Māturīdī affirms that creation occurs not just from God's knowledge, will, and power, but also by virtue of His wisdom and creative ability. This means that human choice is not only the effect of an eternal divine decision ontologically prior to its existence, but is equally the creative spark of eternal divine action as it manifests within the temporal world.

In other words, the human being does not just make a psychologically free choice, but has been created, by an eternally creative action, with the capacity to make an actually free one. Here, it can be argued that the decision of the later Māturīdī school to collapse the attribute of *ḥikma* into *takwīn* can be seen to have profound consequences. An opponent could argue that if the human acts that are created by God's eternal *takwīn* are genuinely free, then, much like Neoplatonic emanation, His creation of them becomes ontologically necessary: His will following their will. However, if God's wisdom is understood as an attribute equal to that of *takwīn*, as initially presented by al-Māturīdī, it becomes conceivable that such a creation occurs on the basis of that eternal wisdom.

This interpretation of al-Māturīdī's theology seems consistent with the view attributed to him and later members of his school that God's wisdom makes inconceivable a certain class of otherwise possible creations. For Māturīdīs, a creator who obligated His servants beyond their abilities,[66] or eternally rewarded disbelievers and damned the believers,[67] is as inconceivable as one who is weak or ignorant.[68]

The key theodical contribution of al-Māturīdī then is not just his defence of God's justice while neither compromising His power, nor the free will of humanity, but his articulation of both divine wisdom and human agency within strict theological parameters. Moreover, his formulation was considered acceptable within the matrix of Islamic intellectual activity that was to become known as Sunnī. Al-Māturīdī's solution deserves wider recognition for innovatively preserving the Qur'anic tension between free will and determinism without resolving it in either direction.[69] In particular, the significance of his affirmation of distinct attributes of *ḥikma* and *takwīn* for the coherence of his position on this ancient philosophical problem was not even recognised by the school that took his name, let alone the wider tradition.

II. Metaethics

Al-Māturīdī places much less emphasis on developing a complete metaphysics of the nature of reality than he does on its theological and moral aspects. This approach, fairly typical for early *kalām*, fits well with the concerns of this book and with the proposal to use his system in a constructive manner. The main purpose of this section is thus an attempt to put his theology to the service of metaethical aims in terms of ontology and epistemology. However, it is worth briefly stating what is known of al-Māturīdī's physical theory with the hope that more substantial constructive work can later be done in putting it into conversation with contemporary approaches.

Ulrich Rudolph presents a compelling argument that al-Māturīdī's implicit metaphysical position is a 'monistic ontology', by which he means that accidents (*aʿrāḍ*; which he also calls *ṣifāt*)[70] are the basic constituents of the material world.[71] Within the broad concept of accidents, he distinguishes between natures (*ṭabāʾiʿ*), which are able to form bodies,[72] and the classical accidents of *kalām*, which describe changing states.[73] Importantly, this means that he rejects the atomism of many Muʿtazilīs, Ashʿarīs, and later Māturīdīs,[74] following instead a model that can be traced to the idea of parts (*abʿāḍ*) held by Ḍirār b. ʿAmr (d. 200/815).[75] The contemporary historian of philosophy Richard Sorabji has attributed the term 'bundle theory' to Ḍirār's work, a classification that would put his thought, and hence that of al-Māturīdī on Rudolph's reading, within a broad family of metaphysical theories that continue to attract discussion today.[76] It may even be possible to see al-Māturīdī as using an early version of a Trope Bundle Theory, in which apparent substances can be analysed in terms of grouped abstract particulars.[77]

Al-Māturīdī also rejects maximal occasionalism, the position that there is only divine causation and that, therefore, God recreates the accidental properties (although not necessarily the bare atoms) of the entire creation at each moment.[78] This theological view became the mainstay of much of the later *kalām* tradition and the physical foundation for the Ashʿarī doctrine of *kasb*.[79] Al-Māturīdī's alternative is what may be called a concurrentist position, in which aspects of causation are attributed both to the creation and to God. Al-Māturīdī's most important theological expression of this is in his theory of human action, as discussed in the previous section.

His opposition to both atomism and occasionalism seems logically related: the idea of constant divine recreation is predicated on ensuring a central position for God in the causation of apparently solid and lasting particles.[80] If, instead, bodies are formed out of unstable natures, God's role is to create them as cohesive structures, to conserve them and to provide the power with which He concurs with them in producing causal effects.[81]

Turning towards metaethics, the key questions are ontological, the nature of ethical statements, and epistemological, the ability of the human being to come to knowledge of them.[82] The ontological position adopted by al-Māturīdī is a form of moral realism in which ethical properties have an objective existence in the created world and the commands of God tally with their value. He treats moral realism as a basic presumption validated by sense experience and induced from the generality of Qur'anic discourse.[83] In the context of the multivariate religious discourse in which his thought developed, among fellow Transoxanian Ḥanafīs, rival Muʿtazilīs, and even Zoroastrian dualists in the eastern Muslim lands around Samarqand, the vast majority accepted at least the basic idea of objective moral values as a given.[84] Despite this, it was to meet a strong challenge over time by an alternative voluntaristic approach, an anti-realist position in which ethical value is subjectively constituted by God's revelation. This seems to have emerged in Iraq at a slightly later period of time.[85]

According to this doctrine, which appears to have been first explicitly formulated by al-Ashʿarī in response to his erstwhile Muʿtazilī colleagues, legal obligation is attributed solely to the omnipotent will of God.[86] Thus, at least theoretically, He could alter the very norms of morality at any moment.[87] Later Ashʿarīs developed increasingly sophisticated and varied arguments against the realist position espoused by Muʿtazilī and Māturīdī theologians without compromising this core emphasis on the divine will.[88]

Part of the appeal of the Ashʿarī perspective was the simplicity of its basic formulation and the aura of absolute otherness and authority that surrounded its conception of the Qur'anic revelation.[89] Another important aspect of the later dominance of voluntarism in Islamic intellectual history was its uncompromising defence of the centrality of God's will in ethics. This was particularly important as a foil to the Muʿtazilī idea of the divine as apparently bound to a human code of values, which, in mirror fashion, they defended via their objectivist stance.[90]

One of the attractions of the theological synthesis of al-Māturīdī is his support of the moral realist position without compromising the autonomy of God's will.[91] This is achieved through his understanding of the attribute of eternal divine wisdom, as outlined in section I. Such a metaethical stance is not only close to the 'Qur'anic view' articulated in the previous chapter, but is significant for the normative analysis of societal justice that will follow.

It is from his doctrine of God's wisdom that al-Māturīdī develops a perspective on divine creation that leads to his moral realism.[92] According to him, it is God's wisdom that allows every action that emerges into being to have two aspects. First, its intrinsic nature, or qualities, the aspect of divine determination that al-Māturīdī calls *ḥadd* (definition) and for which he quotes Q. 54:49, 'We have created all things in due measure (*bi-qadar*).' This is realised by the creation of the act as either good (*khayr*) or evil (*sharr*); beautiful (*ḥasan*) or ugly (*qubḥ*); wisdom (*ḥikma*) or folly (*safah*).[93] At the same time, each act has an aspect in its actualisation within time and place, as well as other extrinsic contexts in which it is explained, such as its reward (*thawāb*) and punishment (*ʿiqāb*).[94] In other words, the moral reality of human action is defined by the interplay between the particularities of its nature and its instantiation within history and relationship to eschatology. This is what Sherman Jackson calls a 'soft' moral ontology: 'all acts/events must be capable of acquiring a teleological status that differs fundamentally from their immediate, practical status'.[95]

This explanation of the intrinsic and extrinsic aspects of acts can again be better understood when related to modern trope theories that posit entities to be defined with reference to their properties, including in some formulations their spatio-temporal locations.[96] Understanding al-Māturīdī's thought to be somewhat equivalent to a trope theory allows easy resolution of two major objections levelled against moral realism by Ashʿarī voluntarism. The first concerns what ontological feature of a certain action existing within the world makes it good or evil. Rather than struggling with how ethical properties can coexist with an atomic account of the world,[97] a trope theory is able to claim that such abstract particulars as, for instance, Zayd's goodness, are ontologically primary. The second issue is what to do about moral exceptions, an issue that plagued some strands of Muʿtazilī thought. If we want to admit that in certain situations, for example, truthfulness could be evil – the classic example is informing a would-be assassin the location of his victim[98] – trope theory allows this by saying that there is a separate abstract particular for each act of truthfulness. While truthfulness can be considered intrinsically good on a conceptual level, it is always found within the world in particular instances, which may sometimes admit exceptions.

The implication of al-Māturīdī's view is that the world is infused with ethical value such that it may provide a foundation for human moral reasoning.[99] Furthermore, as human culture is also part of the world, its movement through history implies a succession of outward forms linked to the underlying Scale, or natural law, which must be reconciled with divine revelation. This thread will be picked up in section III, below.

The ontological divergence between voluntaristic and moral realist perspectives has a close corollary in epistemology. Voluntarists, such as classical Ashʿarīs, hold that ethical knowledge, in the true sense, can only be grounded in revealed scripture.[100] As anti-realists, they do not accept that there are moral entities in the world that can become objects of knowledge. Instead, the morality of human actions is known through God's explicit disclosure in the world through revelation, which reflects His decision to mete out reward and punishment on the Day of Judgement.

For moral realists, such as the Muʿtazila and Māturīdīs, the affirmation of objective good and evil in the world leads naturally to the belief that these values can be known by the human mind. Furthermore, this is true to some extent even in the absence of revelation, as discussed in the previous chapter.[101] (Hourani shows that while it would be technically possible to believe in both objective ethical values and revelation as their sole source of knowledge, there would be no benefit in affirming the former properties, as they would remain perpetually out of reach.)[102]

As the early Ashʿarī moral epistemology was a divine command theory, it was premised fairly straightforwardly on the notion that ethical value could be derived solely from revelation. However, in this form, the theory has a notable flaw, which was exploited ruthlessly by its critics. If it is held that moral knowledge only comes from the command of revelation, then there is no basis on which the obligation to accept revelation can be established.[103] For this reason, the question of epistemology and the role of the mind in morality was examined in greater detail by later Ashʿarīs and those who followed them in rejecting claims to moral knowledge not based exclusively on revelation.

So, al-Ghazālī argues in his *al-Mustaṣfā* that every individual seeks benefit and leaves harm, such that moral obligation is no more than doing what is preferable to seek a known benefit. Encountering a miraculous prophet (later his preserved scripture), motivates enquiry and acceptance, without thereby positing access to objectively real moral knowledge outside of the revelation.[104] Shihadeh points out that this emotivist tendency developed further in later Ashʿarism. Thus, in his final works, al-Rāzī understands ethical value as based on each human judging what will furnish the greatest pleasure and pain. Obedience to God is obligated because the rewards and torments promised by revelation in the Hereafter overwhelm any available in the world.[105] Despite these theoretical developments, later Ashʿarism remained consistent with the early school in affirming that only revelation was capable of providing moral knowledge and establishing moral liability. Their arguments were rather designed to provide their anti-realist ontology with a defensible explanation for how human beings used moral concepts in natural language.[106]

Turning to al-Māturīdī's moral epistemology, he splits knowledge into a number of categories. The first is 'what is known with the outward senses immediately (*mā yuʿlamu bi-ẓāhiri al-ḥawāssi bi-l-badīha*)'.[107] Al-Māturīdī does not mention the phrase *badīhat al-ʿaql* (immediately known) in his discussion of the roots of knowledge in *Kitāb al-tawḥīd*,[108] although later members of the school argued that those things grasped immediately are a part of necessary knowledge, such as the fact that a part is smaller than a whole.[109]

He does not hold detailed principles of morality to be part of such immediate sensory knowledge, although he concedes that the human being by nature (*ṭabʿ*) will incline to the beneficial.[110] Rather, he argues that an *a posteriori* process of reflection and reasoning on the world built up through experience leads to knowledge of the values at the core of human morality.[111] This could take the form of rational arguments for the existence of God, or reflection of the necessity of the basic virtues and moral code. His understanding of human *fiṭra*, based on his understanding of Q. 30:30, is that the human being has a natural capacity to acquire knowledge of the oneness of God, unless the mind is influenced by something else.[112] The same distinction is upheld in al-Māturīdī's commentary on Q. 91:7–10, 'By the soul and how He formed it and inspired it [to know] its own rebellion and piety! The one who purifies his soul succeeds and the one who corrupts it fails.' Here he argues that the inspiration mentioned is the basic capacity to distinguish between good and evil; the knowledge of matters within the world only coming through experience.[113]

This is a further area of difference with the Muʿtazila, who generally affirmed the existence of *a priori* '[a]bsolute general propositions, which are always true in fact in their simple form'.[114] Unlike al-Māturīdī, they saw these as reflecting primary aspects of reality that are applicable to God and humanity equally.[115]

Another category affirmed by al-Māturīdī is the necessity of revelation to provide details of the moral code, which is due to the inevitable differences that arise between individuals in their understanding of what is good and right, and the requirement of a decisive arbitrator in this regard.[116] Therefore, he argues that revelation is not marginalised by the existence of natural moral knowledge, but complementary to it: in laying down specific injunctions and rituals that cannot be determined by the intellect, in comprehensively affirming the objective values of the natural law, and in motivating the adherence to it through disclosure of the reality of the unseen world and the life after death.[117]

Here, too, reason has a part to play in dealing with reports that contain the possibility of error.[118] In his framework, the intellect is the final arbiter, after the reception of sensory information and the arrival of revealed reports, for understanding the moral qualities of acts.[119]

The consequence of this epistemological view is the assumption of moral obligation for those capable of rational reflection even before the sending of a messenger, as commandment and prohibition are attached to their objective moral value.[120] This is, again, a view famously held by the Muʿtazila, but is equally a common early position closely linked to moral realism and preserved by the intellectual tradition associated with Abū Ḥanīfa (d. 150/767), who is said to have declared, 'Had God, Most High, not sent a messenger, recognition of Him by the intellect would have been an obligation upon the sentient (*law lam yabʿath allāhu taʿālā rasūlan la-wajaba ʿalā al-ʿuqalāʾi maʿrifatuhu bi-ʿuqūlihim*).'[121] He is also attributed the statement, 'There is no excuse for anyone of ignorance of his Creator (*lā ʿudhra li-aḥadin fī al-jahli bi-khāliqihi*).'[122] Whether or not these particular words were spoken by Abū Ḥanīfa, it is likely that this position was widely held in the early Muslim community and was especially popular in the regions of Islamic civilisation east of Iraq. Reinhart writes, 'Seen historically it preserves a kerygma in which a dynamic but minoritarian Islam summons – on the basis of moral universals – the non-Muslim or nominally Muslim to conform to the dictates of Revelation.'[123]

While al-Māturīdī's position reflected the early Samarqandī branch of Ḥanafīs, the Bukhārans held a view closer to the Ashʿarīs, that even though morality may be known before revelation, obligation with its attendant rewards and sanctions only arrives with the coming of messengers. The general pattern of the movement of later Māturīdīs towards Ashʿarī positions can be observed by the number of those who adopted this view in subsequent centuries.[124]

Taking stock of al-Māturīdī's metaethics as a whole, both the created order and the divine command act as the grounds for moral obligation. This means that in a sense there are two revelations, one natural and the other supernatural, with each containing signs (*āyāt*) for human beings to read.[125] In this context, Draz refers to the twin lights, revealed and immanent, such that 'only positive divine law can continue and complete natural moral law' and '[i]t is our human reason which tells us to deliver ourselves to divine reason'.[126] While the main focus of this book will turn to the exegetical project of extracting *ḥikma*s for societal justice specifically within the Qur'an, it is important to outline the normative ethical theory within which this activity is meaningful.

III. Normative ethics

Although a wide variety of ethical theories have been discussed within the Islamic intellectual tradition, the dominant normative approach to determining correct action is undoubtedly through *fiqh* and *uṣūl al-fiqh*.[127] In this discourse, a *ḥukm* (pl. *aḥkām*; ethico-legal ruling) is defined as the value of a particular act in terms of the duty of a moral agent to fulfil it. The *ḥukm taklīfī* (commissioning, or defining, ruling), is then 'the address of the Law when it attaches to the actions of legally responsible agents'.[128]

In the main, Muslim jurists derived a five-value classification system for all human action: *farḍ* (obligatory), *mandūb* (recommended), *mubāḥ* (permissible), *makrūh* (discouraged), and *ḥarām* (prohibited). The Ḥanafī school of law used two additional categories: *wājib* (necessary) between obligatory and recommended, and *makrūh taḥrīmī* (prohibitively discouraged) between discouraged and prohibited.[129] For practical purposes these took the value of obligation and prohibition respectively, but reflected the epistemological consideration that lacking definitive evidence, denial of the *ḥukm*'s status would not constitute an act of disbelief.[130]

As discussed above, many moral realists in the early period argue that the *aḥkām* for core aspects of ethics can be known in the absence of revelation. A common position was that the initial status of all other acts is permissibility, although some early Muslim jurists argued for prohibition.[131] Once revelation arrives, this natural law must be integrated in some way within the divine law, which provides many specific rulings. However, the legal theorist still seeks to understand which *aḥkām* can be derived from the scripture and what occasions their presence in particular cases. Zysow analyses the underlying structures of two major theories, proposing that they can be characterised as 'motive models', in which a ruling's *ḥikma* (wisdom, or purpose), causes it to exist directly,[132] and 'sign models', in which the *ḥikma* is inaccessible, but a separate *ʿilla* (indicator, or legal cause) does this job.[133]

El Shamsy argues that discussion about the *ḥikma* of rulings has its origin within third-/ninth-century Baghdadī Muʿtazilī circles.[134] It seems that this theological, rather than juristic, affiliation is important, as a similar theory was shared in the fourth-/tenth-century by Shāfiʿī jurists, such as al-Qaffal al-Shāshī (d. 365/976) and Abū Bakr al-Khaffāf (d. *ca* 345/957), as well as Ḥanafī ones, such as Abū al-Ḥasan al-Karkhī (d. 340/951), the main teacher of Abū Bakr al-Rāzī al-Jaṣṣāṣ (d. 370/981).[135]

Within the Ḥanafī milieu, the Muʿtazilī-influenced al-Jaṣṣāṣ in his *Al-Fuṣūl* defends the sign model, arguing that it is not the place of the jurist to look for the *maṣāliḥ* (benefits) of the ruling, which he thinks can only be known by *tawqīf* (divine stipulation).[136] This accords with his teacher, al-Karkhī, who is perhaps the earliest jurist with an extant text distinguishing between the *ḥikma* of a ruling and its *ʿilla*.[137] For Ḥanafīs, the path laid out by al-Karkhī and al-Jaṣṣāṣ came to dominate juristic discussion. The result is that while the wise purposes of rulings are considered real ethical properties in the world, they are insulated from affecting the derivation of law by a theory of legal kinds in the form of *ʿilal*.[138]

Ashʿarīs such as al-Ghazālī, as metaethical voluntarists, argued that it was God's grace (*tafaḍḍul*) that makes natural reason accord with the content of scripture, despite morality neither objectively existing within the creation, nor human minds having access to it.[139] They therefore developed their own motive theory based on a process of scriptural induction.[140] This alternative method, pursued by philosophically inclined Ashʿarīs, opened up an opportunity for them to directly use concepts

of benefit (*maṣlaḥa*) and higher objectives (*maqāṣid*) within the field of law.[141] Some of the key requirements that were stipulated include the provision of necessary (*ḍarūrī*), certain (*qaṭʿī*) benefits for society at large based on the attainment of universal considerations (*kulliyyāt*).[142]

The *maqāṣid al-sharīʿa*, therefore, are general principles derived inductively from the full gamut of legal rulings with the aim of establishing public benefit or warding off public harm. This theory consists of *ḍarūriyyāt* (necessities), *ḥājiyyāt* (needs), and *taḥsīniyyāt* (embellishments, or enhancements), which work together to secure the interests of human life as a whole.[143] The highest values consist of the preservation of five universals: religion (*dīn*), life (*nafs*), reason (*ʿaql*), progeny (*nasl*), and wealth (*māl*).[144]

The early articulations of these categories make clear that they were initially developed in connection with the rules for specific punishments: apostasy, murder, drinking alcohol, fornication, and thievery, respectively.[145] Their generality, cited as the reason that they can be confidently accepted and broadly used in the absence of scripture,[146] leads to imprecision when applied to the diverse particularities of the law. If the *sharīʿa* was a city, the five universals may be compared to its walls, representing the outer boundary of protection through principles abstracted from its laws. However, the shape of city walls does not tell the whole story of what goes on inside them.

Furthermore, as the system is inherently voluntaristic, the *kulliyyāt* proposed are ultimately grounded in scripture, meaning that, in the formulation of al-Ghazālī, any rule of *maṣlaḥa* based on them can never contradict established scriptural texts.[147] In other words, as critically observed by Ibn Taymiyya, according to the Ashʿarī theory, the benefits achieved by the Law are merely coincidental and do not occur due to God acting with specific *ḥikma*s.[148] The implication is that even if human reason seems to understand that a particular ruling has begun to act contrary to these principles due to the distance from the initial context of revelation, an induced generality cannot override a particular text on which it is based. However, with the concept of *maṣlaḥa* established, the temptation may arise to transform it into a utilitarian cost–benefit analysis, which is where it has often led within modern Islamic thought.[149]

For these reasons, the traditional conception of *maqāṣid* has been criticised for failing to adequately capture the highest values known to the Qur'an and human experience.[150] Some modern scholars have called for the recognition of additional *maqāṣid* with little consensus on how many should be added, or on how the theory as a whole would be modified by the new elements.[151]

These criticisms of the *maqāṣid al-sharīʿa* model are exemplified by its inability to adequately include the idea of justice, which should be central to a discussion of higher values of the *sharīʿa*.[152] Instead, justice has usually been categorised as a 'distant' objective of the *sharīʿa*, with the necessary *maqāṣid* closer and more tangible.[153] This is inconsistent with the theory's approach to the much broader category of *dīn*, as discussed in Chapter 1, which is treated as similar to the other four necessities.[154]

Is it possible, then, to go back and trace an alternative path along a natural law ethics rooted in the moral realism of al-Māturīdī? Such a view would require each ruling to be caused by its own particular *ḥikma*. ʿAlā ʾal-Dīn al-Samarqandī (d. 539/1144) argues for a motive model by stating that 'God's law attaches not to words, but to purposes and grounds.'[155] He quotes his Samarqandī forerunner al-Māturīdī, presumably from one of his lost works on *uṣūl al-fiqh*, who uses the term *ʿilla* for this purposeful cause, 'The legal cause (*ʿilla*) is [defined as] the ontological cause (*maʿnā*) that instantiates the ruling when it is present.'[156] Here Richard Frank points out that in the theological language of the time, such *maʿnā*s are accidents, 'the *intrinsic causal determinants of the thing's being-so*'.[157] According to al-Samarqandī's analysis, the argument returns to al-Māturīdī's theology of God's wisdom. God is the real cause and can act, that is legislate, with or without a means (*sabab*). However, He never acts without wisdom, meaning that, whether human beings are able to fathom it or not, the *ḥukm* is caused by the presence of its *ḥikma*.[158]

This is confirmed by al-Māturīdī's exegesis on the *zakāt* category of *muʿallafāt qulūbuhum* (those whose hearts are to be won over), which Ḥanafīs generally consider abrogated after the time of the Prophet Muḥammad. He uses the same technical term, *maʿnā*, when writing in regard to Q. 9:60:

> In this verse is an inference to the permissibility of abrogation by exhaustive legal enquiry on account of its ontological cause no longer being present (*wa-fī al-āyati dalālatu jawāzi al-naskhi bi-l-ijtihādi li-irtifāʿi al-maʿnā alladhī bihi kāna*).[159]

It may seem strange that al-Māturīdī thinks that a ruling can be abrogated after the time of revelation, but it makes perfect sense within the parameters of his broader motive model. God's wisdom makes it impossible that a *ḥukm* fails to follow its rationally appreciable *ḥikma*. Such a view requires an acceptable theological explanation for abrogation (*naskh*). Al-Samarqandī provides it with a quote from al-Māturīdī's lost *maʾākidh al-sharāʾiʿ*,[160] that 'abrogation is in reality the extrinsic explanation of the duration of time God, Most High, willed for the first ruling (*al-naskhu fī al-ḥaqīqa bayānu muntahan mā arāda allāhu taʿālā bi-l-ḥukmi al-awwali min al-waqt*)'.[161] This is confirmed by statements in al-Māturīdī's *tafsīr*.[162]

So, juristic *ijtihād* is only the apparent cause of the *naskh*; it is really the *bayān* – the extrinsic explanation – of the duration God willed for the ruling.[163] This can be connected to the earlier discussion of al-Māturīdī's metaphysics. If we can posit the initial ruling as a type of trope qualifying certain acts, such as the obligation of paying *zakāt* to the *muʿallafāt qulūbuhum*, then it becoming abrogated means that it has reached the pre-ordained time of expiration in which it is no longer caused by its *ḥikma*.

In light of the above, it is now possible to outline the essential aspects of a neo-Māturīdī natural law ethics. The first principle is that the foundation of morality is in God's eternal wisdom from which He both creates the world with objective moral properties and reveals scripture. Second, as an aspect of the world, which can be accessed by anyone capable of reflection upon experience, the natural law is authoritative over human beings in both the absence of scripture and for those who do not believe in it. However, for those who do affirm revelation, the divine law supplements and perfects the natural law. (The question of drawing the boundary between natural and divine law may be more profitably discussed at the end of this book). Third, what is right is predicated on what is good, meaning that for those aspects of the law that can be known, their particular *ḥikma*s are the ontological causes of their rulings. This teleological aspect would allow the system of rules to change in certain cases even as the underlying moral principles stay constant. Finally, on the social level, the particular wisdoms of the Law are directed towards the ideal condition of justice within society.

I hope that this proposed system can be fully elaborated as a normative ethical theory in a future work. For the present book, creative appropriation of the conceptual resources of al-Māturīdī, and a wide range of classical and contemporary thought, provides a theoretical underpinning for my exploration of Qur'anic societal justice within the context of its first society.

IV. Modelling the just society

If the moral narrative outlined in the previous chapter is visualised as a timeline, starting from an ancient past and continuing to an infinite future, the remainder of this book focuses on the time of the Qur'an's revelation and the just society that it envisages. As Neuwirth writes, in the Qur'an 'the event of the Prophet's inspiration is the crucial fact of salvation history'.[164]

This socio-historical context is the background on which the idea of the just society is explored. In Chapter 1, societal justice was defined as the condition of a society realised by the Wisdom of God's Writ, which matches the Scale of moral value.[165] This definition can be made operative within the normative theory proposed in the previous section as follows: the Wisdom of God's Writ consists of the *ḥikma*s of the *sharīʿa*, the Scale of moral value is the natural law, and societal justice the ideal condition realised by these *ḥikma*s.[166] Moreover, I suggest that it is possible to model the structure of Qur'anic societal justice according to the relationship of these *ḥikma*s. Parts II–IV of this book are precisely the drawing of this blueprint within the applied context of the initial community of Muslims under the guidance of the Prophet Muḥammad.

In seeking to analyse the structure of societal justice, three additional classificatory levels can be added to the basic pair of *ḥukm* and *ḥikma* to clarify the relationship of *ḥikma*s to justice: the spheres of political, distributive, and corrective justice, which have a prior basis in Islamic juristic discourse;[167] thematic subjects; and then thematic topics. These levels correspond to the part, chapter, and section divisions in the book and have been inductively iterated by searching for patterns within the Qur'an's discourse. This schema can be seen in Figure 2.1.

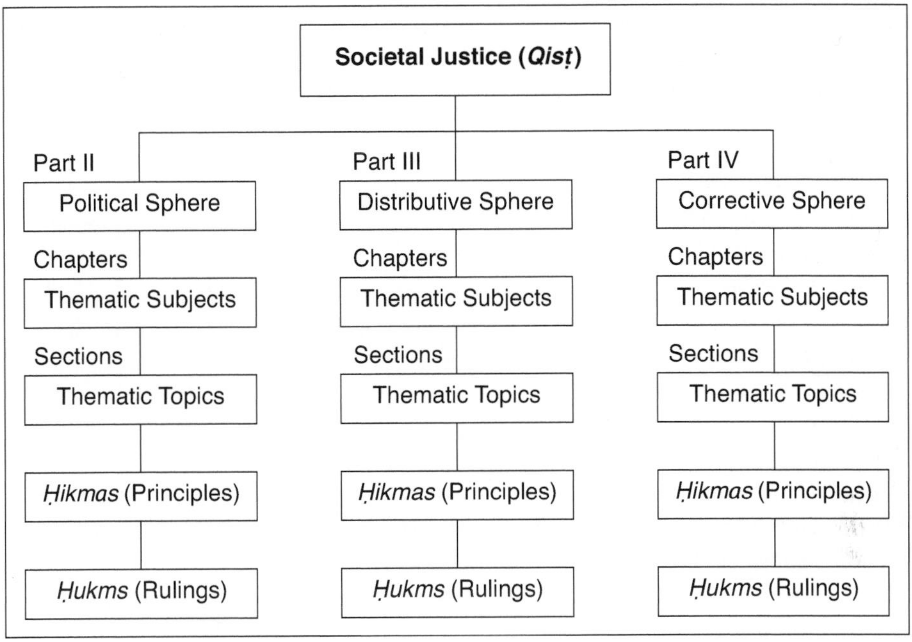

Figure 2.1 Hierarchy of the *sharīʿa* including thematic levels of justice

The decisive question remaining is a methodological one: how can these *ḥikma*s be discovered within the scripture in light of its initial social context? This is the subject of the next chapter.

3

Hermeneutics

So far, a case has been made that the Qur'an contains an implicit meta-theology that can be systematically drawn out within certain fields of analysis. Chapter 2 articulated a theological and ethical model giving a key place to posited *ḥikma*s of societal justice within the Qur'an. This chapter grapples with the role that hermeneutics can play in assisting the extraction of such *ḥikma*s from the totality of Qur'anic material. As a point of departure, I will put forward Farid Esack's suggested criteria for contemporary interpretive theories: utilising multiple genres of Islamic scholarship, particularly *'ulūm al-qur'ān* and *uṣūl al-fiqh* for establishing textual meaning; examining not just isolated occasions of revelation, but 'the *Sitz im leben* of the Qur'ān as an entirety'; and viewing the *tafsīr* tradition as ever-varying approximations of authorial intent.[1]

While these principles are useful general guidelines, to be suitable for my purposes the proposed hermeneutic model must be able to take texts, in the form of discrete passages or verses, from various locations within the scripture and place them into an arrangement that facilitates the analysis of their intra-textual meaning. When drawing upon the connections between them in order to extract their *ḥikma*s, I consider six hermeneutic indices (see Figure 3.1 opposite), each of which comprises a section of this chapter.

The diagram in Figure 3.1 shows how this hermeneutic can be schematised in terms of a process. Qur'anic texts enter first into intra-textual analysis before being studied in terms of *naẓm* (syntax-pragmatics) and semantics, which I consider semi-internal indices. *Niẓām* (textual structure) and socio-historical context provide two different external backdrops against which the various texts are to be read, and the *ḥikma*s of societal justice extracted.

There is a special relationship between *naẓm* and *niẓām*, as they represent the immediate and wider synchronic considerations of the text. There is also a connection between semantics and socio-historical context, as the meanings of words and phrases are known within a historically conditioned lexical context, which is related to the diachronic socio-historical environment in which the text was revealed. The external indices, therefore, represent two ways in which the Qur'an is ordered: as a complete text with its own compositional arrangement, and as an active revelation responding chronologically to the needs of the earliest Muslim community during a period of more than twenty years. A. H. Johns comments in this regard:

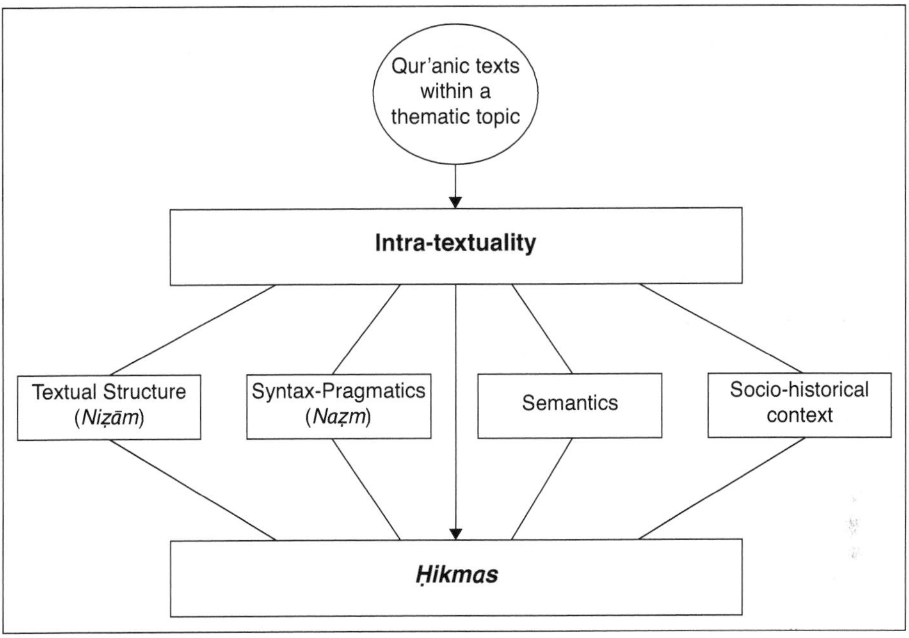

Figure 3.1 The hermeneutic model for extracting the *ḥikmas* of societal justice

> This contextual repositioning of the locutions from the stages of its revelation to the Prophet, and through him to the Companions, guiding their lives throughout a range of circumstances under his leadership to their place in the *muṣḥaf*, reveals emphases and resonances that generate multiple levels of meaning. These modes are as two lungs. To be fruitful, every encounter with the Qur'an benefits from an awareness of the breath supplied by each to experience the levels of meaning it generates.[2]

Neuwirth discusses a similar idea under the rubric of two 'levels of communication': an interior one between the Prophet and his immediate listeners, in which the divine voice speaks mainly to the receiver of revelation, and an exterior one in which the previous listeners have disappeared as active players from the stage, to be replaced by the new readers of the scripture, whom are addressed by the divine voice through the Prophet.[3]

I. Intra-textuality

Interpretation of the Qur'an on the basis of intra-textuality is a fundamental principle of any thematic hermeneutic, because the scripture's content is distributed in such a way that a single topic is returned to in various suras in more or less detail. Intra-textuality is to be distinguished from intertextuality, reading the Qur'an in the light of external texts, such as the Biblical tradition, which I have put under the heading of socio-historical context (see Section V below).

This exegetical principle is famously explained by Ibn Taymiyya (d. 728/1328) as *tafsīr al-qur'ān bi-l-qur'ān* (explanation of the Qur'an by the Qur'an).[4] Significantly, one of the earliest exegetes to systematically apply it to the Qur'an is Abū Manṣūr al-Māturīdī in his commentary *Ta'wīlāt ahl al-sunna*, also known as *Ta'wīlāt al-qur'ān*.[5] It does not seem implausible to suggest that his attention to the Qur'an, especially his adoption of this hermeneutic, is a factor in explaining the close fit between his theological positions and the scripture.[6] A much later development of this approach is found in the modern commentary of Muḥammad al-Amīn al-Shinqīṭī entitled *Aḍwā' al-bayān fī īḍāḥ al-qur'ān bi-l-qur'ān*, in which he takes it as his main interpretive methodology. In his introduction, he outlines his hermeneutic with prominent use of the term *bayān* (explanation) and constructs a typology of its major instances within his work, thereby putting the procedure on a more systematic footing than many exegetes.[7]

This principle can fulfil a number of roles, the most important being clarification of the ambiguous within Qur'anic polysemy (see Section II below), specification of the general expression (*takhṣīṣ al-'āmm*), providing the reason or rationale for a particular injunction, and giving the details or context of what is elsewhere in summarised form. The units for intra-textual analysis in this study potentially range from a single expression to full passages. It is important to point out that, in the words of Abdel Haleem, this 'conciseness or expansion in one place or another depends on *muqtaḍa 'l-ḥāl* (what the situation requires)'.[8] As will be discussed, this is a central element in both the *naẓm* of sentences and the *niẓām* of passages (see Sections III and IV below).

II. Semantics

The Qur'anic vocabulary is complex and multi-faceted. Often a number of different words are employed for the same purpose, yet at other points in the text there is a striking repetition of an identical, or similar, word or phrase. The reason such synonymity can be found even between words with different root meanings is due to the characteristic polysemy of Qur'anic Arabic, a feature called *wujūh al-qur'ān* and recognised from the earliest scholarship upon the scripture.[9] Within the mature discipline of *uṣūl al-fiqh*, a word with multiple conflicting semantic possibilities requiring clarification is termed *mushtarak* (polysemous).[10]

In textual analysis, the semantic possibilities available for each word, or semantic root, must be examined in order to decide which one is present in any particular context. Also, while one word may be used as a near-synonym to another, it often retains an undertone of meaning from the core ideas expressed by its triliteral root, a phenomenon that is far less pronounced in English.

The words of a language do not exist as isolated atoms, but as a semantic web of interrelated significations. Thus, the place of the word within the total structure of the language plays a crucial role in its meaning, as does its use within particular literary contexts. In the case of the Qur'an, there is reciprocity between the word in a particular pragmatic context and other usages both within the scripture and among seventh-century Arabic speakers. When focus is placed on what a particular word means, a definition may be provided through one, or ideally both, of these avenues. In methodological terms, I shall either turn to another place within the Qur'an to better explain the word or phrase – the general rubric of *tafsīr al-qur'ān bi-l-qur'ān* – or to lexicographical material that gives information about the linguistic usage of the Arabians contemporaneous to the revelation.

On the ethical plane, the former route to definition has been studied in detail by Toshihiko Izutsu. Although his work is justly regarded as a seminal contribution to the field, some doubts can be raised about the validity of his epistemological framework. Izutsu presents a picture in which an essentially non-verbal world is named and categorised according to culturally specific language. Implicit in this account is the fact that the specific moral code held by each linguistic community is based on nothing more than the aggregate of its evaluation of various actions.[11] Significantly, he does not see moral phenomena as recognised and named, but constituted through the act of naming itself. Izutsu is thus unequivocal in his espousal of moral conception as culturally relative, a position that sharply contrasts with the Qur'an's own universalist discourse. Nonetheless, his careful examination of Qur'anic language provides a number of different ways in which the text can be used to define its own vocabulary and clarify shades of meaning.[12]

The second method of semantic definition looks outside of the Qur'an to information recorded in lexicons, which are founded on usage within early Arabian poetry and sayings, or the commentary recorded in *tafsīr* texts on the authority of the Prophet, his Companions, and the following generations of Muslims. Certain lexicons have gained special prominence and have become established as standard reference works in the field, such as *Lisān al-ʿarab* by Ibn Manẓūr (d. 711/1312) and *Mufradāt alfāẓ al-qur'ān* by al-Rāghib al-Iṣfahānī.[13] Likewise, in the *tafsīr* tradition, certain texts have gained a substantial reputation as works of authority in linguistic matters, such as al-Zamakhsharī's (d. 538/1144) *Al-Kashshāf*, Abū Suʿūd's (d. 982/1574) *Irshād al-ʿaql al-salīm ilā mazāyā al-kitāb al-karīm,* and al-Rāzī's *Al-Tafsīr al-kabīr*, which is also important as a particularly ethically concerned commentary.[14]

The semantic method adopted in this book, therefore, is to use both of these procedures, internal and external to the scripture, in order to establish key terms and to differentiate the subtleties of meaning between nearly synonymous words. In the frequent cases that the lexicographical sources contain more than one meaning, I will prefer strong internal evidence from the Qur'an if it is available.

III. Syntax-pragmatics (*naẓm*)

I have translated the concept of *naẓm*, an important tool within the hermeneutic model of this study, as the Qur'an's syntax-pragmatics. More properly, it is the interface between these two elements, in which linguistic structures, particularly at the sentence level, are composed in consideration of the intended addressee in order to construct meaning.[15] I distinguish *naẓm* from the related concept of *niẓām*, or wider textual structure, although it is possible to use the former term for both.

Linguistically, *naẓm* refers to the stringing of pearls, and by extension any versified text composed of rhyme and meter, as opposed to prose (*nathr*).[16] The term acquired a technical meaning in its application to the Qur'an by at least the time of al-Jāḥiẓ (d. 255/868–9), who used *naẓm* to describe the miraculous eloquence of its expression, which is closely connected to the theological concept of *iʿjāz* (inimitability).[17]

This idea was developed by a number of scholars in the classical period who were concerned to provide a systematic apparatus for the appreciation of Qur'anic expression. In the process, and particularly through the work of individuals such as ʿAbd al-Qāhir al-Jurjānī (d. 471/1078), the discipline of *balāgha* (rhetoric) was born.[18] Furthermore, as it matured and more sophisticated tools for linguistic analysis became available, it became possible to describe in detail how a particular utterance fitted the contextual requirements of its situation, which was the main purpose of the subdiscipline of *ʿilm al-maʿānī* (contextual semantics).[19] In his *Al-Īḍāḥ fī ʿulūm al-balāgha al-maʿāni wa-l-bayān wa-l-badīʿ*, the rhetorician al-Qazwīnī (d. 739/1338) says, 'This, I mean making the utterance correspond to the requirements of the situation, is what Shaykh ʿAbd al-Qāhir [al-Jurjānī] calls *naẓm*.'[20] Thus, a Qur'anic sentence is analysed to understand how the choice and ordering of words, the intention behind them and their effect on the chosen addressee all come together to form a rich pattern of meaning.[21]

It may be argued, therefore, that the indigenous Arabic rhetorical categories developed for classifying Qur'anic linguistic structures represent an incisive method for appreciating meaning within its ethical texts. This section provides a summary of relevant techniques and an assessment of how they may be used within the wider hermeneutic proposal.

The Qur'anic patterns of address (*mukhātaba*) are multi-faceted, reflecting the variety of different readers they are directed towards. The divine voice switches between modes of address, at times speaking to the Prophet directly, at other times Muslim believers, Scriptuaries, pagans, humanity in general, or even the jinn. There are also moments in which prayers and conversation are directed towards God, either by the assumed voice of the believers (as in Sūrat al-Fātiḥa), a prophet, angel, or even the Devil.

The Qur'an also makes direct addresses during recounted narratives within the text, representing a meta-level of hailing. For instance, a narrative directed ostensibly to the Children of Israel can include an address by God to one of His prophets: 'Remember when Moses prayed for water for his people and We said to him, "Strike the rock with your staff"' (Q. 2:60).

As well as different subjects of address, there is the possibility of varying the address between general and particular in form and meaning; between singular, dual, or plural in structure and intent; and a wide variety of tones and expressions. The classical works of *ʿulūm al-qurʾān* list more than thirty such categories, each with their own subtleties of meaning.[22]

This can be read as part of the Qur'an's distinctive self-reflexive style and omniscient perspective. Abdel Haleem comments:

> The limits of a Qur'anic verse are different from those of an ordinary sentence and may encompass a number of sentences, with different persons, with Allah at the centre of the situation with access to all, speaking from the viewpoint of various aspects of His Godhead about the various persons/things or talking to them from their multiple viewpoints.[23]

Another important aspect of the divine address, according to the communication theories propounded within *uṣūl al-fiqh*, is the assumption of its truthfulness (*ṣidq al-mutakallim*). Not only is this a theological given, but it implies that the non-literal nature of an utterance may be inferred if it is in apparent breach of this condition.[24]

Taking any given sentence, the discipline of *ʿilm al-maʿānī* allows a detailed structural analysis, of which the following are the most important categories: the division into *khabar* (informative), or *inshāʾ* (performative); the modes (*aḥwāl*) of the subject (*musnad ilayhi*), predicate (*musnad*) and structures dependent on the verb (*mutaʿalliqāt al-fiʿl*), according to contextual requirements; the technique of *qaṣr* (restriction); the use of *waṣl* (conjunction) and *faṣl* (disjunction); and the choice of *ījāz* (brevity), *iṭnāb* (lengthiness), and *musāwāt* (medium length).[25]

The distinction between *khabar* and *inshāʾ* is that the former carries a *ḥukm* (valuation) that is capable of being falsified; thus it purports to describe reality.[26] The latter comprises every other utterance that, rather than carrying a description about the world, attempts to influence it, such as orders, prohibitions, questions, and expressions of praise or censure.[27] Thereafter, every sentence is composed of a subject and a predicate, with the latter possibly requiring additional structures if verbal (or carrying a verbal meaning), as well as either being restricted or left unrestricted; conjoined or disjoined from other sentences; and made concise, lengthy or left at a medium length, which is the original state.[28]

In terms of understanding the use of these various forms to fit the requirements of the situation, it is necessary to look at the objective of the speaker and the state of the addressee. In the case of the *khabar*, the assumption is that the objective is to inform the addressee of the *ḥukm*, unless there is an indication that it is to inform the addressee that the speaker knows it, or to mention it for another reason, such as encouragement.[29] As *ʿilm al-maʿānī* was largely developed in order to assist with the interpretation of the Qur'an, the relationship between speaker and addressee is framed in such a way as to have an obvious application to the scripture. The addressee is said to be in one of three states of mind as follows: open-minded to the *ḥukm*, having not encountered it before, for which there is no need for emphasis; already aware of the *ḥukm*, but returning to it to gain certainty, for which emphasis is recommended; and in denial of the *ḥukm*, for which emphasis is necessary.[30] This is the manifest situation, but it can be altered due to the situation of the addressee and the context of the utterance within the text as a whole.[31]

For the *inshā'*, the major distinction is between utterances that call for something not present at the time of the address, such as commands, prohibitions, queries, desires, and calls for attention, and between those that do not, such as praise, blame, and wonder.[32] The objective of the speaker and the state of the addressee again enter into consideration along with the textual context, in determining how the utterance is structured in terms of its fundamental elements.

Having made this brief overview, I shall examine the particularities of analysing ethical texts according to this method. The *khabar* provides informative statements about ethical concepts or the ethics of certain acts, while the *inshā'* directly calls for action or restraint. The *ḥukm*, which is always to be found within the *khabar* structure, is the ethical information within the text, conveyed from God to the Qur'an's audience. It is also important to identify the addressee of an ethical text from its indicators, so that the correct state of mind is understood within its context. Frequently, the Qur'anic style employs the *inshā'* rather than the *khabar* form. As a scripture that puts ethical guidance central, this provides an exhortatory quality that calls directly to action.[33] Identifying these characteristics thus transcends appreciation of eloquent expression to become a useful tool in interpretation, as it enables the reader to better determine the ethical principles underlying the text's normative expressions.

IV. Textual structure (*niẓām*)

The idea of basic textual and moral consistency is used within the Qur'an as one of the arguments for its divine provenance, 'Will they not think about this Qur'an? If it had been from anyone other than God, they would have found much inconsistency in it' (Q. 4:82). This principle was extended by classical exegetes to analyse points of coherence within its language and structure.[34] As has been mentioned, generations of scholars investigating the subject of Qur'anic *naẓm* utilised the concept of *waṣl* and *faṣl* to analyse the connection between sentences within an utterance and their focus on *maqām* (context) implicitly took into account the *sibāq* (preceding textual units) and *siyāq* (following textual units).[35]

Some went further, such as al-Qazwīnī, who concludes his book *Al-Talkhīṣ fī 'ulūm al-balāgha* with a section highlighting the importance of three places in composition: *al-ibtidā'* (the beginning), *al-takhallus* (the transition between the introduction and the objective of the piece), and *al-intihā'* (the ending).[36] He then remarks that 'all the beginnings and endings of the suras are found to be of the most excellent and complete design.'[37] Al-Suyūṭī (d. 911/1505), in *Al-Itqān fī 'ulūm al-qur'ān*, titles a section *munāsabat fawātiḥ al-suwar wa-khawātimihā* (Coherence of the Beginning and Endings of Suras), where he points to the importance of the semantic relationship between the two.[38] However, despite late classical exegetes, such as al-Rāzī and al-Biqā'ī (d. 885/1480), discovering connections (*irtibāṭ*) and correlations (*munāsabāt*) between adjacent verses and suras, there is little effort before the modern period to attempt to deal with the total composition, or unity, of the text.[39]

Recent scholarship on the Qur'an has increasingly placed a degree of emphasis on the analysis of coherence and textual structure at a macro level. The development of the so-called 'sura-as-a-unity thesis', usually following in the footsteps of Ḥamīd al-Dīn al-Farāhī or other twentieth-century exegetes, such as M. A. Draz, Amīn Aḥsan Iṣlāḥī, Sayyid Quṭb, and Muḥammad Ḥusayn al-Ṭabāṭabāʾī, has been a significant turn in contemporary Qur'anic studies.[40] This trend arguably has roots in early Arabic literary criticism and the concept of *waḥdat al-qaṣīda* (the unity of the ode), which was recognised by Ibn Qutayba (d. 276/889) and even earlier by al-Jāḥiẓ, who comments, 'Indeed the most excellent poetry, in my opinion, is that in which the parts cohere and which is fluent in articulation, so you know that it is cast from a single mould and shaped into a single form.'[41]

Of all these authors, some of the deepest theoretical work was done by al-Farāhī, who preferred the term *niẓām*, and seems to be the first scholar in the history of Qur'anic studies to base his entire hermeneutic methodology on the thesis that each sura contains a unique *ʿamūd* (pillar), around which the entire composition turns,[42] which is 'not from its ordered parts, but pervading it as spirit and secret, such that the [manifest] speech is its exegesis and explanation'.[43] Furthermore, he went beyond the sura level to attempt to provide an account of the Qur'an's total structure by positing nine distinct sura groups. His student al-Iṣlāḥī adapted this method to construct an entire commentary in Urdu, in which he reduces them to seven.[44]

A number of criticisms have been levelled at this synchronic approach, the most common being the lack of an agreed methodology for determining the central theme of a sura group, sura, or the internal structure therein. It is thus charged with being too dependent on the subjective opinion of the individual exegete to become a reputable hermeneutic tool.[45] Another critical, although more appreciative view, is that proposed by El-Awa in her book *Textual Relations in the Qur'an*. She notes that coherence does not have to be based on the arbitrary determination of a central unifying theme, but can rely on the more objective notion of a continuum of contextual relevance that unfolds as the text is read.[46]

However, in response to El-Awa's view, A. H. Johns has questioned the wisdom of searching for a single objective basis for sura unity, arguing that the Qur'an's complexity and role as point of contact between divine and human spheres perhaps makes it inevitable that different readers will highlight disparate webs of meaning connecting its elements.[47]

My judgement is that the common insights obtained by scholars from widely different backgrounds in this field are sufficient to support its validity as an area of continued examination.[48] Furthermore, it seems that, as a relatively new development within the long-established discipline of Qur'anic exegesis, it will take some time for it to mature to a stage of greater agreement on method. Until then, the experimentation of different researchers with conceptual schema and terminology should be taken as a sign of scholarly vitality, rather than weakness.

In any case, the particular focus and thematic arrangement of this book puts sustained engagement with the Qur'an at the macro level, in terms of whole sura analysis, or sura order, beyond its reasonable scope. However, as Zebiri comments about thematic and textual unity, '[t]he two concepts are not unrelated; both arise from the modern tendency to take a comprehensive view of the Qur'ān'.[49]

My use of the principle of *niẓām* (following the terminology of al-Farāhī) is primarily for the coherence of meaning within and between passages. Although I provide limited reference to sura-wide concerns, I neither attempt to definitively settle the theoretical question of the nature of structure at the medium or long sura level, nor describe any particular sura's internal textual structure in a comprehensive manner.[50]

Qur'anic passages, or pericopes, consist of no set number of verses, but can be identified by their thematic content, as well as the use of various linguistic markers that point to shifts, or developments, of subject, much like paragraph markers do within modern texts.[51] It is, therefore, often useful to indicate the boundaries of the passage within which a verse relevant to the study is located, and to characterise its theme. At certain points, it may even be possible to go beyond this and provide an analysis of the structure of the material within a passage, as well as its connection to other passages. Despite the inevitable limitations of this procedure, it is still significantly more holistic than typical longitudinal commentaries, which often divorce the meaning of a verse from its surroundings.[52]

Just as the concept of *naẓm* permits a rigorous analysis of each text as an organised discourse in conformity with the requirements of the situation, *niẓām* considers textual structure at the level of passage, sura, and entire text. When a single subject is repeated in different suras within the Qur'an, not only is each occurrence constructed in accordance with the particular local requirements of that linguistic moment, the principle of *niẓām* insists that it is thoroughly woven into the context of each sura's composition.[53] The reality of this insight is that ultimately the *naẓm* and *niẓām* approaches, as they have been defined, are two different levels of analysis, micro and macro, on the same phenomenon of Qur'anic textual composition.

Methodologically, the fruits of *niẓām* spread to all areas of the study of the Qur'an. Thus, it is an important consideration in both semantic clarification and syntactic-pragmatic analysis, helping to establish the meaning of words, as well as the addressees of sentences and places where the usual requirements of the linguistic situation must be left.[54] Another significant use of *niẓām* arises in the interpretation of the Qur'an for the extraction of *ḥikma*s (see section VI below). Interpreting the Qur'an's higher intents involves searching for commonalities between disparate statements, which are identifiable foremost within the Qur'an's own textual structure. Unlike the view of some legal theorists who only grant a connection between adjoining textual units when there is an explicit *qarīna* (indication),[55] the principle of *niẓām* means that I assume relevance unless there is an indication of discontinuity. The logical conclusion of my use of the principle of *niẓām*, then, is that it is integral to Qur'anic understanding, such that I do not consider interpretations that violate its integrity as valid.[56]

V. Socio-historical context

This principle considers the socio-historical context, or Sitz im Leben, of the Qur'an's initial address. The aim is to understand the Qur'anic ethical teachings within the contours of seventh-century Arabia: its society, customary laws, and the broad outline of events that took place during the period of revelation, as well as significant details.[57] Abdullah Saeed describes the reason for this as follows:

> Its concerns, interests and guidance were directly connected with and organically related to the linguistic, cultural, political, economic and religious life, primarily of the people of the Ḥijāz, and more broadly the people of Arabia. Without this connection, revelation would not have made much sense even to the immediate community, let alone as a meaningful guide to humankind.[58]

The Qur'an does not define basic moral terms and other contextual information, as the pragmatic nature of its discourse assumes that the initial audience implicitly grasps how its message may be realised within society.[59] In this book, however, I must supply a minimum level of appropriate contextual information, so that I can adequately reconstruct the scripture's substantive concern with societal justice.[60] It is vital to appreciate that the necessity for the Qur'an to be contextually grounded in this manner does not negate its universality.[61] In fact, the moral narrative presented in Chapter 1 actively demands such a claim. Nonetheless, as discussed in the introduction, an analysis of ethical matters extending beyond the period of Qur'anic revelation in diverse geographical and historical circumstances is beyond the scope of this book.

If the value of an analysis of socio-historical context is granted, then there is a need to clarify how this is to be ascertained. Extant material sources for seventh-century Arabia are relatively scant. This extends to the written text of the Qur'an itself, although for reasons explained in this chapter, manuscript evidence has not been the sole epistemological basis for its textual validation down the centuries. In recent years, discovery of new sources and carbon dating of old manuscripts has led to some notable developments. One of the better-studied finds is the discovery of a codex in Sana'a, Yemen, which (notwithstanding some variant readings) indicates the overall stability of its written text soon after the lifetime of the Prophet Muḥammad.[62]

In terms of the extra-Qur'anic corpus, we possess a vast array of traditional material, today preserved in literary sources from mainly the second/eighth century onwards. Careful studies have shown that in the first century of Islam, this consisted of a mixture of transmitted practice, oral reports, some written documentation and hybrid forms, such as notes used as mnemonic aids.[63] As it appears within the later literary sources, this material is comprised of what I call the '*isnād* genres', due to the ascription of texts by *isnād*s (chains of authorities). The most important of these for this book are those associated with the disciplines of *tafsīr*, Hadith, and *sīra* (prophetic biography).

The sustained post-Goldziher doubts of Western academic scholarship on the reliable transmission of reports dating back to the prophetic era using the *isnād* are so well-rehearsed that I need not repeat them in detail here.[64] The form-critical method of John Wansbrough in his twin publication of *Qur'anic Studies* and *The Sectarian Milieu* in 1977 and 1978, respectively, is an extreme version of this approach. Wansbrough's attempt to be thoroughgoing in his scepticism of the early sources led him to argue that the Qur'anic text settled from a long oral pre-history by approximately 200/815 during the Abbasid period. He therefore treated the traditional Muslim chronology as a justificatory 'salvation history'.[65]

Even Wansbrough did not, however, push his scepticism to the extent of rejecting the Arabic identity of the Qur'an, unlike his contemporary Günter Lüling who published a book in 1974 arguing that its original text could be reconstructed by reading it as strophic poetry written in Pre-Islamic Central Arabian Christian-Arabic.[66] His work is a clear influence on the pseudonymous Christoph Luxenberg's more famous effort in 2000.[67]

These works represent the high watermark of Western scholarly scepticism on the provenance of the Qur'an and the *isnād* genres traditionally used to contextualise it.[68] Although reflecting a period of disengagement from contextual enquiry, such approaches have been debunked by a combination of newly discovered material sources, such as the Sana'a manuscripts, and scholarly argument. One of the basic charges is that, while attractive to some as a thought experiment, this method fails to take into account the cumulative effect of mass corroborative oral testimony.[69] In the terminology of the Islamic tradition, this is called *tawātur* (continuous mass transmission): the principle that at a certain point, corroboration of evidence from diverse sources overruns the concern for systematic assessment of their veracity.[70]

The very existence of the 'Lüling-Luxenberg' school of thought also acts as a challenge to those who operate with a sceptical epistemology, but do not wish to go to their extremes. Such scholars have to explain why they may dismiss traditional reports as unreliable, but are at liberty to use lexicons sourced from the same class of transmitters. If we want to engage with the Qur'an as an Arabic text at all, it seems that we have to accept that the meanings of its words are vouchsaved to us through the same mechanisms of tradition that inform on its context.

Moreover, within academic scholarship, a sustained analysis of the transmission of the early sources has led to a gradual correction in course, away from the empty spaces of extreme form criticism and towards the more familiar topography of source criticism.[71] With the correspondence between report and historical event restored, it has become acceptable once again to probe sources for a reality that they represent. Taking early orally based sources as witnesses that may be scrutinised, questioned, accepted, or rejected as appropriate, the historian is able to escape the charge of circularity: that early Islamic traditional materials are not independent of the events that they purport to portray.

Sinai and Neuwirth argue for such a revival of source criticism, contending that the 'sceptical turn' headed by Wansbrough and others is merely a minor eddy within a larger historical tide. They trace an intellectual heritage from Abraham Geiger's *Was hat Mohammed aus dem Judenthume aufgenommen?* and Theodore Nöldeke's seminal effort to date the scripture's verses, *Geschichte des Qorāns*, in the nineteenth century, to the modern endeavour to situate the Qur'an as an organic element of the wider culture of Late Antiquity, which is the basis for the substantial *Corpus Coranicum* project. The programme that they call for is an effort to assemble the textual background material required to understand a given Qur'anic text, as well as to situate it within 'the diachronically extended sequence of Qur'anic discourses'.[72] Thus a marriage of sorts is implicitly proposed between the wider regional, as well as cultural and biographical, contexts of revelation.

There is no doubt value in situating the Arabia into which the Qur'an was revealed within its broader geographical and historical environs, and giving an accurate picture of the extent of material, as well as religious and cultural, exchange in the sixth and seventh centuries.[73] It is vital to bear in mind, however, that wider Late Antique concerns are principally of relevance to one's reading of the Qur'an insofar as they can be demonstrated to have manifested within the Arabian environment in a particular form. Practically speaking, this means that the study of parallel historical and linguistic material from neighbouring societies of the period (and preceding it), is at best a subsidiary concern, and certainly no replacement for the sources originating within the peninsula itself.[74]

It has also become increasingly clear from methodologically rigorous studies carried out by a loose grouping of scholars, represented in particular by Harald Motzki and Gregor Schoeler, that the dismissal of the *isnād* as a mere tool of pietistic ascription does not hold up to serious scrutiny. Rather, the device was used in a sustained manner in order to transmit information, as evidenced by the correlation between the branches of *isnād*s and their variant *matn*s (texts).[75]

In fact, the achievement of the compilers of the authoritative Hadith works is precisely the simultaneous analysis of multiple strands of tradition, in order to determine those of original provenance, acceptable variants, and later accretions caused by inaccuracy or fraudulent intentions.[76] In other words, Muslim scholars were engaging in *isnād*-cum-*matn* analysis, checking on a massive scale the mutual corroboration of reports in each generation of transmission.[77]

It seems that a lack of familiarity with the actual methodology utilised by traditionists in their scrutiny of hadiths has led many academic scholars to miss this central aspect of the discipline and to uphold the false conception that obsession with the *isnād* led to a neglect of textual differences and incongruities within the *matn*.[78] However, these were actually dealt with as part of the wider assessment of chains, under the terminology of *shudhūdh* (inconsistencies) and *ʿilal* (subtle flaws).[79] On this point, Jonathan Brown argues that subsuming problems in the *matn* within the study of the *isnād* was part of a wider defence of tradition against Muʿtazilī rationalist critique.[80]

It is also useful to view this question from the other side of the equation. The Ḥanafī tradition of jurisprudence, whose early theoreticians in Iraq are often associated with the Muʿtazila, developed sophisticated principles for rejecting *āḥād* (single) reports based on assessment of the *matn*. According to one of the earliest descriptions of the process attributed to the jurist ʿĪsā b. Abān (d. 221/836), this should be done when they conflict with established prophetic practice; a Qur'anic text that cannot be reconciled; general matters of which people would not be ignorant; or they are reports that, although narrated, are inconsistent with their transmitters' own practice.[81]

Returning to the proponents of the mainstream Hadith movement, it seems that the reason their methods are not always appreciated is that, for the most part, their practice was to present only findings in their main collections. They saved discussion of their methodology for specialist works of *ʿilal*.[82] This process can be illustrated with reference to an exception, Abū ʿĪsā al-Tirmidhī (d. 279/892), in his famous *Jāmiʿ* collection (often known as his *Sunan*). He uses his text for a dual purpose: to gather prophetic traditions under the established chapters of law, and also to pull back, to a degree, the curtain on the inner workings of the discipline itself.

The first, and most obvious, distinguishing quality of his work is the presence of comments following each hadith, in which he discusses the practice of various traditionist-jurists, as well as mentioning any other important information about transmission status. He also assigns a rating to each hadith, such as *ṣaḥīḥ* (sound), *ḥasan* (good), and *gharīb* (singly narrated; obscure) in various combinations. Despite defining some of the individual terms, their exact meaning within his personal scholarly terminology has confounded Hadith critics up to the present day.[83] A second distinction of al-Tirmidhī's work for the student of Hadith criticism is that he often intentionally quotes a narration that he knows has a subtle flaw (*ʿilla*), rather than the better attested versions in other collections, such as that of his teacher al-Bukhārī (d. 256/870), in order to teach a particular point.[84] Finally, al-Tirmidhī includes a section at the end of his collection, entitled *Kitāb al-ʿilal* (The Book of Subtle Flaws) in which he not only discusses critical points about various narrators, but provides a number of worked examples, which are meant to illustrate his methodology.[85]

Seen thus, the real benefit of the emergence of the modern *isnād*-cum-*matn* method, is not in recasting the study of history or the authentication of Hadith, but rather in making an understanding of classical Hadith criticism accessible to the non-specialist. Nonetheless, there remains a methodological gap between the classical method and Motzki's *isnād*-cum-*matn* analysis. The most acute point seems to be in the crucial question of how to traverse the so-called common link of a bundle of traditions, the narrator upon which the various branches converge.[86] Motzki allows for this possibility if the 'situation of the sources is favourable'.[87] Moreover, he more or less discounts Muslim *rijāl* (narrator) criticism, which would undermine the point of, in his words, 'critical scholars' developing their own methodology.[88] Motzki does not, however, give a compelling reason to suspend the judgement of Hadith collectors that certain early narrators are corroborated witnesses in general, even if not in each specific report. If his own effort to find dialectical correspondence between *isnād*s and *matn*s plausibly ascribes statements to figures within the first century of Islam, what should be said about the work of those who devoted their lives to this task from the vantage point of only a few generations distance and with access to numerous sources that are forever irrecoverable?

Put differently, we must admit that, in the analysis of Hadith, we are not on an equal playing field with the great canonical collectors, however much it may offend our sense of intellectual progress. As Motzki himself suggests in a thought experiment about the proliferation of *isnād* strands in each generation, we possess only a fraction of the information in their hands, which limits our ability to check their results.[89] He astutely points out that 'the first great collectors and professional teachers' of Hadith, the early second-/eighth-century figures who are associated with the common link phenomenon, often only recorded a single *isnād* for a tradition, although they may have had access to others.[90]

A further point can be deduced from the same logic of the proliferation of *isnād*s over time, which supports reports claiming the total number of transmissions available to a Hadith collector such as al-Bukhārī, including variant *isnād*s for the same (or similar) *matn*, was in the region of 600,000, from which he recorded more than 6,000 in his *Ṣaḥīḥ*.[91] This means that he may have preserved only between one and ten *isnād*s out of approximately 100 in his possession for each *matn*.[92] A parallel situation is plausible for his peers, both the minority whose writings we have and the majority that are no longer extant. When the sheer scale of information processing involved in the Hadith enterprise by the third/ninth century is fathomed, the idea that its pathways of transmission can be adequately reconstructed and assessed based on today's written records looks extremely dubious. It is akin to measuring the slabs of stone composing the pyramids at Giza, and then claiming that we know their sequence and precise method of arrangement better than the people who put them in place.

From this angle, it would seem that the problems Western academic scholars have faced with the 'authenticity question' arise from reasoning the wrong way around. Unable from their historical vantage point to utilise the vast world of oral and written Hadith available in the formative period, they have been forced to use as their raw material only what has survived from that process in written form. It should be obvious that no significant new information can enter the system; even if a new manuscript is unearthed, it would not be unknown to the collectors of the past millennium. This means that, unlike the period of collection, such research can only restrict, never enlarge, the existing corpus of Hadith. However, once it becomes clear that these very sources are themselves the fruit of an immeasurably more complex intellectual process of critical analysis, the case for using these written records to establish an academically admissible core of Hadith crumbles.

A related issue concerns the epistemological value of the Hadith. Exponents of the source-critical method, although less sceptical than some of their academic predecessors, sometimes express grave reservations about obtaining certainty in the detail of historical situations relating to the life and times of the Prophet Muḥammad.[93] Hallaq critiques this kind of academic study upon the Hadith as founded upon the assumption that the canonical *ṣaḥīḥ* collections were seen as certain knowledge, while in reality the vast majority of reports had *āḥād* lines of transmission and were, thus, at best, considered only highly probable.[94] But, as shown by Brown, it is a mistake to think that the lack of epistemological certainty precluded 'historical and operative surety', which is the common currency upon which human life depends.[95]

The present book is ultimately an exegetical exercise, not a historical investigation. With this in mind, I will turn to the practical issue of how I will use contextual information in the chapters that follow. It is useful to adopt the distinction, common to classical and modern source-critical methods alike, between the general sweep of events and historical backdrop that can be established with effective certainty, and the individual details that are necessarily of a probabilistic quality. In terms of the *isnād* genres that may be of value, recognition of the relative strengths of their evidence has long preceded modern studies. Thus, while Muslim tradition has deemed Hadith in the canonical *ṣaḥīḥ* collections reliable, the sources afforded by *sīra* and *asbāb al-nuzūl* (occasions of revelation) outside of these are at a lower degree of authenticity, although not by that measure valueless.[96]

Such sources, whether found in separate collections, the classical *tafsīr* tradition, information from previous scriptures,[97] and the wider geographic context, must be used carefully, but arguably can form a coherent background against which to interpret the Qur'anic text. They also give a framework for the reconstruction of a rough outline of the diachronic order of revelations, which is particularly important for understanding the development of moral injunctions into a more defined legislative form in tandem with the crystallisation of the early community.[98]

Any diachronic analysis must also make at least passing reference to the concept of *naskh* (abrogation), the exegetical use of which has fluctuated within Muslim scholarship. While the early exponent al-Zuhrī (d. 124/742) identifies only forty-two cases of abrogation in the Qur'an, al-Naḥḥās (d. 338/949) finds 138, Ibn Ḥazm (d. 456/1064) asserts there to be 214, al-Suyūṭī twenty, and Shāh Walī Allāh al-Dahlawī (d. 1176/1762) only five.[99] Shāh Walī Allāh comments that certain previous scholars counted many verses within this category that would not be included by their successors and utilises a range of arguments to disqualify as many of al-Suyūṭī's already reduced number of cases as he is able.[100]

This variation highlights the fact that *naskh* as a divine action that abrogates rulings must be distinguished from *naskh* as an exegetical tool, used to reconcile between apparently conflicting scriptural texts. The movement in later scholarship to reduce the occurrences of *naskh*, exemplified by Shāh Walī Allāh, echoes the much earlier approach of Abū Muslim al-Iṣfahānī (d. 322/934) who denied the abrogation of rulings within the Qur'an completely, arguing that *naskh* is that by which Islam abrogates previous dispensations of *sharī'a*.[101] (Fascinatingly, al-Māturīdī argues that abrogation of rulings and *sharī'a*s occurs by a theologically identical process: the expiration of time-limited rules.)[102] The approach of al-Iṣfahānī has sometimes been more or less adopted by Muslim scholars of the Qur'an in the modern period; for example by the Indian Qur'an specialist al-Farāhī.[103]

One of the principle ideas guiding the scholarly shift to a decreasing use of *naskh* is the recognition that the Qur'an does not intend a single monolithic guidance for all situations, but rather presents varying ways to deal with different events. One should therefore seek to harmonise two opposing texts by specifying under which conditions each is applicable. The implication for this study is that *naskh* does not play a major role, especially due to the rule that ethical principles are not abrogated.[104] However, in a few places, I have found an assertion of *naskh* the most compelling solution to a radical shift in legislation during the period of revelation[105] (the question of the possibility of *naskh* after this time, as mentioned in Chapter 2, can perhaps be taken up in another work). Overall, there is a much greater role for *takhṣīṣ al-ʿāmm* (specification of general texts), although it should be noted that in the early period this was often dealt with using the terminology of *naskh*.

The process of *takhṣīṣ al-ʿāmm* is one of the major exegetical and legal uses of the *asbāb al-nuzūl* literature, the other being to tie the Qur'anic text to the wider historical narrative provided by the *sīra* writings.[106] In this book, the general socio-historical context is, in most cases, of greater importance than the individual events that may be linked with particular verses, especially considering the relatively low credibility of much *asbāb al-nuzūl*. Furthermore, alongside historical events, early scholars often recorded as *asbāb al-nuzūl* the kinds of situations to which a particular verse was held to apply.[107] However, there are places in which the particular revealed context of a verse, if it can be recovered, may have an impact on interpretation, particularly if it is to specify what otherwise appears to be a general expression.

Muslim scholars give two main conditions for the operation of the *sabab* (cause, or occasion). It must chronologically precede the verse in question and be an event contemporaneous with the era of revelation.[108] It is notable that the second condition is not followed by some earlier figures, such as al-Wāḥidī (d. 468/1076), who allowed the *sabab* to be a historical event mentioned in the revelation, for instance the story of the Prophet Abraham given in Q. 2:260, or the events described in Sūrat al-Fīl.[109]

Uṣūl al-fiqh uses the terminology of *khāṣṣ* (specific) and *ʿāmm* (general) for the idea of specification. Here *khāṣṣ* denotes specified individuals, while *ʿāmm* refers to a text applying to every individual of a class. Al-Suyūṭī gives as an example of a *khāṣṣ* text, Q. 92:17, 'The most pious will be kept away from it [Hell] (*wa-sa-yujannabuhā al-atqā*)', in which he argues that *al-atqā* (the most pious) refers specifically to the Companion Abū Bakr based on the use of the definite article *alif lām*.[110] This usage is called *maʿhūd li-l-dhiʾn* (known referent), which refers to something that is definite due to the audience already being aware of it.

Expressions with *ʿāmm* wording apply to all members of a class. The definite article *alif lām* can also be used here for definition of the class (*taʿrīf al-jins*) as a kind of ideal type, for instance, *al-muʾmin* (the believer), or for each member within a class (*al-istighrāq*), such as *al-muʾminūn* (the believers).

A number of cases can be identified in which specification of an otherwise *ʿāmm* wording is indicated by an expression: exceptions using *illā* (except); descriptions of a quality shared by all members of a class; conditions fulfilled by all members of a class, using *in* (if), *idhā* (when), or *hattā li-l-ghāya* (until …);[111] and substitutions in which the whole class is substituted for specific members using *man* (the one who).[112]

A foundational maxim for juristic study of the Qur'an is 'a ruling is according to the generality of wording, and not the specificity of its circumstances of revelation'.[113] However, despite the majority of Muslim scholars accepting this formulation, which effectively allows the maximum deductive inferences to be drawn from Qur'anic texts, they agree that if a relevant *qarīna* can be established, the text is specified by its *sabab*.[114] It is also possible for an *ʿāmm* text to be specified according to the language or sense of the verse itself,[115] another verse of the Qur'an,[116] or a hadith (which can also be the source of information about the *sabab*, if it is known).[117]

A minority opinion is that even with general wording, and in the absence of other specifying evidence, texts that were revealed in specific circumstances can only be applied to other cases by *qiyās* (analogy),[118] or through the prophetic tradition, 'My judgement upon the individual is my judgement upon the group.'[119]

A final area of interest within this discussion is a phenomenon by which the analysis of *asbāb al-nuzūl* intersects with *naẓm* and *niẓām*. Al-Suyūṭī states that through its definiteness, the *khāṣṣ* verse is closer to the *sabab* than the *ʿāmm* verse, and acts as a bridge between the two within the scripture's composition.[120] He illustrates this with Q. 4:51, which is *khāss* because of its *sabab*, which refers to a pair of Jews who did not honour their commitment to tell the pagans what was in their scripture regarding the Prophet, 'Do you not see how those given a share of the Scripture, [evidently] now believe in idols and evil powers? They say of the disbelievers, "They are more rightly guided than the believers."'

This specific incident about the concept of *amāna* drives the scripture to next mention trusts in general in Q. 4:58, 'God commands you [people] to return things entrusted to you to their rightful owners, and, if you judge between people, to do so with justice: God's instructions to you are excellent, for He hears and sees everything.'[121]

Rippin argues that this is a self-created 'problem' for al-Suyūṭī, in which pursuit of a general meaning that he wishes to derive for legal purposes leads to a 'possible rupture' to the specific meaning of a passage.[122] I would argue, however, that perhaps al-Suyūṭī has rather astutely identified a characteristic feature of the Qur'anic instructional style, as I have also found this relationship between verses during the present study.[123]

In such situations, there are three levels of definition interacting: a specific socio-historical event, the *sabab*; the revelation of *khāṣṣ* verses according to this *sabab*; and the revelation of *ʿāmm* verses, which follow the *khāṣṣ* ones within the sura's *niẓām* and draw general principles from the specific cases. These general verses can even have been revealed at an earlier time than their specific counterparts, as while a *sabab* must chronologically precede the revelation of its verse, the positioning of verses for the consideration of *niẓām* is not restricted in this way.[124]

Overall, socio-historical context is a crucial consideration within this book's hermeneutic, as it forms the backdrop against which the Qur'an's immediate discourse of societal justice must be read to tease out the underlying structure. I have argued for the effective certainty of the mass-transmitted general narrative of the *sīra* and for giving orally transmitted reports about early Islamic history consideration according to their strength within a hierarchy of *isnād* genres. Finally, I have discussed how the related concepts of *naskh*, *asbāb al-nuzūl*, and *takhṣīṣ* fit within the exegetical method.

VI. Extraction of *ḥikmas*

Within the Islamic intellectual tradition, the discipline of *uṣūl al-fiqh* ostensibly deals with the extraction of rulings from scriptural texts. However, Sherman Jackson provides the important and challenging insight that formal theoretical speculation about the principles underlying the *sharīʿa* is principally used for the justification of the pre-existing corpus of legal rulings, which were derived in a non-formalistic manner.[125] That is not to say that the methods used within the genre bear no relation to the process by which a jurist practices *ijtihād*. But, as developed within history, *uṣūl* theories serve the principle function of justifying an evolving corpus of legal rules within a juristic school, by claiming to codify the understanding of natural language users.[126]

In this book, I seek to use the resources of this discipline in a related, yet distinct way. Rather than primarily justifying *aḥkām*, I intend to defend the *ḥikma*s extracted from the text through the preceding five indices discussed in this chapter. This differing objective leads to two major areas in which my approach varies from *uṣūl al-fiqh* theories: scope and comprehensiveness.

From as early as al-Shāfiʿī's (d. 204/820) *Al-Risāla*, effectively the founding text of the genre,[127] there is a commitment to treating the Qur'an and Sunna as a single utterance.[128] In light of the scope of this book, I focus on the overarching moral principles of the Qur'an, treating the Sunna as the Prophet's practical implementation of them during his life. This means that I put material from the *sīra* and Hadith corpora under the category of socio-historical context – part of the effort to reconstruct the meaning of the Qur'an for its first audience.

Second, although I stipulate that understanding a text's *ḥikma* requires a clarification of its meaning, it is not always necessary to exhaustively detail its *ḥukm*(s). This is because the characteristically indeterminate nature of *ḥikma*s means that they can usually be extracted from texts without requiring the same level of specification.

Beside these caveats, I make use of the basic toolkit of linguistic analysis provided by the authors of *uṣūl al-fiqh*. My neo-Māturīdī normative theory, as outlined in Chapter 2, fits well with use of the terminological categories of the Ḥanafī school as a starting point.[129]

An important principle that the Ḥanafīs uphold is termed *al-tanṣīṣ lā yadillu ʿalā al-takhṣīṣ* (stipulation does not indicate specification), sometimes discussed within works of *uṣūl al-fiqh* as a negation of the principle of *mafhūm al-mukhālafa* (contrary implicature).[130] The basic question that this principle seeks to answer is one of linguistic inference: does the mention of something about a certain case (x) imply the negation of the same about its counterpart (other than x). For example, if someone is told to pay a certain sum in gold (x), does that imply that they cannot pay its equivalent in silver (other than x)? Zysow argues that each of the two possible answers has its own internal logic. In effect, the Shāfiʿī position, which accepts *mafhūm al-mukhālafa*, deals with cases beyond the explicit terms by nullifying them and hence would limit the payment to gold. The Ḥanafī position, which accepts *al-tanṣīṣ lā yadillu ʿalā al-takhṣīṣ* and rejects *mafhūm al-mukhālafa*, leaves everything beyond the explicit terms open for potential analogy.[131] Thus, silver would not be excluded and could be the subject of analogy.[132]

Returning to the Qur'an, I find *al-tanṣīṣ lā yadillu ʿalā al-takhṣīṣ* more consistent with its linguistic patterns and the concept of *naẓm*. The scripture has many ways of signalling restriction through the use of appropriate words and sentence structures.[133] If these are not present, it does not seem justified to draw the inference that other terms are negated.

What remains is to search for the *ḥikma*s of the *sharīʿa* that lead to the ideal condition of justice in a society. Based on my adoption of the motive model that argues the cause of a *ḥukm* is its purpose, or *ḥikma*, I propose that the *ḥikma* of a text can be identified by the same particles used by jurists to identify the *ʿilla*.[134] This can often be done through the presence of particles, principally *kay* and *li-ajli* (on account of), as well as *lām*, *bāʾ*, *an*, *in*, and *inna*. There are also expressions that implicitly denote *taʿlīl* (attribution of the legal cause), either with *fāʾ al-taʿqīb* (immediate succession), or by their overall sense.[135]

Of course, in many cases within the Qur'an, the *ḥikma* of a particular injunction, statement, or narrative, is not mentioned so explicitly that it can be identified by the presence of a particle or term. Here, it is the ethical interpretation of the text, according to the indices that I have mentioned, read against its socio-historical background, which allows it to be known. This process is essentially the subtle teasing out of connections between the Qur'an and its context, as well as between texts sharing a common *ḥikma* and, at a higher level, the coherence of the total system of *ḥikma*s.

However much that consistency is desired through setting down rules by which this may take place, the reality is the process of abstraction that the search for such correspondences entails is something that one may intuitively accept as valid, without being able to pinpoint quite how it works. Douglas Hofstadter writes, 'Getting from the story to the story's gist, something that occurs swiftly yet almost invisibly in a human mind, is as central a mystery of cognitive science as any that exists.'[136]

This fact was realised by Muslim scholars and explains, in part, their introduction of formal systems to justify and to some extent regulate their process of derivation from the sources.[137] Nonetheless, deferral to the pre-*uṣūl* master jurists of the formative period reflects an implicit acknowledgement that their rule-based systems were principally to defend, not conduct, *ijtihād*. In this, they anticipated the German philosopher Friedrich Schleiermacher (d. 1834) who said about hermeneutics as a craft, 'Art is that for which there admittedly are rules. But the combinatory application of these rules cannot in turn be rule-bound.'[138]

When making a serious effort to interpret any text, let alone one as open to varying nuances of meaning as the Qur'an, there is no escape from, and there should be no shame in, searching for original solutions to the problems one has set. In fact, the true purpose of theoretical work is to provide the map to take one to the edge of what is known, so that real exploration can begin.

4

Historical Context

To understand principles of societal justice within the Qur'an on an abstract level requires deep appreciation of their concrete embodiment within history. This chapter studies the features of Arabian society in the sixth and seventh centuries CE as the contextual background on which the Qur'anic discourse takes place. The focus is on two interrelated dimensions: the general patterns of Northern Arabian life, influenced to a degree by their wider geographical environment, and the particular local aspects that intersect with the life of the Prophet Muḥammad and his community, especially in Mecca and Medina.[1] The analysis is split into three sections, reflecting the thematic content of Parts II, III, and IV of the book: socio-political, socio-economic, and socio-judicial context.

It is useful to briefly discuss the sources upon which such a study can be made. As discussed in more detail within the previous chapter, the relative paucity of material evidence for this period of history and the need to rely, to greater or lesser extent, on sources drawn from the *isnād* genres, has led to widely divergent views not just on what is known, but what can be known. The approach taken in this book is to try to make sense of a broad range of transmitted information, but with a healthy critical awareness of the epistemological weight of the various materials.

Besides the well-known works of *sīra*, Hadith and *tārīkh* (history), some of the most useful primary sources for building up a background to Arabian history and society prior and contemporary to the life of the Prophet Muḥammad are classical geographically specific works that reflect sources no longer extant. Three books deserve special mention: al-Azraqī's *Akhbār makka wa-mā jā' fīhā min al-āthār* and Ibn Ḥabīb's *Kitāb al-munammaq fī akhbār Quraysh*, both of which are focused on Mecca, and al-Samhūdī's *Wafā' al-wafā bi-akhbār dār al-Muṣṭafā*, which deals with Medina. In this chapter, I also engage with the voluminous secondary literature on the period and endeavour to fill in gaps and suggest resolutions to established problems when possible.

I. Socio-political context

In pre-Islamic Arabia, political action was dominated by the tribe (*qabīla*), in which all members traced their lineage to a real (or at least perceived) common eponymous ancestor.[2] In the words of Henry Sumner Maine, 'The earliest and most extensively employed of legal fictions was that which permitted family relations to be created artificially.'[3]

Although the tribe was unified for important common purposes, such as warfare against other tribes, local political affiliation took place at the level of the clan (*ʿashīra*), a sub-division branching from the descendants of the main tribal ancestor. This was also the level of organisation at which outsiders bereft of a tribal affiliation could attach themselves as clients (*mawālī*) and benefit from its protection. In the Ḥijāz of the sixth century, Arabians living in established settlements had quite recently been, to some degree, nomads (*aʿrāb*, or Bedouin). They thus retained a common culture and social organisation with their Bedouin counterparts, although the differing reality of settled life exerted a certain pressure that manifested in various areas of society.

The political leadership of an Arabian clan was based largely on competence in managing the community's affairs, which implied political influence and, given the pre-eminence of family, was usually found in those senior enough to command a wide loyalty from descendants and wider kinship networks. The result for the tribe as a whole could be the dominance of a single figure, or the existence of multiple poles of authority competing for hegemony. In either case, the situation was fluid and constantly negotiated as the passing of time and circumstance led to the strengthening and weakening of various parties.[4]

The development of the camel as a riding beast of war by at least the beginning of the Common Era, possibly associated with the invention of a specialised saddle, led to this animal becoming a decisive instrument of aggression in Northern Arabia, far outstripping other available technologies.[5] Not only were all parties, settled and nomadic alike, subsequently obliged to utilise the camel in this way, but this played a part in restricting the major powers of the Byzantine and Sassanid empires in their attempts to claim territory within Arabia. They were effectively required to make use of tribal vassals, such as the famous Ghassanid and Lakhmid dynasties, as regular armies were unsuited to conflict in the desert.[6] The Byzantines, for instance, by making judicious use of local Nabataean troops, including those mounted on camels, were able to install a legion to patrol a northern region of the Ḥijāz from approximately 100 CE.[7]

A closer look at the particular political development of the Prophet Muḥammad's tribe, Quraysh, in the generations immediately preceding his lifetime is very useful for understanding Qur'anic material with relevance to political justice, as well as the socio-political environment in which it was revealed. In analysing the development of Quraysh from the time of the figure known as Quṣayy, according to the available sources, it will be argued that because the process by which this particular nomadic tribe became sedentary was based at first around the religious pilgrimage site of the *ḥaram* (sanctuary) of Mecca, functions of power were associated with offices connected primarily to its sacred rites. Over time, the popularity of the pilgrimage, alongside internal politics and regional economics, led to the dominance of clans involved more with warfare and trade, both through these offices and outside of them.

The traditional narrative states that during the fifth century a powerful leader of the Quraysh, Quṣayy b. Kilāb b. Murra, seized control of the ancient sanctuary of Mecca from the previously dominant tribe of Khuzāʿa. Quṣayy is also credited with founding around the sanctuary a permanent city, as opposed to a temporary encampment, and establishing a number of offices, which he gave to his eldest son, ʿAbd al-Dār.[8] These were as follows: Dār al-Nadwa, the building in which the *malaʾ*, the deliberative council of clan chiefs, was hosted; possession of the keys to the Kaʿba (*hijāba*); possession of the battle standard in war (*liwāʾ*); providing water to the visiting pilgrims (*siqāya*); hosting them with food (*rifāda*); and allowing the mounts (camels and horses) permission to travel in trade and war (*qiyāda*).[9] Of particular note in the initial period was the institution of *rifāda*, which seems to have become the focal point for a kind of rudimentary taxation that Quṣayy made Quraysh concede as a moral duty.[10]

The wider importance of these institutions was to make Mecca the major regional centre for pilgrimage and trade, *umm al-qurā* (lit. Mother of the Villages),[11] independent (*laqaḥ*) of external political, economic, and religious control from Persia or Byzantium.[12] This is particularly significant given the development of Byzantine influence on the Northern Arabian–Syrian border through their Ghassānid potentates from 490 CE and the Persian Sassanid hegemony of a region of Northern Arabia stretching from Bahrain in the East to Medina in the West through the Lakhmid dynasty.[13]

Although still capable of acting as a unified force in times of crisis, the extended family of Quraysh was later split into a number of dominant clan factions. The first significant alignments emerged in the generation of the grandsons of Quṣayy. Hāshim (himself the Prophet Muḥammad's great-grandfather) along with his two brothers, ʿAbd Shams and al-Muṭṭalib, led a faction of clans, known as the Muṭayyabūn, against their rivals, the Aḥlāf.

The result of the disagreement was a settling of the balance of power that favoured the former, who took the duties of watering and feeding the pilgrims, as well as leading the mounts. The latter group held on to the largely ceremonial duties of holding the keys to the Kaʿba and the battle standard, while Dār al-Nadwa was shared between the two groups.[14] This power-sharing is significant, because the *malaʾ*, as the body deciding tribe-wide action, was perhaps the most important political institution of Quraysh. Although it was mainly a deliberative body and relied on gaining general assent from the assorted clan factions, its centrality to Meccan politics meant that neither side would accept it dominated by the other.[15]

A further development of these alliances, which occurred during the youth of the Prophet, was the *ḥilf al-fuḍūl*, a pact formed to recover a debt owed to a Yemenī trader by a Meccan from the clan of Sahm.[16] It was constituted from the majority of the clans that made up the Muṭayyabūn: Hāshim, al-Muṭṭalib, Asad, Zuhra, Taym, and perhaps al-Ḥārith b. Fihr. Although ʿAbd Shams (the forerunner to Banū Umayya) and Nawfal had been part of the Muṭayyabūn, as recently ascendant powers they felt no need for a renewed alliance.[17] The formation of this alliance was subsequent to the wars of Fijār,[18] in which Ḥarb b. Umayya b. ʿAbd Shams, who had inherited the duty of *qiyāda,* was the supreme Meccan leader.[19] The underlying motivation for the series of Fijār conflicts may have been the desire to establish control of the important marketplace of ʿUkāẓ and the trade routes leading through the Najd towards al-Ḥīra in the north over the rival tribes of Hawāzin and Banū Thaqīf.[20]

This expansion of Qurashī territorial ambition took place against the background of the decline of Sassanid influence in Northern Arabia. In this environment, the financing of regional caravan trade by leading members of Quraysh was increasingly viable. This led to an emphasis on military strength and political alliances to maintain *īlāf* (security pacts) guaranteeing safe passage for caravans. Such developments boosted the prestige of Banū Umayya and led to the reported rivalry between Ḥarb b. Umayya and his cousin ʿAbd al-Muṭṭalib b. Hāshim who held the pilgrimage offices of *rifāda* and *siqāya*, alongside trade interests, and otherwise would have been the most influential clan leader within the tribe.[21] Evidence for this is found in reports that in the Year of the Elephant, approximately 570 CE and the traditional date for the birth of the Prophet Muḥammad, ʿAbd al-Muṭṭalib is quoted as one of only two notables to remain in Mecca to feed the people threatened by the Abyssinian army, in accordance with his duties. The other is Shayba b. ʿUthmān, who held the position of *ḥijāba* and could have been expected to stay to defend the Kaʿba.[22]

The parallel establishment of the ritual practices of *ḥums*, a term denoting a special religious status for the Quraysh and allied tribes,[23] might have had some connection with attempting to bolster the pilgrimage offices in the face of the competition of mercantile power. Particularly interesting is a report mentioning that a pilgrim from the people of *ḥill* (outside the immediate vicinity of the *ḥaram*) should not bring in food with them to eat, but were to be dependent on the *rifāda*.[24] By the time of the Prophet's full maturity and the beginning of the period of Qur'anic revelation, the traditional importance of *rifāda* and *siqāya* had broken down somewhat, and were performed with a certain prestige, but little real power, by Banū Hāshim through the Prophet's uncles Abū Ṭālib and al-ʿAbbās, respectively.[25] Banū Umayya and its politics of mercantile power allied to the ceremonial office of *qiyāda* increasingly vied with Makhzūm and other clans for pre-eminence.

Mahmood Ibrahim presents a convincing argument that a changed economic landscape was central for providing Banū Umayya with an advantage over its clan competitors.[26] I add to this explanation the contention that this clan continued to benefit from holding the traditional Qurashī office of *qiyāda*. The significance of this office may have been overlooked in the literature because it is omitted by the influential author of *sīra*, Ibn Hishām (d. 218/834). One conceivable explanation for this lacuna is that his major source, Ibn Isḥāq (d. 150/767), may have prepared his text for the prince al-Mahdī (d. 169/785), the son of the Abbasid ruler of the time, al-Manṣūr (d. 158/775).[27] Such a focus on the historical leadership role performed by Banū Umayya may have been omitted due to political sensitivities.

Whether or not this speculation is correct, it is difficult to make sense of the reports about Meccan political action throughout the period without positing the continued importance of the office of *qiyāda*. For instance, ʿUtba b. Rabīʿa, who is recorded as holding *qiyāda* prior to Abū Sufyān b. Ḥarb,[28] is the person acknowledged to have the authority to lead the Quraysh back into Mecca without fighting at the Battle of Badr.[29] It seems that while the clan of Makhzūm through al-Walīd b. Mughīra and his nephew Abū Jahl was becoming increasingly influential, the office of *qiyāda* continued to be passed through the family of Umayya. Eventually, with the death of ʿUtba at Badr it reached Abū Sufyān, who had previously had to remain content with the ceremonial battle standard, which he had inherited from his father Ḥarb, following Fijār.[30] This explains his position as leader of the Meccan forces after Badr until his conversion just before the Conquest of Mecca in 8/630.[31]

By the sixth century, Medina, a fertile oasis consisting of a number of sprawling agricultural settlements, was populated by two main groups. Of these, the earlier inhabitants were Jewish tribes, most significantly the Banū al-Naḍīr, Banū Qurayẓa, and Banū Qaynuqāʿ, followed by other assorted smaller families. These were diaspora Jews, possessing both a full religious culture, including knowledge of Hebrew and Aramaic, and fully integrated into Arabian culture and livelihood. It is likely that both migration and conversion from indigenous Arabians played a part in their composition.[32]

The second main presence in Medina was the pagan Banū Qayla, formerly a nomadic tribe from Yemen, which consisted of two main clan branches, the ʿAws and the Khazraj, and thereafter divided into numerous sub-clans loyal first to those of their common stem, and then to Qayla as a whole. There is also mention of other small groups, perhaps the remnants of a Northern Arabian presence in the oasis preceding Jewish settlement.[33] Al-Samhūdī states that the first to practise agriculture in Medina and to build houses and fortresses were the ʿAmālīq (Amalekites).[34] However, the known territory of this nomadic group is significantly to the north of the Ḥijāz between the Sinai Peninsula and the Southern Levant, as suggested in Genesis 14:7, so this seems doubtful. Furthermore, the ʿAmālīq have taken on an ubiquitous role in Islamic narratives of the ancient past that is difficult to square with any solid evidence.[35]

While Mecca was proud of its independent status since its inception as a settlement, Medina, more northernly and accessible to the broader Near East region, had not escaped imperial overtures. Until about the middle of the sixth century, Medina was administered on behalf of a Sassanid *marzubān* (governor) based in the East Arabian port of al-Zāra (proximate to modern-day Qaṭīf). It is possible that the Jewish tribes of al-Naḍīr and Qurayẓa were themselves, or were allied to, the agents through which this was managed, as it is reported that they used to collect a tax from the other inhabitants of the oasis.[36]

Following this, the growing strength and numbers of the combined Banū Qayla put them first on an equal footing with the Jewish tribes and then through political intrigue allowed the capture of many of their 'houses, wealth and fortresses'.[37] This mainly took place in the central area of the settlement that would later become the residence of the Prophet and his community.[38] These developments did not leave the Jewish contingent entirely without political influence. The three most significant tribes still possessed the best fortifications within the city and, heavily armed, were known as *ahl al-ḥalqa wa-l-ḥuṣūn* (the people of weaponry and fortresses).[39] However, this fact alone does not prove that the Jews of Medina held political dominance: it could equally be taken as a sign of insecurity. Overall, it seems their influence came through utilising their assets to affect the balance of power between the ʿAws and Khazraj through temporary strategic alliances.[40]

By the latter years of the sixth century, during the reign in al-Ḥīra of King al-Nuʿman b. Mundhir IV (r. *ca* 580–602 CE), there is evidence that Persian influence was briefly reasserted on Medina. The crowning of ʿAmr b. al-Iṭnāba of the Khazraj as a kind of proxy king, with al-Zāra bypassed, temporarily ceased the feuding between the two Medinan clans and reversed the arrangements for Sassanid taxation, which became paid by the Jews.[41] Thereafter, decline of al-Ḥīra as a regional force, concurrent with the end of the Lakhmid dynasty at the death of its king, spelled the end of external influence on Medina, plunging the ʿAws and Khazraj into renewed mutual conflict and variable alliances with the Jewish tribes.

The most significant battle between the two Qayla branches was that of Buʿāth, which took place in 617 CE, about five years before the Prophet Muḥammad's hijra. ʿAws, by this time the weaker of the factions, tried to use an alliance with Banū Qurayẓa and al-Naḍīr to overcome the dominant Khazraj. The battle went in the favour of ʿAws, but ultimately resulted in the killing of the leaders of both sides, with the exception of ʿAbd Allāh b. Ubayy of the Khazraj, and another less important Khazrajī clan leader, who had prudently stayed aloof from the conflict.[42]

The aftermath was a tense period of truce, in which various efforts were made to find a more permanent resolution to the political stalemate. The most important of these was a series of meetings at the site of pilgrimage outside Mecca in ʿAqaba, held at first between the Prophet Muḥammad and six converts from Khazraj in 620 CE. This gathering was reconvened with minor ʿAws representation the following year and a formal pledge of allegiance, known as the Pledge of Women (*bayʿat al-nisāʾ*),[43] before the definitive Pledge of War (*bayʿat al-ḥarb*) that immediately preceded the hijra in 622 CE.[44] During this time there was an effort between some elements within the two clans for rapprochement, which it was hoped could be achieved by calling their people to embrace the religion and political authority of the Prophet.[45]

During the same period, Ibn Ubayy had managed to bring Banū al-Naḍīr back into alliance with Khazraj and to secure an alliance with Qaynuqāʿ.[46] Along with his supporters, he had apparently negotiated his imminent crowning as King of Medina, presumably as the last really powerful member of the older generation of clan leaders.[47] Thus, although the arrival of the Prophet to the city curtailed this latter development, it seems that the need for political stability under a strong leader was an important common factor shared in the rapid spread of Islam there. The 'near crowning' of Ibn Ubayy is also likely a significant factor in his reluctant acceptance of the Prophet Muḥammad's emerging role within the community and leadership of the 'hypocrites' during the unfolding Medinan era. Recent research has also put forward the hypothesis that the Byzantine emperor Heraclius may have used his influence with the Ghassanids to ease the arrival of the Muslims to Medina, thereby neutralising any Persian attempt to ally with the Jews of the city.[48]

II. Socio-economic context

The different life patterns of nomadic and settled communities are significant for the study of socio-economic conditions in pre-Islamic Northern Arabia. The Bedouins of Arabia practised a subsistence economy, based on the herding of camels, goats, and sheep. For necessities beyond this, they made use of the markets, whether in established settlements, or seasonal trade fairs. At the point of hardship, and even before, they would conduct raids, the famous *ghazw*, upon settlements, or the temporary encampments of their rivals. This was a direct result of the vulnerability of their domestic wealth, which, as it was based on their herds, could easily starve, escape, or be plundered.[49]

Stable settlements, on the other hand, allowed the practice of agriculture – although this was usually only possible within oases – as well as trade, crafts, and other developed industries. With increased wealth, tribes could build up territorial control and ultimately exact tribute, profit from control of markets, and even become involved in financing longer distance trade, or domestic moneylending. The symbiosis between nomad and settler can be witnessed in the latter's use of the Bedouins as guides and guards when travelling across the harsh empty desert, as well as employing them to fight in their wars.[50] Dangerous as the nomadic Arabians were, it was their settled brethren who ultimately had the upper hand due to their greater economic sophistication.[51]

The ancient *ḥaram* in Mecca had long been an important regional centre for pilgrimage and trade. The sanctity of the land for Arabians guaranteed its attractiveness as a neutral location for the exchange of wares, especially within the four sacred months each year.[52] Furthermore, the location of Mecca as a Northern Arabian staging post on the Incense Road, which still ran from Southern Arabia to the Mediterranean, allowed the Quraysh to participate in the profitable caravan trade.[53] But, lacking power outside of the *ḥaram*, they were at first limited to hosting other merchants in the trade fairs that accompanied the religious rites, and apparently were not, before the generation of the Prophet's great-grandfather, Hāshim b. ʿAbd Manāf (d. *ca* late fifth century), significantly involved in external trade themselves.[54]

Gene Heck has argued that ongoing hostilities between the regional powers of the Byzantine and Sassanid empires led to a ravaging of the market for the luxury goods that had been the previous mainstay of trade and created demand for the export of a higher volume of more basic goods produced on the Arabian Peninsula itself.[55] Mining of gold and silver provided the basic investment capital,[56] while the export commodities included the following products: agricultural produce from local fertile regions such as al-Ṭaʾif, livestock, jewellery, smithed metal goods, leather goods, textiles, and perfumes.[57] Imported goods were equally diverse,[58] with caravans returning loaded with fresh goods from the major trading centres of the Levant, Yemen, and Iraq. The import of grain to feed the inhabitants of barren Mecca is especially highlighted in the sources.[59]

It seems that, by the generation of Hāshim, the income for the Quraysh provided by their hosting of pilgrims had become supplemented and possibly even supplanted by the mercantile possibilities the changed regional economic landscape offered. The political basis for Mecca's trading boom at this time was the development of *īlāf* for the safe passage of not only its own caravans, but others that it guaranteed.[60]

There is some disagreement as to the exact process by which treaties were agreed. Shiblī Nuʿmanī quotes reports from Ibn Saʿd that the first pact was made with Byzantium by Hāshim, allowing Qurashī merchants to trade without incurring taxes; thereafter agreements with local Arabian tribes followed.[61] Serjeant suggests that the Byzantine connection is exaggerated, and construes the pacts as having developed first in the Arabian Peninsula before being extended.[62] Heck sees the increase in trading and development of pacts as a simultaneous one as Quraysh moved into the commercial and administrative vacuum caused by the warfare between the two northern imperial powers.[63]

There are further competing narratives concerning agreements with other nations. One report has Hāshim travelling first to Abyssinia, which was praised as a trading stop, and then Yemen, Syria, and Iraq. With each he is said to have made a pact.[64] In another version, each of the four sons of ʿAbd Manāf conclude an agreement with a regional power and gain security from the tribal chiefs that controlled the route: Hāshim in Syria, al-Muṭṭalib in Yemen, ʿAbd al-Shams in Abyssinia, and Nawfal in Persia.[65]

Although the elder brother, ʿAbd Shams, possessed the duty of *qiyāda* and is described as a man 'perpetually travelling', it is Hāshim who is most famed within the sources for concluding the *īlāf*. According to tradition, it was due to a famine requiring a supply of grain that Hāshim became involved in trade and had even more success than his elder brother, arousing the jealousy of the latter's son, Umayya b. ʿAbd Shams.[66] The antagonism between supporters of the political claims of Banū Hāshim and those of the Umayyad caliphate in the formative period of Islamic history puts a question mark over this story. What is clear is that in the generations before the birth of the Prophet Muḥammad, Quraysh was in ascension as both a political and economic power within the region.

The major threat to Mecca during this time, the Abyssinian Abraha's campaign to destroy the Kaʿba in approximately 570 CE, can partly be seen as an effort to assert dominance over the Northern Arabian trading network, extending existing control of Yemen in the south. The lack of success led to the opposite occurring. In the words of M. J. Kister, '[It] is evident that the failure of the expedition helped to expand the trade of Mecca, to set up close relations with the tribes, to establish its influence and to strengthen the institutions already built up by Quraysh.'[67]

Kister goes on to link this to a report about the establishment of the market of ʿUkāẓ fifteen years after these events.[68] However, if the Prophet's birth is dated to approximately the Year of the Elephant (*ca* 570 CE), then by the time of the fourth War of Fijār, fourteen years later, ʿUkāẓ was already an established trade fair, such that al-Nuʿmān b. al-Mundhir, the king of Ḥīra, was ready to send a caravan to it.[69] It seems that the reference of 585 CE for ʿUkāẓ must instead refer to the aftermath of the fourth War of Fijār, which cemented Qurashī control over it.[70] Michael Bonner argues that ʿUkāẓ had no established king who would levy a specific tax on those wishing to transact, although he does not dispute that it was administered by varying tribes.[71] He also counters some of the mercantile assumptions presented in this chapter by emphasising elite control over Arabian marketplaces as connected more with gift-giving and prestige.[72]

The wealth generated by intensified trading was accompanied by an influx of immigration into the city; new manufacturing and service professions emerged in response to economic demands, and traditional collective tribal structures were modified in response.[73] Without, however, suitable alternative mechanisms for the redistribution of wealth within society, and with its monopolisation by a few dominant clans, not to mention the charging of exorbitant usurious loans and deceitful practices within the marketplace, the ground was laid for a socio-economic crisis with an accompanying moral dimension.[74]

The economy of Medina, an oasis settlement built on fertile volcanic land, was underpinned by its agricultural produce of dates,[75] as well as fruits, grains, and vegetables. The Prophet Muḥammad is reported to have made the invocation, 'Bless us in our fruits,' over the first fruits of the season in Medina.[76] The Qur'an mentions in Q. 80:24–32, a Meccan passage, but clearly referring to the vibrant oases of the Ḥijāz:

> Let man consider the food he eats! We pour down abundant water and cause the soil to split open. We make grain grow, and vines, fresh vegetation, olive trees, date palms, luscious gardens, fruits, and fodder: all for you and your livestock to enjoy.

Agriculture in Medina seems to have proceeded according to a form of sharecropping, in which landlords would allow their land to be cultivated in return for a specific portion of the harvest.[77] The pagan Arabians of ʿAws and Khazraj were primarily herders and agriculturalists,[78] but had not fully left the psychological mentality of the Bedouin *ghazw* – forcefully taking possession of herds and properties according to the opportunities presented – which lead to analogous property insecurity, yet lacking even the escape valve of the empty desert.[79]

The Jews within Medina were highly skilled, having introduced techniques of irrigation and hand pollination into the date plantations,[80] and were also distinguished for their winemaking, tailoring, and smithing, especially of weaponry and jewellery.[81] Their appellation of *ahl al-ḥalqa wa-l-ḥuṣūn* was based, in part, on their craft expertise.[82] It is also reported that there were 300 goldsmiths living in Zuhra close to the centre of Medina, the vast majority of whom were Jewish.[83] The expulsion of Banū Qaynuqā', usually dated to 2/624,[84] who were apparently extremely well-equipped for warfare, resulted in the Muslims seizing a considerable amount of weaponry. The Prophet Muḥammad is reported to have personally taken three bows, two suits of armour, three spears, and three swords.[85]

The sources reveal that at the time of the Prophet's hijra there were four markets in the settlement as a whole. Two were controlled by Jewish tribes, including the centrally located market of Banū Qaynuqā', the most significant in Medina, and the other two by pagans.[86] Of these, the one known as al-Ṣafāṣif near Qubā' was owned by the Banū Jahjabā, who were among the clans of the Banū 'Amr b. 'Awf, of the 'Aws.[87] Lecker admits to mistakenly attributing the market called Muẓāḥim to the Khazrajī leader 'Abd Allāh b. Ubayy, based on it sharing the name of his tower-house.[88] Nonetheless, given the proximity of this market to the Prophet's mosque, understood to be built on land from Banū al-Najjār of the Khazraj,[89] it is not at all implausible to suppose it could have been a Khazrajī market, counterbalancing the one owned by the 'Aws.[90]

The explicit stipulation made by the Prophet that the market he established soon after arriving in the town would be without taxation, suggests that high taxes were common practice.[91] It is also clear that caravans arrived at Medina, in order to transact within its markets,[92] and it is possible that local and longer distance trade was organised by the population of the settlement, particularly the Jews, unless Mecca had a means of dominating the routes through its pacts with Bedouin tribes.[93]

The family structure of the time was extended, and included wider kin, whom would frequently live together, or in close proximity. Despite the presence of matrilineal structures in Arabia,[94] the genealogical background of the tribes of the Ḥijāz demonstrates that patrilineal organisation generally, although not completely, dominated society. In other words, individuals in both Mecca and Medina tended to be named after their fathers and marriage was organised around the male. However, particularly in the latter settlement there are instances of individuals named after their mothers, such as 'Abd Allāh b. Ubayy, who is also known as Ibn Salūl.[95] These differences are explained by the variety of marriages acknowledged to have existed in the pre-Islamic period.

Presumably the most common marriage was the sometimes polygynous patrilineal type that continued into the Islamic era.[96] Nonetheless, a number of alternative forms of marriage existed, which reflect different combinations of matrilineal and polyandric practices. One kind, known as *nikāḥ al-istibḍā'* (marriage of seeking nobility) apparently involved the husband and wife seeking a different father of greater 'nobility' for the prospective child.[97] Other types of marriage made paternity very uncertain, either due to allowing a number of men to visit the mother over the time of conception, or through the practice of a woman advertising her sexual availabity with a banner outside of her residence. In such cases the child would be attributed to one of the potential fathers.[98] Finally, it can be remarked that the common practice of wet nursing cemented ties within the wider family.

Although sources for the details of slavery as a social institution in the pre-Islamic period are fairly scant, it is evident that it was integrated into Ḥijāzī life in a manner that paralleled other Late Antique cultures. There were several ways in which a person could be enslaved, including on the battlefield, if captured by bandits, and by being born into bondage.[99] As such, in theory, a slave in Mecca or Medina could come from any tribal, or ethnic, background. In practice, it seems that the typical patterns of pre-Islamic slavery meant that many Ḥijāzī slaves were originally from Arabia, rather than outside the peninsula.[100]

Slaves worked as labourers in the various types of economic activities described above, as well as providing domestic service and fighting in their masters' wars.[101] It seems that manumission was fairly common, especially in the case of children issuing from the cohabitation between masters and their bondswomen.[102] When other slaves not related to their masters were freed, they were considered *mawālī* of the tribal unit along with its allies (*ḥalīf*s).[103]

III. Socio-judicial context

Arabia of the sixth and early seventh century, with no centralised authority, nor generally recognised legal system, was a dangerous place. When disruptions threatened the internal social order of the tribe, there was an effort to deal with them according to customary notions of right and wrong. If disagreement ensued, or conflict emerged between rival tribes, the main recourse was to seek arbitration from a recognised source of higher authority, a *ḥakam* (arbitrator). The historian al-Yaʿqūbī states,

> The Arabians used to have arbitrators (*ḥukkām*) who they turned to in their affairs, and from whom they sought judgement in their disputes, inheritance, wells (lit. waters), and retaliation (lit. blood), because they had no religion to turn to for legal ordinances. Therefore, judgement was carried out by people of nobility, truthfulness, trustworthiness, leadership, age, diligence and experience.[104]

Despite this search for reliable arbitration, the potential for bias and corruption among such figures is obvious. The lack of a basic constitution, or set of practical ethical principles in a context where all had loyalties towards kin, could lead very easily to partisanship. In terms of traditional Bedouin values, the loyalty of a tribesman to his compatriots' decisions, even if judging them to be misguided, is proverbial. The famous couplets of Durayd b. al-Ṣimma, who had warned the other notables of his tribe against a raid that was ultimately to take the life of his brother,[105] illustrates the tendency:

> I gave them my command at Munʿaraj al-Liwā,
> They will never clearly see guidance 'less by light of the morrow.

> When they disobeyed me, I was still from them,
> Though I saw their error and I was not rightly led.
> Am I except from Ghaziyya? If she errs, I err,
> And if Ghaziyya goes aright once more, I go aright with her.[106]

The phrase 'Am I except from Ghaziyya? (*hal anā illā min ghaziyya*)' equates the poet's identity entirely with the will of his tribe: even though he is fully aware of its mistake, he is powerless to stand aloof. Although this depiction may be romantic, it also reflects a certain reality of the commitment required in the collective life on the margins that nomadic existence entailed. By the end of the sixth century, however, it seems that such a sentiment was beginning to be disrupted within certain settled tribes of the Ḥijāz as part of a wider process of societal change connected with concurrent political and economic developments. An example of this is the emergence of the *ḥilf al-fuḍūl* in Mecca.[107]

There was thus a social tension in Arabia between the general sentiment of partisanship and the expectation that a *ḥakam* would uphold a higher standard of morality according to the popular conception of *murūʾa* (Arabian chivalric virtue).[108] Moreover, it is likely that even the most impartial of arbitrators would judge based on an implicit hierarchy of social status, with a leader worth more than a person of less renown; a member of a prominent clan worth more than one from a weaker group; a male generally worth more than a female; and a freeman worth more than a slave.[109] The *ḥakam* (usually a man, but occasionally a woman)[110] would often be someone possessed of real political standing – that is, a tribal or clan chief – as well as of perceived wisdom. This is because the qualities of judgement desired for arbitration were the same as those regarded important for leadership.[111] Furthermore, contesting parties could expect the decision of one with social influence to be widely respected and upheld.

Also significant in pre-Islamic Arabia was the role played by the *kāhin* (soothsayer) as an arbitrator. Rather than the worldly wisdom and authority claimed by the chief as *ḥakam*, the *kāhin* relied on the supernatural grounds of a reputation for magic and mastery of the jinn. As one would expect from a more specialised vocation, the extant sources seem to indicate a fewer number of *kāhin*s.[112] Jones also argues that they had a greater social importance in settled as opposed to nomadic life.[113] The rulings of the *kāhin* were often considered more definitive than that of the *ḥakam*, due to their quasi-divine sanction, which could explain why matters of inter-tribal and inter-clan significance were taken to them.[114] An example of this is the narrative of the famous intended sacrifice by the Hāshimī ʿAbd al-Muṭṭalib of his son ʿAbd Allāh (the Prophet Muḥammad's father). This prompts a visit to a female *kāhin* in Medina, in which he is accompanied by ʿAbd Allāh's maternal aunts from the influential clan of Makhzūm.[115]

As mentioned above, the city of Mecca had, by the lifetime of the Prophet Muḥammad, its own political dynamics and established institutions based on the competition between clan factions.[116] Over a period of time this led to an increasingly formal role for *ḥakam*s in dealing with issues of dispute. It is said that 'in order to avoid wickedness they were chosen by mutual consent and that none of them would strive to overpower the rest of Quraysh'.[117] The individuals who are reported as having acted in this capacity of arbitrator are unsurprisingly the leaders of influential clans, figures such as ʿAbd al-Muṭṭalib and, in the following generation, al-Walīd b. al-Mughīra of Makhzūm.[118] There are also reports that ʿUmar b. al-Khaṭṭāb was responsible for resolving disputes between the clans on behalf of Banū ʿAdī, while Abū Bakr would apportion blood money on behalf of Banū Taym.[119] However, these may derive from later attempts to build a suitable pedigree for their eventual caliphates. Qurashī inter-clan arbitration and agreements with other tribes were often carried out at Dār al-Nadwa.[120] For instance, a pact is recorded to have been made there between Banū Hāshim and the tribe of Khuzāʿa under the auspices of ʿAbd al-Muṭṭalib.[121]

Occasional inter-tribal arbitration was also carried out in the annual market of ʿUkāẓ, which was for a period of time managed by the Banū Qays.[122] The likely branch was that of the Hawāzin, who were geographically proximate and who worshipped an idol named Jihār there.[123] It seems probable that the report of the transfer of this function to the leader of Banū Tamīm in the period immediately preceding the rise of Islam is a reflection of the Hawāzin's loss of control of ʿUkāẓ and the trade routes leading to the Najd due to the wars of Fijār.[124] Overall, during the lifetime of the Prophet Muḥammad, Meccan society possessed adequate resources for dealing with the range of quasi-legal matters that it encountered, although it faced the usual problems with ensuring security of life and property characteristic of Northern Arabian society.

Unlike independent Mecca, which had evolved its own institutions of arbitration and redress, Medina, which had been at times externally controlled during the fifth and sixth centuries, suffered from political, and therefore judicial, instability. Thus, by the early seventh century, when the ʿAws and Khazraj were looking for a central point of authority, part of their motivation was to guarantee a sustainable order of redress. The Jewish community, with a fixed code drawn from its scriptures and a religious hierarchy of rabbis, was less affected internally,[125] although still not entirely free from its own disputes.[126] They also required a system that could adequately deal with the realities of their interaction with the pagans living in their midst. Thus, a convergence can be noted between the general political needs of Medina at the time of the Prophet's hijra, and the subset of specifically judicial ones.

An important aspect of any stable and peaceful society, let alone one achieving a measure of justice, is a general security for life.[127] If this is violated, even the most simple of tribal societies requires that there should be some kind of redress for the victims of the crime, as well as responsibility to be borne by the perpetrator, or family thereof.[128] The Arabia into which the Qur'an was revealed was no exception to the general rule, and there existed a sophisticated pattern of customary procedures for redress in the case of murder or lesser infringements. This was sought directly by the kinship group of the person or persons slain, and was generally 'a slain for our slain, a prisoner for each one of us captured, and goods for our goods'.[129]

This makes clear the generic nature of retribution between lineages – the killing of a member of kin in kind was more important than bringing the responsible individual to account directly.[130] Also, depending on a particular tribe's custom, additional killings might be required in order to satisfy its sense of honour.[131] Understandably, the result of this could be the development of extended feuds, in which further retaliations were made back and forth for each new victim.[132]

An effective route out of the cycle of violence was the payment of *diya* (blood money), a settlement between the aggrieved family and aggressor paid by an established group of liable kin known as the *ʿāqila*. However, pride could lead to social stigma for the acceptance of payment ahead of retaliation, as recorded in these lines of poetry:

> What wretched kin you are
> To a kinsman oppressed!
> You have been diverted from avenging your brother
> By a bit of minced meat and a lick of meagre milk.[133]

The interaction of these various aspects of the retaliation system commonly practised in seventh-century Arabia meant that in certain places in which multiple tribes were in rivalry, such as Medina, extended blood feuds had reached the level of a malignant social problem.[134]

After concern about redress for the slain, Arabian tribal society had some interest in rights due against stolen property, whether it was reckoned in captives, animals, or goods. In practice, however, the vulnerable nature of the principal form of tribal wealth, the camel, led to the emergence of a curious fact. For the Bedouin, '[i]t is easier to steal camels than to defend them. Possession, in other words, is inseparable from a capacity for theft.'[135] From this, it follows that the *ghazw* was not enacted as an act of criminality, but of necessity: 'Raiding per se was not a crime but a duty incumbent on any respectable man, an ecological adaptation which enhanced one's own tribe's wealth, diminished that of foes, and kept herds from becoming too inbred.'[136]

The redress for the theft of members of one's herd was simply to replace the stock from that of another rival and did not require direct compensation like the *diya* for murder. Of course, raids for property, if detected, could often turn into murderous conflicts, and brigandage was a perpetual danger on travel routes if sufficient protection of armed guards, or safe passage, was not arranged. Within Arabian settlements, the previously nomadic mentality with respect to property did not greatly change in the period preceding Islam. However, theft would have been difficult to carry out without entering into physical conflict, and risking the resulting blood feud.[137]

Reports from the period give a mixed picture in terms of regulating sexual relationships and the concern for preserving known paternity, so it seems that this was determined by the customary practice of marriage as it varied from tribe to tribe. Thus, in some tribes the punishment for what would be seen in Islam as fornication was death, including by stoning, while in others it was openly accepted.[138]

To conclude, by the beginning of the seventh century, Northern Arabian society was undergoing change in response both to external economic opportunities and internal social and political challenges. At the same time, there was a great deal of continuity with the past for nomad and settler alike. The coming of the Qur'an to Arabia irrevocably altered this calculus of civilisational development, shaping first the people of the Ḥijāz, and then Arabia, and eventually much of the world. Fascinating though it is, the story of this societal change is not the main subject of this book, but rather the background against which analysis of the Qur'anic discourse on justice in the next three parts occurs.

Part II

Political Justice

5

Politics

Relationships of power embodied in political structures are a given of complex human societies. The Qur'an acknowledges the reality of power, or dominion (*mulk*), while morally necessitating it to be bound to stewardship of the earth (*khilāfa*), under which justice is to be upheld. Discussion of this theme within the scripture is set upon a broad canvas, in which successive nations are tested with their capacity to use their power to uphold God's commands and keep to the Scale.

In the first section of this chapter, I focus on the question of legitimacy in governance, paying special attention to the Qur'an's paradigmatic use of the *khalīfa*s of the Children of Israel. I will ultimately argue that while framing legitimacy according to revelation has an understandably central place in the scriptural discourse, doing so according to qualities of justice and piety as understood through a natural law framework is not thereby ruled out. The second section assesses the reciprocal relationship between just governance and the communal duty of loyalty to it within Medinan verses.

I. Legitimacy

A key topic of investigation for the theme of political justice within the Qur'an pertains to the legitimacy to rule, or to govern, the Muslim community. Interestingly, statements on the subject of God-pleasing rule are overwhelmingly made through the exemplary stories of previous nations, rather than as a ready-formulated political manifesto directed towards the Prophet Muḥammad and his followers.[1] This has led some commentators to perhaps underplay the presence of this topic.[2] On the contrary, the Qur'an does not remain silent on questions of political import, but speaks after its own fashion, in which the religious has its own political dimension.[3] Muhammad Asad argues that rather than providing detailed political legislation, it gives a number of principles to be applied in any particular system of government.[4] In the language used within this book, it provides *ḥikma*s for which *aḥkām* must be sought, a neat inversion from other topics studied. The overall purpose of the sphere of political justice is to provide leadership over the establishment of societal justice as a whole, including governance over the more prescriptive distributive and corrective spheres.

Within the Qur'an, the issue of the disposal of power among humanity, whether for justice or injustice, is treated as part of the story of prophetic history. This is a narrative in which the powerful within successive nations are tested with the responsibility of leadership as the political expression of their stewardship (*khilāfa*). The patterns that emerge from these lessons of sacred history serve as a backdrop to the instruction that the Prophet Muḥammad is given to successfully forge his community within his immediate social and political context.

The key words that inform the enquiry into the Qur'anic concept of political legitimacy are those derived from *mulk* and *khalīfa*.[5] The Qur'an acknowledges in Q. 3:26 that *mulk*, in the sense of real sovereignty, is ultimately held only by God:

> Say, 'God, holder of all authority (*mulk*), You give authority to whoever You will and remove it from whoever You will; You elevate whoever You will and humble whoever You will. All that is good lies in Your hand: You have power over everything.'

However, this verse also makes clear that certain people and groups tend to assume coercive power over others. Al-Iṣfahānī defines *mulk* in this human sense as 'the capacity [by a ruler] for administration of command and prohibition amongst the general public, which is specific for politics'.[6] He further identifies two varieties of linguistic use of the term *mulk* within the Qur'an: the taking of possession and control in terms of political authority (Q. 27:34), and having the strength to acquire authority, whether it is actualised or not (Q. 5:20).[7]

These two aspects are traced in the famous thesis of Ibn Khaldūn (d. 808/1406) in his *Muqaddima*, as *mulk* and *ʿaṣabiyya* (group identity), respectively. He gives an account that aims to demonstrate why human society needs a ruling authority, and that this power is characteristically assumed by a group with members sharing certain qualities. It is this phenomenon of social unification to establish *mulk* that he calls *ʿaṣabiyya*.[8] Ibn Khaldūn's approach is especially fascinating due to his synthesis of classical Islamic disciplines and empirical study of the phenomenon of political power within human history.[9]

In the course of his analysis, he makes a three-fold distinction between different possible configurations of political power within society. The first is *mulk* in its raw form, which is based upon the ruling power's domination of those weaker than it, which arises due to the dynamics of human nature. The second and third are more rarefied forms of *mulk* in which the raw power of *ʿaṣabiyya* is tempered by recourse to a political law. If this law is developed by intellectuals and people of importance within society, then it tends towards becoming a rationally grounded polity (*siyāsa ʿaqliyya*), which acts to secure material benefits and ward off harm. If the law is based on executing the divine commands then it becomes a religiously grounded polity (*siyāsa dīniyya*), which benefits its members both in the world and the Hereafter.[10] Ibn Khaldūn's analysis thus concurs with Khadduri's classification of Islam as a divine nomocracy, 'a system of government based on a legal code; the rule of law in a community'.[11]

Returning to the Qur'anic concept of *khalīfa*, and, by extension, *khilāfa*, some commentators express reservations about its political interpretation. For instance,

Qamaruddin Khan, in his *Political Concepts in the Qur'an*, states: '[P]hilologically or according to ancient usage, or according to the Qur'anic texts themselves, not even the slightest idea of representation or delegation is contained in this word.'[12] However, study of the word's root, *kh-l-f*, contains exactly this connotation among its meanings,[13] and it is used in this sense in the Qur'an in Q. 7:142, when Moses tells his brother Aaron upon leaving his community for his retreat on Mount Sinai, 'Take my place among my people (*ukhlufnī fī qawmī*).'

It seems the modern resistance in some quarters to drawing any connection between the Qur'anic term *khalīfa* and politics is perhaps a response to use of the title of caliph by Umayyad rulers after the Prophet,[14] which profoundly influenced lexicographers and exegetes to understand the word more or less exclusively in terms of its later historical manifestation.[15]

I argue that studying the word as deployed within the Qur'an itself reveals it to have a paradigmatic political function within the scripture's moral narrative. If the basic idea of the *khalīfa* within the Qur'an is the human steward charged with a duty to live according the moral Scale that God has set within creation, then in the social sphere this implies upholding justice, establishing His law and rectifying worldly corruption. Such a function can be seen as a logical consequence of the *amāna* given to human beings – as they are able to obey or disobey God, so they must take responsibility for the just regulation of their society.

The social nature of human life means that the personal aspect of moral responsibility that impinges upon the conscience is matched by a collective one, in which it must be negotiated within the power relations that characterise society. The Qur'an plays on the linguistic meaning of the plurals of *khalīfa*, *khalā'if* and *khulafā'*, by opening up a temporal dimension whereby each nation is the successor of the one who comes prior to it and is charged with inheritance of stewardship.[16] Among a believing community actively trying to fulfil its primordial convenant with God, the realities of human life require support for governance that simultaneously exercises political authority and stewardship.[17]

It is important to bear in mind how the ethical discussion broached in Chapter 2 affects such a position. A voluntaristic theory makes the descent of revelation the crucial moment for the emergence of morality within human history and the opportunity for political authority to be held in God's name. In this vein, Hamid comments, 'Establishing justice means that people strive to connect the revelation with the land, so that sovereignty will be God's alone and human beings will be equal under His revealed commands.'[18] The normative theory proposed in this book holds that human beings were already equal under the natural law before the arrival of revelation. Therefore, there has been an opportunity for the faithful holding of stewardship in every age. Revelation, or divine law, is God's favour and assistance for human beings to succeed in this test.

This analysis also relates to the articulation of Qur'anic political philosophy. Rather than positing an anarchic state of nature that is only removed through Ibn Khaldūn's *'aṣabiyya*, or the social contract of Thomas Hobbes or John Locke,[19] a natural law theory is able to act as the basic ground for the responsibilities of governor and governed alike. In fact, the Qur'an states that the initial state of humanity was of a single community (*umma*), which along with concepts such as *fiṭra* and the Scale presumes a known moral order.[20]

With this conceptual sketch in place, it is possible to delve into a more detailed textual analysis of *khilāfa* within the Qur'an as it pertains to political legitimacy. The focus will be on a thematic thread that is traced first through a number of prophetic communities, before considering that of the Children of Israel in greater depth.

An important point to bear in mind when reading verses of the Qur'an that ostensibly refer to figures at a vast historical distance from the Prophet Muḥammad is that, very often, the passages dealing with such issues are addressed directly to him, rather than other potential recipients of their content.[21] In itself, this is not surprising, as much of the scripture is addressed directly to the Prophet. However, it is of particular relevance for the theme of political justice, which contains relatively few direct commands, as the specific content of historical narratives are shaped so as to constitute a form of instruction for him and by extension his community.[22]

Furthermore, considering the trajectory of the Prophet's mission and the hijra from Mecca to Medina, it emerges that the Qur'anic material revealed in the former phase, rather than apolitical, is concerned, in part, with building a historical precedent for the wielding of prophetic power.[23] The Prophet is provided with instances from the past in which leaders have possessed both spiritual and temporal authority, while his followers are made aware of their rich heritage as a believing community.[24] This is also important due to the revelation adding unity upon lines of belief to that of family and tribe.[25] The Meccan revelations, therefore, provide a historical preamble for themes of political action that only emerge in practice within the environment afforded by Medina.

Returning to the Qur'anic discourse upon *khilāfa* within sacred history, it should be appreciated that aspects of *niẓām* could be taken to indicate its significance. Q. 6:165, the final verse of Sūrat al-Anʿām, points towards the thematic core of the following sura, al-Aʿrāf,[26] which focuses on the temporal and prophetic succession between Adam, Noah, Hūd, Ṣāliḥ, Lot, Shuʿayb, Moses – whose people 'inherit the land' – and finally the Prophet Muḥammad himself:

> It is He who made you *khalāʾif* (stewards, successors) in the land and raises some of you above others in rank, to test you through what He gives you. [Prophet], your Lord is swift in punishment, yet He is most forgiving and merciful.

Within Sūrat al-Aʿrāf, Q. 7:4 hints towards the substantive theme to follow: 'How many towns we have destroyed! Our punishment came to them by night or when they slept in the afternoon.' This sura does not treat the destruction of the peoples of previous prophets as inevitable, but the consequence of moral choices. They fail to rectify corruption and to manifest justice according to the divine Scale and thereby are unable to establish stewardship of the earth as instructed by their messengers. The narrative sequence is preceded by an extended prelude in Q. 7:4–58, dealing with the story of Adam and including a number of injunctions addressed to his descendants, which re-emerge as distinct themes later in the sura.

Important verses include Q. 7:29, 'Say, "My Lord orders justice (*qisṭ*)"'; Q. 7:56, 'Do not corrupt the earth after it has been set in order', which is echoed in the story of the Prophet Ṣāliḥ and the people of Thamūd, 'Do not spread corruption in the land' (Q. 7:74), as well as the narrative of Shuʿayb and the people of Madyan (Q. 7:85–6).[27] Between these is the story of the people of Lot (Q. 7:80–4). The word used to describe them in their sexual practice is *musrifūn*, which refers to waste or excess, as previously mentioned in Q. 7:31, a way of moving out of balance or harmony with creation.[28]

Like other prophetic narratives in the Qur'an, Q. 7:96 confirms that it is upon failure to establish stewardship and hold back corruption and inequity that a people are destroyed.[29] Thereafter, Q. 7:97–100 uses the example of these past peoples to cause the present 'inheritors of the land', the Quraysh, to reflect on the coming of their messenger,[30] before revisiting the previous nations once more in Q. 7:101–2, 'We found most of them did not honour their commitments; We found that most of them were defiant (*wa-mā wajadnā li-aktharihim min ʿahdin wa-in wajadnā aktharahum la-fāsiqīn*).'

At both the beginning and end of this passage two elements are emphasised: belief in God and actions in conformity to God's Law.[31] The implication is that the nation that collectively fails to have *taqwā*, being instead characterised as *fāsiqūn*, is one in which the duty to hold back corruption from society is abandoned, and thus is deserving of destruction.

Concern with social corruption leading to humanity falling short in the Scale is also highlighted at the beginning of the lengthy exposition of the story of Moses and his people in Q. 7:103. Following the defeat of Pharaoh's sorcerers, a similar expression is used to goad him to continue to act against the Children of Israel, 'The leaders among Pharaoh's people said to him, "But are you going to leave Moses and his people to spread corruption in the land and forsake you and your gods?"' (Q. 7:127).

The resolution comes in Q. 7:137 in which the oppressed Children of Israel inherit 'the east and west of the land that We had blessed (*mashāriqa al-arḍi wa-maghāribahā allatī bāraknā fīhā*)'. The phrase *mashāriqa al-arḍi wa-maghāribahā* literally means the sun's points of rising and setting upon the earth and idiomatically denotes a vast extent.[32] In Q. 28:5–6, the divine address mentions about Moses's people:

> We wished to favour those who were oppressed in that land, to make them leaders, inheritors, to establish them in the land (*wa-nurīdu an namunna ʿalā alladhīna istuḍʿifū fī al-arḍi wa-najʿalahum aʾimmatan wa-najʿalahum al-wārithīn wa-numakkana lahum fī al-arḍ*).

The word *al-arḍ* in all three occurrences within these verses may seem *ʿāmm* in its expression, yet, in at least one case, Q. 28:5, it is more likely *khāṣṣ* due to the well-known context that the site of the captivity of the Children of Israel was Egypt, hence the translation 'that land' above.

The Qur'an is less explicit about the location of the land that they are to inherit, although the obvious assumption is that the audience know from the Biblical tradition that it is Palestine. Furthermore, there is an allusion towards this in Q. 7:137 in the phrase 'that We had blessed (*allatī bāraknā fīhā*)', which acts as a quality shared by the area around *al-masjid al-aqṣā* as mentioned in Q. 17:1, and so can specify the *ʿāmm* expression.[33] The vast extent of that domain is a likely reference to the reign of Solomon, which is yet to come, while the moral lesson is expressed in the final part of Q. 7:137, 'Your Lord's good promise to the Children of Israel was fulfilled, because of their patience, and We destroyed what Pharaoh and his people were making and what they were building.' That is, the obvious material achievements of their civilisation were rendered worthless, because the internal dimension was corrupt. Meanwhile, God provides the Children of Israel with the opportunity to establish stewardship over their promised land.

The *khilāfa* of the Children of Israel, as presented in the Qur'an, has a prelude in Moses's speech to his people in Q. 5:20:

> Moses said to his people, 'My people, remember God's blessing on you: how he raised prophets among you and made you kings (*jaʿalakum mulūkan*) and gave you what he had not given to any other people.'

It is possible to see the word *mulūkan* in this verse as either an eloquent metaphor for their entry into a state of mastery over their own affairs and freedom from the servitude they suffered in Egypt, as well as their pre-eminence over the surrounding peoples, or use of the past tense to convey glad tidings of a future kingdom.[34] This latter interpretation is bolstered by the following verse, Q. 5:21, in which it becomes apparent that Moses used his speech to urge the Children of Israel to enter the Holy Land.

The story of the Israelite political dynasty represented by the figures of Saul, David, and Solomon is principally told within the Qur'an in two passages: Q. 2:246–51 and 38:17–40. In this instance, the verses that narrate the earlier historical events of the rise of Saul and David (Q. 2:246–51) are Medinan and were revealed after the Meccan verses that deal with the testing of the kingship of David and Solomon (Q. 38:17–40).

The passage Q. 2:246–51 is centred on the divine election of Saul as king of the Israelites, his leadership of his reluctant people in the battle to recapture their land, and the rise to prominence of David by slaying the enemy chief, or champion, Goliath. The culmination of the sequence is David's elevation to king himself, which is the starting point of Q. 38:17. Aside from the *malaʾ* of the Children of Israel, and the Israelite and Philistine armies, this narrative contains four main individual actors:

Saul, Goliath, David, and the unnamed prophet who confirms Saul's kingship over the chiefs (identified as Samuel in the Hebrew Bible).[35]

It is possible to see in each of the four figures a paradigm for personal leadership reflected in early Islamic history. The Prophet Samuel represents prophecy without political power, analogous to the condition of the Prophet Muḥammad while in Mecca. David represents prophecy with political authority, like his condition in Medina. Saul represents just rule, which is the condition of the Prophet's successors, either the *khulafāʾ rāshidūn* (the well-guided successors), according to the Sunnī perspective, or the Imams of Ahl al-Bayt (lit. People of the House; the Prophet's family), according to the Shi'a one.[36] Finally, Goliath represents the unjust rule found within the Umayyad caliphate and afterwards.[37]

Saul and Goliath are the main counterparts in the narrative of Q. 2:246–51, both non-prophet worldly leaders, but contrasting in their support and opposition to prophetic guidance. The appointment of Saul as king, for which the Qur'an uses the terms *baʿatha* (sent, raised) and *iṣṭafā* (chosen) in Q. 2:246 and 2:247, respectively, is mentioned in the context of the request by the chiefs of the Children of Israel to their prophet for a ruler to lead them in war. The historical background to this need is the settling of the Philistines in the five city-states of Ashdod, Gaza, Ashkelon, Gath, and Ekron in the southern coastal plain of Palestine in the mid-twelfth century BCE and the consolidation of their power up until the time of Saul:

> The Philistines were better armed and better organized and the Israelites were obliged to combine into a larger unit if they were to maintain the position they had achieved. Combining into a larger unit meant having a leader of the larger unit, one with a higher status than that of a tribal chief.[38]

In the Qur'an, the chiefs object to the selection of Saul on the grounds that they are more deserving and wealthy. This may reflect the statement in 1 Samuel 9:21 that Saul was from the tribe of Benjamin, the smallest of the Israelite tribes. Q. 2:247 affirms Saul's intelligence and strength, 'He increased him abundantly in knowledge and stature (*wa-zādahu basṭatan fī al-ʿilmi wa-l-jism*).'[39] Samuel asserts God's right to choose whoever He wants for political authority in phraseology that echoes Q. 3:26 on the giving of sovereignty and announces a sign of Saul's rulership – the return of the Ark of the Covenant. This sacred chest, in which Samuel states, there is 'tranquility from your Lord and relics of the followers of Moses and Aaron, carried by the angels' (Q. 2:248) can be understood as equivalent to a mobile *qibla* (prayer direction) for the Children of Israel in that time.[40]

The association of this spiritual artefact with Saul's legitimacy to rule is an indication of the connection between religious and political authority within the Qur'an. It is never enough for a ruler to be merely a competent worldly administrator. Whether male, as usually found in the Qur'an, or female, as in the case of the Queen of Sheba,[41] he or she must have suitable personal qualifications, including a high degree of piety. The discussion below on the Israelite dynasty of David and

Solomon also demonstrates that the Qur'anic vision of the responsibility of the just ruler is such that even prophet-kings are tested to ensure the perfection of their servitude to God.

The Qur'an does not give a definitive answer to the question of Goliath's role within the Philistine army, as it uses the ambiguous phrase 'Goliath and his warriors (*jālūt wa-junūdihi*)'. This could mean that he is the commander, or just the most fearsome individual fighter. The Biblical account in 1 Samuel 17:4 uses the phrase *īsh habbīnayim* (lit. the man of the middle) to describe Goliath, which has been translated as 'champion', according to the interpretation of Rashi, 'a mighty warrior who would leave his camp and stand alone between the warring armies, challenging the opposing force'.[42]

While Goliath and Saul within the Qur'an are similar in their great physical prowess and ability to lead in battle, it is precisely the aspect of legitimacy, underscored by their spiritual states, that differentiates them. Goliath represents brute force devoid of any higher spiritual meaning, while Saul has similar worldly power, but is legitimised in the sight of God through his connection to prophecy and his ability to rule under the spiritual direction of Samuel. This is encapsulated in the Qur'an by the attribution of *ʿilm* to him.

While the Biblical passage 1 Samuel 17:8–11 portrays Saul cowering with the rest of the Israelite army before the challenge of Goliath, the Qur'an presents Saul as a brave king with no aspersions cast upon his valour or legitimacy. In Q. 2:249, he determines those from his army who are true believers, ready to put their trust in God, by forbidding them to drink more than a handful of water from a river.[43] The succinct Qur'anic style draws a maximum of moral commentary from a minimum of details. For the full contrast between the two groups in Saul's army to be maintained, it is necessary to read the verb *qālū* (they said) in the following key sentence as referring to those who failed the test by drinking freely from the river, 'When he crossed it with those who had kept faith, those [who stayed back] said (*qālū*), "We have no strength today against Goliath and his warriors."'[44]

David, who is only mentioned in the final verse of this sequence (Q. 2:251), eclipses the achievements of Saul by killing Goliath, and is subsequently given *mulk* and *ḥikma* by God, as well as being 'taught what He willed'. Exegetes usually understand *ḥikma* here to refer to prophecy.[45] In Q. 38:20, too, it is mentioned that David's kingdom was strengthened and he was given *ḥikma*, which indicates the temporal precedence of his political authority. This fits with the Hebrew Bible, which despite mentioning that David has the Prophet Nathan as an advisor in 1 Kings 1:23, hints that he becomes a prophet in his own right after being established as King of Israel with the phrase, 'The spirit of the Lord spoke in me (2 Samuel 23:2)'.[46] Given that Biblical texts also place the death of Samuel (1 Samuel 25:1) before the death of Saul (1 Samuel 31:1–6), al-Rāzī does not seem to be correct in arguing that David immediately inherited prophecy when Samuel died, just as he inherited kingship from Saul.[47] An interesting Qur'anic exegetical view is that no one combined these two roles before David.[48] This may relate to the fact that he is the only individual directly addressed by the divine as a *khalīfa* within the scripture in Q. 38:26.[49]

The final statement of the narrative sequence in Q. 2:251 is important for encapsulating one of the key principles at work within the story, the moral justification for jihad, 'If God did not drive some back by means of others (*wa-law lā daf'u allāhi al-nāsa ba'ḍahum bi-ba'ḍ*), the earth would be completely corrupt, but God is bountiful to all.'[50] Thus, the exercise of force through *khilāfa* can be the means of ensuring rectification of the world.

Within the life of the Prophet Muḥammad and his community, these verses are generally held to have been revealed in the early part of the Medinan period. Nöldeke puts them before the battle of Badr and sees in them an indication that the Prophet discerned a first battle with his people could not be further delayed.[51] Iṣlaḥī makes the fascinating observation that the battle of Saul and the Israelites against the Philistines, as depicted in 1 Samuel 17:1–3, is strikingly similar to the layout of the Muslims and Qurashī pagans at Badr, with both armies pitched up on hillsides overlooking a central valley.[52]

More important than any physical correlation, however, is the moral force of the story in inspiring a numerically inferior, although righteous, group to overcome a larger army, 'How often a small force has defeated a large army with God's permission! God is with those who are steadfast' (Q. 2:249).[53]

Iṣlāḥī argues that the period of Israelite history mentioned in the passage has characteristics that parallel the situation of the Muslim community in Medina. Just as the Israelites had to flee their homes and then fight to regain their *qibla* in the form of the Ark of the Covenant, so too were the Muslims forced to make the hijra and then fight for their *qibla*, the Ka'ba in Mecca.[54] This context can be related to the condemnation in Q. 2:217 of those who 'prevent access to the Sacred Mosque, and expel its people'.

Q. 38:17 continues the explication of David's *khilāfa* with a shift away from the address of scorn towards the Prophet Muḥammad's Meccan tormentors in the previous passage. The new tone is one of tenderness (*taḥannun*),[55] in recounting God's favours upon David, 'Have patience with what they say and remember Our servant David, the possessor of strength in abundance. Indeed he was penitent.'

This tenderness is likely related to the difficulties suffered by the Prophet upon the sickness and death of his uncle Abū Ṭālib, an event that some commentators relate to Q. 38:6, based on the prominent connection between the term *al-mala'* and tribal politics.[56] The guidance that the Prophet receives for his interaction with his tribe is not predicated upon their punishment, but relates to the story of David, one of the Qur'anic prophets who rules over his nation, rather than witnessing its destruction.

The Qur'an's vision of this previous prophet is one in which spiritual qualities are balanced with worldly power and judicial responsibility is twinned with the skills required for governing. This profile prefigures the role the Prophet Muḥammad was to later play in Medina. Q. 38:20 mentions, 'We strengthened his kingdom, gave him wisdom and decisive speech (*faṣl al-khiṭāb*).' This last quality is important for political activity and neatly mirrors that of the Prophet Muḥammad, who is reported in a hadith to have said, 'I was sent with comprehensive speech (*jawāmiʿ al-kalim*).'[57]

It also becomes apparent that part of the reason this sura mentions the story of David, followed by that of Solomon and Job, is to show that God always tests his prophets by placing upon them difficulties and afflictions.[58] Thus, in Q. 38:21–5, there is a scene in which two disputants enter David's chamber and demand judgement, an incident that he understands afterwards as a test, eliciting his prostration.[59] His act of humility is accompanied by a divine admonition of the grave responsibility that comes with his position in Q. 38:26:

> O David, Indeed We have made you a steward in the earth. Judge between people with truth and do not follow your desires so that you are diverted from the path of God (*yā-dāwūdu innā jaʿalnāka khalīfatan fī al-arḍi fa-ḥkum bayna al-nāsi bi-l-ḥaqqi wa-lā tattabiʿi al-hawā fa-yuḍillaka ʿan sabīli allāh*).

Unlike Q. 2:30, which stresses the intimacy of personal interest in the creation of humanity through the first-person singular, this verse is in the first-person plural of majesty, which emphasises the power of God. Possibly this form is used due to the command and prohibition in the verse. The word order also highlights the role of the *khalīfa*, rather than the location of the earth. By the time of the Prophet David, the earth is well-established as the place of stewardship; the point is his responsibility to implement just rule and judgement.[60] Thus, 'with truth (*bi-l-ḥaqq*)' may be understood as David's personal quality of fairness, contrasted with following mere passion, that is to establish social justice.[61]

Furthermore, Q. 38:26 is echoed in the later Medinan verse:

> So judge between them with what God has revealed and do not follow their whims in regard to what has come to you of truth (*wa-an uḥkum baynahum bi-mā anzala allāhu wa-lā tattabiʿ ahwāʾahum wa-ḥdharhum an yaftinūka ʿan baʿḍi mā anzala allāhu ilayka*). (Q. 5:48)[62]

This means that part of a narrative seemingly revealed to the Prophet Muḥammad to comfort him in the face of his people's rejection in Mecca re-emerges as a legislative command in the midst of the religious other in Medina. It is possible to see the former verse as having a preparatory effect on the Prophet and the political function that he was called to adopt in the latter phase of his prophecy.

The next figure in the narrative of Sūrat Ṣād is David's son, the Prophet Solomon, who is mentioned in Q. 38:30–40. He is introduced with the verse, 'We bequeathed Solomon for David, what a wonderful servant! He was penitent (*awwāb*).'[63] Unlike David, who is understood to have started life as a humble shepherd, Solomon is born into the luxury of kingship and receives training from his father in judging from a young age (Q. 21:78–9). In one sense, then, his initial position represents the limit of worldly privilege and the challenge of making use of it without becoming corrupted.

In terms of miracles, the Qur'an describes David in several places as experiencing the mountains and birds join him in his praise of God,[64] as well as receiving a revealed scripture: the Zabūr (Psalms).[65] Solomon is given further control and mastery over aspects of the creation: the wind, the animal kingdom, and even the jinn.[66] Sūrat Ṣād is the place within the Qur'an where the spiritual context of the first attainment of these powers is expressed, allowing a greater insight into the qualities of the ideal Qur'anic steward.

In some passages of the Qur'an, Solomon's military power is described in terms of the full flourishing of these favours after the events described in Sūrat Ṣād. A particularly good example is Q. 27:17, 'Solomon's hosts of jinn, men, and birds were marshalled in ordered ranks before him.' This contrasts with Q. 38:31, in which he admires a less exotic parade of horses, 'disciplined chargers (*al-ṣāfināt al-jiyād*)'.[67] The next verse, Q. 38:32, mentions that his love for good things, usually understood to mean his horses, is 'on account of the remembrance of my Lord (*ʿan dhikri rabbī*)'. Another rendering is 'on account of my Lord's Torah'.[68] The praise of the horses can be interpreted as referring to their importance for the defence of the realm, which is religiously commendable.[69]

When the horses' speed causes them to disappear from sight, Solomon calls them back in order to stroke their necks, which honours them as steeds of battle, as well as indicates his personal leadership.[70] This fits with Q. 27:19–20 in which he is later even attentive to the fear of an ant, and to the absence of a single hoopoe from his forces.

Q. 38:34, 'Indeed We tested Solomon and threw upon his throne a body, then he turned in repentance (*wa-la-qad fatannā sulaymāna wa-alqaynā ʿalā kursiyyihi jasadan thumma anāb*)' has been explained within the exegetical literature through a number of stories, often involving an impostor jinn stealing his signet ring and taking his position as ruler for a period of time.[71] Another opinion is that the phrase *alqaynā ʿalā kursiyyihi jasadan* refers to Solomon as gravely ill, such that he became, according to classical Arabic usage, as if 'a body without a spirit', or 'a mere skeleton'.[72]

Interestingly, both of these explanations are based on the idea of role reversal: Solomon, born to great wealth and power, is tested by being reduced to a state of powerlessness, a reminder for him that real authority is in the hands of God, and that he is only a delegated representative. The verb *anāba* is used in this verse for the meaning of turning back to God in repentance, yet the word can also connote the delegation of authority. The root meaning of *nawb* is that of returning to something again and again.[73] In the context of the Qur'anic concept of *khilāfa*, it is the responsibility of stewardship that God entrusts time after time, as nations rise and fall, and people live and die.

Echoing David's rise from humble prostration to *khalīfa* in Q. 38:26, Solomon prays in Q. 38:35, 'Lord forgive me! Grant me a kingdom (*mulk*) inappropriate for anyone after me.' The result of this prayer includes control over the wind, and the jinn, 'every kind of builder and diver and others chained in fetters' (Q. 38:36–8). This is equivalent to control over the four elements. He is able to manipulate the element of air directly via the wind, while through fire, represented also by the jinn, he is able to exert his will over the earth (building) and the water (diving).[74]

Although Solomon is told 'give or withhold as you wish without account' (Q. 38:39), the purpose of his kingdom is not the gain and disposal of power, but working for the sake of God with gratitude. Q. 34:13 makes this point with the command, 'Work thankfully House of David (*i'malū āla dāwūda shukran*)', while Solomon exclaims upon being brought the throne of the Queen of Sheba, 'This is from the generosity of my Lord, so that He may test me as to whether I am thankful, or ungrateful' (Q. 27:40).

The incident in which Solomon is brought the throne also reflects the governance principle of *shūrā* (consultation), which comes from the root *sh-w-r*, meaning the gathering or extracting of honey from its wild sources. Thus, *shūrā* is the extracting, or drawing forth, of someone's opinion in a like manner.[75] In mirrored passages, Solomon and the Queen of Sheba both exemplify this quality in discussion with their advisors. Upon receiving a letter from Solomon, the Queen says, 'Counsellors, give me your counsel in the matter I now face: I only ever decide on matters in your presence' (Q. 27:32). After rejecting her gift, Solomon turns to his own council, 'Counsellors, which of you can bring me her throne before they come to me in submission' (Q. 27:38).

There is also a parallel with the instruction to the Prophet Muḥammad in Q. 3:159, 'Consult with them about matters, then, when you have decided on a course of action, put your trust in God: God loves those who put their trust in Him.' This verse identifies a semantic association between the concept of *shūrā* and that of *tawakkul* (placing trust in God).[76] The significance of this seems to be that the Qur'an insists on both qualities being present within, and complementary to, the life of a believer. In other words, it is wrong to consult the people for the best course of action, but not trust in God for the ultimate safeguarding of one's affairs; yet it is also wrong for trust in God to cause one to neglect consultation.

Returning to the Qur'anic narrative of Solomon, it is obvious that he is both the inheritor of his father's kingdom and his *khilāfa*. However, while the former came with birth, the latter was accepted only after testing, both in terms of mental faculties (as in Q. 21:78–9) and physical and spiritual endurance in the face of worldly tests. The lesson is that wealth is of no use if one becomes intensely physically deprived. Rather, for one caught in such a trial, spiritual reserves are all that remain.

Within the Qur'an, Solomon represents the furthest extent of worldly power, even to the point of mastery over the unseen realm of the jinn. The conclusion to be drawn is that no king or ruler, however powerful they may become, can outdo the feats of Solomon. Thus, the principles and limits that the Qur'an applies to his case, apply to all. This is characteristic of the Qur'anic style, which often moves to the upper or lower limit of any comparison in order to implicitly encompass all of the intervening range. As a rhetorical strategy, this phenomenon is known in Arabic as *istiqṣā' al-ḥujja* (taking the proof to its limit).[77] An example is that even after Solomon's death, his lifeless body, propped up by his stick, still exerts 'power' over his jinn servants who continue to work for him (Q. 34:14). This image also indicates that Solomon has no intrinsic share in his own authority, and that, by extension, even the most mighty within worldly terms faces absolute impoverishment in front of the divine. In the words of Asad, 'God is the ultimate source of all human power and glory, and that all the achievements of human ingenuity, even though they may sometimes border on the miraculous, are but an expression of His transcendental creativity.'[78]

A general observation that emerges from these prophetic narratives is the blurring of the functions of political ruler and judge. This is, of course, quite normal for societies of late antiquity and even into the medieval period. For instance, in England, '[t]he research of many scholars has failed to find any text earlier than the middle of the tenth century which explicitly assigns the right of holding a court to any lord other than the king'.[79]

The role of a judge is that of possessing an authority to apply the law impartially in cases of dispute or infraction. The prophets charged with carrying out this duty within the Qur'an are usually the few granted leadership and political authority over their people: Moses, David, Solomon, and Muḥammad. Similar to this is the pious king, of which the pre-eminent example is Dhū al-Qarnayn, the protagonist of Q. 18:83–98. He is an important paradigmatic figure of the just and righteous ruler within the Qur'an and need not be identified with a particular historical personage. There is an inconclusive discussion about whether he was a prophet, in which an intriguing piece of evidence is found in God's direct address to him in Q. 18:86, 'We said, "O Dhū al-Qarnayn (*qulnā yā-dhā al-qarnayn*)"'. Al-Qurtubī comments, quoting Abū Naṣr al-Qushayrī, 'Either he was a prophet, so it is *waḥy* (revelation), or he was not, so it is *ilhām* (inspiration).'[80]

Dhū al-Qarnayn uses the rulership granted to him by God in order to punish those who had done injustice (Q. 18:86–7), and restore balance, by means of his famous barrier, to a land in which Gog and Magog were sowing corruption (Q. 18:92–7).

In all these cases, these figures apply God's Law, whether through revelation, or natural law. Thus, their authority in both ruling and judging is one of delegation, in the terminology used within this chapter, *khilāfa*. This is contrasted within the scripture with the absolute – and unjust – regimes of unbelieving despotic kings who implicitly or explicitly claim divine authority for themselves. In some cases, these figures are named, such as Pharaoh in Q. 20:71 and 43:51; in others described, but unnamed, such as the king who disputes with the Prophet Abraham in Q. 2:258 (usually associated with Nimrod);[81] or merely alluded towards, such as Q. 11:59, '[ʿĀd] followed the command of every obstinate tyrant.'

It does not, however, necessarily follow from the fact that ruling and judicial authority are often in practice merged within a single individual, that there is a corresponding lack of awareness of the possibility for conceptual distinction between the two within the scripture. The Prophet Joseph in the Qur'an provides a good example, as he does not become the ruler of Egypt, but the governor of the nation's storehouses (Q. 12:55). Nonetheless, he acts autonomously as a judge when his brothers unknowingly visit him (Q. 12:58–93).[82] A further point is that it is theologically inconceivable that he would serve on an unjust king's behalf, yet the Qur'an provides no indication that the latter ruled according to a revealed law.

Returning to the question of what constitutes legitimate ruling authority for the Muslim community according to the Qur'an, the study of these narratives has led to the following conclusions. A ruler is legitimised by recourse to the Law, whether its outlines are known in the absence of revelation, its details received directly through prophecy, or indirectly by those following in a prophet's footsteps, who must reconcile it with the natural law.[83] This is because, in reality, sovereignty is envisaged for God alone and the person who takes it must do so on the basis of a form of delegation (*khilāfa*).[84] Four possibilities for rule are implicitly illustrated within the Qur'an: just rule on the basis of natural law; just rule on the basis of divine and natural law (including prophetic rule); unjust rule in contravention of natural law; and unjust rule in contravention of divine and natural law.

Although the texts that have been examined explicitly endorse a form of personal absolute rule in which a monarch holds court with advisors, this undoubtedly reflects social contexts in which this was the norm. Interestingly, while the rejection of Saul's appointment by the Israelite chiefs confirms Ibn Khaldūn's notion of *ʿaṣabiyya* as a dynamic in social affairs, in the cases of both Saul and David the legitimate leader is divinely elected. Solomon represents the principle of dynasticism, although the story of his testing and elevation to an even greater kingdom indicates that family succession is only valid when the recipient is worthy.

The obvious conclusion to draw from the fractious events in the first century of Islam is that the Qur'an neither provides a definitive set of criteria for the precise identity of who should lead the Muslim community following the death of the Prophet Muḥammad, nor a political theory for succession.[85] One could argue that the very lack of an explicit statement agrees with the Sunnī view that leadership may be held by any qualified individual of the Prophet's tribe of Quraysh, or even outside of this, provided the condition of sufficient *ʿaṣabiyya* is met.[86] Alternatively, the parallels with the Prophet David noticed above, as well as Qur'anic references to other prophets and the Ahl al-Bayt, could provide support for the Shi'a position that legitimate authority should remain in his family.[87]

II. Loyalty

Having discussed the question of legitimate leadership, I shall now briefly address the other element of this relationship: the duty of community to be loyal to just governance.[88] Within the Qur'an, this is principally expressed in discourses from the Medinan period associating obedience of the community to the Prophet with obedience to God. A salient example is, 'Say, "Obey God; obey the Messenger." If you turn away, then he is responsible for his duty and you are responsible for your duty' (Q. 24:54).

The major passage in which the political authority of the Prophet Muḥammad is mentioned in depth is Q. 4:58–83. This can mostly be dated to 3–4/625–6 following the Battle of Uḥud, in which the Medinan Muslim community had been stretched to its utmost in conflict with its opponents from the Quraysh.[89] It is important, therefore, to read this passage in the context of the pressure of the external threat from the Quraysh and, inside Medina, the potential for the 'fifth column' of hypocrites to ally with the generally antagonistic Jewish tribes remaining in the city. This scenario was to play a part in the expulsion of Banū al-Naḍīr during the same period.[90]

In these verses, the address alternates between the Prophet and the believers, emphasising the duties of each. The principle of a reciprocal relationship between ruler and ruled can be extracted from Q. 4:58–9. Here, those in authority are told, 'God commands you to return trusts to their people and when you judge between people, judge justly' (Q. 4:58), while the governed community are addressed, 'O you who believe, obey God, obey the Messenger, and those in authority amongst you. If you differ about any matter, refer it to God and his Messenger, if you believe in God and the Last Day' (Q. 4:59).[91]

The immediate *sabab* of Q. 4:58 is said to be the incident after the Conquest of Mecca in which ʿUthmān b. Ṭalḥa b. ʿAbd al-Dār is returned the keys to the Kaʿba in line with his ancestral duty of *ḥijāba*, although it obviously has a much wider application.[92] In the case of Q. 4:59, the term 'those in authority (*ulū al-amr*)' has been related within narrations to commanders chosen by the Prophet who are to return back to him if differences emerge between them.[93] By extension, these words could also refer to political leaders in general. However, another influential possibility is that it refers to the ulema and their authority in guiding one's religious affairs.[94]

With the basic principle outlined, verses Q. 4:60–4 deal with the response of the hypocrites. They are condemned for turning away from the Prophet for judgement, which is one of the major concerns of Sūrat al-Nisāʾ.[95] Q. 4:60 contrasts loyalty with those who claim to believe in what was revealed to the Prophet and those before him, 'yet summon one another to the judgement of the rebellious one (*yataḥākamū ilā al-ṭāghūt*)'. The word *ṭāghūt* is used in both single and plural to denote those rebellious to God, or worshipped in His stead and is connected within the Qur'an to idols, diviners, the Devil, and particular opponents of the Prophet.[96] The most plausible and consistent meaning is 'the Devil, or devils', depending on the linguistic construction and context.[97] Q. 4:60 thus denotes the exact opposite of calling to God's judgement.[98] This basic meaning of the word *al-ṭāghūt* can be retained without necessarily rejecting the narrations that it specifically concerns Kaʿb b. al-Ashraf, a satirical poet and 'hypocrite' who sought judgement from the leader of Banū al-Naḍīr, rather than the Prophet Muḥammad.[99]

Q. 4:61–4 responds sharply to this and thereby directs the discourse towards the next major statement about the Prophet's authority:

> By your Lord, they will not be true believers (*fa-lā wa-rabbika lā yuʾminūna*) until they let you decide between them in all matters of dispute, and find no resistance in their souls to your decisions, accepting them totally (Q. 4:65).

In terms of *asbāb al-nuzūl*, this has been related to the dispute between the companion al-Zubayr and a member of the Anṣār over a garden.[100] However, arguably the textual structure, as suggested by Q. 4:60, implies that the verse was revealed in regard to the hypocrites or Jews of Medina, and then subsequently related to the story of al-Zubayr, which is entirely valid for a *sabab al-nuzūl*.[101]

The language of *fa-lā wa-rabbika lā yuʾminūna* is extremely emphatic. The first *lā* can be read as a rejection of their claim to believe, or as emphasis for the complement of the oath, 'they will not be true believers'.[102] Another possibility is that the first *lā* rather strengthens the oath 'by your Lord' itself, as in Q. 56:75, 'Indeed I swear by the locations of the stars (*fa-lā uqsimu bi-mawāqiʿi al-nujūm*).'[103]

Ultimately, these are different nuances rather than substantive differences in the meaning, which is a rebuttal of the hypocrites' superficial claims to faith. Such emphatic language reveals that the linguistic *ḥukm* of this statement, although ostensibly directed towards the Prophet, is in reality for the hypocrites who come to it with a mind of rejection and severe doubt.[104] This is consistent with the Qur'anic style, which generally treats direct address from God as an honour, such as in the following linguistic patterns: Q. 2:21, 'O humanity (*yā-ayyuhā al-nās*)'; 4:59, 'O those who believe (*yā-ayyuhā alladhīna āmanū*)'; 66:1, 'O Prophet (*yā-ayyuhā al-nabī*)'; 2:40, 'O Children of Israel (*yā-banī isrāʾīl*)'; and 3:65, 'O Scriptuaries (*yā-ahl al-kitāb*)'.

When outright disbelievers and hypocrites are addressed, this is typically either done with speech conveyed via the Prophet, such as in Q. 109:1, 'Say, "O disbelievers (*qul yā-ayyuhā al-kāfirūn*)"', or they are spoken about in the third person, a rhetorical distancing. An example of this is Sūrat al-Munāfiqūn, in which the hypocrites are discussed, yet not once directly addressed.

Q. 4:66–79 continues to discuss the back-sliding of the hypocrites in battle and gives counsel to the believers to be on their guard against their arguments to avoid fighting for His sake.[105] Q. 4:68–9 echo Q. 1:6–7 in Sūrat al-Fātiḥa and provide an expansion of what is meant by 'the straight path, the path of those You have favoured (*ṣirāta alladīna an'amta alayhim*)':

> [If they had done what they were told we would have] guided them to a straight path. Whoever obeys God and the Messenger will be among those He has blessed (*an'ama allāhu 'alayhim*): the messengers, the truthful, the martyrs, and the righteous – what excellent companions these are! (Q. 4:68–9)

Thus, obedience to the Messenger is again put beside that of God and stands at the very epicentre of the *dīn*, with the eschatological reward clear.

In Q. 4:80, the argument is taken to its furthest extent, 'Whoever obeys the Messenger obeys God.' This is because a messenger is an emissary who represents the one who sends him. At the same time, 'If some pay no heed, We have not sent you to be their keeper' (Q. 4:80) implies that people may enter a political community willingly and may leave it in the same way. In the following verse, the Prophet is told explicitly about those who say they obey, but then plot by night against him, to 'leave them alone, and put your trust in God' (Q. 4:81). Thus, while the Prophet is the temporal focus of authority, he is himself subject to its ultimate source, God.

The final significant verse in this passage is Q. 4:83, which mentions what the Muslim community should do with news, whether of peace (*amn*), or war (*khawf*). The people are criticised for spreading it around when they should instead have referred it back to the Messenger and those in authority (*ulū al-amr*), so that 'those of them seeking its meaning would have found it out (*la-'alimahu alladhīna yastanbitūna minhum*)'.

This verse indicates that any individual report should not be taken as giving an accurate representation of the state of a battle. Only people of knowledge and wisdom are able to see the ultimate repercussions of a situation, and taking the issue of morale into consideration, to make the judgement of whether this should be immediately publicised among the community.[106]

The language used in Q. 4:83 also returns to the question raised about Q. 4:59, of whether political authority is meant by the phrase *ulū al-amr*, or rather the ulema. Here, the idea of connecting key security matters to those in authority with the ability to extract their essential meanings would perhaps suggest the latter.[107] The two interpretations are not necessarily in conflict, however, as *alladhīna yastanbitūna minhum* can be read as partitive of the people of authority, implying that there is a select group that have authority in both knowledge and command. To make good leadership decisions requires the ability to understand events of importance for the community in a profound way. This also accords with the Prophet's practice of sending people of knowledge to govern and lead, such as Mu'adh b. Jabal to Yemen, in the famous narration.[108] In fact, both Q. 4:83, and especially Q. 4:59, due to its imperative form, are used extensively by later Muslim political theorists.[109]

Taken as a whole, it is not difficult to see how the Qur'anic data can be used to support the dominant Sunnī theological paradigm mandating obedience to even an oppressive ruler.[110] One could argue, however, that this discourse within the Qur'an is forged on the relationship between the community and the Prophet, a figure who rules by virtue of his prophetic office. Thus, the general *ḥikma* seems to be that just as legitimate authority is predicated upon establishing justice in harmony with the natural law, so too is loyalty of the people to be earned not assumed.[111]

Even if legitimate and governing a loyal population, the ideal governance envisaged by Qur'anic ethical discourse will inevitably come into contact with communities composed of people with differing beliefs. Chapters 6 and 7 deal with the questions of peace and war that emerge in these circumstances.

6

Peace

The previous chapter explored the concept of stewardship within the Qur'an's vision of the just society and its implications for the politics and governance of a Muslim community. Attention will now turn to how a community that intends to enact revealed laws should deal with the political reality of other traditions and religions within the world.

Rather than starting from the concepts assumed within the genre of politico-legal writing known as *siyar* (international relations),[1] I shall develop an interpretation of the underlying ethical concepts from a contextual reading of key passages concerned with this theme. The resulting model for interaction between the Muslim community addressed by the Qur'an and its non-Muslim counterparts will be explored in this chapter and the following one. The former will deal with peaceful relations through formal, or informal, treaties, as well as active alliances. The latter will focus upon the breakdown of this positive relationship leading to hostility and outright war.[2]

In brief, I shall argue that the initial normative state of affairs between a Muslim community and others is peace. As discussed in the previous chapter, a natural law reading of the Qur'an makes this the ethical basis for human relationships, even if the opposite is often realised within history due to human failing. Ideally, peaceful relations are formalised in distinct treaties. In the context of seventh-century Arabia, wherein a state of warfare in their absence would be assumed by other parties, making such covenants was a practical political requirement. Moreover, if agreement and trust grows between the two communities, they may choose to enter into an active alliance. Likewise, treaties may be rescinded if not honoured, and a state of hostility, leading to raiding or war, may take their place.

A key point is that, depending on particular circumstances, any of these possibilities may hold in engagement with any independent community, irrespective of religion. Thus, I shall argue on the basis of the natural law framework, as well as Qur'anic discourse, that the underlying ethics of just political action do not vary between pagans and Scriptuaries, with the exception of a limited number of practical and ritual considerations. The qualification of an 'independent' non-Muslim community is of importance and refers to a community possessing its own security arrangements through an army or militia. This contrasts with the situation of non-Muslims whose security arrangements are provided by the Muslim community, a matter that I shall consider in Chapter 7, in connection with the concept of jizya, or tribute.

I. Peace treaties

The relations that the Qur'an enjoins upon its first recipients within the Muslim community with respect to the pagans of the Arabian Peninsula, and especially those of the Quraysh, can be split into two main periods. The first, before the hijra to Medina, was based upon patience and fortitude, and is reflected by the Prophet eschewing the use of force against his tribe, as reflected in numerous Qur'anic verses.[3] Although he received a degree of political protection from his uncle, Abū Ṭālib, many of his community did not, precipitating the emigration of some to Abyssinia during the Meccan period.[4] That this stage, which I have termed prophecy without political power, was entirely pacifistic is further supported by the permission to fight given in the Medinan verse Q. 2:216, to be discussed in Chapter 7.[5]

The second period, after the hijra, contains the Qur'anic moral instructions for interaction between the Muslim community and the pagans outside of Medina. Due to the hostility of the relationship with many of them, especially the Quraysh, during the post-hijra years, they are contingently often centred on war and conflict. Nonetheless, as will be shown, the Qur'anic discourse promotes toleration and living in peace for those who neither oppress, nor act dishonourably with respect to their treaties.

That the main interaction with pagans is outside of Medina reflects the effectiveness of the Prophet's preaching within Banū Qayla, the tribe of the Anṣār, in the wake of success at the Battle of Badr in 2/624: only a small number remained within the settlement.[6] The most notable exception is the sub-clan of the ʿAws called the ʿAws Allāh, which is reported to only have embraced Islam following the Battle of Khandaq in 5/627. This is possibly explained by their close proximity to the Jewish clans of Banū al-Naḍīr and Banū Qurayẓa in the south-eastern region of Medina.[7]

The second main group that requires discussion are Scriptuaries (Ahl al-Kitāb), who occupy a special place within the Qur'anic discourse by virtue of their possession of previous dispensations of the divine Law. Although the Qur'an nowhere gives a definition of this group, there is a clear indication from the name itself, as well as Q. 2:62 and Q. 5:69, that their essential characteristics are monotheism and belief in a revealed scripture. As these verses include the Sabians along with Jews and Christians, the term does not seem limited to the latter two groups. Some scholars have argued for this restriction using Q. 6:156, 'Lest you say that Scripture was only revealed to two communities before us'.[8] However, it would seem that this verse cannot be decisive as it puts the statement into the mouths of the pagan Quraysh who may not have been aware of other scriptural communities.

It is useful to make some further brief remarks on the Qur'anic terminology for Scriptuaries. The descendants of the Prophet Jacob are often called the Children of Israel (*banū isrāʾīl*), based on the appellation he is given in Q. 3:93 and 19:58. Technically, this should refer to his patrilineal descendants, although it seems to be used as a general term for the Arabian Jewish communities contemporaneous with the Qur'an, even though they may have included converts. Other common terms, such as *alladhīna hādū* and *al-yahūd* (Jews), as well as *qawm mūsā* (community of Moses) in Q. 7:159 and *ahl al-dhikr* (People of the Torah) in Q. 16:43 and 21:7, refer to members of this community from the time of the Torah.[9]

The Qur'an uses the word *al-naṣārā*, literally Nazarenes, for Christians.[10] This refers to the locality of Nazareth as the site for the activity of Jesus and his disciples and is a name for the early Christians in the New Testament in Acts 24:5.[11] Another Qur'anic term is *ahl al-injīl* (People of the Evangel), as mentioned in Q. 5:47.

The reference to Sabians (*al-ṣābiʾūna*) is fairly obscure. The most likely candidate seems to be the Elchasaites, a scripturally focused monotheistic community, with qualities somewhere between Jews and Christians, which was still numerous in southern Iraq by the time of Ibn Nadīm in the fourth/tenth century.[12]

Of the Scriptuaries, greater emphasis within the Qur'an is placed on the Jews than on the Christians due to their prominence in Medina.[13] However, there were a number of established communities of both religions within the Arabian Peninsula as a whole during the sixth and seventh centuries. Notable examples outside of the settlement of Yathrib (Medina) include the sizeable Jewish community in Khaybar to the north, as well as a presence in al-Ṭāʾif close to Mecca.[14] In the case of Christians, the most significant population was in Najran to the south, alongside various others, including certain tribes and, according to some reports, monasteries in Wādī al-Qurā relatively close to Medina.[15] Overall, however, both the scale of the Christian presence in the Ḥijāz and the evidence for it is considerably less than its Jewish counterpart.[16]

There appears to be only limited direct contact with Jews and Christians during the Meccan period, although some passages, such as Q. 7:138–71 within the late Meccan Sūrat al-Aʿrāf, do deal with theological questions arising from the Prophet's mission.[17] The Medinan period, beginning from the hijra in 622 CE, is more focused on the question of the political relationship between the Muslim community, now in charge of its own security, and others. From the outset, the Prophet's entry into Medina, a city already housing Jews and pagans, was a peaceful affair.[18]

The two main words used for peace treaties within the Qur'an are *ʿahd* (pl. *ʿuhūd*) and *mīthāq*. As well as a political agreement, these words can refer to a spiritually binding pledge, or covenant, as discussed in Chapter 1.[19] The association of these two terms is clear in Q. 2:26–7, in which the *fāsiqūn* are defined as 'those who break their covenant (*ʿahd*) with God after its binding (*mīthāqihi*)'. This usage accords with the linguistic origin of the word *ʿahd* as something entrusted for safekeeping,[20] as well as *mīthāq* in the rope, or fetters, used to bind prisoners, or animals.[21]

The Qur'anic lexicon contains other words that, while semantically similar, are not used within the current thematic topic. The verb *aṣlaḥa* (to make peace) in Q. 49:9 concerns a truce between fighting believers, while both *aṣlaḥa* and the related noun *ṣulḥ* are used for the peaceful settlement between husband and wife following marital strife in Q. 4:128.[22] In the Qur'an, these terms based on the root *ṣ-l-ḥ* are not used in the context of peace treaties with non-Muslims. The word *dhimma* means a compact of security given by a dominant party to a less powerful one and is only used within the Qur'an in a particular passage of Sūrat al-Tawba. In Chapter 7, the question of *dhimma* will be discussed and the distinction between it and the peace treaties under consideration here will be addressed.

Although the Prophet and Muslim community avoided armed conflict with pagans during the Meccan period, this flared up considerably following the hijra. Discussion of the initial legislation of warfare will follow in the next chapter. After the success of the Muslims at Badr, and the continuing hostility invoked by the humiliation of Qurashī defeat, injunctions directly concerned with peace treaties are found in Q. 8:55–61. The desirability of making a treaty to avoid outright warfare is alluded to in Q. 8:56 and mentioned explicitly in Q. 8:61. It is clear that the condition for such a treaty is the trustworthiness of the other party, as stated in Q. 8:58, 'And if you learn of treachery on the part of any people, throw [their treaty] back at them, for God does not love the treacherous.' Q. 8:60 encourages Muslims in times of war to adopt a military posture that keeps their enemies at bay, 'Prepare whatever forces you [believers] can muster, including warhorses, to frighten off God's enemies and yours, and warn others unknown to you but known to God.' That this is not a call for the unilateral building up of weaponry is shown by Q. 8:61, which commands the Muslims to incline towards peace with their opponents if they show signs of leaving hostility themselves. Furthermore, this is echoed in Q. 4:90, which mentions about people with whom the Muslim community already have a treaty, or who do not want to fight, 'If they withdraw and do not fight you, and offer you peace, then God gives you no way against them' (Q. 4:90).

Some early exegetes argue that this provision for concluding peace treaties is abrogated by the instruction to fight in Q. 9:5.[23] However, quite apart from the restricted nature of Q. 9:5 when read in textual and socio-historical context,[24] there is no need to posit abrogation as the two different rulings do not conflict, but rather are to be applied in different circumstances.[25] In fact, Q. 9:5 takes into consideration the previous statement in Q. 8:58 about those who betray their treaties.

Al-Shāfiʿī is said to have set ten years as the maximum limit for a treaty between a Muslim community and non-Muslims who are not in a covenant of *dhimma* and paying jizya, due to reports that these were the original terms of the Truce of Ḥudaybiya between the Muslims and pagan Quraysh in 6/628.[26] I do not find this a compelling view, however, as there is no evidence that the Prophet was seeking to legislate a maximum limit for treaties and the principle of *mafhūm al-mukhālafa* is needed to infer this.

The Qur'anic discussion about the Jewish community after the hijra takes place against the backdrop of the Covenant of Medina, the document used by the Prophet to lay out a formal legal framework between the Muhājirūn, Anṣār and some Jewish tribal groups.[27] As there is no specific reference in the extant text to the three most influential Jewish tribes, Banū al-Naḍīr, Qaynuqāʿ, and Qurayẓa, there is some difficulty in determining whether they were party to the agreement, which would amount to a formal alliance (*walāʾ*). Watt thinks that it is likely that they would have been included, but their articles were dropped from the updated document after they were expelled from Medina.[28] Lecker gathers a number of conflicting reports about an agreement drawn up between the Prophet Muḥammad and the leaders of these clans, concluding that they were at least bound by a non-belligerency treaty.[29] Another angle from which to approach this question is to look for evidence that suggests that these tribes brought their inter-tribal disputes before the Prophet as a *ḥakam*, a role specified within the text of the Covenant:

> Whatever happenstance or difference occurs between the parties to this agreement (lit. *ṣaḥīfa*: scroll), such that its ill effects are feared, it should be returned back to God, Mighty and Majestic, and to Muḥammad the Messenger of God, may God grant him blessings and peace.[30]

A plausible connection can be drawn between this statement and the passage of Sūrat al-Māʾida in Q. 5:41–50. Although this sura is generally considered to be from the later Medinan period,[31] it is clear that these verses presuppose the live interaction between the Prophet and members of the Jewish tribes of Medina. Hadiths directly relating Q. 5:42 to the question of the Prophet judging between the factions of Banū al-Naḍīr and Qurayẓa would put these verses no later than 4/625, when the former tribe was expelled from the city.[32]

This passage both critiques the historical fidelity of Jewish and Christian communities to their scriptures and reconciles their freedom to continue within the legal bounds of their traditions with the authority over them granted to the Prophet Muḥammad. Q. 5:41 mentions hypocrites and Medinan Jews that say to each other regarding him, 'If you are given this ruling, accept it, but if you are not, then beware!' This is often taken to refer to the well-known story of the Jews who were exposed by the Prophet for trying to cover up the verses in the Torah mandating stoning for the adulterer.[33] In Q. 5:42–3, Banū al-Naḍīr and Qurayẓa are characterised as ready to use the Prophet's worldly authority within the city to gain some advantage without truly accepting his spiritual authority over them:

> If they come to you [Prophet] for judgement, you can either judge between them, or decline – if you decline, they will not harm you in any way, but if you do judge between them, judge justly (*bi-l-qisṭ*): God loves the just – but why do they come to you for judgement when they have the Torah with God's judgement, and even then still turn away? These are not believers.

The Medinan Jews are here merely given the option to seek the Prophet's decision concerning their internal disputes; likewise, he is under no obligation to give them a judgement. However, if he does choose to sit in judgement over them, he is commanded to do so with justice (*qisṭ*). The rhetorical question near the end of Q. 5:43 lampoons the litigants for turning away from their scripture, which contains comprehensive legal injunctions, to seek judgement from a prophet whom they deny.

Therefore, after further criticism of those among the rabbis who would alter the revelation for worldly gain, there comes the conclusion in Q. 5:44, 'Those who do not judge according to what God has sent down are unfaithful.'

The idea that Scriptuaries should maintain fidelity to the rules within their revealed tradition is continued with respect to the followers of the Evangel in Q. 5:46–7. In Q. 5:46, Jesus is referred to as a confirmer (*muṣaddiq*) of the Torah, which acts as a prelude to Q. 5:48's announcement that the Prophet Muḥammad's revelation has a similar confirmatory role towards previously revealed dispensations and is a guardian (*muhaymin*) over them.[34] This verse also intimates that God's division of humanity into different religious communities is predicated on the wisdom of testing each of them based on what they have been given.[35] Finally, the Prophet is exhorted to be true to his revealed message (Q. 5:49), before the passage ends with the rhetorical questions, 'Do they want judgement according to pagan ignorance? Is there any better judge than God for those of firm faith?' (Q. 5:50)

In a general sense, 'judgement according to pagan ignorance' can refer to choosing a particular judge in order to receive a favourable ruling.[36] More specifically, it can be related to allegations that the Jews of Medina would abandon their scriptural norms when punishing murder.[37] In the context of the thrust of the passage as a whole, the broader point is that if the inheritors of previous revealed traditions fall into dispute, they should resolve their issues with the prophet in their midst, as mentioned in the text of the Covenant.

II. Alliances

The term for alliances within the Qur'an is *walāʾ*, which derives from the idea of a connection forged between two things.[38] Sūrat al-Mumtaḥana, which is dated between the conclusion of the Truce of Ḥudaybiya in 6/628 and the Conquest of Mecca in 8/630, deals extensively with alliances and their revocation (*barāʾ*).

The first section of the sura, Q. 60:1–3, prohibits the community of believers from an act of *walāʾ* with those who had driven them out of Mecca, 'You who believe, do not take My enemies and yours as your allies, showing them friendship' (Q. 60:1). The exegetical literature relates this to the incident of a letter sent by a Muslim in Medina called Ḥāṭib b. Abī Baltaʿa to secretly warn the Meccans about the planned conquest so as to protect his family and property.[39]

The crucial word is *al-mawadda* (friendship; love), which is used twice in Q. 60:1, and again in Q. 60:7. In each of these cases, *mawadda* signifies the cordial relations that are usually a precondition for a formal agreement of *walāʾ*, indicated here by the word allies (*awliyāʾ*) and in Q. 60:9 by the verb *tawallā*.

The rationale for this prohibition is given in Q. 60:2, which expresses that any temporary willingness on the Meccan side to temper hostilities is but a tactical move to be followed by renewed aggression if the opportunity arises. The root of this enmity is their wish for the Muslims to leave their newfound faith – the real desire hidden beneath the outward friendship. This characterisation of the opponents highlights their injustice, one of the sura's main themes. The Qur'an contrasts this starkly with the moral imperative for Muslims to remain just.

The section Q. 60:4–6 narrates the story of the Prophet Abraham and his companions leaving their people and rejecting their idolatry as a parallel to the Muslim community and their disbelieving kinsfolk in Mecca. The word used to express this dissociation is *burāʾ*, which is from the same root as *barāʾa*. The latter is an alternative name for Sūrat al-Tawba and the term expressing the exact opposite of *walāʾ* in Q. 9:1, 'A release (*barāʾatun*) by God and His Messenger from the treaty you [believers] made with the pagans [is announced].' This verse will be discussed in the next chapter.[40]

It should be remembered that Abraham's example of *burāʾ*, like that of the nascent Muslim community, is not in response to differences in belief alone, but to the persecution he receives on its account. It is for this reason that in the prayer of Q. 60:5, his party call out, 'Lord, do not expose us to mistreatment (*fitna*) at the hands of the disbelievers.' *Fitna* here refers to the kind of oppression that had forced the Muslims to make hijra to Medina as mentioned in Q. 60:1 and 60:9, and explains the resonance of this particular narrative with the injustice faced by the Prophet and his companions.

Q. 60:7–9 comprise the conceptual heart of this sura, taking the context of the tension and confrontation between the two communities and distilling ethical principles for the just practice of *walāʾ*. The pivotal statement is found in Q. 60:8:

> He does not forbid you to deal kindly and justly with anyone who has not fought you for your faith or driven you out of your homes: God loves the just (*lā yanhākum allāhu ʿan alladhīna lam yuqātilūkum fī al-dīni wa-lam yukhrijūkum min diyārikum an tabarrūhum wa-tuqsiṭū ilayhim inna allāha yuḥibbu al-muqsiṭīn*).

The principle of *al-tanṣīṣ lā yadillu ʿalā al-takhṣīṣ* allows the rejection of the inference from this verse that the Muslims may refuse to deal justly with those who have fought them for their faith or driven them from their homes. Q. 5:8 also points to the same conclusion, explicitly stating in reference to similar acts of oppression that 'hatred of a people' should not divert from justice.

The meaning of *tabarrūhum*, rendered as 'dealing kindly' above, may be veracity in word and oath, especially with respect to agreed treaties.[41] Some exegetes follow this line of thinking in referring it to the tribe of Khuzāʿa and their entry into alliance with the Prophet at Ḥudaybiya,[42] specifically the Kaʿb b. ʿAmr branch.[43] The phrase *tuqsiṭū ilayhim* (deal justly) would thereby imply carrying out these specific commitments in all fairness.[44] Moreover, it is not entirely clear whether this clan were Muslim at the time; if they had already joined the Prophet's community, they would not have needed to be specifically mentioned in the negotiations.[45] It should be noted that, even so, it seems many of the Kaʿb b. ʿAmr did embrace the faith thereafter. Describing the attack on them two years later by the Banū Bakr and Quraysh that led to the end of the Ḥudaybiya treaty and the Conquest of Mecca, their leader, ʿAmr b. Sālim al-Khuzāʿī, emphasises, 'We were killed and we had entered Islam (*qutilnā wa-qad aslamnā*).'[46]

In Q. 60:9, it is explicitly stated using a particle of restriction (*ḥaṣr*), that *walāʾ* is only (*innamā*) prohibited with those guilty of fighting the Muslims for their faith, driving them out of their homes, or helping others to expel them. While it goes without saying that such people are unjust, the Qur'an takes this judgement further to declare that those allying themselves with such people are themselves oppressors (*al-ẓālimūn)*.

Ethically speaking, four categories are instantiated by these verses as follows: members of the Muslim community who act justly in regard to *walāʾ*; those of them who act unjustly by allying with enemies; non-Muslims who act justly by refraining from persecution; and, finally, the oppressive enemies themselves. The conclusion to be drawn is that the Qur'an acknowledges justice as a quality that can be present or absent in an individual irrespective of their faith, at least with respect to the practice of *walāʾ*, and, by logical extension, other political, social, and legal relationships. In the words of MacIntyre, 'When in the ancient world justice was extended beyond the boundaries of the *polis*, it was always as a requirement of theology.'[47]

This possibility for a peace treaty to be used as the starting point for a Muslim community to enter into an alliance with people of other faiths sharing its political objectives is an important precedent. It reflects the metaethical insight of a shared social space populated by real ethical qualities that can exist in those who do not necessarily believe in the Qur'an's message. As such, it interestingly contrasts with the conclusion that Izutsu reaches when discussing the 'fundamental moral dichotomy' between belief and disbelief,[48] and his asseveration that the Qur'an treats revelation as 'the final yardstick of justice'.[49]

7
War

The previous chapter dealt with the mutual relationships of Muslims and non-Muslims between political communities in the Qur'an. The principle was established that the fundamental basis for relations is peace, which leads to formal treaties and even alliances (*walā'*). In this chapter, I will discuss the right of disavowal (*barā'*) for a community when such treaties are breached. This can lead to jihad, a just war predicated on self-defence or the removal of corruption in the land, including preserving freedom to worship God.[1] Jihad may put the community in a position of political authority over its opponents, able to exact a jizya, or tribute, paid in lieu of participation in the standing army. Such security, or *dhimma*, is usually associated in Muslim tradition with Scriptuaries, although the term itself is used exclusively in the Qur'an for relationships with pagans and there is no scriptural reason to assume it must be limited to the former group. Furthermore, I will argue that these injunctions need not be read as abrogating the different types of treaty-based arrangements discussed in the previous chapter, nor obligating the Muslim community to perpetual offensive jihad against others.

It may be helpful to begin by outlining the Qur'anic basis commonly adduced for the belligerent interpretation just mentioned. This can be implicitly connected to what was termed a voluntaristic political theory in Chapter 5.[2] If the Qur'an is assumed to bring morality to an amoral world then it is a logical consequence that the only way that human beings can experience the justice of God's Law is to be under the political authority of the Muslim community.

A starting point is the classical view that certain late verses, such as Q. 9:5, which commands fighting against pagans, and Q. 9:29, which does so against Scriptuaries, abrogate earlier regulations concerning war and peace.[3] This perspective became so well-established on a juristic level that even such a thoughtful figure as al-Māturīdī adheres to it without significantly questioning its assumptions. For example, although al-Māturīdī claims that disbelievers are not fought on account of their disbelief, he confirms that if they do not answer the invitation to faith they are indeed fought until they are compelled to accept Islam.[4] However, the jizya, a tribute, may be taken in lieu of continued war from Scriptuaries (which for Ḥanafīs like al-Māturīdī includes everyone except pagans from the Arabian Peninsula).[5]

The *ḥikma* of this state of affairs, he avers, is that each group is given a test within the wordly life, whether this is fighting, or paying jizya.[6] Furthermore, classical proponents of this theory, which is more or less constant within legal schools,[7] as well as modern adherents such as Sayyid Quṭb, combine this with a reading of *li-yuẓhirahu ʿalā al-dīni kullihi* in verses such as Q. 9:33,[8] to demonstrate that non-Muslims at a global level must be continually fought until they embrace the faith, or submit to pay jizya in the case of those taking the ruling of Scripturaries.[9]

The analysis to follow will provide a different approach to the same Qur'anic materials with the aim of discovering *ḥikma*s related to the wider structure of societal justice. Starting with reasons given for the legislation of jihad at the beginning of the Medinan period, attention will then be paid to the breakdown of peaceful relations with the major Jewish tribes. Afterwards, I will read the key passage Q. 9:1–37 as responding to two particular contexts of treaties being broken, one by pagans in Q. 9:1–28 and another by Scripturaries in Q. 9:29. This will be followed by a discussion of the ethical basis by which the Muslim community can leave treaties, enter into hostilities, and establish a formal compact of security upon defeating its opponent's forces.

Before the Battle of Badr, the first significant conflict between the Muslim community in Medina and the pagan Quraysh remaining in Mecca, a revealed verse strengthens the resolve of the former who are reluctant to enter into war, 'Fighting is ordained for you, though you dislike it' (Q. 2:216). The legislation of fighting is made as a response to the aggression that the Muslim community faced from their antagonists in Mecca and is justified through appeals to the principle of religious freedom. Q. 22:39–40, revealed soon after the hijra,[10] reads:

> Those who have been attacked are permitted to take up arms because they have been wronged – God has the power to help them – those who have been driven unjustly from their homes only for saying, 'Our Lord is God.' If God did not repel some people by means of others (*wa-law lā dafʿu allāhi al-nāsa baʿḍahum bi-baʿḍ*), many monasteries, churches, synagogues, and mosques, where God's name is much invoked, would have been destroyed. God is sure to help those who help His cause – God is strong and mighty.

The wisdom underlying this permission for the use of force is explained in Q. 22:40 as the Muslim community's expulsion from their home and also their place of worship in Mecca. This is then linked to a broader point that God wants His servants to protect all of the houses of worship belonging to Scripturaries. That fighting is sometimes required to avert the destruction of these buildings can be read as implying the right to religious practice. A second rationale is supplied by Q. 4:75, which was revealed a few years later, most likely after the Battle of Uḥud and is a continuation of the lengthy discourse in Sūrat al-Nisāʾ directed towards the hypocrites discussed in Chapter 5. The addressees of this verse are asked why they would not fight in the way of God when 'oppressed men, women and children are calling out, "Our Lord, let us leave this city of unjust people"' (Q. 4:75). Here, taking up arms in jihad is predicated on helping people – likely Meccans – who are praying for God to provide them with support and relief from injustice.

Q. 2:190–5 provides more detailed ethics on how defensive jihad should be practised: the response must be proportionate to the original attack, and should be respectful of sacred times and places, as well as accompanied by keen spiritual awareness. Thus, in Q. 2:193, 'Fight them until there is no more persecution, and worship is devoted to God. If they cease hostilities, there can be no [further] hostility, except towards aggressors.'

In a number of cases, entering into jihad requires the revocation of formal peace treaties. The earliest example in the Qur'an is between the Muslim and Jewish communities in Medina. It is found in Sūrat al-Ḥashr, which was called Sūrat al-Naḍīr by early Muslims on account of its commentary on the expulsion of this tribe in 4/625.[11] The main discussion is in the passage Q. 59:2–7, of which the start of Q. 59:2 sets the tone, 'It was He who drove those Scriptuaries who broke faith (*kafarū*) out from their homes at the first gathering of forces.'

Here the verb *kafarū* has been translated as '[they] broke faith' rather than 'disbelieved', as the reference is to the political rather than theological unfaithfulness of Banū al-Naḍīr.[12] While there is a degree of uncertainty about whether they were bound by the Covenant of Medina, reports indicate that, at the very least, a treaty agreed with the Prophet was violated.[13] The principle that can be extracted from this verse is not then just the revocation of transgressed treaties, but the possibility of forced expulsion in the case of treachery.

Within *sīra* literature, Banū Qaynuqāʿ are usually said to have been expelled from Medina two years earlier in 2/624.[14] An alternative view is found in hadiths that suggest that the Prophet banished all the remaining Jews of Medina, including Qaynuqāʿ, after the incident with Banū Qurayẓa (see below).[15] Although the Qur'an does not clearly refer to Qaynuqāʿ, the phrase *li-awwali al-ḥashr* (the first gathering of forces) could be taken as consistent with there being no expulsion before 4/625.[16]

Likewise, Muslim tradition considers Banū Qurayẓa to have broken their treaty obligations by negotiating with the sieging army of Quraysh and its allies during the Battle of Khandaq in 5/627.[17] Again, there is only an allusion to this in Q. 33:26–7:

> He brought those Scriptuaries who supported them down from their strongholds and put panic into their hearts. Some of them you [believers] killed and some you took captive. He passed on to you their land, their houses, their possessions, and a land where you had not set foot: God has power over everything.[18]

Various traditions give details about the circumstances to which this verse refers. The Jews of Qurayẓa are said to have asked a former ally and trading partner from the clan of ʿAws, Saʿd b. Muʿādh, to decide their punishment. Their reasoning was based on the lenient terms that the Khazrajī ʿAbd Allāh b. Ubayy had previously managed to secure for Banū al-Naḍīr. However, rather than banishment, Saʿd is said to have sentenced the male combatants to execution, the women and children to captivity, and their property to be seized by the Muhājirūn.[19] It seems possible that this judgement is modelled on the following verses of the Torah:

> But if it [the city] makes no peace with you, but makes war against you, then you shall besiege it; and when the Lord your God gives it into your hand you shall put all its males to the sword, but the women and the little ones, the cattle, and everything else in the city, all its spoil, you shall take as booty for yourselves; and you shall enjoy the spoil of your enemies, which the Lord your God has given you (Deuteronomy 20:12–14).

If it is also true that the Prophet approved this decision by Saʿd, declaring it as the judgement of God, it may reflect the principle of scriptural communities adhering to the law contained within their own books.[20] However, there do not seem to be any examples of the Qur'an validating collective punishment, which adds a degree of weight to alternative interpretations. One such view is the apologetic argument provided by Barakat Ahmad who uses both an analysis of the sources and various logistical considerations to assert that a mass execution is not credible and must be an exaggeration.[21] His conclusion is that Saʿd used the term *muqātil* (combatants) with respect to the leaders of Banū Qurayẓa to exclude the old and rabbis. He thereby arrives at a reduced executed figure of about sixteen, rather than the 600–900 suggested by Ibn Isḥāq (and not found in well-attested hadiths).[22]

Exegetes give various possibilities for the 'land where you had not set foot (*arḍan lam taṭaʾūhā*)' in Q. 33:27, including Byzantium, Persia, Mecca, and Khaybar, the cluster of strongholds to which Banu al-Naḍīr had fled after their expulsion and had helped fund the participation of the nomadic Ghaṭafān in the siege of Medina.[23]

The Qur'anic passage under discussion for the remainder of this chapter is at the beginning of Sūrat al-Tawba. Like much of the Qur'an, the material confronts the exegete with a hermeneutic challenge: it deals with particular, even exceptional, circumstances, yet is to be read as a wellspring of universal principles. This sura, also known as Barāʾa due to its opening revocation of a treaty with certain pagans, is the only one in the ʿUthmānī *muṣḥaf* (codex) that does not start with the *basmala*.[24] Early Muslims offered different explanations for this fact. One proposal is that the Prophet Muḥammad passed on before clarifying its location in the Qur'an, so it was placed as a continuation of Sūrat al-Anfāl due to the connection in meaning. Another suggestion is that the two suras are actually just one, as it is said that there are seven *ṭiwāl* (long) suras, and joining them together meets both this number and the necessary length. Finally, it is mooted that the *basmala* signifies a security (*amān*), while Barāʾa was revealed in order to revoke treaties.[25]

An important insight is to see Q. 9:1–37 as a single cohesive passage, and, as will be mentioned below, there is evidence that it was publicly recited as such. Stern criticism of certain pagan tribes in failing to meet their treaty commitments in Q. 9:1–28 segues into an order to fight Scriptuaries who fail to pay the tribute that they owe, followed by a rhetorical likening of some of their beliefs to idolatry in

Q. 9:30–2. In Q. 9:33–7, the further thread that ties the two together in the Qur'an's judgement becomes clear: failure to sanctify what God has made sacred.

The sura begins, 'A revocation from God and His Messenger to those pagans with whom you made a treaty. Therefore, travel in the land four months and know that you will not escape God, and that God disgraces the disbelievers' (Q. 9:1–2). Two points can be noted: the addressee shifts from the believing community in Q. 9:1 to the pagans discussed in Q. 9:2, and for this second address to be effective, it would have to be communicated directly to those with whom the treaty was revoked. The next verse highlights the significance of the public recital of this disavowal, 'A proclamation from God and His Messenger to all people on the Day of the Great Pilgrimage (*yawma al-ḥajji al-akbar*): "God and His Messenger are released from [treaty] obligations to the pagans"' (Q. 9:3).[26]

A hadith provides a context for the public conveyance of the first part of the sura on the Day of Sacrifice in the hajj led by Abū Bakr, which is dated to 9/631.[27] Recital of Barāʾa was combined with the prohibition of pagan participation in hajj from the following year and the practice of circumambulating the Kaʿba naked.[28]

The year 9/630–1 is known within the *sīra* as the 'Year of Delegations (*ʿāmm al-wufūd*)', because of the numerous representatives of tribes that came to Medina from all over Arabia to pledge their allegiance to the Prophet. Nonetheless, some tribes held out against Muslim hegemony over the peninsula. The passage in its entirety, and particularly Q. 9:1, 10, and 13, make clear that the revocation applies to a treaty with specific idolaters. Q. 9:5 mentions that at the end of the 'sacred months (*al-ashhuru al-ḥurum*)', these belligerent pagans could be attacked.

Reflection upon this dating provokes an exegetical problem that deserves a satisfactory conclusion. A pronouncement during the hajj would be dated to Dhū al-Ḥijja, yet this would mean the period of four months in Q. 9:2 would extend beyond the remaining sacred months in Q. 9:5, including the rest of Dhū al-Ḥijja and Muḥarram of 9–10/631 (Rajab and Dhū al-Qaʿda of 9/630–1 would have already passed).

I suggest that the best solution is to read the initial limit of four months in Q. 9:2 to have been set at the beginning of Shawwāl 9/631, which would mean that the entire period also includes the consecutive sacred months of Dhū al-Qaʿda, Dhū al-Ḥijja, and Muḥarram.[29] Commissioning representatives at the hajj to recite the first part of the sura points to an intention to widely disseminate the new rules between the Muslims and certain pagans. If this is the case, then Q. 9:5, in referring to the end of the sacred months, counts down towards the same period set out in Q. 9:2, providing a public warning that the period of grace ends in Muḥarram.

The gap between the revelation of the verses in Shawwal and their recitation on the Day of Sacrifice is reduced if narrations are taken into account that claim that the hajj in 9/631 really took place in Dhū al-Qaʿda due to the Arabian practice of *al-nasīʾ*, or adjustment of months.[30] Such an idea is supported by the Prophet's words in the *khuṭbat al-wadāʿ* (farewell sermon) during the hajj of the following year, 'Time has returned to its state the day God created the heavens and the earth, and truly the number of months according to God is twelve; of them, four are sacred.'[31]

Some reports suggest that approximately the first forty verses of the sura were recited at the hajj in question.[32] In the light of this information, Q. 9:1–37 is a plausible passage that could have been conveyed to the diverse peoples gathered in pilgrimage, including various groups of pagans. These verses contain a number of interlinked themes, including the revocation of treaties and the warfare following it, as well as the renewal of sacred institutions. Q. 9:38 broaches the new topic of hypocrites among the believers, moving the discourse to the internal affairs of the community.

Q. 9:5, sometimes called the sword verse (*āyat al-sayf*), reads in full:

> When the forbidden months are over, wherever you encounter the pagans, kill them, seize them, besiege them, wait for them at every lookout post; but if they turn [to God], maintain the prayer, and pay the prescribed alms, let them go on their way, for God is most forgiving and merciful.

A common exegetical strategy is to read the word *al-mushrikūn* (pagans) in this verse, and repeated several times in the passage, as *ʿāmm* and, therefore, declaring war upon every pagan, except for various restrictions taken from other verses of the Qur'an, or the Sunna.[33] However, the language of the passage makes it more likely to refer back to the specific pagans mentioned in Q. 1–3, meaning that *al-mushrikūn* should be read as *khāṣṣ* with *alif lām* used for *maʿhūd li-l-dhiʾn* (known referent).[34] Looking at the passage as a whole, it appears that two kinds of pagans are continuously contrasted: those whom the Muslims must fight, because they do not honour their treaties, in Q. 9:1–3, 5 and 8–14, and those with whom they may keep peaceful relations, because they are trustworthy, in Q. 9:4, 9:6, and 9:7.

The distinctions that can be drawn between these two sets of verses demonstrate the continuation of a nuanced approach to warfare up until the end of the Medinan period. Q. 9:4 clarifies that pagans who have fulfilled their obligations are to fully retain their treaties for whatever term has been agreed and provides no reason to assume that renewal would be prohibited at that point. Q. 9:6 allows pagans to seek the protection of the Muslim community, to hear the Qur'an and then be taken to a safe place. This ability to grant safety would seem to apply to any Muslim, although some commentators restrict it to the community's leader.[35]

Q. 9:7 begins by rhetorically questioning the very idea of concluding a treaty with (untrustworthy) pagans with the phrase, 'How could there be for the pagans a treaty? (*kayfa yakūna li-l-mushrikīna ʿahd*)', expressing condemnation.[36] However, it immediately gives the parenthetical exception of those who entered into an agreement at *al-masjid al-ḥaram* in Mecca, which may refer to those local groups, such as various clans of the Banū Bakr, who had not yet embraced Islam.[37] The following verse, Q. 9:8, clarifies, 'How, when if they were to gain the upper hand from you, they would not respect their ties of kinship with you, nor give you security (*dhimma*)?' Thus, those that would behave appropriately are not to be included in the disavowal, a point highlighted in Q. 9:12, 'But if they break their oath after having made an agreement with you, if they revile your religion, then fight the leaders of disbelief – oaths mean nothing to them – so that they may stop.' Again, fighting the pagan tribes is predicated upon them breaking their oaths and committing aggression.[38]

The Qur'an does not accord peace treaties with pagans its highest value, which is reserved for their embrace of the faith and practice of its major obligations (Q. 9:11). Furthermore, despite political tolerance based on sound treaties, there is an unequivocal concern in Q. 9:17–19 and 9:28 that the central religious institution of the Sacred Mosque in Mecca is to be neither kept, nor attended, by pagans. This is because, while restricting the right to political and religious autonomy would not be just, the case is different with respect to God's sanctuary, which must be kept free from idolatry.[39]

What about the analogous case of Scriptuaries? This question can be answered by a close consideration of Q. 9:29, which is the only verse in the Qur'an that explicitly mentions the concept of jizya, or tribute. As such, classical Muslim exegetes have tended to reify it as 'the jizya verse' and treat it as an independent source of legislation without fully situating it within its textual, or socio-historical context.

It is imperative to highlight that the practice of jizya, tribute paid by a conquered, or militarily outclassed, party for the protection of its stronger counterpart, was well-known to seventh-century Arabians. In the century before the hijra both the Jews and pagans of Yathrib had collected such a tax on the others inhabiting the oasis.[40] The earliest report referring explicitly to tribute taken by the Prophet Muḥammad's Muslim community seems to pertain to the Christian tribe of Kalb, located in the territory of Dūmat al-Jandal, due north of Medina and on the intersection of trade routes going to Iraq and the Levant. In 6/627, the prominent Companion ʿAbd al-Raḥmān b. ʿAwf led a force there to secure an agreement of jizya.[41] This is significant for chronologically preceding Q. 9:29, which, based on the surrounding material within the sura, is usually dated to about 9/630–1.[42]

Below, I develop the suggestion of Abdel Haleem that jizya represents a pre-existing political solution affirmed within the Qur'an in certain circumstances, rather than a new institution legislated by Q. 9:29.[43] Before exploring the implications of this understanding, it is useful to give an explanatory translation of Q. 9:29:

> Fight those who do not [truly] believe in God and the Last Day, who do not sanctify what God and His Messenger have sanctified, and who do not obey the religion of truth, from amongst those given scripture, so that they pay their jizya readily as tributaries.

In this verse, the word *min* in 'from amongst those given scripture (*min alladhīna ūtū al-kitāb*)' is a partitive expression that specifies the conditions that such Scriptuaries must fulfil. The syntax of the Arabic is significant here, too, as the phrase 'those given scripture' is delayed until after all of the conditions, except those related to the jizya itself. This gives a rhetorical effect of cautious qualification to the statement about fighting Scripturaries, contrasting with a verse such as Q. 9:7 within the previous passage, which makes a broad statement about pagans before restricting it.

The first specification 'those who do not [truly] believe in God and the Last Day' reflects the irreligiosity of the people in question. Such Scripturaries are thereby implicitly contrasted with those in Q. 2:62 and 5:69 who are positively affirmed in these twin beliefs.

Next, they are described as those 'who do not sanctify (*ḥarrama*) what God and His Messenger have sanctified'. The verb *ḥarrama* is often translated as 'forbid', yet a number of considerations suggest the meaning is to sanctify, or treat as sacred. The previous verse, Q. 9:28, specifically bans pagans from the Sacred Mosque (*al-masjid al-ḥarām*), while Q. 27:91 reads, 'I have only been commanded to worship the Lord of this land, which He has sanctified (*rabba hādhihi al-baldati alladhī ḥarramahā*)'. Relevant too is the *niẓām* of this passage as a whole, which concludes in Q. 9:36–7 with condemnation of those who adjust the calendar in order to desacralise a month. The reference to the sacred implied in Q. 9:29 could include the mosque, the rituals established by the Prophet Muḥammad for his followers, and even the oaths and treaties under discussion in the last chapter.

The third qualification given in Q. 9:29 is 'who do not obey the religion of truth (*wa-lā yadīnūna dīna al-ḥaqq*)'. Abdel Haleem makes the astute observation that *yadīnūna* cannot here mean 'to practise as a religion', as it does not take the particle *bi*.[44] He therefore does not translate *dīn al-ḥaqq* as 'religion of truth', but 'rule of justice'. However, *dīn al-ḥaqq* is a known Qur'anic phrase, which reappears in the same sura in Q. 9:33, as well as in Q. 48:28 and 61:9 in contexts that make any reading besides 'religion of truth' implausible.[45] It is possible, however, to take the primary verbal meaning of obey for *yadīnūna*, while retaining the usual signification of *dīn al-ḥaqq*. The nature of this obedience is specified in the final phrase of the verse as being in the matter of jizya.

Q. 9:29 concludes, 'so that they pay their jizya readily as tributaries (*ḥattā yuʿṭū al-jizyata ʿan yadin wa-hum ṣāghirūn*)'. The particle *ḥattā* can mean 'until', or 'so that' among other possibilities. Here, the point is not general warfare until the class of all those mentioned in the verse pay, but rather specific warfare so that they pay what they owe. This meaning is also derived from the definite article *alif lām* of *al-jizyata*, translated above as 'their', an example of *maʿhūd li-l-dhiʾn*. In this passage, it points beyond the Qur'anic text to the actions of the human actors to which it refers. In other words, people may be fought to collect the jizya they owe.

Much has been made by exegetes of the phrases *ʿan yadin* (lit. out of hand) and *wa-hum sāghirūn* (lit. while they are submitted), extracting from them everything from a humble manner of payment[46] to a model of political organisation.[47] My reading is that the first refers adverbally to readiness to pay their jizya, while the second refers to their status as tributaries.

In sum, the so-called jizya verse, like the remainder of the first part of Sūrat al-Tawba, is responsive to a particular situation. It refers to the rebellion of certain carefully specified Scriptuaries who had evidently begun to refuse to pay the jizya that had been arranged upon their military defeat, or their surrender and petition for *dhimma*.

The mere existence of jizya and the Qur'anic endorsement of a tributary relationship in Q. 9:29 does not, therefore, imply the abrogation of any of the previous verses that have been mentioned. Likewise, the call to fight those who rebel against their jizya does not mean that treaties cannot be concluded with those maintaining standing armies. Neither does it suggest a policy of universal conquest and subjugation. However, in support of this latter idea, Q. 9:33 is often read as follows, 'He is the one who has sent His Messenger with guidance and the religion of truth to manifest it over all religion (*li-yuẓhirahu ʿalā al-dīni kullihi*), despite the dislike of the pagans.' Semantic issues were raised with this reading in Chapter 1.[48] There are also compositional problems with this approach. The verse does not come directly after Q. 9:29, but rather follows a critique of the beliefs of Jews and Christians in Q. 9:30–1 and the statement in Q. 9:32 that 'God insists on perfecting His light', suggesting the meaning is successive conveyance of the message until it is complete.

The overall purpose of Q. 9:29 appears to be guidance on how the tributary regime in the territory under the authority of the Muslim community is to be maintained, particularly in the face of potential revolt. In this context, it is interesting to note that the area of Dūmat al-Jandal, in which jizya was taken from the tribe of Kalb in 6/627 and from Kinda in 9/630, rebelled three years later in the early post-prophetic era.[49]

If the proposed reading is accepted, then the only people who may be fought to force them to pay their jizya are those for whom a treaty of protection has been contracted. A well-known example of such a treaty was concluded with the delegation sent in 10/631 by Christians from Najran. This acknowledged the protection of their places of worship and priests in return for a jizya of 2,000 garments and confiscation of a range of military equipment, to be returned upon the outbreak of sedition in their land.[50]

Jizya, then, is the standard mechanism for dealing with communities who, whether due to conflict, or a wish for protection, do not maintain their own military independence. Therefore, they can be placed under the security (*dhimma*) of the Muslim community, while continuing to operate their own systems of internal governance and religious rites. The Qur'an considers them, once they have rejected the Prophet Muḥammad's call, as autonomous communities with their own laws, which they remain free to follow, despite the moral obligation to recognise God's final messenger. However, if they disagree among themselves they can offer their questions to the Prophet who is able to act as an arbiter. This reading of Q. 9:29 does not abrogate the verses in Sūrat al-Māʾida discussed previously, but rather coheres with them.[51]

A further query is whether the mention of jizya in relation to Scriptuaries disbars it from those who do not fall into this group. The basic exegetical principle to be used here is again *al-tanṣīṣ lā yadillu ʿalā al-takhṣīṣ*. Simply put, the mere fact that certain Scriptuaries are to be fought so that they pay their jizya should not lead to the conclusion that it is prohibited to collect it from others, such as pagans.[52]

This also relates back to the definition of Scriptuaries and whether other traditions can take their rulings in some cases. For instance, hadiths suggest that the Prophet declared that jizya was to be taken from Magians and that he sent Abū Ubayda b. al-Jarrāḥ to Bahrain to collect it from them.[53]

Another issue pertains to the capture or group surrender of pagans at the time of the Prophet. Here, it would seem that tribute in the form of jizya would be taken from them and *dhimma* provided.[54] Therefore, despite differing rhetoric and criticism of beliefs and practices, the main distinction in terms of conflict with Scriptuaries versus pagans at the time of the Prophet relates to the banning of the latter from the Sacred Mosque and rituals of the hajj.

This interpretation conflicts with some hadiths within the canonical collections that suggest that, at the very end of his life, the Prophet intended to expel all non-Muslims from the Arabian Peninsula. One set of hadiths asserts this specifically for Jews and Christians.[55] However, it should be noted that these hadiths rely on the testimony of a single figure, Abū al-Zubayr Muḥammad b. Maslama, who is not accepted by al-Bukhārī without corroboration.[56]

The only hadith that al-Bukhārī records relating to the expulsion of Scriptuaries is a narration in which the Prophet Muḥammad is with Abū Hurayra outside of a Jewish Bayt al-Midrās in Medina. The Prophet says, 'I want to drive you out from this land. If any of you have any property, sell it. If not, know that the land is for God and His Messenger.'[57] The precise context is not clear, but given the difficult relationship between Muslims and Jews within Medina in the period, it is likely that his words refer to the immediate area of the city.[58] It is only with his chapter heading that al-Bukhārī associates this hadith with the Arabian Peninsula as a whole.

The weight of hadith evidence points to an expulsion event for Scriptuaries during the caliphate of ʿUmar b. al-Khaṭṭāb.[59] However, in a recent article, Harry Munt has pointed out that this might have been conflated with the later Umayyad Caliph ʿUmar b. ʿAbd al-ʿAzīz, who is associated with expulsions in the *Muṣannaf* of Ibn Abī Shayba; or partially due to a lack of clarity over the borders of the peninsula, it may have effectively never happened at all.[60]

On the normative plane, it is important to weigh these fairly isolated narrations against Q. 5:5, which regulates relationships between Muslims and Scriptuaries in the context of the completion of the Writ to the Prophet Muḥammad.[61] It is hard to imagine the kind of interchange in marital relations between communities envisaged within this verse in conjunction with a policy of expulsion from the Arabian Peninsula.

The case for the intended expulsion of pagans is a bit more secure, due to the severe criticism meted out to them in the Qur'an and the lack of a parallel religious law. Also, the hadith that mentions 'expel the pagans' as one of the Prophet's final commands is accepted by al-Bukhārī, Muslim, Abū Dāwūd, and al-Nasāʾī.[62] However, on the weight of the evidence from the Qur'an, this does not need to be understood as an absolute statement, but as referring to those who refused to coexist peacefully with the Muslim community. Rather, as shown in the present chapter, the Qur'anic discourse is consistent with agreed treaties, as well as the principles of *dhimma* and jizya, being applied to pagans, whether inside or outside the Arabian Peninsula.

Overall, the picture is that, with the exception of certain ritual matters relating to the sanctuary in Mecca, non-Muslim communities are free to practise their religions as they see fit, with peace as the basic state of affairs, notwithstanding the possibility of both alliance and hostility. Although the duty of stewardship is to establish a just order in accord with the moral Scale that God inscribes into the world, other communities are free to organise themselves politically and are able to establish polities according to the basic principles of natural law. A proviso is that they must not do so with belligerent intent and, therefore, in order to safeguard the Muslim community, it is necessary to have enough martial power to ensure security. This is because, in some cases, it is only the proper use of force that can hold corruption at bay, and establish societal justice, including the basic freedom to adhere to one's existing beliefs and traditions.

Focusing once again on the broader development of ideas within this book, the ideal should have emerged of just governance with a loyal population, which is able to deal with other communities in peace and war. Such leadership cannot stand apart from a wider socio-economic settlement within society. This requires a fair distribution of wealth and balancing the demands of the self-interest of community members with the collective welfare of the group. Moreover, the varied roles and responsibilities within marriages and the broader family must be understood, as well as the needs of the present population versus those of future generations. These are the subjects of Part III.

Part III

Distributive Justice

8

Trade

The question of how goods should be justly distributed within a society is one of the perennial questions addressed by political philosophers. The Qur'an does not present an explicit theoretical model in response to this issue, but rather legislates on a range of practical socio-economic concerns with a particular concern for morality and, in later revelations, law.

This chapter deals with the ethics for the acquisition of wealth and is divided into two sections. The first deals with the theme of upright trading in general, while the second examines the specific condemnation of the practice known as *ribā*, which is approximated by the English term usury. These thematic topics are concerned with the procedural aspect of distributive justice, the facilitation of just transactions between people in society. Unlike the following chapter, there is no concern to allocate or rebalance the goods of society according to a specific pattern or rationale. Rather, space is created for enterprise and competition in trade, but within a sphere of moral rectitude that restricts the range of contracts that may be entered into. Furthermore, when just trade is abandoned, it leads to the spread of corruption, requiring an effort to return society to the initial state of right dealing (*iṣlāḥ*), as will be discussed in the narrative of the Prophet Shuʿayb.

I. Fair trade

The Qur'an defends the basic personal right to possess wealth and property as the foundation of human livelihood and economic activity. This right is not absolute, however, as each person is seen to be, in reality, merely a steward over the bounty bequeathed by God to the community as a whole.[1] The moral outlook of the Qur'an, embodied also in its legislation, thus implicitly strikes a balance between the needs of the group and those of the individual.[2]

A fundamental constituent of settled society, trade is given considerable attention within the Qur'an as the means by which individual wealth is acquired.[3] It was the profession of the Prophet Muḥammed before his prophetic calling, as well as many of his forbears. Within the early Meccan Sūrat Quraysh, the intimate relationship between this tribe and the practice of caravan trading is recalled in glowing terms, 'In order [to preserve] the security of the Quraysh (*li-īlāfi quraysh*), their security in the [trade] journeys of the winter and summer' (Q. 106:1–2).

The particle *li* in the phrase *li-īlāfi quraysh* is best understood as a *lām al-ta'līl* (attributive), which assigns a cause to the last sentence of the preceding sura.[4] This describes God's annihilation of the People of the Elephant – the Abyssinian army that was raised with the intention of destroying the Kaʿba in Mecca – with the evocative phrase, 'So He made them as if razed cornstalks (*fa-jaʿalahum ka-ʿaṣfin maʾkūl*)'. A single sentence is then composed between the two suras, as follows, 'So He made them as if razed cornstalks, in order to preserve the security of the Quraysh, their security in the [trade] journeys of the winter and summer' (Q. 105: 5–106:2). The compositional interlink between Sūrat al-Fīl and Sūrat Quraysh establishes the connection between defence of the realm, usually the job of the political authority, and the practice of trade. However, the Qur'an cites divine intervention of a kind appropriate for the House of God, rather than conventional modes of defence.

While these verses confirm the honour of Quraysh's trading, those that follow in the sura present them as honoured keepers of the House of God, blessed with security and livelihood. The sura concludes, 'So let them worship the Lord of this House, who provides them with food to ward off hunger and safety to ward off fear' (Q. 106:3–4). As a whole, then, Sūrat Quraysh has a symmetrical structure. The first and last statements on security pacts and safety from fear are related, as are the second and penultimate on trade journeys and provision to defeat hunger. The central term urges the worship of God, and links it to the House of God, the Kaʿba, which is the central hub for trade and worship alike. In fact, the inviolable status of the *ḥaram* was the basis for the emergence of a trade centre in an agriculturally barren valley, while the pacts said to be concluded by the Prophet's great-grandfather Hāshim were made to supply much-needed grain during a famine in Mecca.[5]

With trade the lifeblood of the Meccan economy, it should not be surprising that a number of the verses of the Qur'an revealed in the city focus attention on scrupulous practice of it. Later verses during the Medinan phase of the Prophet's life take this general ethical framework and add more precise injunctions in response to the conditions of the time.

Q. 6:152 commands, 'Give full measure and weight, according to justice (*wa-awfū al-kayla wa-l-mīzāna bi-l-qisṭ*).' *Awfū* is the plural imperative of the verb *awfā* (root *w-f-y*), which means to pay, or render fully, someone's right, or due.[6] *Kayl* refers to a measure of capacity and *mīzān* to a scale for weight. Therefore, to transact with *qisṭ* here is essentially to be upright and fair in trading and not to cheat by withholding goods or produce. Q. 17:35 is similarly worded, 'Give full measure when you measure, and weigh with accurate scales: that is better and fairer in the end (*wa-awfū al-kayla idhā kiltum wa-zinū bi-l-qisṭāsi al-mustaqīmi dhālika khayrun wa-aḥsanu taʾwīlan*).' The main difference between this verse and Q. 6:152 is that *al-qisṭ* is replaced with *al-qisṭās al-mustaqīm* (accurate scales).[7]

If Q. 6:152 calls for giving full measure according to a standard of just dealing, Q. 17:35 highlights the use of the correct measuring scale to reach this end. In the phrase *dhālika khayrun wa-aḥsanu taʾwīlan*, exegetes have identified *taʾwīl* as referring to the consequence of the action, literally the best, or most beautiful, state to which it returns. Thus, a person who follows this practice of scrupulousness will gain a good reputation and an increase in trade within their worldly life, as well as safety in the Hereafter.[8]

Linguistically, these exhortations to fair trade are of the *inshā'* form, performative utterances to influence reality. The pattern is continued in similar verses within the narratives of the Prophet Shuʿayb.[9] He is mentioned a number of times in the Qur'an and is characterised as calling for social justice along with the unadulterated worship of God.[10] The three passages with greatest significance for the present theme are Q. 7:85–6, 26:181–3, and 11:84–8.

Q. 7:85-6 is within Sūrat al-Aʿrāf, a sura that has already been analysed in the context of the theme of social and religious corruption.[11] In Q. 7:85, the particle *fā'* is used in the phrase 'So give full measure and weight (*fa-awfū al-kayla wa-l-mīzāna*)'. This connects his commands for social rectification to the *bayyina* (clear sign) that he has produced as a prophet, using it as the proof for his authority to reform their practice.[12] A. H. Johns argues that this verse echoes Q. 7:8–9, 'On that Day the weighing of deeds will be true and just', thereby linking human trade to God's precise measuring of deeds in the Hereafter.[13] The call for just trading is closely paralleled by the discourse in Q. 26:181–3, while in Q. 7:86, Shuʿayb extends his demand for social justice, prohibiting his people from sitting 'in every pathway, threatening and barring those who believe in God from His way, trying to make it crooked'.[14]

Q. 11:84–8 relates an enlightening polemical discussion between Shuʿayb and his people. In Q. 11:84, after commanding his people to worship God, declaring His unicity, and calling for them to trade scrupulously, he says, 'I see you are prospering, but I fear you will have torment on an overwhelming Day (*innī arākum bi-khayrin wa-innī akhāfu ʿalaykum ʿadhāba yawmin muḥīṭ*).'

In terms of *naẓm*, Shuʿayb's statement, 'I see you are prospering (*innī arākum bi-khayrin*)', which is something obvious, uses the particle *inna* for additional emphasis. The manifest situation has been left due to a connection to the preceding prohibition: the fact that the people of Madyan are wealthy makes their cheating even more indefensible.[15] The next emphatic device, used in the phrase 'I fear (*wa-innī akhāfu*)' returns to the usual requirement of the situation according to their denial of eschatological punishment. In other words, in this passage Shuʿayb castigates his people for dishonesty in the marketplace when they are already prospering, as it will lead them to a destructive end. While previous verses highlighted the corrupting effect of immoral trading on society, here the wisdom of avoiding these practices is given from the perspective of its ultimate result in the life to come.[16]

The response of Shuʿayb's community in Q. 11:87 underscores the theme of distributive justice, 'They said, "O Shuʿayb, does your prayer command that we leave worshipping what our fathers worshipped, or doing what we like with our wealth? Indeed you are forbearing and rightly guided (*innaka anta al-ḥalīmu al-rashīd*)." They are not only incredulous that Shuʿayb's personal devotion should have an impact on their own belief and worship, but that it is possible for it to have bearing on their disposal of wealth.

Here, the people of Madyan make three points in argumentative response to Shuʿayb. First, they insist on adhering to the same worship practised by their ancestors regardless of his warning; then they contend that it is only fair for the sphere of worship to be separated from transactions and property; and, finally, they twist words that ordinarily denote praise to mean their opposite through an implicit mocking tone. By this, they turn, 'Indeed you are forbearing and rightly guided' into a sardonic statement, castigating him for what they perceive as a lack of tolerance (*ḥilm*) and right guidance (*rushd*).[17]

Shuʿayb responds in the following verse (Q. 11:88) and answers each of their objections. To the first point regarding worship, as in Q. 7:85, he replies that he is acting on clear evidence (*bayyina*) from his Lord. Answering their argument that they should have free disposal of their wealth, he stresses that he does not set one standard for them and another for himself. Rather, he points out that, like them, he is provided with provision (*rizq*), but acknowledges it is a trust from God, either helping the rectification, or furthering the corruption, of the created order. Finally, he responds to their scorn by stating that he does not see himself as guided except with the facilitation of God.

This passage continues until Q. 11:95 with further polemics on either side. It ends with those who did not believe in him struck with a blast such that it was 'as if they had never lived there (*ka-an lam yaghnaw fīhā*)', of which the root verb *ghaniya* also has a connotation of being wealthy or free of need. This may allude to a fitting contrast between their state in life and in death.[18]

The Medinan verses on the topic of fair trade usually flesh out the general principles proclaimed in Mecca with specific details. An arguable exception to this is the cluster of verses beginning Sūrat al-Muṭaffifīn, which is variously said to have been revealed in Mecca; on the way to Medina from Mecca; or to be the first sura revealed in Medina, possibly even within the initial hour.[19] These verses read, 'Woe to those who give short measure, who demand of other people full measure for themselves, but give less than they should when it is they who weigh or measure for others!' (Q. 83:1–3) There seems to be a significant connection between the proposed time of revelation for this sura and the Prophet's early activity in Medina, which included setting up a marketplace as a rival to others already present within the city.[20] As with the narrative of the Prophet Shuʿayb, the justice that the Qur'an invokes within the discourse of fair trade is a general ethical quality held by Muslim and non-Muslim alike.

Q. 2:188 prohibits both the wrongful consumption of wealth and the bribing of arbiters (*ḥukkām*), an obvious injustice and a means for further exploitation.[21] The phrase 'Do not consume your wealth (*lā taʾkulū amwālakum*)', which comes from the root *ʾa-k-l*, connects this verse with two major economic prohibitions within the Qur'an: *ribā* and usurping the inheritance of orphans.[22]

This root is found also in the Medinan verse Q. 4:29, which contains a fundamental principle for trade. It states, 'You who believe, do not wrongfully consume each other's wealth but rather trade by mutual consent (*yā-ayyuhā alladhīna āmanū lā ta'kulū amwālakum baynakum bi-l-bāṭili illā an takūna tijāratan ʿan tarāḍin minkum*).' Q. 4:29 is placed within the *niẓām* of Sūrat al-Nisāʾ after specific legislation for protecting the property of orphans (Q. 4:2–10) and inheritance (Q. 4:11–12). The analysis of verses Q. 4:2–10 in Chapter 11 will demonstrate that they are *khāṣṣ*, as they are inseparable from specific events within the early Medinan community.[23] Moreover, they drive the composition towards the *ʿāmm* principle embodied in Q. 4:29.[24]

The use of the vocative form *yā-ayyuhā* (O you!) indicates that what follows is to be paid special attention.[25] Every *bāṭil* (false, or wrongful) manner in which to gain wealth is prohibited by the first part of the verse. Al-Rāzī mentions two alternative definitions of *bāṭil* in this context: everything that is not permissible according to the revealed law and everything that is taken from people without them receiving something in exchange.[26]

The former view reflects a voluntaristic perspective towards ethics and, as would be expected from a scholar with a background in Ashʿarī theology, al-Rāzī favours it in his *tafsīr*.[27] However, his criticism of the second view, that trying to set an economic rationale for the *bāṭil* would lead to the prohibition of charity and gifts, as nothing is outwardly received in exchange, is not very convincing.[28] Such things are not part of trade to start with.

The phrase *illā an takūna tijāratan ʿan tarāḍin minkum* cannot be coherently read as using the common *istithnāʾ* (exceptive) form to make unlawful consumption of wealth legitimate if it is mutually agreed. Instead, the exception should be taken as nullified (*al-istithnāʾ munqatiʿ*), which is when 'the [subject of] exception is not included in the original set (*li-ʿadami dukhūli al-mustathnāʾ fī al-mustathnāʾ minhu*)'.[29] This makes the meaning of *illā* 'but rather trade' and what follows it the form of a command to the effect that lawful trade must be made with agreement between the parties.[30] This not only gives a very large role for considerations of custom in reaching mutual agreement under the Law, but conversely implies that unjust transactions are those that do not take account of contracts arrived at through the use of natural reason.

The Qur'anic prescription of contracts to regulate economic activity reaches its most detailed form within the longest verse in the Qur'an, Q. 2:282, or the so-called *āyat al-dayn* (the verse of debt), with Q. 2:283 as its adjunct. These two verses near the end of Sūrat al-Baqara follow important passages about first charity (Q. 2:261–74) and *ribā* (Q. 2:275–81). In terms of *niẓām*, the textual order is as follows: first the virtue of giving is extolled, before being contrasted with the grave sin of *ribā*, a comparison that is also made explicit within the text, 'God blights *ribā*, but blesses charitable deeds with multiple increase' (Q. 2:276). The specific case of a debt is considered thereafter because it is a neutral aspect of commerce, neither praiseworthy like charity, nor condemnable like *ribā*.

In this book, these three topics will appear in reverse order, because the thematic structure dictates that Q. 2:282–3 is united with the other verses discussing the basic principles of fairness in trade. The second section of this chapter discusses the Qur'anic condemnation of *ribā* as a special case of a prohibited financial practice. The treatment of charity in Chapter 9 reflects the duty of the individual to support the welfare of the community.

Q. 2:282 provides step-by-step instructions for the proper recording of a debt in significant detail: al-Qurṭubī extracts no less than fifty-two *masā'il* (legal points) from it.[31] The verse begins, 'You who believe, when you contract a debt for a stated term put it down in writing (*yā-ayyuhā alladhīna āmanū idhā tadāyantum bi-daynin ilā ajalin musammā fa-ktubūhu*).' In Arabic, a *dayn* (debt) is generally defined as anything that is not present,[32] which explains the statement later in the verse, 'But if the merchandise is there and you hand it over, there is no blame on you if you do not write it down.' Al-Rāzī glosses the opening sentence as *idhā ta'āmaltum bi-mā fīhi dayn* (when you transact such as to involve a debt), because understanding *tadāyantum* literally would mean both parties trading in debt, which is prohibited. There are thus two valid possibilities: a deferred payment, or a forward payment, also known as a *salam* contract.[33] The use of the imperative in *fa-ktubūhu* is understood by the majority of jurists to imply recommendation rather than obligation.[34]

The remainder of the verse concerns the precise details that ensure the contract drawn up between the parties accurately records their commitments, as well as specifying the evidentiary requirements of the witnesses. The fact that various external actors play a role in this process highlights the importance of community support for upholding justice between individuals.

At each stage, a high degree of scruples is required. The scribe is to write impartially and the debtor is to dictate honestly, both described as *bi-l-'adl*, and if a guardian takes his place, then the obligation for just action falls on him. Although it is the debtor's responsibility to repay, he or she is also given the job of dictating the amount to the scribe. As there is an obvious danger of lessening the amount owed in this situation, the need for *taqwā* is invoked. Nonetheless, dictation of the sum falls to the debtor as the weaker party, in whose hands corruption is likely to be less damaging than if this power was also given to the creditor.[35] A further safeguard against disagreement emerging from debts is provided by independent witnessing, which is recommended in the following terms:

> Call in two men as witnesses. If two men are not there, then call one man and two women out of those you approve as witnesses, so that if one of the two women should forget the other can remind her. Let the witnesses not refuse when they are summoned.

This part of the verse has also been extended to justify the requirement of two women instead of one man in witnessing in a great many other areas of Islamic law.[36] This does not, however, seem justified from the text of the Qur'an. Other verses that explicitly mention establishing points of public law upon a number of witnesses, such as two for bequests in Q. 5:106 and four for the punishment for fornication in Q. 4:15 and 24:4, do not specify gender, but rather take the masculine plural form that can be used collectively for both males and females. The language of Q. 2:282 thus marks it out as an exception to the general rule, not a basis to restrict it.

A number of modern scholars have concurred with this analysis on a contextual basis, arguing that the rule is due to the general unfamiliarity of women with commercial transactions at the time of revelation, especially in Medinan society prior to the coming of the Prophet.[37]

After an encouragement for witnesses to take part, the discourse returns to the virtues of keeping a written record of the debt and its duration, which include it being 'more just (*aqsaṭ*) in God's eyes, more reliable in testimony, and more likely to prevent doubts arising between you'. The term *aqsaṭ*, used for the justice of the practice, can be contrasted with the attribution of *ʿadl* to the scribe and the guardian of a debtor with legal incapacity. The difference between the terms here is that *ʿadl* manifests internally as the impartiality called for in situations of this kind. *Qisṭ* refers to the quality of the practice itself and its positive social consequences.[38] Q. 2:282 concludes with the injunction to neither harm scribe nor witness, as putting pressure on the external actors leads to prejudicing the transaction.[39] The next verse, Q. 2:283, gives two simpler alternatives to this formal written process in the more constrained conditions of a journey: taking a security deposit, or trusting one's debtor.[40]

The scriptural materials concerning the moral guidelines for trade that have been analysed above demonstrate that the general praise of scrupulous trade, along with the paradigmatic figure of the Prophet Shuʿayb fighting against its corruption within the Meccan Qur'an, gives way to more specific principles, and even procedures, to ensure the establishment of distributive justice within the Medinan community. I read these principles as extremely flexible, allowing community members to freely initiate contracts of trade within a social order built upon natural law foundations. As the next section shall show, the presence of a similar movement may be proposed for the related theme of the prohibition of *ribā*.

II. Prohibition of *ribā*

The Qur'an's most severe transactional prohibition concerns *ribā*, a word that linguistically connotes increase.[41] Although the scripture provides no exact definition for this term, its textual usage and socio-historical context lead to the conclusion that it is a wider concept than its closest English equivalent, usury. While usury refers only to money loaned on interest, *ribā* refers to an unjust increase in one person's wealth at the expense of another, a practice that apparently took two main forms among the Arabians before and during the lifetime of the Prophet Muḥammad.

The first kind of increase, called *ribā al-nasīʾa*, which is the type mentioned in the Qur'an, was made by an interest-bearing loan of various kinds. The interest could be fixed by agreement for the end of the period, paid monthly with strict terms for non-payment, or added upon failure to make payment in a deferred sale.[42] The second kind, known as *ribā al-faḍl* and discussed in the Hadith literature, consisted of the uneven or delayed exchange of gold, silver, wheat, barley, dates, and salt, six classes of fungible items, those 'precisely or acceptably replacing or replaceable by another item'.[43]

In the Qur'an, *ribā* may be seen as forming a system along with almsgiving and trade in which their values are respectively prohibited, obligated, and permitted.[44] The prohibition of *ribā*, and other forbidden types of transaction, is thus a means to restrain the abuse of natural differentials in wealth within society, such that the rich are not able to make their livelihoods at the expense of the poor. At the same time, the moral, and later legal, obligation of almsgiving sustainably redistributes the standing wealth of the rich to various needy societal groups. Unless corrupted in some manner, trade is permitted and encouraged, as it becomes a means for wealth to enter into the community and subsequently flow within it.

The verses mentioning *ribā* extend from the middle of the Meccan period (Q. 30:39), until the time of the surrender of Banū Thaqīf in 9/630, or afterwards (Q. 2:275–81), and demonstrate the well-known Qur'anic legislative technique of *tadrīj*, or *tadarruj* (graduation). This is characterised by the revelation first making known the fundamental principles underlying a certain rule – giving its audience time to adjust – before commanding or prohibiting in a definite form. It is to be distinguished from the alternative case in which the ruling holds from the outset, but the detailed explanation or specific punishment is delayed, for instance, consuming the wealth of orphans, or *zinā* (fornication).[45]

As with trade more generally, the response to socio-economic injustice within the Meccan Qur'an is tied to the basic Qur'anic message of moral responsibility before God that psychologically readies the community to accept the more comprehensive legislation introduced in Medina.[46] In other words, natural law is to be united with faith before it is perfected by divine law.[47]

The *ḥikma* of the prohibition of *ribā* is explained in Q. 30:39, the earliest verse on the subject and usually associated with the middle of the Meccan period.[48] Q. 30:39 reads:

> Whatever you lend out in usury to gain value through other people's wealth will not increase in the sight of God (*wa-mā ātaytum min riban li-yarbuwa fī amwāli al-nāsi fa-lā yarbū ʿinda allāh*), but whatever you give in charity, in your desire for God's approval, will earn multiple rewards.

The critical phrase is *li-yarbuwa fī amwāli al-nās*, in which the particle *fī* can be read as denoting a parasitical relationship between creditor and debtor with the *lām* before the verb expressing *taʿlīl*.[49] In other words, *ribā* is wealth that grows through that of others and reduces the prosperity of the people rather than adding value to the economic arena. Rosen argues that such gains are made by the creditor without 'adequate reciprocity'.[50]

This interpretation of Q. 30:39 differs from the opinion favoured by al-Qurṭubī and a number of classical exegetes, in which it is taken to refer to a gift given by someone in the hope that more will be received in return.[51] I suggest that there are two reasons why it is more appropriate to understand Q. 30:39 as referring to *ribā* proper. First, the oppositional relationship of *ribā* with charitable giving is present in other Qur'anic verses dealing with this term: Q. 2:275–6, 3:130–4, and 4:161–2, and, second, according to Fazlur Rahman:

> The Meccan verses of the Qur'an are replete with the denunciation of the economic injustice of contemporary Meccan society, the profiteering and stinginess of the rich, and their unethical commercial practices such as cheating in the weight and measurements, etc., how is it possible then that the Qur'an would have failed to condemn an economic evil such as *ribā*?[52]

Furthermore, Q. 30:41, which closely follows Q. 30:39, states, 'Corruption has flourished on land and sea as a result of people's actions and He will make them taste the consequences of some of their own actions so that they may turn back.' As demonstrated in the analysis of narratives concerning the people of Madyan, and the Prophet Shuʿayb, there is a close semantic link in the Qur'an between wrongful economic practice and the spread of corruption within society.[53]

The first Medinan verse to mention *ribā* is Q. 3:130, which is most likely placed after the battle of Badr and before Uḥud in the period 2–3/624–5. This timing accords with the received dating of Sūrat Āl ʿImrān,[54] as well as a hadith concerning a figure called ʿAmr b. Uqaysh who would not at first enter battle at Uḥud as a believer due to his wish to profit from the usurious loans he had lent.[55]

Q. 3:130 reads, 'You who believe, do not consume usurious interest, doubled and redoubled (*lā taʾkulū al-ribā aḍʿāfan muḍāʿafatan*). Be mindful of God so that you may prosper.' Rahman focuses on the language of 'doubled, redoubled', seeing the swift multiplication of debt from a credit-based loan as the *ʿilla* for prohibition – by which he obviously means *ḥikma* – such that it acts as the basis for the general rule.[56] However, my preference is to understand the *ḥikma* of the prohibition to have been explained in Q. 30:39; with an outright ban delayed until revelation of Q. 3:130 when the Muslim community reached the appropriate stage of development. The hadith of ʿAmr b. Uqaysh supports the hypothesis that this verse completely outlawed *ribā*, as do the later verses Q. 4:161 and Q. 2:275–81, which assume this ruling. It is characteristic of the Qur'anic style that it makes its prohibition in the most emphatic language and with the most extreme example, including *a fortiori* everything less than it.[57]

Q. 4:161 deals briefly with the question of *ribā* in the context of explaining God's restriction of the Jewish sacred law based on a number of transgressions, including 'for taking usury when they had been forbidden to do so'. From its placement in Sūrat al-Nisāʾ and discussion within the same passage of dialogue between the Prophet and the Jews, it is likely to have been revealed in 4–5/626–7. For the topic at hand, the main point is that the Qur'an calls upon Muslims to avoid emulating the Jews in failing to live up to the prohibition of usury and even taking it as a livelihood.[58]

The final passage involving *ribā* within the Qur'an is Q. 2:275–81. There are good reasons to believe it is of late Medinan provenance, with Q. 2:281 sometimes said to be the final Qur'anic verse to be revealed.[59] Al-Rāzī records several *asbāb al-nuzūl* narrations for Q. 2:278, 'You who believe, beware of God: give up any outstanding dues from usury, if you are true believers.' The command is likely to either relate to those who entered into Islam after the Conquest of Mecca in 8/630 and still had usurious contracts in place, or to those of Banū Thaqīf from al-Ṭāʾif who likewise wished to continue to collect *ribā* after their conversion in 9/630.[60]

The language of this verse supports the view that a prohibition was already in force at the time of its revelation, and that its role is to encourage proper implementation. Furthermore, the sequence does not begin in Q. 2:275 with mention of the rule, but rather a statement warning of the eschatological consequences of failing to heed it, 'Those who take usury will rise up on the Day of Resurrection like someone tormented by the Devil's touch.'

The sentence following this in Q. 2:275 provides the rationale for the punishment, 'That is because they say, "Sale is like usury," but God has allowed sale and forbidden usury (*dhālika bi-annahum qālū innamā al-bayʿu mithlu al-ribā wa-aḥalla allāhu al-bayʿa wa-ḥarrama al-ribā*).' This statement, put into the mouths of opponents of the Muslim community, could be expected to have been ordered the other way around: 'usury is like sale', thereby legitimising their practice. The order in the verse is thus a rhetorical reversal. The individuals in question are under pressure for their continued consumption of *ribā*. When accused, they go on the offensive against their interlocutors, arguing that one may as well say that sale is like *ribā*, as there is no difference between the profit made from the interest due at the end of a loan and from selling goods at a margin.

Sherman Jackson has analysed the Qur'anic response to this argument as open to two diametrically opposed interpretations. One approach, taken by al-Ṭabarī (d. 310/923), explains that *ribā* is not like trade only by virtue of God having forbidden usury and permitted trade.[61] The other, exemplified by Rashīd Riḍā, argues in the opposite direction, stating that the type of increase between the two is different in kind and their permission and prohibition relate to their underlying benefit and harm.[62] Jackson describes this divergent understanding in terms of 'whether there is an ontic index of moral right and wrong ontologically, and not just noetically, inscribed upon creation'.[63] In other words, this question of interpretation exactly mirrors the theological debate between the voluntaristic and moral realist conceptions of the *sharīʿa* discussed in Chapter 2.[64]

The natural law framework taken within this book supports further exploration of the latter option and an assessment of the underlying *ḥikma* for the distinction in the kind of profit gained within sales and usury. A person who buys for a certain price and sells at a profit has to take possession and financial responsibility for the merchandise, which comprises real objects of sale. In the time between purchase and resale there is the possibility of market conditions changing and thus an element of risk in their transactions. The person who lends *ribā* is not selling a real object, but rather is making profit by selling a debt. The seller of this intangible debt is not subject to the normal risks experienced in trade, but instead is able to make the assets 'gain value through other people's wealth' (Q. 30:39). This underscores the deeper realisation that the prohibition of *ribā* is a measure intended to cut the roots of exploitation within society by setting a limit on the type of profit that human beings may accrue from their voluntary contracts.

Verses Q. 2:278–80 deal with integrating those who were previously involved in usurious transactions into the community, a particular concern in the latter years of the Medinan period.[65] The warning of 'war from God and His Messenger (*ḥarbin min allāhi wa-rasūlihi*)' in Q. 2:279 is unique within the Qur'an and demonstrates the emphasis that the scripture places on eliminating this mode of economic activity and its attendant social problems.

This condemnation of *ribā* is put into even starker relief by its consistent contrast with verses devoted to charity in the Qur'an. Rather than money being multiplied to the detriment of the vulnerable in society, it is to be given to benefit the vulnerable for the sake of God and multiplied by His grace in terms of spiritual rewards. The word *zakāt* is used in three of the four *ribā* verses: taking the basic meaning of alms, or charity, in the Meccan verse Q. 30:39; while in Q. 2:277 and 4:162 it has the more technical meaning of obligatory alms, as shown by its conjunction with the 'establishment of prayer'. The place of this redistribution of wealth within the Qur'anic system of societal justice is the subject of the next chapter.

9

Alms

If the right to wealth is protected through a system of fair procedures for transactions and the prohibition of false and exploitative practices, especially *ribā*, what can be said about redistribution? I propose that, in the Qur'an, individual possession of wealth is predicated upon the same principles of collective stewardship, grounded in natural law, that were discussed in relation to the governance of political communities. One's right to cultivate and to profit from the resources of the world is thus tempered with a duty towards the community to redistribute the goods acquired for the benefit of those in greater need. Although there are a number of modalities in which this concept of alms is found within the Qur'an, it is possible to trace a consistent pattern throughout the entire period of revelation, the ethical imperative meeting the specific social requirements at each time.

The Meccan verses that touch upon this topic develop a Qur'anic critique of the moral failings of society in terms of greed and selfishness, arguably connected to a decay of old Arabian chivalric virtues of generosity due to a settled, and increasingly mercantile, life.[1] The early revelations of the Qur'an provide a sharp commentary on these qualities, often presented in a terse, powerful style. Thus, in Q. 89:18–20, 'You do not urge one another to feed the needy (*miskīn*), you consume inheritance greedily, and you love wealth with a passion.'[2] Miserliness is also strongly connected with worldliness and rejection, or ignorance, of a Hereafter in which such actions will be held to account. Thus, Q. 102:1– 2, 'Striving for more distracts you until you go into your graves', and Q. 104:1–3, 'Woe to every fault-finding backbiter who amasses riches, counting them over, thinking they will make him live forever.' Even within the worldly life, the dire consequences of wealth without social conscience is emphasised, as in Q. 17:16:

> When We decide to destroy a town, We command those corrupted by wealth [to reform], but they [persist in their] disobedience (lit. We command those who were its affluent ones, so they led a dissolute life within it; *amarnā mutrafīhā fa-fasaqū fīhā*). Our sentence is passed, and We destroy them utterly.[3]

The Qur'an enjoins the giving of alms known as *zakāt* (the word *ṣadaqa* is also used) as a moral duty that combats both negative internal qualities and outward societal harm. *Zakāt* comes from the root *z-k-y*, which connotes purification and growth for the giver, as well as benefit for the recipients. The spending of a small proportion of one's wealth is understood as cleansing for the rest, which thereby increases in blessing. Meanwhile, the inner heart is also purified and made to expand as greed and miserliness are challenged.[4]

These meanings are alluded to within Q. 9:103, '[Prophet] take from their wealth alms (*ṣadaqan*) to cleanse and purify them (*tuṭahhiruhum wa-tuzakkīhim*), and pray for them – your prayer will be a comfort to them. God is all hearing, all knowing.' As the word *ṣadaqa* is indefinite, it is possible that it refers specifically to an amount taken from the wealth of certain sinful people about whom the verse was revealed, as mentioned in Q. 9:102, rather than the obligatory *zakāt*, with exegetes divided on the issue.[5]

In the Meccan Qur'an, there are six main categories of people who are mentioned as appropriate recipients of alms: relatives, the needy (*masākīn*), beggars, travellers, orphans, and captives.[6] The word *zakāt* is used occasionally in a legally undefined, but not thereby voluntary, way. For instance, in Q. 41:6–7, 'Woe to the idolaters, who do not pay the prescribed alms (*zakāt*) and refuse to believe in the world to come!', and, in Q. 30:39, 'But whatever you give in charity (*zakāt*), in your desire for God's approval, will earn multiple rewards.' The word *ḥaqq*, used frequently in these verses, demonstrates that it is considered a right of the needy to receive aid from those able to spare it, although how much and how often to give is left to each person's discretion.[7]

The Qur'an warns against profligacy and admonishes to avoid excess in giving and withholding, as in Q. 17:29 and 25:67. Furthermore, Q. 17:28 makes clear that if a person does decide to hold back, he or she is expected to at least say something in order to console those in need. A pre-existing social practice of giving a harvest tithe to the poor is seemingly confirmed by Q. 6:141, 'Give its due the day of harvest (*wa-ātū haqqahu yawma ḥaṣādihi*)' and the story of the Owners of the Garden (*aṣḥāb al-janna*) in 68:17– 33.[8]

Within the Medinan phase of revelation, the fact that almsgiving was previously made incumbent upon the Children of Israel is mentioned in Q. 2:83 and 5:12.[9] Such discourses form part of the Qur'anic argument, implicit in verses such as Q. 2:43 and 4:162, that the Jews of Medina should believe in the Prophet who has come to them with a confirmation of this divinely sanctioned practice.

The Medinan verses also gradually develop the basic principle of wealth redistribution into a legal institution with a number of key features. There are two main lines of development that can be observed in the Qur'an. The first is a widening and refining of the categories of recipients in response to the new social needs within Medina until they reach the final form recorded in Q. 9:60. The second development concerns the growth of institutional structures in the Medinan Qur'an from the discretionary moral roots laid down within the Meccan revelations. *Zakāt* emerges as a pillar of Islam alongside the ritual prayer laying claim to a mandated set proportion of an individual's wealth, which is ultimately collected by community officials. The Qur'an establishes this in outline only. Hence, a large number of classical scholars view the word *zakāt* in the Qur'an as *mujmal* (ambiguous), requiring explanation from the Sunna of the Prophet.[10]

Both of these strands in the development of the fully developed pillar of *zakāt*, and the closely related topic of war booty, can be explored through three Medinan stages. I treat these as broad phases that are not necessarily reflected within other themes. The first is the early Medinan, in which the amount of the obligation is not formally set, but the categories of recipients are slightly expanded from those in Mecca. The second is the middle Medinan, in which this obligation is set, but is not centrally collected, and the recipients have been further enlarged, particularly by 'those in God's path', a reference to the equipping of expeditions. The last is the late Medinan, in which *zakāt* is collected by its own officials, and is divided within the final eight classes of beneficiaries. These can be analysed as four pairs, each one fulfilling a particular need: subsistence, compensation, emancipation, and supply.

The early Medinan stage of *zakāt* includes the verses Q. 2:215 and 2:271–7 referring to the period before the Battle of Badr in 2/624, Q. 8:41 dealing with the spoils of war after Badr in 2–3/624–5, and Q. 59:7–8 discussing booty after the siege of Banū al-Naḍīr in 4/625. This stage includes all of the categories mentioned within Mecca and adds two more: those in bondage (*fī al-riqāb*) and the poor (*al-fuqarāʾ*). The first of these, which is found in Q. 2:177, represents a more general category than the (war) captive (*asīr*) mentioned in Q. 76:8, as it also includes slaves.[11] The category of *al-fuqarāʾ* is of particular interest, because there is a need to clarify its differentiation from that of the *masākīn*, especially in its emergence as a distinct category in Q. 9:60.

Linguistically, *faqīr* (pl. *fuqarāʾ*) can take a number of meanings in classical Arabic. One of the most common definitions is a person who is not absolutely destitute, but lives at the level of bare subsistence. It is quoted in a verse by al-Rāʿī, 'As to the *faqīr* whose milch camel has sufficient for his household and nothing (more) left to him.'[12] It can also refer to someone who has been incapacitated, such that they cannot carry out their usual trade.[13] While the class of the *miskīn*, the needy, is mentioned extensively throughout the Meccan period and into the Medinan, the earliest Qur'anic usage of the term *fuqarāʾ* as a category deserving alms is within Q. 2:271–7. The verse Q. 2:273 states:

> [Give] to the poor (*fuqarāʾ*) who have been restricted in God's way and cannot travel in the land (*uḥṣirū fī sabīli allāhi lā yastaṭīʿūna ḍarban fī al-arḍ*). The unknowing might think them rich because of their self-restraint, but you will recognise them by their characteristic of not begging importunely. God is well aware of any good you give.

This verse describes the *fuqarāʾ* to whom alms should be given and can be split into two halves. In the first half, the situation of these people is discussed with a linguistic construction that allows for a number of interpretations. It is possible that as a result of their sacrifice for the sake of God, they have been prevented from travelling in the land to trade, which was their customary source of income.[14] Alternatively, the meaning could be that their poverty restricts them from travelling in expeditions, or jihad, for the sake of God.[15] The two ideas are not mutually exclusive and the verse can also be read as saying that preoccupation with fighting has left them unable to partake in their normal trade.[16]

It is clear that Q. 2:273 discusses a particular group of *fuqarāʾ* in Medina, likely the new arrivals from Mecca.[17] This is confirmed by Q. 59:8, which immediately follows the verse describing the booty gained by the Muslims from the siege of Banū al-Naḍīr in 4/625 (see below), 'The poor emigrants (*al-fuqarāʾi al-muhājirīn*) who were driven from their homes and possessions, who seek God's favour and approval, those who help God and His Messenger – these are the ones who are true – [shall have a share].'[18]

Interestingly, although this verse clarifies the identity of the *fuqarāʾ*, it does not settle the interpretation of Q. 2:273. Both the first explanation, that it refers to them giving up their wealth and trade for the sake of religious freedom, and the second one, that it means that they need help to set out on campaigns, remain plausible. In either case, the *fuqarāʾ* are to be treated as a special individual category to which a share of community wealth, whether from the spoils of war, or personal wealth, is due.

In the second half of the verse, a further way to recognise the *fuqarāʾ* is given. Their quality of restraint, which to an ignorant person appears a mark of self-sufficiency, is actually the very sign that despite the smallness of their means, they do not abandon their dignity. In a hadith, the Prophet is reported to have said, 'The poor person is not the one for whom a date or two or a morsel or two is sufficient, but the poor person is he who is too shy to beg. Recite if you wish, "They do not beg of people importunely"' (Q. 2:273).[19]

The other main groups in Q. 59:7 who are eligible for the spoils of war have been mentioned previously, and are the same categories introduced in Mecca: kin, orphans, the needy, and travellers. The exception is that the phrase 'for God and for the Messenger' is never applied to categories of *zakāt* – only booty.

A subtlety of the Qur'anic diction here is that the particle *lām* is used before the name of God (in the sense that the gains are really for His sake) and repeated for the Messenger and for kinsfolk, which can thus be understood as the Prophet's kin.[20] Thereafter, *wāw* alone is used to conjoin for the other groups, a fact that leads some Shi'a exegetes to understand that the orphans, poor, and travellers meant are those from the Prophet's household specifically.[21] The rationale of the division of booty in this way can be connected to the responsibilities that the Prophet had taken on by 4/625 in terms of community leadership, which required a share of the total gains. These included sustaining those with no other support network and provisioning the army in defence of his people.[22]

The phrase following the main statement of categories in Q. 59:7, 'this is so that they do not just circulate among those of you who are rich (*kay lā yakūna duwalatan bayna al-aghniyāʾi minkum*)', provides the *ḥikma* not just for this particular rule, but for a key aspect of the social mechanism of *zakāt* as a whole. As wealth does not really belong to the person who stakes a temporary claim to it, so it must not be kept permanently away from the others in society who may have more need for it.[23] Furthermore, as is exemplified in the case of the Prophet Shuʿayb, a society that becomes unbalanced in the relationship between members, such that it sees extremes of wealth and poverty, becomes socially corrupt.[24] The Qur'an greatly encourages giving as much as one is able, with the amount of *zakāt* the minimum that must be redistributed.

Although uncertainty in dating means that a middle Medinan stage cannot be precisely defined, it is coherent to posit a phase of development in the institution of *zakāt* after the setting of its obligation and amount, yet prior to its collection according to the final categories mentioned in Q. 9:60. Islamic tradition records a range of views about when the fixed obligation of *zakāt* began. One view is that this happened in the second year after the hijra just before the obligation of fasting, which would fit with its general placement after prayer and before fasting in the list of the pillars of Islam.[25] Another view is that this happened after the command for fasting sometime between 2/623 and 5/627, based on various traditions, which are also used to discount a narration about the defined obligation coming in the ninth year.[26]

As well as an obligation sitting firmly beside the ritual prayer in importance, the middle Medinan verses place increasing emphasis on a new recipient of giving, the person 'in God's way (*fī sabīli allāh*)', which is a term used primarily for someone engaged in the proselytising, reconnaissance, raiding, and sometimes outright war known as the *maghāzī*. An example is Q. 4:95, 'Those believers who stay at home, apart from those with an incapacity, are not equal to those who commit themselves and their possessions to striving in God's way.'[27]

The later Medinan stage confirms the obligation of *zakāt* and provides for it to be collected by representatives of the community's leadership. The key verses are Q. 9:58–60 and are usually thought to date to 9/630, the same year that officials were sent out to collect the appropriate shares of public wealth, particularly herds and agricultural produce.[28]

These verses begin with the mention of criticism received by the Prophet about his division of alms. Exegetes link this to an incident in which the figure known as Dhū al-Khuwayṣara says to him, 'Be just!' To which he replies, 'Woe upon you! Who is just if I am not just?'[29] This becomes the context for the affirmation of the various categories of recipient in Q. 9:60:

> Alms are only for the poor, the indigent, those who administer them, those whose hearts are to be won over, those in bondage, the indebted, for God's cause and travellers. An obligation from God, He is omniscient, wise (*innamā al-ṣadaqātu li-l-fuqarāʾi wa-l-masākīni wa-l-ʿāmilīna ʿalayhā wa-l-muʾallafati qulūbuhum wa-fī al-riqābi wa-l-ghārimīna wa-fī sabīli allāhi wa-bni al-sabīli farīḍatan min allāhi wa-llāhu ʿalīmun ḥakīmun*).

This verse does not include close relatives or orphans within its eight categories, but adds three new recipients: those who administer [the alms], those whose hearts need winning over, and those in debt. The result, as suggested by Mustansir Mir, is a system of four pairs each with a slightly different function.[30]

The first two, the poor and the needy, deal with the subsistence required to live. Given the legal implications, there is unsurprisingly considerable disagreement among exegetes concerning the difference between the terms *fuqarā'* and *masākīn* used in this verse.[31] As has been discussed, Qur'anic usage points to the *masākīn* as those who are in need of alms in order to continue to live, whether they are very poor, or entirely destitute. The *fuqarā'* are characterised by being unable to carry out their normal trade for some reason and restrained in revealing their poverty. While previous verses such as Q. 2:273 and Q. 59:8 illustrate this category with reference to the Muhājirūn, Q. 9:60 arguably makes their essential qualities a general group of need, no matter who possesses them.

If the *fuqarā'* comprise a category suffering from less dire poverty than the *masākīn*, it is natural to seek to explain their precedence on the list. One possibility is that raising a person entirely out of the state of poverty has a greater social benefit than giving handouts to the more deprived. Such people may only need a little bit of help to establish themselves within normal economic activity, which would include paying their own *zakāt* and contributing to helping others out of poverty.[32]

The next group, consisting of *zakāt* administrators, and those whose hearts are to be won over, is based around the reception of some kind of compensation or consideration. The people appointed to the job of *zakāt* collection are not expected to do so without any payment for their time and effort, and are sometimes considered one of the few groups that are allowed to receive from the collected funds without necessarily being in a state of need themselves.[33] There is also a longstanding difference of opinion over whether their wage is set by the ruler, or is according to their work.[34] Al-Jaṣṣāṣ uses this category to argue against giving *zakāt* on a private basis, proposing that each person who pays outside the existing system of collection cannot pay a contribution towards the wages of the collectors, which harms the poor in the long term.[35]

'Those whose hearts are to be won over' are described by exegetes as originally consisting of various groups: senior non-Muslim tribal elders, who are paid to prevent their harm to Muslims and even to assist them against other hostile tribes, those encouraged by gifts to enter into Islam and stay within the faith, and new Muslims supported to prevent them returning to disbelief.[36] However, 'Umar b. al-Khaṭṭāb is held to have considered this, unlike the other categories of *zakāt*, a temporary concession for the time when the number of Muslims was very small and was followed in this by early Ḥanafī jurists.[37]

The third pair is centred on the meaning of emancipation, as it concerns those in a form of bondage, whether through slavery, or heavy debts. The question of debt is fairly straightforward, although it may be remarked that some jurists were keen to establish the principle that distributed *zakāt* must be taken into possession by an individual, so it cannot be used for paying off the debts of the recently deceased, nor to purchase the burial shroud.[38]

A similar line of reasoning is connected to the difference of opinion among jurists as to whether '*fī al-riqāb* (to free slaves)' refers generally to paying for their emancipation, or specifically to helping *mukātab*s, indentured slaves who enter into a contract with their masters to pay for their freedom (usually in instalments). The stated opinion of the Ḥanafīs and Shāfiʿīs is to refer the verse to the *mukātab*, as opposed to the view of the Mālikīs, although there are a number of different opinions narrated from Mālik (d. 179/795) himself.[39] One of the arguments used by Ḥanafīs is that if the *zakāt* is used to buy the freedom of a slave, this would entail that it is directly received by the owner who is not a valid recipient.[40]

More broadly, the Qur'an acknowledges the existence of slavery within the society that it immediately addresses, using the institution for didactic purposes in Q. 16:71 and 30:28. However, its main discourse about slaves deals either with regulating their marriage (Q. 4:3, 4:25, and 24:32) or encouraging their emancipation (Q. 90:13 and 2:177), binding it into the expiations for certain oaths (Q. 5:89 and 58:3), or as part of the obligatory alms (Q. 9:60 and possibly 24:33).

The so-called *mukātab* verse, Q. 24:33, has a known obscurity in its language, such that al-Māturīdī admits that it would seem to be about teaching the Qur'an, except that it has been universally understood in the formative period as about indenture.[41] More recently, Patricia Crone has argued that discussion of the emancipation of slaves is incongruous in a passage concerned with chastity.[42] She supports this with the contention that in the part of Q. 24:33 that mentions 'those of your bondspeople who desire *al-kitāb*, write it for them (*fa-kātibūhum*) if you see good in them', the word *al-kitāb* must refer to the marriage contract. Based on this, she argues that this part of the verse is a loose paraphrase of Q. 24:32 and the first part of Q. 24:33, which enjoin marrying off single members of the community, including male and female slaves, and encouraging them to abstinence if they cannot wed. She considers it a secondary consideration that this would imply that the concluding phrase of Q. 24:32, 'God is Bountiful and Omniscient', should be positioned after the first part of Q. 24:33.[43]

Interestingly, Crone's assumption that it is obvious that the Qur'an is simply paraphrasing itself in these two verses is not shared by early Muslims who understood *kātibūhum* as relating to indenture, nor by al-Māturīdī's *uṣūlī* notion that the word *kitāb* is to be read as the Qur'an in the absence of other evidence.

It seems that Crone's argument is effectively based on considerations of *niẓām*. Although she makes a plausible case, one way that she can be challenged on structural grounds is with reference to Cuyper's ideas of Semitic composition. Within his 'law of the shift of the centre', it is in the central term of a concentric structure that a new 'antithetical element' is introduced, before the system concludes.[44] I suggest that it would be possible to recast Q. 24:32–3 as a concentric structure focused on the idea of chastity with the contested sentence as the central term. Understood in this way, it would not at all be implausible for *kātibūhum* to refer to the identure contract, especially as it would lead to a non-redundant meaning for the remainder of Q. 24:33:

> Those of your bondspeople who desire a contract of indenture, write [it] with them if you know they are trustworthy and give them from God's wealth, which He has given you. Do not [thereby] force your young bondswomen into prostitution when they desire chastity, so as to seek the goods of worldly life (*wa-lladhīna yabtaghūna al-kitāba mimmā malakat aymānukum fa-kātiabūhum in ʿalimtum fīhim khayran wa-ātūhum min māli allāhi alladhī ātākum wa-lā tukrihū fatayātikum ʿalā al-bighāʾi in aradna taḥaṣṣunan li-tabtaghū ʿaraḍa al-ḥayāti al-dunyā*). Whoever compels them, truly God remains after their compulsion forgiving and merciful.

If the word *khayran* is to be the condition for writing a contract of indenture, there is a need to understand its precise meaning. Early jurists gave a wide variety of interpretations to the word, including truthfulness, wealth, a trade, trustworthiness, and an ability to fulfil the contract.[45] Considering the next part of the sentence about financially helping them, the possession of wealth does not seem a decisive criterion, while specifying possession of a particular trade is too restrictive. The intended meaning would seem to be the internal qualities of trustworthiness (including truthfulness) and the ability to fulfil the contract.[46]

A second question is the meaning of the imperative in *fa-kātibūhum*. Mālik, with reference to Q. 5:2 and 62:1, views it as encouragement, not obligation.[47] Al-Māturīdī argues that it could not have been obligatory, otherwise generations of Muslims would not have left slaves without giving them this contract.[48] This argument is hardly decisive, as it ignores the conditional construction of the injunction. Al-Ṭabarī says that it is indeed obligatory as there is no countervailing argument and in this he is following various early figures, including Ibn ʿAbbās, ʿAṭāʾ, and ʿUmar.[49] Thus an obligation to emancipate via the *mukātab* contract, only restricted by the suitability of the bondspeople for entering into its responsibilities, would seem to best serve the Qur'an's emphasis on manumission.

The phrase '*wa-ātūhum min māli allāhi alladhī ātākum* (and give them from God's wealth, which He has given you)' constitutes the main piece of evidence linking this verse with Q. 9:60 and the broader discourse of *zakāt*.[50] In particular, it can be understood as stating that the collective wealth of the community must support the *mukātab* in seeking freedom.

Given the above interpretations, it is possible to see the relationship between the category of *zakāt* known as *fī al-riqāb* and the indenture contract as two parts of a single emancipatory system. Rather than a universal proclamation of emancipation, it seems that the Qur'an, in the context of a time of widespread slavery, uses a more graduated approach. By ordering those who own bondspeople to identify those suitable for a contract of indenture, it ensures that they are only freed when ready to live without the protections that servitude also offered. The contract itself provides financial compensation for the owner and a period of transition for both parties, including the opportunity for the *mukātab* to earn in the same manner as free people. The setting of a category of *zakāt* for this purpose means that everyone in the community has a share in the emancipation of the enslaved and thus a responsibility in helping them as *mawālī* (freed slaves).[51] The provision of funds also lowers the threshold for a bondsperson to be eligible for the contract, as he or she would not necessarily need to be capable of earning the entire amount.

The above points are important when considering the next part of the verse, 'Do not [thereby] force your young bondswomen into prostitution when they desire chastity, so as to seek the goods of worldly life.' This is usually treated by exegetes as an entirely separate injunction based on a *sabab al-nuzūl* report that ʿAbd Allāh b. Ubayy had slaves that he compelled to work as prostitutes.[52] My reading is that it is a warning against greed for the earnings of the indenture contract, or stinginess in paying towards it from *zakāt*, which could both lead to a premature contract for bondswomen, thereby effectively forcing them into prostitution to pay for their freedom. Mālik records a narration from ʿUthmān b. ʿAffān that supports this understanding, 'Do not give the burden of earning to your bondswoman without a trade, as she will earn by prostitution.'[53]

The final pair in Q. 9:60 concern the idea of supply, such as equipping a person for work done in the path of God, particularly battle, or helping a traveller return home. There is some discussion in the classical literature about whether a rich person could be given *zakāt* in order to fight in jihad. The Ḥanafīs generally hold this to be impermissible, although al-Jaṣṣāṣ states that it is allowable if someone does not possess the equipment for war, such as a mount and weapons, which are surplus to his needs at home, or if he finds himself in a state of need after he has set out to fight.[54] It should be noted that the assumption is that the Muslim community is without a standing army.[55]

Ibn al-ʿArabī (d. 543/1148) responds to any restriction of this category by arguing that it amounts to making an addition upon the text of the Qur'an, which, according to the Ḥanafīs' own principles, should only be possible on the basis of the Qur'an itself, or a *mutawātir* (mass transmitted) hadith.[56] It seems, however, that the usual Ḥanafī position is founded in a more basic interpretive presumption that the *ʿilla* of each of the categories, except that of the administrators and those whose hearts are to be reconciled, includes the state of neediness.[57] For this reason, al-Shaybānī is also quoted as allowing alms to be given to the person too poor to undertake the hajj.[58]

Some exegetes, such as al-Rāzī, consider the possibility of a more expansive meaning to the phrase *fī sabīli allāh*, which, according to its manifest (*ẓāhir*) meaning, does not directly refer to a person, and arguably could be applied to anything of general and broad benefit for the community.[59]

Travellers (*ibn al-sabīl*), the last category of the eight mentioned in Q. 9:60, are also widely considered to be eligible for support even if not poor, as long as their wealth is inaccessible to them, the consideration being towards effective need at a point in time.[60] It is also narrated that some early jurists considered *ibn al-sabīl* to be the category that should be utilised to help the pilgrim restricted from performing the hajj.[61]

The comprehensive range of societal benefits supported by these different categories and the emphasis of their obligatory nature points towards the development of a structural system of redistribution by the end of the Medinan period. This system is intended to realise the overarching principle that private wealth is a trust held by God's stewards that must flow back for the benefit of society as a whole. The individual *ḥikma*s that have been uncovered represent the purposes, in terms of distributive justice, that the particular system of rules must fulfil.

10

Marriage

Through the Qur'anic lens, family is the basic unit linking individual human actors with the wider society. As such, in both its immediate and extended forms, family is only made possible by the binding force of marriage. This institution places responsibilities on a couple who should strive to provide a stable family unit for nurturing children. It also gives an outlet for the human needs of love, companionship, and sexuality. At the same time God uses it as a test: husbands and wives can go through strife and even divorce, which must be managed justly. Another way that marriage can end is through the death of one of the partners, leaving widows and widowers. I will analyse these potential life cycles of the marriage in the present chapter. After that, in Chapter 11, I will discuss the important Qur'anic theme of inheritance, the means by which family wealth is justly redistributed to the extended family, as well as the special case of orphans.

Many of these elements may be found by reading between the lines of the first verse of Sūrat al-Nisāʾ:

> People, be mindful of your Lord, who created you from a single soul, and from it created its mate, and from the pair of them spread countless men and women far and wide; be mindful of God, in whose name you make requests of one another, and of severing the ties of kinship: God is always watching over you (Q. 4:1).

The address here is *yā-ayyuhā al-nās* (O people!) not *yā-ayyuhā alladhīna āmanū* (O believers!), as might be expected from the legislative Medinan verses that follow. This is contextually appropriate due to the subject matter concerning the origins of humanity. The verse repeatedly stresses the importance of *taqwā*, first in conjunction with a statement of God's creation and the spread of humanity using the word *rabb*. *Taqwā* is mentioned again in connection to the mutual requests made in the name of God; such networks of reciprocal claims are at the heart of the concept of human society.[1]

The last reference to *taqwā* in Q. 4:1 is implicit in the *wāw* before *al-arḥām* (lit. the wombs; ties of kinship), which is used for *ʿaṭf* (conjunction) with the imperative verb *ittaqū* (be mindful!).[2] Thus, the address moves from a call for pious awareness of God at the level of the societal macrocosm to the same at the microcosm of one's familial relationships, the blueprint for social organisation.[3] The verses that follow in the sura's *niẓām* are tied to these initial commands and concern the topics of marital relationships, orphans, and inheritance.

I. Contract and responsibilities

The principal term used for marriage within the Qur'an is the word *nikāḥ*, which also has the linguistic signification of sexual intercourse, or a contract.[4] The Qur'anic approach to this institution emphasises its importance as a divinely ordained blessing, yet is pragmatic in allowing its dissolution. Thus, despite the important spiritual dimensions to marriage within the Qur'an, its basic status is a contract conducted between two individuals, as opposed to a sacrament as developed within the Christian tradition.[5]

The purpose of marriage is encapsulated in the Meccan verse Q. 30:21, 'And from His signs is that He created spouses from among yourselves (*min anfusikum*) for you to live with in tranquillity: He ordained love and kindness (*mawaddatan wa-raḥmatan*) between you. There truly are signs in this for those who reflect.'[6]

The language here recalls the idea in Q. 4:1 that God places human souls in harmonious pairs. Al-Zamakhsharī quotes on the authority of al-Ḥasan al-Baṣrī the interpretation of *mawadda* as sexual union and *raḥma* as children, which brings to the fore the implicit Qur'anic view of parenthood as the real reason for marriage.[7] This emerges also in Q. 2:187, highlighting the physical nature of the relationship between husband and wife, 'You are permitted to lie with your wives during the night of the fast: they are garments to you, as you are to them.' The institution of marriage is thus presented as a source of protection and caring company for both husbands and wives, which provides the environment in which children can be nurtured.

The importance of marriage for chastity within society is underscored by Q. 24:32–3, which follows legislation directed at the purification of the public sphere. These verses start with the command, 'Marry off the single among you.' In the first part of Q. 24:33, the *ḥikma* for this is made clear, 'Let those who are unable to find marriage stay chaste until God enriches them from His bounty.' The Qur'anic focus on chastity is strongly tied to the idea of known paternity: children should be aware of their parentage and receive due inheritance and other rights.[8]

Q. 64:14–15 presents another purpose for marriage, that one's family is a *fitna*, a word meaning trial, derived from the practice of placing gold in fire to test its purity.[9] This links back to God's creation of the worldly life as a test for the soul.[10]

One of the consistent features of the Qur'an's discourse on marriage is use of the term *maʿrūf*, meaning what is customarily recognised. This is significant not only for its consideration of human custom, but for Qur'anic approval of it as reflective of justice. In terms of the wider proposals made in the present book, this is intimately connected to the arguments for a natural law framework to Qur'anic ethics that I have articulated.[11] In other words, to do what is *maʿrūf* is to do what is commonly agreed to lead to justice and to facilitate the practice of life as an expression of indebtedness to God. Despite this tendency to validate customary practice, the marriage contract in the Qur'an differs from its pre-Islamic form, often in order to limit the abuse of male power over female wives and daughters that was rife at the time of revelation.

As mentioned in Chapter 4, pre-Islamic Arabia had a number of types of marriage, although it seems that the one accepted within the Qur'an, the so-called *zawāj al-buʿūla* (a marriage consisting of an offer and acceptance, with dower paid by the husband), was dominant in the Ḥijāz within both settled and nomadic communities.[12]

It is generally reported that pre-Islamic Arabians of the Ḥijāz were able to marry an unlimited number of wives.[13] The Qur'anic revelation led to a restriction, as told through the story of Ghaylān b. Salama al-Thaqafī from Ṭāʾif who had ten wives and was ordered by the Prophet Muḥammad to choose four to retain after converting.[14] This limited form of polygyny is also accepted within Q. 4:3, 'If you fear that you will not deal fairly with the orphans, you may marry those that seem good to you from amongst the women, two, three, or four.' This verse is closely connected with treatment of orphans at a specific point in the history of the early community and will receive further treatment in the next chapter.[15]

Moreover, those who interpret the verse as an indication towards an idealised social system, remove the apodosis 'you may marry' from the presence of orphans and widows at the time, as well as its relationship to the protasis 'if you fear that you will not deal fairly with the orphans'. Nowhere in the Qur'an is there a call for Muslims to marry multiple wives, except when attached to this condition.[16] Thus, the Qur'an does not establish it as a general rule.

Another important condition for polygynous marriage is equity (*ʿadl*), which is mentioned in Q. 4:3 as the reason for a man to marry a single freewoman, or bondswomen. This point is reiterated in Q. 4:129, 'You will never be able to treat each of your wives with absolute equity, however much you desire to do so. Do not be so impartial that you leave one like something hanging (*ka-l-muʿallaqa*).' This last expression is usually interpreted as neither providing the treatment that a wife deserves, nor divorcing her.[17] The argument made by some contemporary scholars that this latter verse amounts to active discouragement of polygynous marriage is not, however, very convincing.[18] Rather, the verse gives the practical advice that although complete equity between multiple wives may not be possible, the husband should not be obviously biased towards any one of his spouses. The Qur'anic concern with known paternity for children would seem to be one of the reasons for the absence of provision for polyandrous marriages, although these were known among Arabian communities before Islam.[19]

The Qur'an acknowledges the concubinage of bondswomen, a common social practice at the time of revelation, as mentioned in Q. 23:6 and 70:30, '[those who guard their chastity,] except with their wives or their bondswomen (*illā ʿalā azwājihim aw mā malakat aymānuhum*)'. It also permits free men to marry bondswomen if they fear they will not remain chaste. As they would also have the option of concubinage, or manumitting their own slaves and marrying them once free,[20] it would seem that this was an option given to poorer members of the community for whom marriage to a bondswoman owned by another was cheaper than marriage to a freewoman, or purchase of a concubine. This is confirmed by the wording of Q. 4:25,[21] which provides guidance for such marriages with women – possibly captives of war – who should be married with the permission of their masters (*ahlihinna*) once they have made themselves chaste, including completing their *ʿidda* (waiting period of three menstrual cycles).[22] The consistent Qur'anic *ḥikma* of protection of paternity, as shown below in this chapter, means that a bondswoman married in this way would no longer be sexually available to her master.

Q. 4:19 unambigously prohibits a man inheriting a wife from a family member, 'O you who believe, it is not permissible that you inherit women against their will.' This refers to an apparently common practice in pre-Islamic Arabia, in which it was customary for a brother, or other male relative, to step into the marriage of his deceased sibling.[23] Even a son could inherit the wife of his father, although the marriage was known as *maqt* (detestable), a word used in its explicit condemnation in Q. 4:22.[24] In Yathrib, this would be announced by the inheritor throwing his garment over the woman; if no relative chose her, she could be prevented from remarrying for the rest of her life.[25]

Although pre-Islamic Arabians were familiar with dower paid by the husband at the time of marriage, it seems that the guardian of the bride would usually take possession of it, either for expenses in taking the couple into his house, or for himself.[26] Al-Māturīdī makes the interesting argument that this comes from previous dispensations of the divine law and is abrogated in Islam. He adduces the story of the Prophet Moses and the conditions of his betrothal to a daughter of the old man, usually said to be the Prophet Shuʿayb, who features in the narrative of Sūrat al-Qaṣaṣ:[27]

> [The father said], 'I would like to marry you to one of these daughters of mine, on condition that you work for me for eight years. It is your choice if you wish to complete ten. I do not want to make any hardship for you: God willing you will find me an upstanding person' (Q. 28:27).

In Q. 4:4, the Qur'an uses language that stipulates ownership of the dower belongs to the wife alone, 'Give women their dower as an obligation (*wa-ātū al-nisāʾa ṣaduqātihinna niḥlatan*).'[28] It also cannot be taken back following divorce in normal circumstances, as shown in Q. 4:20, 'Even if you have given them much gold, do not take anything back from it' and Q. 2:229, 'It is not permissible for you to take back anything that you have given them, unless you both fear that you cannot uphold God's limits.' This seems closely connected to the idea that the dower is to act as insurance against the financial insecurity that would result from a divorce suddenly enacted by the husband. It also seems to be a kind of compensation, or counterbalance, to granting him the unilateral power of divorce. When a wife wishes to divorce her husband, she is to give up part of her dower.[29]

Thus, the Qur'an's reform of pre-Islamic marriage contracts keeps the basic elements of the *zawāj al-bu'ūla*, but secures the status of the wife as a fully consensual participant in the contract. Within the interpretive frame of this book, one may say that such a shared role is essential for the marital relationship as a pair of God's stewards, weaving the social fabric according to the values set within creation. This is the cornerstone of the collaborative social justice between genders alluded to in Q. 9:71, 'Believing men and women are supporters of each other. They enjoin common standards of justice (*bi-l-ma'rūf*) and forbid that which is not recognised as such (*al-munkar*).'

The strictly Qur'anic view of marriage, then, seems opposed to the notion that the agreement of the bride's guardian (*walī*) is a necessary component of the contract. This is reflected by the Ḥanafī school of law, which relies on Q. 2:232, 'When you divorce women and they have reached their set time, do not prevent them from remarrying their husbands if there is mutual agreement between them according to what is customarily recognised (*an yankiḥna azwājahunna idhā tarāḍaw baynahum bi-l-ma'rūf*).' The Ḥanafīs argue that the use of the word *yankiḥna* in the active tense means that a marriage contracted by a woman acting alone is valid. If her guardian forcifully prevents her from going ahead, that is an act of oppression.[30]

A final aspect of marital legislation that the Qur'an necessarily innovates is the question of marriage between Muslims and people adhering to different religions. Unsurprisingly, marriage between Muslims and pagans is prohibited in Q. 2:221. This rule is also found in Q. 60:10–11, where it includes some details pertaining to the repayment of dower to the former pagan husbands of women who join the community of believers. Permission is granted for male Muslims to marry chaste Scriptuaries in Q. 5:5. The rationale behind this allowance, and not its converse, would seem to be connected to the upbringing of children and the assumption that they would be raised according to the religion of their father.

The question of the marital roles of husband and wife in the Qur'an is famously tied to interpretation of the first part of Q. 4:34. It begins, 'Men support women with that which God has given to some of them ahead of others and with what they have spent from their wealth (*al-rijālu qawwāmūna 'alā al-nisā'i bi-mā faḍḍala allāhu ba'ḍahum 'alā ba'ḍin wa-bi-mā anfaqū min amwālihim*).'[31] That this refers to husbands within marriage is signalled by the rest of the verse that obviously deals with inter-marital relations. Linguistically, it can be read as reflective of the typical situation at the time of revelation, in which men were usually in the social position to earn more than their wives.[32] The traditional reports about the successful trading career of the Prophet's wife Khadīja serve as an exception to this rule.[33]

However, the Qur'an does not come to document Arabian social practice, but to reform it. Therefore, rather than using the binary of descriptive versus prescriptive forms, it can be read as normative in the sense that men are to act as supporters to women when God gives them more capacity to earn. Here one can again utilise the principle that stipulation does not indicate specification,[34] leaving the possibility of cases in which the wife earns more and supports her husband. This links to Q. 4:32, two verses prior, which states in the context of trade and wealth creation:

> Do not wish for what God has given to some of you ahead of others (*wa-lā tatamannaw mā faḍḍala allāhu bihi baʿdakum ʿalā baʿḍ*). For men is the portion they have earned and for women the portion they have earned: so ask God for his bounty, He is knowledgeable about everything.

Thus, although there may be a biological aspect to the question of marital roles insofar as childbirth and maternal nurturing may reduce the ability to earn, this reflects a general tendency – more a rubric than a strict rule.[35] The next part of Q. 4:34, 'what they have spent from their wealth (*bi-mā anfaqū min amwālihim*)', can be understood as a single fixed payment that complements the dynamic process of earning. Many early figures interpret it as the dower,[36] which is also referred to in Q. 60:10–11 with the same word, *anfaqū*, and is strongly emphasised in the sura.

Q. 4:34 continues, 'Righteous wives are devout, guarding the private matters that God has entrusted them to preserve (*fa-l-ṣāliḥātu qānitātun ḥāfiẓātun li-l-ghaybi bi-mā ḥafiẓa allāhu*).' The phrase *bi-mā ḥafiẓa allāhu* can be interpreted in various ways, especially with respect to whether *allāh* is read with *naṣb* (accusatively) or *rafʿ* (nominatively). I have followed the more common latter possibility, which takes the sense of *istaḥfaẓa* (to entrust).[37] As shall be seen in Chapter 13, the Qur'anic concern with private boundaries is centred on the idea of wealth, chastity, and reputation.[38] It would seem that the situation envisaged is one in which the husband has gone out to work and his wife is expected to guard these private matters. This concords with a prophetic commentary recorded on this verse to the effect that the 'private matters' are the wife's own self and her husband's wealth.[39] It does not exempt men from the same level of devotion and vigilance, although it may imply that, to the extent that women do stay at home, these qualities may be tested more in this setting.

The Qur'an's approach to parenting in its wider sense takes in a great number of the stories of past prophets, as well as exemplary figures, such as Luqmān the Wise (Q. 31:12–19). Many of these figures are portrayed as fathers, mothers, or children and reflection upon them can lead to insights about *tarbiya* (cultivating, or nurturing children; a word used in verbal form in Q. 17:24). Much of the relevant material is from the earlier, Meccan phase of the revelation, which is focused on instilling faith and morality. During this period, there is a condemnation of the Arabian practice of burying unwanted daughters. Criticism of this as a social injustice is also used to attack the belief – popular in Mecca and its environs – that God has daughters, such as in Q. 16:57–8.[40]

In the Qur'anic picture of parental roles and responsibilities within marriage, the main issues surround the earliest stage of a child's life and the provision for nursing.[41] An acknowledgement of the difficulty of the early years of life upon mothers is found in the Meccan verse Q. 46:15, 'We obliged man to treat his parents with excellence: his mother carried him and gave birth to him with great difficulty – his bearing and weaning took thirty months.'

Q. 2:233 sets the maximum period of nursing at two years, a number that provoked an obvious exegetical challenge for Muslim scholarship, as twenty-four months plus the normal nine-month term equals thirty-three – three more than Q. 46:15 sets for pregnancy and weaning. Al-Qurṭubī presents two possible solutions. The first is that if a mother has a nine-month term, she should stop nursing after twenty-one months, only completing the two years if giving birth at six months. The second is that Q. 46:15 only refers to the last six months of the pregnancy, because the child is not large enough to be a heavy burden in the first trimester.[42]

Q. 2:233 states that the mother's 'provision and her clothing are the responsibility of the child's father, according to what is customary (*wa-ʿalā al-mawlūdi lahu rizquhunna wa-kiswatuhunna bi-l-maʿrūf*)'. Here, the construction implies that while maintenance is mandatory, its amount is customarily set. The distinction between this obligation and the marital support in Q. 4:34 is that the responsibility falls upon the man in his role as father rather than husband, as indicated by the expression *al-mawlūdi lahu* that singles out his personal relationship to the child. This has certain consequences in the provision given to divorced or widowed pregnant women, as will follow.[43] Q. 2:233 goes on to mention that if the father dies, his heir must continue to bear this responsibility.[44]

The same verse makes clear that neither mother, nor father, should suffer hardship on account of bringing up the child and that they 'shall not be blamed if, following consultation and mutual agreement, they decide to wean their child'. Likewise, a wet nurse may be employed, as long as there is mutual agreement between the father and the child's mother and payment is agreed at a customarily recognised rate.[45]

The Qur'an's strong emphasis on the link between parents and children does not negate the possibility of adoption, although it is careful to distinguish between it and ties of blood. Q. 33:5 states that adopted sons (*adʿiyāʾ*; lit. those invited) are to be named after their (biological) fathers – a practice that is called more just (*aqsaṭ*) in the sight of God. However, if perhaps this information is not known, then they are 'your brothers in the faith and protégés (*ikhwānukum fī al-dīni wa-mawālīkum*)'. The next verse, Q. 33:6, goes on to further strengthen family ties, here possibly at the expense of the brothership (*muʾākhā*) that the Prophet had struck between the Muhājirūn and Anṣār upon first entering Medina.[46] Perhaps the most plausible interpretation of the verse, which as part of Sūrat al-Aḥzāb is usually dated to 5/627, is that while one would have previously inherited from the other, as possibly alluded to in Q. 4:33, the development of the community led to the abrogation of this and the return to usual family relationships.[47]

Q. 33:37 continues this theme through the personal ordinance given to the Prophet Muḥammad concerning his marriage to Zaynab bint Jaḥsh, the divorced wife of his freed slave and adopted son Zayd b. Ḥaritha.[48] The verse suggests that this marriage was divinely ordained to teach the point that the prohibition of fathers marrying their sons' ex-wives, and vice versa, does not apply in the case of adopted sons.[49]

II. Marital strife

Marriage, an institution that brings the lives of two human beings into intimate association, is a microcosm of society at large. Filled with its own triumphs, celebrations, disasters, and wars, there is a need for just procedures to regulate the strife that, if not inevitable, is often to some extent unavoidable. The Qur'an's focus on piety and good conduct is itself a wellspring of counsel for dissatisfied spouses. However, the scripture provides specific injunctions for those who go beyond the usual travails of married life and become characterised by what it terms *nushūz* (enmity).[50]

The term appears twice in the Qur'an, in Q. 4:34 and 4:128, applied to a recalcitrant wife and husband, respectively. The latter verse is couched in general language and can be rendered as, 'If a wife fears enmity or alienation from her husband, neither of them will be blamed if they come to a peaceful settlement, for peace is best' (Q. 4:128). The exegetical literature usually reads this as referring to a problem generated by polygyny, in which a wife experiencing enmity and neglect from her husband on account of his recent additional marriage, may suggest giving up part of her dower, support, or share of his time, in order to avoid a looming divorce.[51] In this regard it is related by exegetes to Q. 2:229, which regulates *khulʿa* (compensatory divorce).[52]

One of the traditional approaches to analysing a verse such as Q. 4:128 is to connect it to a particular *sabab al-nuzūl* and effectively specify its range of meanings according to that situation. This is commonplace despite the theoretical position that the specific *sabab* should not specify the general expression.[53] The method applied in this book attempts to frame the verse within a socio-historical context that, where possible, is broader than individual anecdotes, as well as using the concept of scriptural *niẓām*.

As will be discussed in the next chapter, Q. 4:128 may be read as one part of a passage between Q. 4:127 and 4:130 connected with Q. 4:3, dealing with the widowing and orphaning in Medina caused by the Battle of Uḥud in 3/625.[54] Such an observation predicates an understanding of the verse's *ḥikma* upon the subtle interplay of text and context.

The meaning of Q. 4:128 for the life of the early community, therefore, relates to the challenge that the remarriage of widows due to Uḥud posed to the existing marriages in Medina. The Qur'anic discourse is concerned, first, with keeping marriages intact and harmonious. The arrival of a new wife doubtless brings stresses to an existing marriage that can only be resolved through compromise. The very generality of the language of *ṣulḥ* (peaceful settlement) used within the verse leaves the details to be worked out according to the particular needs of the situation. This means that there are a wide range of potential solutions, from the husband's withdrawal of some degree of spousal support, to the first wife's request for extra money or time – a possibility envisaged by early exegetes.[55]

Equally, the verse is relevant to the problems that may emerge within a single marriage. If a husband persistently behaves badly towards his wife, or ignores her, it is prudent to try to see if any aspect of their shared life can be adjusted to ensure their mutual happiness. Usually this requires some compromise from both members of the couple. As Q. 4:128 continues, 'Souls bring with them stinginess; if you do good and are mindful of God, without doubt He is well-acquainted with all that you do.'

A further point is that the Qur'an couches dissatisfaction in the marriage from the wife's side in the language of conciliation. This both suits the context, as well as the basic pattern of the marriage envisaged in the Qur'an, in which a direct divorce is at the behest of the husband alone. In other words, a wife cannot 'threaten' her husband with immediate divorce if his behaviour is bad, although she can request a compensatory divorce – a possible interpretation of the *ṣulḥ* mentioned in the verse – or go to a community authority (its qadi according to the Islamic juristic tradition), as will be seen in Q. 4:35 presently.

Q. 4:129 continues the passage's discussion of polygynous marriage, remarking that, while absolute equity may not be humanly attainable, an unsatisfactory situation should not be allowed to continue without resolution, with the wife left suspended between marriage and divorce.[56] Instead, God promises to enrich them if they do separate (Q. 4:130). Thus, just as fear of poverty should not prevent marriage (Q. 24:32), neither should it stop divorce when the couple's relationship cannot be remedied.

The other Qur'anic reference to *nushūz* is in Q. 4:34.[57] The second half of this verse with the suggestive phrase *wa-ḍribūhunna*, which has usually been understood as 'strike them', has engendered significant controversy, particularly in recent years. The apparent clash between the verse and 'modern values' has led to the assessment of Jonathan Brown that it is 'the ultimate crisis of scripture in the modern world'.[58]

After the first part of Q. 4:34, which deals with the responsibilities of wives, the verse continues:

> Those (wives) from which you fear enmity, admonish them (*fa-ʿiẓūhunna*), swear off from them in the marital beds (*wa-hjurūhunna fī al-maḍājiʿ*) and strike them (*wa-ḍribūhunna*). However, if they are agreeable towards you, do not seek a means against them – God is exalted, great.

The *naẓm* of this verse is to set up a conditional situation and three types of recourse for recalcitrant spouses. Admonition, indicated by *fa-ʿiẓūhunna*, can be understood in the sense of a spiritual warning, or counsel, emphasising God's punishment in the Hereafter.[59] The next two imperative verbs are preceded by *wāw*, which allows some jurists, such as al-Shāfiʿī, to read them as stages in a temporal sequence.[60] But Ḥanafīs, many later Shāfiʿīs, and other schools reject *tartīb* (order) for *wāw*, understanding it as indicating a simple conjunction.[61]

Another option for husbands is to abandon such wives in bed (*wa-hjurūhunna fī al-maḍājiʿ*), which is usually interpreted as either withholding conjugal relations, or refraining from speaking to them there.[62] This first idea can be developed by reading it as an oath to abstain from sexual relations for a period of time. The Qur'an mentions in Q. 2:226–7 that if such an abstention extends to four months, it constitutes a divorce of the type called an *īlā'* within later juristic literature. This would provide a very serious warning about the direction that the marriage was heading.

This seems to concord with an incident in the life of the Prophet Muḥammad in which he vowed to stay away from his wives for one month due to an act of collusion between them, leading to the revelation of the verses Q. 66:1–5.[63] The point is expressed at the end of a long hadith in which the Prophet returns after twenty-nine nights and his wife ʿĀ'isha says, 'O Messenger of God, you swore that you would not enter in upon us for a month.'[64] This leads to the revelation of the verse giving the choice (of divorce),[65] which is extended to all of his wives.[66]

The third possibility mentioned in Q. 4:34 for husbands facing enmity from their wives is to strike them, the *ẓāhir* meaning of *iḍribūhunna.* Like the English verb 'strike', the verb *ḍaraba* has an extremely wide semantic range depending on its linguistic context. Its use with a direct object can convey physical striking, from tapping to heavy beating, as seen in Q. 7:160, '[Moses] tap the stone with your staff (*iḍrib bi-ʿaṣāka al-ḥajar*)' and Q. 8:12, 'Strike above the necks and beat every fingertip (*fa-ḍribū fawqa al-aʿnāqi wa-ḍribū minhum kulla banān*).'[67] Al-Iṣfahānī gives as a general abstract definition, 'the falling (*īqāʿ*) of one thing onto another'.[68]

Looking at the context of the verse, physical violence as a means of marital control already existed within Arabian society and appears to have gone against the inclination of the Prophet. It seems that he first prohibited husbands from striking their wives outright, but then rescinded the ban after it caused social uproar.[69] The usual *sabab al-nuzūl* mentioned for Q. 4:34 is the personal complaint of an Anṣārī woman whose husband had hit her. The Prophet is said to have ordered *qiṣāṣ* (talion), an equal injury to be given to him in kind, precipitating the revelation of Q. 4:34 and the withdrawal of her right to retribution.[70] This leads to a curious tension between Q. 4:34 and the attitude of the Prophet, which is encapsulated in the words, 'I wanted one thing and God wanted another.'[71]

The modifying phrase *ghayra mubarriḥ* (without injury), which is applied to the permission to strike, appears in two different hadith clusters in the canonical collections, both of which place it within the Prophet's *khuṭbat al-wadāʿ*. The first is the long hadith of Jābir b. ʿAbd Allāh recorded by Muslim, Abū Dāwūd, and Ibn Mājah,[72] while the second is the shorter hadith reported by ʿAmr b. al-Aḥwaṣ recorded by al-Tirmidhī and Ibn Mājah.[73] It seems that with the possibility of striking affirmed by revelation, the Prophet tried to make sure that it was understood by his community in a way that did not cause harm. Some commentators use these traditions to limit the striking to a non-injurious and possibly symbolic gesture, by suggesting use of the toothstick (*siwāk*), or folded handkerchief (*mandīl*), although others have allowed more latitude.[74]

Continuing with the verse's *naẓm*, the verbal root *ṭ-w-ʿ* in the sentence beginning, 'if they are agreeable towards you (*fa-in aṭaʿnakum*)' is commonly understood as to obey, or to obey despite anger.[75] However, *ṭāʿa* is also the antithesis of *kurh* (aversion), so the meaning could refer to the state of a wife without enmity.[76] Therefore, it may be read as warning husbands not to engage in any of these methods if their wives are agreeable.

The next verse, Q. 4:35, switches the address towards the community with the construction, 'If you fear division between them appoint an arbiter from his family and her family (*wa-in khiftum shiqāqa baynihimā fa-bʿathū ḥakaman min ahlihi wa-ḥakaman min ahlihā*).' The indication of domestic unrest could directly refer to the action taken in the previous verse, for instance the husband spending an extended period away from his wife, or there could be other signs. The point seems to be that the community, and particularly the family on both sides, should be aware of problems within the marriage and be on hand to help resolve conflict before it becomes fatal to the relationship. Thus, the verse suggests arbitration from both sides as a final chance to avoid divorce.

With the overall *ḥikma* of this Qur'anic passage understood, like Q. 4:129, as the attempt to rectify one's marriage in the face of a difficult spouse, it is possible to return to the tension noticed above in the contextual application of the verse in the life of the Prophet. Understanding that each rule is distinct from, and dependent upon, realisation of its *ḥikma*, makes it possible that the Prophet's desire for a marital ethics without recourse to physical disciplining was an aspiration that could not be met in his socio-historical setting.

This can be related to an issue with wider implications than Q. 4:34 alone, highlighted by Kecia Ali in her book *Sexual Ethics and Islam*. She questions the Qur'an's use of androcentric language in sexual relationships, addressing husbands and assuming their control, while wives are seemingly left passive and 'othered'.[77] While Ali seems willing to excuse androcentric language as addressing those with greater power in the historically normative structures of marriage, divorce, and polygamy, she finds this 'less convincing with regard to intimate sexual relations between husband and wife'.[78]

Aysha Hidayatullah goes further in theorising about the apparent dissonance that contemporary feminists observe between those Qur'anic verses stressing male–female mutuality and those reinforcing hierarchy. She states that such scholars should acknowledge the possibility that any assumed conflict may be a product of their own historically conditioned viewpoint.[79] In other words, she argues that in seeking to understand the meaning of the Qur'an, one should not assume that it upholds modern standards of equality and justice, which may have been alien to its first audience.

Notwithstanding the caveats that I have already made about the nature of any reading or interpretation of the Qur'an,[80] I do not think that historically relativising its basic moral principles does justice to the ethical claims of the scripture, or natural law. Rather, it is possible to acknowledge a system of wise purposes that retain universal validity even as the rules by which they are instantiated may need to shift according to time and place. Seen in this way, the problem of androcentrism in the Qur'anic address on sexuality is not of a different magnitude from that pertaining to structures of marriage and divorce. If we are willing to accept that the social context of revelation mandates justice to be established through reform of the *zawāj al-buʿūla*, addressing those with greater power in it, why can we not assume that this also holds true for the unspoken codes of sexual intimacy?

In any case, it is a brute fact of the Qur'anic discourse that, while many of its injunctions are gender neutral in meaning – if not in grammar – when it does make a gender-specific address, it is virtually always directed to the male believers, whether or not the subject is related to marriage or sexuality. The main exception is in the personages of the Prophet's wives, who in Q. 33:30–4 are addressed directly and even told, 'You are not like any other women' (Q. 33:32). Earlier in the same sura, al-Aḥzāb, comes the famous sentence, 'The Prophet is closer to the believers than their own selves and his wives are their mothers' (Q. 33:6). Again, in Q. 66:4–5, which are from the verses critical of the Prophet's wives in Sūrat al-Taḥrīm, two and then all of them, are directly addressed. An additional consideration in this pattern of address, therefore, may be to emphasise direct communication between God and the Prophet's wives, who were to become key figures in the history of the early community.

III. Divorce and widowing

Sometimes a marriage cannot be saved and the result is divorce, which in the Qur'an can take a number of forms. As with the initial marriage contract, the starting point for understanding the Qur'anic discourse on divorce is through the practices of the pre-Islamic Arabians, particularly those of the Ḥijāz. The overall shape of these customary procedures was retained by the Qur'an, but reformed in line with its moral vision.

In the culture that preceded Islam, it was common for men to make oaths that, while not counting as a formal divorce, acted in a similar way by indefinitely denying a wife her marital rights. Two well-known varieties of such oath were the *īlāʾ* and *ẓihār*, both of which were used by a husband to forswear from sexual relations with his spouse, although the latter did so through a considerable insult.

The *īlāʾ* was formerly used by husbands to leave their wives for months or even years.[81] The Qur'an, in Q. 2:226–7, limits this to a maximum of four months, after which divorce is enacted, although the husband may stop this occurring by breaking his oath and paying an expiation of the type mentioned in Q. 5:89, which is to feed ten indigents, or clothe them, or free a slave. If these are not found, one may fast for three days.

In pre-Islamic Arabia, *ẓihār* was an imprecation along the lines of, 'you are to me like my mother's rear (*ẓahr*)', which would also allow a husband to deprive his wife of her rights without allowing her to remarry.[82] The Qur'an, in Q. 58:2–4, castigates the practice and stipulates that before a husband making such a statement can have sexual relations with his insulted wife, he must make an expiation. This is weightier than the penalty for breaking a regular oath, requiring him to free a slave. If he is unable to do this, he must fast for two continuous months, or, failing this, feed sixty indigents. As it functions like an *īlā'*, if it remains in place for four months, it too arguably results in divorce.[83] Thus, the Qur'an simultaneously solves the problem of wives under *īlā'* and *ẓihār* being indefinitely suspended, while allowing a regulated place for oaths of abstention, which I argued remain important as an option in times of marital strife.

It seems that, within the Ḥijāz, formal divorce was usually in the hands of husbands. However, in some cases the family of the wife could intimidate, or beat, the husband into instigating it, while, in certain Bedouin communities, wives could perform divorce without words by turning their tent in the opposite direction.[84] It is also reported that divorce was not considered final, but rather men could pronounce a divorce and then revoke it an unlimited number of times – leading to obvious abuse.[85]

In articulating the Qur'anic moral structure pertaining to divorce and relating it to the wider theme of distributive justice, recourse can be made to three main suras. The most detailed material is to be found in Sūrat al-Baqara, in the passage Q. 2:224–37, with relevant material also in Sūrat al-Nisā'. Finally, Sūrat al-Ṭalāq (Divorce), also sometimes called Sūrat al-Nisā' al-Quṣrā (the Shorter Sura of Women),[86] contains supplementary regulations.

In the remainder of this chapter I will discuss the following topics: the principles of divorce before setting of dower and consummation of the marriage, four degrees of divorce discussed by the Qur'an, maintenance to be provided to the divorced woman, and regulations for widows.

Q. 2:236 permits divorce before dower and consummation, emphasising that the husband should give provision according to need in a customary manner. If a divorce is made after the dower is given, but before consummation between the spouses, Q. 2:237 specifies that half is kept by the wife, unless she waives her share, or this is done by 'the one holding the marriage tie (*bi-yadihi uqdatu al-nikāḥ*)'. Early exegetes interpreted this as meaning either that the husband can equally waive his share of the dower, or that the woman's guardian can waive it on her behalf.[87] The first position seems stronger based on the unequivocal Qur'anic stance that wives own their dower; moreover, a choice for both parties is consistent with the other divorce scenarios to be discussed.

Q. 33:49 declares generally in the situation of divorce before consummation that there is no *'idda* for the wife. The *ḥikma* of this is evidently that its primary purpose of protecting paternity is not applicable. This verse also states that the husband must 'provide for them (*fa-matti'ūhunna*)'. It would seem that if the dower has not been set, the wife should be given provision in proportion to the relative wealth of the husband, as described in Q. 2:236.[88] If it has been set, then she will receive her half, as in Q. 2:237, with any additional provision merely optional. For this reason, some early authorities held Q. 33:49 to be abrogated – although one may argue that this means specified – by Q. 2:237.[89]

The ethical structure of divorce in the Qur'an following the payment of dower and consummation can be subdivided into four categories based on the attitudes of the parties and the arrangements made, particularly with respect to ownership of the dower.

The first category is prohibited outright and thus sinful in divorce. It includes husbands, as mentioned in Q. 2:231, who 'hold onto their [wives] harmfully (*tumsikūhunna ḍirāran*)', not finalising the divorce despite their unhappiness. This is similar to the situation described in Q. 4:129.[90] It is also interdicted in Q. 2:229 and Q. 4:20 for divorcing husbands to unilaterally take back any of the dower. This is given a rhetorical intensity by the phrase in Q. 4:21, 'How when you have lain together and they have taken a heavy covenant (*mīthāqan ghalīẓan*) from you?'[91] For wives, it is prohibited at the time of divorce to conceal their pregnancy (Q. 2:228), which is part of the Qur'an's wider concern with establishing paternity.

Second, there is a category of divorce that the Qur'an considers to be permissible in certain circumstances, in which the wife allows some of the dower to be returned to the husband. This is usually called a *khulʿa* and may reflect a situation in which the wife is keener to dissolve the marriage than her spouse. Q. 2:229 mentions that this is for a husband and wife who cannot keep to God's limits, presumably referring to a husband unwilling to divorce without financial inducement, despite the marriage having become dysfunctional and both falling into sinful behaviour. However, some exegetes have understood Q. 2:229 to be addressed to arbitrators (as in Q. 4:35) who will take some of the dower and give it to the husband when it is the only way to secure the divorce.[92] Q. 2:229 uses the expression *lā junāḥa ʿalayhimā* (there is no blame upon them), which makes clear that, under the circumstances, the compromise is not sinful, although it may be undesirable. Q. 4:19 aims to ensure that a husband cannot abuse the *khulʿa* by intentionally treating his wife badly, hoping to get back part of her dower. However, the husband may legitimately claim a remittance if it is his wife who is guilty of acting in a flagrantly lewd manner (*bi-fāḥishatin mubayyina*).

The third category of divorce mentioned in the Qur'an is according to what is *maʿrūf* and corresponds with the *ṭalāq* (divorce) found in juristic literature. When pronounced by the husband, the wife's three-month *ʿidda* begins, although reconciliation is recommended (Q. 2:228). This verse also states that the rights of wives are equal to their obligations, according to what is customary, although men have a particular degree (*daraja*) over them. The context would perhaps suggest that this refers to the legal power to initiate divorce unilaterally, which is balanced by the institution of dower.

Q. 65:1–2 provides more details about how divorce should be performed. The *ʿidda* is to be observed correctly, none of the dower should be returned to the husband, and it should be witnessed by two just people. Referring to the option for the husband to revoke this type of divorce, the language used in Q. 65:2 is 'so keep them according to what is customary or split from them likewise (*fa-amsikūhunna bi-maʿrūfin aw fāriqūhunna bi-maʿrūf*)'. A similar phrase is found in Q. 2:231 with *sarriḥūhunna* (release them) replacing *fāriqūhunna*. Overall, in this key passage within Sūrat al-Baqara, the word *maʿrūf* is used no less than eleven times, emphasising the flexibility in arrangements beyond the minimum guidelines set by the scripture. This Qur'anic usage exemplifies the argument that a natural law normative ethics is not vitiated by the existence of a divine law, but complements it.

The final category of divorce is the same as that just discussed, but has the additional quality of being performed with *iḥsān*, going beyond a customary notion of justice to aim for the highest moral standard. This term is used in Q. 2:229, which limits the number of revocations to a maximum of two, before a final decision must be made. The verse reads, 'Divorce is twice, so a retention according to what is customary, or a release with excellence (*al-ṭalāqu marratān fa-imsākun bi-maʿrūfin aw tasrīḥun bi-iḥsān*).'It would seem that the word *iḥsān* is used instead of *maʿrūf* in this verse due to considerations of *naẓm*. As mentioned under the second category, Q. 2:229 goes on to discuss the case of a couple unable to keep to God's limits and the allowance for the husbands to retain some of the dower. Implicitly, then, a level of conduct that goes beyond what is expected, for instance by additional generosity and kindness, is contrasted with the lower one. Another possibility is that *iḥsān* here is an allusion to the requirement of *nafaqa* (provision) following the third divorce (see below).

That divorce is made irrevocable on its third pronouncement is lightened in Q. 2:30 by allowing remarriage of the couple following the wife's marriage to a different husband. Q. 2:32, as has preceded, enjoins family members to refrain from stopping wives remarrying their previous husbands if there is mutual agreement.[93]

Sūrat al-Ṭalāq foregrounds the importance of the *ʿidda* in the Qur'anic rules for divorce by beginning with a direct address to the Prophet and the male believers. In Q. 65:1, 'O Prophet, when you all divorce women, divorce them so their waiting period can start and count the waiting period carefully. Be aware of God your Lord. Do not expel them from their homes unless they have committed a manifest indecency (*fāḥishatin mubayyina*).'

This last injunction is due to the strong connection of the *ʿidda* and its associated maintenance with the protection and support of any unborn children from the marriage – the unconsummated marriage does not receive an *ʿidda* at all. This can be contrasted with the dower that is meant for the divorced wife herself. At the same time, Q. 65:1 is consistent with Q. 4:19 in lowering the requirements to be met by husbands when their wives have been guilty of lewd behaviour. In the case of unfaithfulness, the paternity of the child is in question and so too is the divorced wife's right to remain in the husband's accommodation.

Q. 2:241 states that divorced women are to be given *matāʿ* (maintenance) according to what is *maʿrūf* and that this is a duty for people of *taqwā*. Although this is open to interpretation, it would seem to be an emphatic way to enshrine a general duty for believers, rather than a specific one for the best among them, just as no one seriously questions the generality of *hudā li-l-muttaqīn* (guidance for the pious) in Q. 2:2.[94]

More detail is provided in Q. 65:6, which states:

> House them where you house yourselves according to your means and do not act adversely to them so as to restrict them. If they are pregnant, provide for them until their child is born. If they nurse for you, pay them for it and consult between yourselves in a good way. If you make things difficult for each other, someone else can be employed to nurse for the father.

Although this verse is clear about the obligation of *suknā* (housing), commentators debate over whether the irrevocably divorced wife receives *nafaqa*, a matter not in question for one revocably divorced. The main positions are as follows: the Ḥanafīs and al-Thawrī hold that *nafaqa* should be given whether or not the wife is pregnant; Mālik that it is only given when she is pregnant (and if it is affordable for the husband, in one narration); and al-Shāfiʿī, al-Layth, and al-Awzāʿī that it is not given even if she is pregnant.[95] This means that the latter figures argue that the verse's enjoinment of *nafaqa* for the pregnant divorcee specifically refers to the scenario in which the divorce can still be revoked.

In agreement with the first of these three interpretations, there does not seem to be a compelling reason to restrict the verse to revocable divorce alone, or to reject implicit provision for the wife so housed.[96] Likewise, the instruction to provide for pregnant wives until the child is born in Q. 65:6 can easily be read as an extension of the *nafaqa*. This is because the raison d'être of the *ʿidda* is to establish whether or not the marriage has produced any offspring. It is only when three menstrual cycles are complete that this possibility is negated. Therefore, the precautionary approach towards the needs of the potentially unborn child is to provide the *nafaqa* for the duration of the *ʿidda* and then to extend it as required during the pregnancy. That this is the purpose of the *nafaqa* is further supported by the fact that, upon birth, the divorced wife's *suknā* and *nafaqa* are replaced with payment for nursing.

As well as divorce, the Qur'an envisages the situation in which women are widowed by their husband's death. In Q. 2:234, the length of *ʿidda* to be observed by the widow is given as four months and ten days. After that time, which ensures that the paternity of any child conceived just before the husband's death is correctly ascribed, widows are free to remarry. Q. 2:235 then mentions the etiquettes to be observed in proposing to them. Provision for the widow is set in Q. 2:240 as a bequest (*waṣiyya*), which extends for up to a year while she continues to live in the house of her deceased spouse and presumably does not remarry. Al-Qurṭubī mentions that the majority of exegetes interpret Q. 2:240 as the initial situation, with this time period abrogated by the four months and ten days of Q. 2:234 and the bequest abrogated by the formal inheritance for wives in Q. 4:12.[97]

This may be an occasion in which the notion of abrogation is not very helpful in trying to determine the underlying principles at work. It would seem that the *ʿidda* of four months and ten days is meant as the point upon which a widow can remarry if she is not carrying a child. If she is pregnant then, as mentioned in Q. 65:4, the *ʿidda* lasts until the birth, which could be either sooner or later than this. In fact, it is interesting that the time period set in Q. 2:234 is almost half the usual nine-month term. The bequest of one year's *suknā* and *nafaqa* covers all of a potential pregnancy and some months beyond. After this, payment for the child's nursing would be the responsibility of the deceased's heirs as mentioned in Q. 2:233.

In the case of the divorced wife, *nafaqa* is based upon the potential or actual support of the unborn child and is paid for by the ex-husband. For the widow, the envisaged bequest is to be provided irrespective of whether she has an unborn child and comes from the husband's estate. It does not follow from this that such widows, who may have with them orphaned children from the marriage, should be forced to leave their homes after four months and ten days if they have not remarried. Rather, they should be allowed to remain in their houses for the full year and to grieve the loss of their partner fully as indicated in Q. 2:40.

However, whether the funding of this period should be treated as an independent bequest or subsumed within the widow's share of inheritance would seem to depend on the broader question of the principles of inheritance. These will be discussed in the next chapter, along with assessment of the Qur'anic treatment of the orphan in general.

To recap, the theme of marriage and divorce in Qur'anic law, although in an outward sense intimately entwined with the social norms of seventh-century Arabian society, reveals a consistent inward pattern at a universal level of morality. In general, it includes principles dealing with the whole gamut of the forming and breaking of relationships around marriage. As well as directed to the environment in which the Qur'an was revealed, the discussion of these various aspects is explicitly predicated on the intuitive moral sense of human agents, through the idea of the *maʿrūf*.

11

Inheritance

The institution of inheritance is part of the reciprocal responsibilities of human society, acting as the nexus through which wealth is redistributed to future generations.[1] The two basic strands to this theme within the Qur'anic discourse are the general case of bequests and legislated inheritance, as well as the special case of caring for orphans and protecting their inheritance until the time that they reach full maturity. Three considerations prompt starting with the topic of orphans first: the discussion of widowing at the end of the previous chapter, the Qur'an's sustained focus on their welfare, and the fact that this is the order observed within the *niẓām* at the beginning of Sūrat al-Nisāʾ. This sura is a key location for the articulation of the present theme, in which discussion of the particular case of orphans widens to encompass shares of inheritance and other economic matters.

I. Orphans

The Qur'an singles out orphans with the concern that their share of inheritance, held in trust, is not squandered. A number of Meccan verses repeat this basic injunction in different rhetorical styles, so as to drive home the central moral principle. Once the Muslim community settled in Medina, the emergence of armed conflict led to the likelihood of a significant increase in the number of orphans. The Medinan verses concerned with this theme articulate it more fully and in the most detailed passage concerning orphans, Q. 4:2–10, combine it with social legislation concerning marriage and inheritance issues.

The word in the Qur'an for orphan is *yatīm* (pl. *yatāmā*), which in classical Arabic arguably has a more precise meaning than is conveyed by the English equivalent. The verbal noun *yutm* means solitude or isolation and *yatīm* is an intensive form linguistically denoting the one left alone.[2] More precisely, the term is used for a child whose father dies before he, or she, reaches puberty and ceases to be applicable once this milestone is reached.[3] That is because, upon reaching maturity, the orphan is able to take responsibility for disposal of inheritance and managing earnings. The concept of the orphan is therefore closely tied to the idea of provision, due to the father's assumed role as the primary supporter of the family.[4]

By utilising this term, the Qur'an directs attention to one of the groups in society most in danger of exploitation by others. In fact, the repetition of this theme in a number of Qur'anic verses and the powerful language used, demonstrates both that this was a real social problem and an important strand of the Qur'anic moral message. Again, this may be read as a rhetorical point: if a society fails to care for its orphans, how can it lay any claim to justice?

Analysis of this topic reveals substantive distinctions between Meccan and Medinan verses related to both the changing external environment and developing internal social conditions of the Muslim community. The Meccan verses mention the singular form *yatīm*, with the exception of Q. 18:82, which uses the dual *yatīmayn* in its story of two orphans within the narrative of Moses and al-Khaḍir.[5] This indicates that the former revelations are as much concerned with giving the concept of the orphan a special place in the moral world of the community, as they are with dealing with the social problem in Mecca.

With the Meccan foundations in place, the Medinan verses focus exclusively upon the practical ramifications of orphaning on society, particularly after its increase due to various armed conflicts in the period after the hijra. In consequence, the verses revealed during this time use the plural language of *al-yatāmā*, in the sense of known members of society whose rights are in immediate need of defence.[6]

The Meccan verses concerning orphans can be broadly split into two categories: those that stress, in powerful and concise language, the importance of their care, all located in the short suras at the end of the Qur'an, and those that emphasise the preservation of the wealth held in trust for them. The former set the fundamental moral orientation towards the orphan, while the latter act as a catechismal prelude to the explication of the theme in the Medinan period.

Sūrat al-Duḥā contains the Qur'an's most personal address to the Prophet Muḥammad concerning his own early life as an orphan. In it, the reminder in Q. 93:6, 'Did we not find you an orphan and give you care', is complemented by the command in Q. 93:9, 'Do not treat the orphan with harshness'. Likewise, the Prophet is asked in Q. 107:1–2, '[Prophet], have you considered the person who denies the Judgement? It is he who pushes aside the orphan.' Q. 89:17–20 alludes to the consumption of inheritance alongside a reference to orphans, a theme that develops significantly in later revelations, 'No indeed! You [people] do not honour orphans, you do not urge one another to feed the poor, you consume inheritance greedily, and you love wealth with a passion.' This is paired with the next sura in Q. 90:12–15: 'What will explain to you what the steep path is? It is to free a slave, to feed at a time of hunger an orphaned relative.'[7]

The same theme is found in Q. 18:82, in which al-Khaḍir explains to Moses that he rebuilt a wall about to fall, because of an inheritance waiting for a pair of orphans underneath it. This is continued in Q. 6:152 and 17:34, which are both generally considered to be within late Meccan suras, and contain the identical sentence, 'Do not go near the orphan's property, except with the best [intentions], until he reaches the age of maturity.' This injunction anticipates the central theme of the later Medinan verses, which expand on how guardians should treat orphans.

In Sūrat al-Baqara, the issue of orphans, like a number of other matters of social concern, is presented in Q. 2:220 as a reply to be delivered by the Prophet to his community using the introductory formula *yas'alūnaka 'an* (they ask you about) and its response *qul* (say). Here the answer given is as follows:

> It is good to set things right (*iṣlāḥ*) for them. If you combine their affairs with yours, remember they are your brethren: God knows those who spoil things (*al-mufsid*) and those who rectify them (*al-muṣliḥ*). Had He so willed, He could have made you vulnerable too. He is almighty and wise.

In characteristic style, the Qur'an creates a dichotomy between the corrupters and rectifiers of the social order by presenting a powerful argument in succinct form. It acknowledges that an orphan has already suffered great loss in worldly affairs, so the duty of the guardian is to improve their quality of life as much as possible by administering all entrusted inheritance in the best way.

Two conditional sentences follow. In the first of these, 'If you combine their affairs with yours; remember they are your brethren (*in tukhāliṭūhum fa-ikhwānukum*)', the grammatical apodosis (*jawāb al-sharṭ*), here *fa-ikhwānukum*, is not a consequence of the initial condition. In other words, orphans are to be considered one's brethren in faith whether or not one takes on responsibility for their maintenance alongside one's own family. For this reason, to translate the expression requires additions to the front of 'they are your brethren', such as 'remember'[8] and 'be warned'. The real judgement is elided for rhetorical effect but made clear by the pointed affirmation that God knows the *mufsid* from the *muṣlih*: do not usurp their wealth. The second conditional sentence is used to drive home the point by eliciting empathy with the use of the hypothetical particle *law*. The ones asking about orphans are clearly in a position of relative strength, yet they are made to reflect on the fact that they could have been at the mercy of others.

The most detailed Qur'anic passage dealing with the question of the protection of orphans, Q. 4:2–10, is found in Sūrat al-Nisā'. Here the above general ideas enter into the socio-historical context of a particular set of problems faced by the Medinan Muslim community in 3–4/625, the year following the Battle of Uḥud.[9] The death of men in the fighting led to an unprecedented number of orphans within the small community. Al-Bukhārī collects a report that mentions seventy deaths at the battle.[10] In another hadith, the Companion Jābir mentions the death of his father at Uḥud causing the orphaning of his nine sisters.[11]

Q. 4:2 expands on the allusive language in Q. 2:220, beginning with a general command, 'Give orphans their wealth.'[12] This is followed by prohibition of two ways in which property held in trust is appropriated. The first, 'Do not replace [their] good things with bad (*lā tatabaddalū al-khabītha bi-l-ṭayyib*)', has been explained as taking the orphan's well-fed beast and giving back an emaciated one, or to take sound money and replace it with counterfeit.[13] The more general point is that although, given the period that trusteeship lasts, it may not be realistic to return exactly the same items of wealth that were entrusted, the guardian must ensure that an equivalent standard of property is returned.

The second prohibition concerns the further step of usurping the property of orphans entirely. The verse reads, 'Do not consume their wealth joining it with your property (*lā ta'kulū amwālahum ilā amwālikum*)', which depends on the meaning of the particle *ilā*. Most plausible is that it modifies the normal sense of *akl al-māl* (consumption of wealth) to mean 'joining it with one's own', that is, usurping it. Another interpretation is that *ilā* has the meaning of *ma*ʿ (with), a usage found in Q. 3:52. Thus: 'Do not consume their wealth along with your own.'[14]

The Qur'an declares such actions *ḥūban kabīran*, a great sin, or injustice.[15] The word and its close relation, or dialect variant, *ḥawb*, found in this verse according to the reading of al-Ḥasan al-Baṣrī, has a connotation of loneliness, grief, and lamenting.[16]

The next verse, Q. 4:3, has often been studied more for the Qur'anic permission for polygyny than its context relating to the treatment of orphans.[17] There are various explanations for the details of the particular social problem addressed by the verse and its legislated solution. A common one is that it refers to orphan girls that guardians were tempted to marry without providing dower and thus they should marry other women instead to avoid the injustice.[18] Another view is that the guardians wanted to marry the orphans, so they could retain access to their property.[19] This could be related to Q. 4:127, in which *mā kutiba lahunna* (lit. what is written for them) is interpreted as the inheritance of orphans.[20] Overall, it would seem that the difficulties with orphans relates to the long-term development of the family structure and the exploitation of weaker members, as much as to particular historical events.[21]

Analysing Q. 4:3 in the light of both frames, I assume that the orphans of Uḥud would go under the guardianship of the men of their clan to ensure protection of their inheritance, which was likely to include such wealth as livestock or land requiring management. The guardians could be tempted to usurp this wealth, so the advice (in imperative form) came to marry the mothers of the orphans, providing for their nurture and protecting themselves from acting with injustice.[22] This gloss of Q. 4:3 may be suggested, 'If you fear you will not deal fairly (*in khiftum allā tuqsiṭū*) with the orphans [of Uḥud under your guardianship], you may marry those that seem good to you from amongst the [widowed] women [their mothers], two, three, or four.'

The linguistic basis for this interpretation is to understand the definite article (*alif lām*) in both the word orphans (*al-yatāmā*) and women (*al-nisā'*) as *maʿhūd li-l-dhiʾn*, rather than indicating the class of orphans or women as a whole (*taʿrīf al-jins*). *Ab initio* these terms have the potential to be interpreted as either *khāṣṣ* or *ʿāmm*, depending on the use of the definite article. Arguably there is a stronger case for the former based on socio-historical context and scriptural *naẓm*. This leads to the implication that the *ḥukm* in this verse is only directly applicable to the particular historical case in question (in contrast to its *ḥikma*). The rule that the consideration for a ruling comes from the generality of the wording, and not the specificity of its circumstances of revelation is inapplicable if the wording is interpreted as being, in actuality, specific.[23]

It may be that a single man would act as a guardian for a number of children from different women and the verse would then allow for up to four such women to be married, although he would not be obliged to do so, as is shown by the phrase *mā ṭāba lakum* (those that seem good to you). However, the second part of Q. 4:3 makes clear that fair treatment is to be given to each wife, 'If you fear that you cannot be equitable [to them] (*fa'in khiftum allā ta'dilū*), then marry only one, or from your bondswomen: that is more likely to make you avoid bias.'

Thus, establishing one type of justice for children should not lead to causing another type of injustice among spouses. Marrying just one of the widows is given as an option in this case, or instead taking another person's slave as a wife. The point seems to be that if there is a danger of injustice due to the sparsity of means, whether it results in the consumption of the orphan's wealth, or unfair treatment to spouses, it is better to just marry a single wife, or to take the more affordable step of marrying a bondswoman. Although this is not as good as marriage to the mother of the orphans under one's care, it still ensures that a female figure is provided for them.[24]

The following verse, Q. 4:4, can be understood as part of the same discourse, as it indicates that the previous call for equality between wives includes fairness in respect of the amount of dower paid to each of them. If the husband has taken on the care of orphaned children, he may feel that he should not have to pay a dower as he has already done their mother a favour, or that he should adjust the amount that he gives to each based on the number of children supported.[25] The Qur'an rejects these assumptions and uses Q. 4:4 to emphasise the requirement of the dower, an instituted protection for the wife in case the marriage is not successful, 'Give women their bridal gift as an obligation, though if they are happy to give up some of it for you, you may enjoy it with a clear conscience.'[26] Thus, the women are given the choice to return some of the dower in order to assist the husband in managing the practical burden of taking on additional dependants.

One may compare the language in Q. 4:4, 'if they are happy to give up some of it for you (*fa-in ṭibna lakum 'an shay'in minhu nafsan*)', in which the subject of the verb *ṭibna* is the feminine plural, with Q. 4:24, 'there is no blame on you in what you mutually agree to do with it after fulfilling the obligation (*wa-lā junāḥa 'alaykum fī mā tarāḍaytum bihi min ba'di al-farīḍa*)'. In Q. 4:4, the widows are in a vulnerable position and so they are given the unilateral choice whether to remit a portion of their dower. Q. 4:24 expresses the general state of affairs in marriage and makes partial remission of the dower a mutual decision between the parties. Also, the *niẓām* of the passage as a whole deals with the more pressing case for marriage – to fulfil the needs of specific orphans – before dealing with marriage in its regular social manifestation.

Further support for this interpretation can be found in Q. 4:127:

> They ask you [Prophet] for a ruling about the women. Say, 'God Himself gives you a ruling about them. You already have what has been recited to you in the Scripture about

the orphans of the women (*yatāmā al-nisāʾ*) – from whom you withhold what has been prescribed for them (*mā kutiba lahunna*) and whom you wish to marry – and [also about] helpless children, God instructs you to treat orphans fairly: He is well aware of whatever good you do.'

Evidently members of the Prophet's community desired clarification about a particular situation regarding women. The existence of the question in the first place, the reference to Q. 4:3 as a past revelation, and the discussion of resolving marital discord in Q. 4:128–30 can be understood as pointing to some problems with the new marriages to the widows of Uḥud.

When the Prophet is asked about 'the women', the Qur'an responds about both them and the welfare of the children involved. First the Prophet is told to tell the questioners that God Himself will deliver the ruling. This highlights for them that a direct Qur'anic response will follow. The community is reminded about what has already preceded in Q. 4:3 with the phrase *yatāmā al-nisāʾ*, which can be read as the 'orphans of the [widowed] women'. Al-Rāzī criticises the Basran grammarians for treating this as a possessive construction (*iḍāfa*), rather than a partitive one, such as, 'the orphaned from amongst the women'.[27] However, I suggest that as well as making more contextual sense, the possessive rendering is more semantically coherent: *al-nisāʾ* refers to adult women, while *yatāmā* means those before the age of puberty.

In the next part of Q. 4:127, a relative clause summarises the point made in Q. 4:3–4, that if one wishes to marry the mothers of the orphans, then one must pay their proper dower: *mā kutiba lahunna*. In other words, when the questioners ask for a ruling about managing their polygynous marriages, they are told that they have already been instructed to enter into these marriages in the best way. This acts as preliminary advice for the verses Q. 4:128–30, which provide the ruling in question, as mentioned in the previous chapter.

The foregrounding of the orphans, just as in Q. 4:3, is to stress the importance of the children for whose benefit the marriages were conducted. The phrase in Q. 4:127, 'and [also about] helpless children (*wa-l-mustaḍʿafīna min al-wildān*)' alludes to a previous recitation about such children in the Scripture, due to the *wāw* grammatically linking to *yatāmā* in the previous sentence by *ʿatf* (conjunction).[28] This is likely to be a reference to Q. 4:9, 'Let those who would fear for the future of their own helpless children (*dhurriyyatan ḍiʿāfan*) if they were to die show the same concern [for orphans].' The verse concludes with a repeated call to establish justice in the treatment of orphans, and a reminder that God is well aware of any good in this regard.

Revisiting the first passage of Sūrat al-Nisāʾ, in Q. 4:5–10 the immediate context of the aftermath of Uḥud gives way to a more general discussion about the proper guardianship and transfer of property within the family. Q. 4:6 commands guardians to assess orphans for fitness to receive their wealth at marriageable age. This would appear to further support the view that Q. 4:3 and 4:127 do not refer to the marriage of male guardians with female orphans, but rather to their mothers. Q. 4:7

broaches the issue of mandatory inheritance, which is dealt with in detail in the next section of the sura, Q. 4:11–12, as well as closing it in Q. 4:176. The Qur'an's call in Q. 4:9 for its addressees to consider how they would feel if their own children were in an analogous situation presents a psychological argument to those who may be tempted to usurp the wealth of the orphans under their care. They should rather fear God and 'speak out for justice (*wa-l-yaqūlū qawlan sadīdan*)'. Q. 4:10 strengthens the force of this injunction with the eschatological result of the prohibited actions, 'Those who consume the property of orphans unjustly are actually swallowing fire into their own bellies: they will burn in the blazing Flame.'[29]

The *ḥikma* for the Qur'an's emphasis on the inheritance of orphans, then, reflects the fact that, as children, they are the future of society, yet they are without the fundamental benefit of the protection and support of their parents. The duty of generational justice thus devolves upon the entire community and becomes a trust given to those who take the responsibility of guardianship over them.

II. Bequests and shares of inheritance

Generational distributive justice, although emphasised most for orphans, is important too for other members of the family and stated beneficiaries. The Qur'an uses two concepts for this matter: the bequest (*al-waṣiyya*) and defined shares of inheritance (*al-farā'iḍ*) for specific individuals. The Qur'anic presentation of the rules pertaining to inheritance is one of the more complex topics of legislation within the scripture, especially as it is expressed in fractions. An explanation for this level of detail is the potential for inheritance to 'stir conflict in society or between individual members of a single family'.[30]

General procedural rules for bequests are dealt with in Q. 5:106–8, which focuses on establishing just witnessing for a dying person's testament. The principle in this situation is that as such a person will not be alive to check that their will has been carried out correctly, and as the amounts are not specified by scripture, it is vital that their wishes are accurately conveyed. Like Q. 2:282, the passage Q. 5:106–8 details each step that should be taken to ensure the scrupulous discharge of the duty. It emphasises the role that the entire community should play, including making the witnesses swear to their trustworthiness directly after having prayed, and, if needed, being ready to replace them with others who are more reliable.[31] A particular point of interest for the argument developed within this book is that Q. 5:106 mentions 'two just people from amongst you, or two from other than you (*dhawā ʿadlin minkum aw ākharāni min ghayrikum*) if you were afflicted by death whilst travelling'. Here, the quality of *ʿadl* is explicitly attributed to the non-Muslim witnesses.

The question of whether the bequest is to be considered obligatory and how it is related to the specified shares of inheritance in Q. 4:11–12 is subject to various interpretations. A number of early Kufan figures, including al-Shaʿbī and al-Nakhaʿī, interpret the bequest as having been a recommendation from the outset.[32] However, the language of Q. 2:180, which includes the phrase *kutiba ʿalaykum* (it is prescribed for you) with respect to parents and close relatives, is more likely to indicate a duty. The same is implied with respect to widows in Q. 2:240, as mentioned in the previous chapter.[33]

Despite this, many scholars consider the obligation to make a bequest to be abrogated by the obligatory shares of inheritance in Q. 4:11–12, or at least in the case of those who are set to inherit, as indicated in reports, including one about the Prophet's *khuṭbat al-wadāʿ*.[34] In one hadith, Ibn ʿAbbās states, 'Wealth used to be inherited by the son, while the parents received a bequest. Then God abrogated whatever he wanted of that practice.'[35] This could suggest that the Qur'anic injunction of an obligatory bequest for parents in Q. 2:180 was meant as a transitional stage between pre-Islamic priority for male descendants at the expense of ancestors and the more comprehensive legislation to follow in Sūrat al-Nisāʾ.

Q. 4:11–12 repeats the statement 'after payment of any bequests or debts' four times, emphasising the importance of making any bequests before division of the estate. I should note that David S. Powers has argued that the replacement of bequests by specified shares of inheritance is a legal development from the post-prophetic era.[36]

Q. 4:11, in beginning with inheritance for children, expands on the summarised injunction of Q. 4:7.[37] The share of sons is not specified, but is put at a ratio of 2:1 in relation to daughters, which is strong evidence that the Qur'an retains the principle that sons, or the nearest agnatic relatives, receive the remainder after other shares are given. In another report ascribed to Ibn ʿAbbās there is the statement, 'Give the obligatory shares of inheritance to whoever they are due. Then, whatever remains belongs to the closest male relative of the deceased.'[38] The rationale behind such a division is the assumption of male responsibility for both dower when getting married, and provision for the family thereafter. If these needs are not there due to the absence of sons, the largest single shares of inheritance fall to daughters: half for an only child, a division of two-thirds of the estate for more.

Parents are discussed next and take a sixth each in the case that the deceased has left children and has no brothers. This rises to one-third for the mother if there are no other inheritors, with again the unstated assumption that the father would take two-thirds. However, it is adjusted to one-sixth and five-sixths respectively if the deceased left brothers, which reflects the need to aid them and their families, typically done through the clan's patriarch. Note that the brothers themselves do not receive a share in this situation, so part of the redistribution of wealth is deferred until the death of their parents.[39]

One of the important developments of the Qur'anic inheritance laws compared to the pre-Islamic system, then, is the protection of shares for both parents and children simultaneously, which was impossible when closer agnatic relatives excluded more distant ones. The *ḥikma* of this is expressed in the wording in Q. 4:11, 'You cannot know which of your parents or your children is more beneficial to you (*ābāʾukum wa-bnāʾukum lā tadrūna ayyuhum aqrabu lakum nafʿan*)'.

Q. 4:12 continues to add to the rulings of the previous verse by dealing with two distinct issues. The first is the matter of spouses, which immediately follows that of children and parents. Again, prioritising a significant share of the estate for children impacts the legislation, as husbands receive half of their wives' inheritance if the latter were childless, a quarter if not. Wives receive half as much if they are widowed, a quarter and an eighth respectively, reflecting the recurring assumption that the male needs more to provide for others, and presumably for paying a new dower upon any remarriage.

The second issue that Q. 4:12 addresses is the shares due from the individual known as the *kalāla*, a term that, although considered somewhat obscure, is usually understood as either a deceased person with no ascendant or descendant heirs, or their inheritor.[40] Using this classical definition of the term, the second part of Q. 4:12 can be translated as follows:

> If a man or a woman dies leaving no children or parents, but a single brother or sister, he or she should take one-sixth of the inheritance; if there are more siblings, they share one-third between them. [In all cases, the distribution comes] after payment of any bequests or debts, with no harm done to anyone: this is a commandment from God: God is all knowing and benign to all.

That brothers and sisters should be considered after children, parents, and spouses and only if there are no ascendant or descendant heirs is perfectly understandable given the preceding principles. What is puzzling, however, is that the brothers and sisters of the *kalāla* are to equally share one-third. The other legislation in the passage would lead to the assumption that brothers and sisters would receive inheritance at a ratio of 2:1, as in the case of children. This part of the verse was evidently confusing for the early community, as an answer providing a more expected rule is given to a question in Q. 4:176, which is placed at the end of the sura:

> They ask you [Prophet] for a ruling. Say, 'God gives you a ruling about inheritance from someone who dies childless with no surviving parents. If a man leaves a sister, she is entitled to half of the inheritance; if she has no child her brother is her sole heir; if there are two sisters, they are entitled to two-thirds of the inheritance between them, but if there are surviving brothers and sisters, the male is entitled to twice the share of the female.'

An obvious way to reconcile the *kalāla* rulings in Q. 4:12 and Q. 4:176 is to invoke *naskh* of the former by the latter. However, this solution is not very satisfying due to Q. 4:12's placement within the same passage as the other final rules of inheritance and the difficulty in justifying the shift in rule.

It is therefore, in part, within the literature of variant readings that Muslim scholarship has classically justified the distinction between Q. 4:12 and Q. 4:176. A reading from Saʿd b. Abī Waqqāṣ adds 'from the mother (*min al-umm*)' to the phrase 'brother or sister' in Q. 4:12, which suggests that the verse deals with uterine siblings, those related through the mother alone.[41] This would imply that Q. 4:176 is for germane siblings, those related through the father.

Whereas the recipient of the uterine *kalāla* gets one-sixth, whether male or female, and any number of brothers or sisters equally share one-third, the germane equivalents are treated as if they are the sons and daughters of the deceased, with the same rules regarding inheritance: full for a sole brother, half for a sole sister, two-thirds for more than one sister, and a share of 2:1 male to female for a mixture of brothers and sisters. The *ḥikma* in this distinction would seem to be that, in the case of the uterine *kalāla*, it is possible that the recipient's father is still alive, while this is not possible for the germane equivalent. The financial benefit of one's living father over one's mother, both in terms of immediate support and future inheritance, is thus assumed to compensate for the lessened share.

The existence of the above apparent discrepancy has led to a number of contemporary scholars writing lengthy works focused wholly or partially on the *kalāla*, with Powers, who tackled the subject in books published in 1986 and 2009, the most prominent among them.[42] Powers' central hypothesis is that the word *kalāla* found today in Q. 4:12 has been emended after the lifetime of the Prophet from its previous form in which it allowed designation of a *kalla* (daughter-in-law) as an heir alongside a wife.[43] This, however, puts a more substantial engagement with his contention outside the scope of the present study, as I have restricted myself to the ʿUthmānī codex with – at most – some consideration of the tradition of canonical *qirāʾāt* and attested variant readings.

Overall, the Qur'anic discourse maintains a fine balance between the apparent pre-Islamic assumption that inheritance is for the nearest male agnatic relatives and its new provision of defined shares for daughters, parents, spouses, and siblings. This means that, like rules pertaining to the marriage contract in the previous chapter, and *qiṣāṣ* in the next one, the Qur'an reforms the existing social institutions of tribal Arabia to benefit the position of women, while retaining their basic structure. In this case, the principle that women are to have a protected claim for inheritance alongside men is declared in Q. 4:7, 'For women, a share from what parents and close relatives leave, whether it is small or large, a mandatory share.'

More generally, my analysis of distributive justice within the Qur'an in this part of the book has shown a chronological development in each thematic area. The moral concern to uphold natural justice through ensuring the existence of fair commercial practices and redistributing wealth according to need, develops through the period of revelation, becoming embodied in legislated duties within the *sharīʿa*. Thus, at a minimum, the just division of the community's wealth is ensured by actively reaching the positive parameters set by the Law. The next chapter considers the boundaries that, if broken through criminal action, require corrective action to rebalance society.

Part IV

Corrective Justice

12

Public Crimes

Building upon the study so far, I submit that a transgression of the moral order requires a certain rebalancing of society to match the Scale, returning it to equilibrium and harmony. In certain instances when this is not achieved at a personal level, the Qur'an mandates that it is enforced societally.

Analysis of the Qur'anic system of corrective justice in terms of its internal purposes and coherence requires a number of principles to be borne in mind. The scripture makes plain that despite the importance of the societal quest for justice, perfect recompense for all acts is only found in the Hereafter.[1] The society envisaged within the Qur'an is centred on this belief and therefore the highest ideal in responding to a disruption of the moral scale is an internal correction based on forgiveness, encouragement for repentance and reform, and the covering of private sins. When such disruptions become public crimes, because of their social consequences, the desire of the criminal to confess, or the need for the victim to air their grievances, then the circumstances change and an external correction is required through punishment, unless there can be public conciliation.

Worldly justice should not then be understood as standing in place of the requital of the Hereafter, but rather as fulfilling three major purposes: repentance, deterrence, and compensation for victims. Repentance is the means by which the perpetrator rectifies his or her relationship with the divine and should be made for all sins, especially major ones, although God reserves the right to forgive in any case.[2] Its function is to ward off the much greater punishment awaiting in the Hereafter. M. A. Draz remarks that acting sinfully gives the conscience a sense of imbalance, a kind of disequilibrium between the ideal of the moral code, and the reality of its own self. Remorse follows, but to be effective it must be utilised for repentance, which can be seen itself as a kind of sanction, a duty that becomes obligatory due to the neglect of a previous duty.[3]

The existence of judicial punishment deters other members of society, warding off the particular harm associated with the crime, and maintains social stability. Michel Foucault identifies three elements typical of pre-modern physical punishment – the type legislated by the Qur'an – which enable it to fulfil its deterrent function. It must be painful to some degree; it must 'mark' the victim, either by a physical scar left upon the body, or in terms of public humiliation; and it must create a social spectacle.[4] He identifies this last component as critical for the effectiveness of deterrence due to the role that it ensures for the populace at large. Deterrence works not just because the spectators are afraid, but because 'they must be the witnesses, the guarantors, of the punishment, and because they must to a certain extent take part in it'.[5] Another way to put this is that the community, or society at large, must bear its share of responsibility for the punishment.

Finally, the specific victim of the crime is to be compensated for the harm received. The compensation can take a number of forms. It may be a statement of contrition and plea for forgiveness,[6] in some cases accompanied with material restitution, or it may be through the psychological closure offered by punishment of the criminal. This latter element, although acknowledged as an expected human response, is at a lower level than the value of forgiveness, as here the *iḥsān* of the victim's cultivation of mercy is superior to acting solely according to a strict sense of *ʿadl*. However, that is only provided that he or she is satisfied that the moral reform of the criminal is real and that this person does not pose a continuing threat to society. Likewise, for victims to waive due compensation for the sake of their own forgiveness represents greater moral excellence than taking it.

These principles run throughout Part IV of this book. In the present chapter, I will present them in the context of public crimes, which are those actions causing such serious disruption to the social fabric that their investigation by the governing authority for the sake of society as a whole cannot be avoided. Within the Qur'anic discourse, these crimes are murder (*qatl*) and brigandage (*ḥirāba*), each of which represents a threat to the safety and security of the community.

I. Murder

The crime of murder, intentionally depriving an innocent person of life, is the most severe act that a person can commit against another human being. The Qur'an is unambiguous in both condemning it and allowing capital punishment in response to it in certain circumstances. There are texts in three suras that must be investigated within the Qur'anic treatment of this issue: Q. 17:33, Q. 2:178–9, and Q. 5:27–45. The verse in Sūrat al-Isrāʾ is from the Meccan period and is meant to have a purely moral impact. This lays a foundation for the verses in Sūrat al-Baqara and Sūrat al-Māʾida, which were revealed in Medina with a direct legislative impact on the management of community affairs.

Q. 17:33 is addressed to people in general, both believers and disbelievers in the Qur'anic message, which is clear from the verses calling for *tawḥīd* that frame its passage in Q. 17:22[7] and Q. 17:40. The verse sits within a series of moral prohibitions that were propounded in Mecca as part of the Qur'an's manifesto of reform for the vices of Arabian society. Q. 17:33 reads:

> Do not take life, which God has made sacred, except by right (*wa-lā taqtulū al-nafsa allatī ḥarrama allāhu illā bi-l-ḥaqq*): if anyone is killed wrongfully, We have given authority to the defender of his rights, but he should not be excessive in taking life, for he is already aided [by God].

The key principle is enshrined in the prohibition of the first sentence, which comes under the category of *inshā'*. From the *naẓm* of the verse in its passage, and in its linguistic construction, it is obvious that the *alif lām* of *al-nafs* is for *ta'rīf al-jins*, that is, the class of every life, or soul, is sacrosanct. The use of *lā* and *illā* is the most common form of *qaṣr*, here exempting the prohibition on killing to those for which there is a *ḥaqq*, or right. The word *al-ḥaqq* in this construction is *'āmm*, and in order to specify its content, it is necessary to look elsewhere in the Qur'an, in particular the series of verses Q. 5:27–45.[8]

The term that the Qur'an uses for the retaliation of murder is *qiṣāṣ*, which is the verbal noun of the verb *qāṣṣa*, meaning a retaliatory slaying to make someone even.[9] It would seem that its original signification is to follow behind someone and, by extension, 'pursuing and finding the murderer'.[10]

The Qur'anic legislation of *qiṣāṣ* is in Q. 2:178:

> You who believe, fair retribution is prescribed for you in cases of murder: the free man for the free man, the slave for the slave, the female for the female (*al-ḥurru bi-l-ḥurri wa-l-'abdu bi-l-'abdi wa-l-unthā bi-l-unthā*). But if the culprit is pardoned by his aggrieved brother, this shall be adhered to fairly, and the culprit shall pay what is due in a good way. This is an alleviation from your Lord and an act of mercy.

A number of narrations exist within the *asbāb al-nuzūl* literature purporting to explain the particular circumstances under which Q. 2:178 was revealed. Al-Suyūṭī records a tradition that, just prior to their embrace of Islam, two pagan neighbourhoods fought, presumably in the vicinity of Medina. After they accepted Islam they came to settle their affairs, with the wealthier and more numerous demanding the retaliatory slaying of a free man for each slave, and a male for each female of theirs.[11] According to this account, the verse was revealed to forbid this and other similar practices. There is also a more general narration in which the verse is a response to the pre-Islamic practice of excessive and unfair retribution due to a tribe's sense of honour or prestige, rather than connecting it to a particular incident.[12]

Some classical Muslim scholars interpret 'the free man for the free man, the slave for the slave, the female for the female' as a specification (*takhṣīṣ*) of the general legislation of *qiṣāṣ* just preceding it, using various linguistic arguments.[13] However, given the above context and the principle that *al-tanṣīṣ lā yadillu 'alā al-takhṣīṣ*, it may be suggested that the freeman is punished for the freeman he has slain from any tribe, and so on for the others, without thereby assuming that *qiṣāṣ* is not followed in other possible combinations between them.[14] Thus, the verse does not conflict with the principle of 'a life for a life' mentioned in Q. 5:45 and rather than perpetuating the pre-Islamic practice of a basic hierarchy for the value of human life, it refutes it within its tribal context.

The main continuity with the previous system is the provision for the payment of compensatory *diya* (blood money) in place of retaliation, at the behest of the family of the slain. Q. 2:178 states, 'This is an alleviation from your Lord and an act of mercy', raising this payment in status compared with pre-Islamic tribal norms, as well as Mosaic law. Q. 2:179 introduces one of the *ḥikma*s of the injunction, 'Fair retribution saves life for you, people of understanding (*wa-lakum fī al-qiṣāṣi ḥayātun yā-ūlī al-albāb*).' This form of address indicates those with a greater capacity for insight into the divine purpose by ennobling them as well as urging them to protect life.[15]

Before relating *qiṣāṣ* in the Qur'an to the wider structure of justice, I shall analyse a significant passage from Sūrat al-Māʾida, Q. 5:27–45, which deals in greater depth with the moral question of the right to take a life within society and related issues of crime and punishment. In terms of *niẓām*, it is part of a larger textual unit, which besides the prohibition of murder focuses on the punishment for brigandage in Q. 5:33–4, thievery in Q. 5:38–9, and the Prophet as a judge over Jews and Christians in Q. 5:41–50.[16]

The passage begins, in Q. 5:27–31, by recounting the story of Abel and Cain – its only appearance in the Qur'an – which provides a powerful moral context for the discussion of murder and its consequences, as well as other questions of law and order. In terms of explicit linguistic markers, Q. 5:27 announces its thematic shift from the preceding historical discussion of the community of Moses in Q. 5:20–6 with the device, 'Recite for them the real story of the two sons of Adam (*wa-tlu ʿalayhim nabaʾ ibnay ādama bi-l-ḥaqq*).'[17]

The story of Cain's unjust murder of Abel is followed by Q. 5:32:

> On account of [his deed] (*min ajli dhālika*), We decreed to the Children of Israel that if anyone kills a person – unless in retribution for murder (*bi-ghayri nafs*) or spreading corruption in the land (*fasādin fī al-arḍ*) – it is as if he kills all humanity, while if anyone saves a life it is as if he saves the lives of all humanity.

This is part of an address directed simultaneously to the Prophet and his community, as well as to the Jews of his time, legislating for the former, while warning the latter about wrongdoing in the light of their community's past actions. Al-Zamakhsharī remarks that, in terms of structure, *min ajli dhālika* treats the incident of Cain and Abel as a *sabab* for the decree to the Children of Israel.[18] Despite this connection between Q. 5:31 and Q. 5:32, there is no use of *wāw* to indicate *waṣl*. In terms of *naẓm*, such a *faṣl* can occur for a number of reasons. Here it seems to be *kamāl al-ittiṣāl* (complete connection), in which the second utterance is synonymous, emphatic, or explanatory to the first.[19] It thus takes the place of *ʿaṭf al-bayān* (explicative apposition) in providing explanation.[20] The rhetorical effect of this *faṣl* is to highlight the close relationship of cause and effect between the world's first murder and the principle revealed to the Israelites.

The story of Abel and Cain is mentioned in Genesis 4:1–25 with the same essential meaning, but some differences in detail and circumstance. One of the key verses is 4:10, 'Then He said, "What have you done? The voice of your brother's blood (*dimī*) cries out to Me from the ground!"'

The Hebrew word *dimī* is in the plural form, which can be defined as 'blood in quantity, hence sometimes of blood shed by rude violence, and of blood-stains'.[21] The Sanhedrin, a codification of Jewish Law from the second century CE, quotes rabbinic authorities of the Mishnah in explaining the significance of this plural form in Genesis 4:10 for the legal formulation of the law of retaliation:

> Know moreover, that capital cases are not like non-capital cases: in non-capital cases a man may pay money and so make expiation; but in capital cases the blood of the accused and of his posterity may cling to him (the witness) to the end of the world. For so we find it in the case of Cain, who slew his brother, as it is written: the voice of the bloods of thy brother cries to me from the ground; – not the blood of thy brother, but the bloods of thy brother – his blood and that of his posterity ... For this reason man was created one and alone in the world: to teach that whosoever destroys a single soul is regarded as though he destroyed a complete world, and whosoever saves a single soul is regarded as though he saved a complete world.[22]

This is the scriptural reference mentioned in Q. 5:32, which does not state that it is to be found in the Torah, in contrast with the law of talion in Q. 5:45. The phrase 'We decreed (*katabnā*) to the Children of Israel' is compatible with the Mishnah according to the Rabbinic tradition. This comprises binding teachings of the sages, which are traced back to the oral revelation given to Moses in parallel with the written Torah.[23]

The connection between the story of Abel and Cain, and the moral lesson decreed for the Children of Israel, is that the killing of a person does not merely stop at him, but cuts off all of the unborn generations that would have followed in his lineage. This is the reason for the Jewish prohibition of blood money in place of the retaliatory killing. The Qur'an's reference to *diya* as an alleviation (*takhfīf*) is more literally rendered 'lightening', and can be taken as a reference to this stricture of the Mosaic Law.[24] This does not indicate a reduction in the severity of murder between the two *sharī'as*,[25] but rather represents the chance for forgiveness and conciliation between the families of the victim and perpetrator. Such a reform is also part of the Qur'an's positioning as a balanced middle between the rigour of the Law of Moses and the call of Jesus for his followers 'to turn the other cheek' in the same situation (Matthew 5:38–9).[26] This would signal the universality that was to mark the 'final sacred law'.[27]

Q. 5:32 also specifies a second circumstance besides murder in which there is a *ḥaqq* for capital punishment. This is in the phrase 'spreading corruption in the land', which is directly connected to Q. 5:33–4, the following verses that legislate against brigandage.

I have discussed the sequence that immediately precedes Q. 5:45 in Chapter 6. In the current context, the most relevant part is Q. 5:42–3, which relates to the Prophet's authority to judge over the Jews of Medina if they come to him.[28] Hadiths indicate that this refers to the practice of the Jewish tribes of Banū al-Naḍīr and

Qurayẓa, in which the former would insist on a retaliatory killing, based on their nobility, when they were infringed against, but would give only a payment in the converse situation.[29] Other reports have al-Naḍīr insisting on paying half, but taking full blood money.[30] This practice clearly derived from the surrounding pagan custom, rather than their own revealed law, so after castigating those rabbis who altered the scripture, there is a restatement of the Torah's law of talion in Q. 5:45:

> In the Torah We prescribed for them a life for a life, an eye for an eye, a nose for a nose, an ear for an ear, a tooth for a tooth, an equal wound for a wound: the one who gives clemency, it will serve as atonement for him. Those who do not judge according to what God has revealed are doing grave wrong.

The phrase 'the one who gives clemency, it will serve as atonement for him (*fa-man taṣadaqa bihi fa-huwa kaffāratun lahu*)' is another addition to the law of talion and refers to the possibility of the injured party, or their representative in capital cases, forgoing retaliation, so as to seek God's forgiveness for their own sins.[31] This is again a lightening of the strict judgement in the Torah, 'If there shall be a fatality, then you shall award a life for a life; an eye for an eye, a tooth for a tooth, a hand for a hand, a foot for a foot; a burn for a burn, a wound for a wound, a bruise for a bruise.'[32]

The fact that the Qur'an confirms this law of the Torah and then legislates an extra condition may be taken as evidence that Q. 5:45 – including the *qiṣāṣ* of 'life for a life' regardless of faith – is intended as part of Qur'anic legislation, although this has been doubted by some exegetes.[33] Moreover, the normative weight of Q. 5:45, confirmed from a previous revealed dispensation, gains further credence based on the above interpretations of Q. 17:33 and Q. 2:178.[34]

It should now be possible to draw some conclusions about the underlying moral structure pertaining to *qiṣāṣ* in light of the general system outlined at the beginning of this chapter. The concern that the offender repents for their sin ideally emerges when paying the *diya*, which is a type of material restitution. This, however, requires *iḥsān* in the form of forgiveness from the victim's family, an allowance that the Qur'an terms a mercy. If retaliatory killing is demanded, then this repentance is not negated, but rather is still incumbent upon the killer before his or her execution.

Regardless of whether *qiṣāṣ* is enacted in any given case, it acts as a deterrent with the intention of stabilising society. The fruit of this stability is the protection from further loss of life, which is the major societal *ḥikma* mentioned in Q. 2:179. The sanctity of life is a value to be extended absolutely to all members of humanity, but can be waived in two exceptional cases: those persons who have themselves taken a life without right, and those who severely transgress and corrupt the normal social order. As shall be seen in the next section, this latter case primarily means to threaten the community as belligerents. Likewise, although the fundamental sanctity of human life is universal, *qiṣāṣ* is not applied to those who kill belligerents in situations of war, or self-defence.

A final observation concerns the intersection between society as a whole and the victims of killing. Unlike the crimes that shall be discussed in the next chapter, the grave consequence of murder for a community makes it an absolutely public matter. The need for family to grieve, to pray at the funeral, and for inheritance to be determined, as well as possible changes in the guardianship of children, makes it impossible for a murder, once discovered, to be intentionally kept out of the public eye. Furthermore, there is obviously no opportunity for the slain to offer their forgiveness, so this falls upon the next of kin who must be informed, making it also by this measure a community affair.

This all means that the possibility for the victim (here representative) to forgive the perpetrator – an essential aspect of Qur'anic corrective justice – does not happen in the private sphere, but is legally regulated in public. The value of this forgiveness is extolled each time that retaliation is mentioned within the Qur'an: in Q. 17:33, the family of the slain are told they are already 'helped'; in Q. 5:45, they are encouraged that forgoing retaliation will act as an expiation for their sins; while in Q. 2:178, it is anticipated that the culprit will be pardoned by his 'brother'.

A few words should be said about the accidental killing of believers, which is discussed in Q. 4:92. Three cases are given depending on the community from which the deceased originates. If it is someone from within the community of Muslims, then the expiation is made of freeing a believing slave (*taḥrīru raqabatin muʾminin*) and providing a compensatory payment (*diyatun musallamatun*) to their people, although this can be waived by them (*yaṣṣaddaqū*), just as mentioned for *qiṣāṣ* in Q. 5:45. The same rules apply for a killed believer from a tribe with a peace treaty (*mīthāq*), except there is no expectation for the payment to be waived. Finally, in the case of a hostile tribe, only the expiation is made.

It can be seen that while the internal value of repentance for accidental killing, represented by manumission of a believing slave, is constant, elements of corrective justice vary depending on the political circumstances. Although the values of compensation and forgiveness from the victim's family are most fully realised within the community of believers, the former is also extended to any tribe enjoying peaceful relations, whether or not they are Muslims themselves. These specific rules, then, cohere with the broader point made within Chapter 6 that justice is capable of extension beyond the immediate community as a quality known through shared appreciation of the natural law.[35]

This concept of public crimes explains some of the procedural differences between *qiṣāṣ* on the one hand, and the punishments usually known as the *ḥudūd* on the other. According to my analysis, the key distinction is not over whose right, or *ḥaqq*, is infringed, but over whether the matter unavoidably enters into the public sphere, like murder, or does so only as a last resort, as will be seen in Chapter 13.

II. Brigandage

The punishment for the crime of *ḥirāba* in Q. 5:33–4 is connected with the more general term *baghy* (aggression, or rebellion), which is mentioned in suras revealed in Mecca. The famously comprehensive Q. 16:90 mentions, 'God commands justice (*ʿadl*), moral excellence (*iḥsān*), and generosity towards relatives and He forbids what is shameful, blameworthy, and oppressive (*al-baghy*).'[36] Q. 7:33 provides an additional qualifier, 'Say [Prophet], "My Lord only forbids disgraceful deeds – whether they be open or hidden – and sin and unjustified aggression (*al-baghya bi-ghayri al-ḥaqq*)".'

The phrase *bi-ghayri al-ḥaqq* implies, like Q. 17:33 with respect to killing, that despite the usual prohibition, there are certain cases in which overpowering someone may be acceptable. This idea is expanded in Q. 42:39–43. Although Sūrat al-Shūrā is Meccan, an undefined number of verses have traditionally been considered to derive from the Medinan period,[37] especially if, as in this passage, they are connected to themes such as armed conflict.[38] Thus, in Q. 42:39, '[What God shall give is better and more lasting for] those that defend themselves when they are oppressed (*idhā aṣābahum al-baghyu hum yantaṣirūn*).' As well as acting to defend one's own community, Q. 42:42 affirms going on the offensive against oppressors, 'There is only cause to act against those who oppress people and transgress in the land against all justice (*innamā al-sabīlu ʿalā alladhīna yaẓlimūna al-nāsa wa-yabghūna fī al-arḍi bi-ghayri al-ḥaqq*)'.

Again, the process is of basic Meccan moral instructions being extended into a rule-based framework within Medina. The prominent place given to pardon and forgiveness in Q. 42:40 and 42:43 is also notable.

A final stage is reached in the so-called *ḥirāba* verses, Q. 5:33–4:

> Those who wage war against God and His Messenger and strive to spread corruption in the land (*alladhīna yuḥāribūna allāha wa-rasūlahu wa-yasʿawna fī al-arḍi fasādan*) should be punished by death, crucifixion, the amputation of an alternate hand and foot, or banishment from the land: a disgrace for them in this world, and then a terrible punishment in the Hereafter, unless they repent before you overpower them – in that case bear in mind that God is forgiving and merciful.

These verses require careful scrutiny from several angles. First, the identity of the punished group must be established with reference to the language of the verse and relevant contextual information. Next comes analysis of the *niẓām* of the verse in relation to the rest of the sequence extending from Q. 5:27, which was discussed in the previous section. Finally, there is the question of fitting the legislation propounded in these verses within the wider schema of Qur'anic punishment, and ultimately justice.

The language used in the verse obviously excludes the class of believers. As it is not possible to literally wage war against God, this stands for complete rejection of Him, raising violent opposition against His Messenger and seditious activity.

The group referred to may either be existing opponents from another religious affiliation, or belligerent apostates from the Muslim community. Al-Bukhārī in his *Ṣaḥīḥ* uses Q. 5:33 as the title of his first section within his 'Chapter of those from the People of Disbelief and Apostasy who Wage War (*kitāb al-muḥāribīna min ahl al-kufr wa-l-ridda*)'. He puts in it a single hadith:

> A group from [the tribe] of 'Ukl[39] came to the Prophet and accepted Islam, yet did not find that the food and drink available within Medina agreed with them, so the Prophet ordered them to take the camels held as alms, so that they could drink from their urine [as medicine] and milk. They did that and became sound in constitution; then they apostatised and killed the camels' shepherds, [fleeing while] urging the camels ahead of them. [The Prophet] set out in their tracks, until he came upon them, and punished them by amputating their hands and feet and putting out their eyes. Thereafter, he did not leave them until they had died [from dehydration].[40]

The elements contained within this event are apostasy, followed by murder and theft, while the implementation of the *ḥirāba* punishment arguably consisted of amputations for stealing the camels and executions for the killing of their shepherds.[41] Blinding them could be considered a discretionary punishment, although it is interesting that some versions of this hadith mention crucifixion as well, a further link to Q. 5:33.[42] Sean Anthony argues that this could merely refer to leaving them exposed in the desert to die, in which case blinding would ensure that they were unable to escape.[43] Another exegetical strategy is to mention that the punishment of blinding was either abrogated, or prevented from happening, by the revelation of Q. 5:33.[44]

There is also the possibility that, instead of violent apostates, the Children of Israel are alluded to with the phrase 'those who wage war against God and His Messenger' in Q. 5:33, which follows immediately from 'many of them continued to commit excesses in the land (Q. 5:32)'. The banishment given to the Jewish tribes of Qaynuqā' and al-Naḍīr and even the reported execution of the combatants of Qurayẓa could also potentially fit within this interpretation of Q. 5:33.[45] A concern with this view, however, is that it implies a form of collective punishment that is incompatible with Qur'anic ethics, which are predicated on individual moral accountability.[46]

In essence, then, the character of the group mentioned in Q. 5:33 is that it is composed of those who reject the Qur'an's message, are armed and belligerent, and are either living outside, or rejecting a peaceful role within, the Muslim community. It is thus distinct from Muslims who diverge from the main body as a result of political differences, while remaining believers, as mentioned in Q. 49:9–10.[47]

Placing the *ḥirāba* punishment within the structure of corrective justice, it is obvious that the crime it concerns is, like murder, necessarily within the public sphere. The place of forgiveness is extremely prominent in Q. 5:34, which stipulates a unique condition within Qur'anic punishment, 'unless they repent before you overpower them – in that case bear in mind that God is forgiving and merciful'.

As it is a basic Qur'anic principle that repentance is accepted until the death throes, the significance of this condition must relate to the punishment meted out to the belligerents within the world.[48] The captured criminals may avoid the harsh punishments described in the verse if they desist from their actions and repent.

Socially, the existence of such punishments has a deterrent function as discussed for *qiṣāṣ*. In this case, the intention is the increase of social stability primarily in the areas outside of settlements, rather than inside, and the protection of the routes of travel between them. In fact, jurists often discussed the implications of this verse under the title *ḥadd qaṭʿ al-ṭarīq* (the penalty for highway robbery; lit. for cutting off the path).

The primary victim of this type of offence is the community as a whole, and so the potential for pardon is at the behest of the authorities and couched in those terms, as evidenced by the plural forms used throughout. The Qur'an does not specify whether persons otherwise fulfilling the criteria for pardon could have their punishment for killing, injury, or property offences waived. Ḥanafī jurists argued that this was not possible, as they have impinged upon a *ḥaqq* of God, which cannot be forgiven by humankind.[49] Shāfiʿīs hold a similar position.[50] The argument presented in this chapter and the next is that the Qur'an always allows the possibility for forgiveness. As the above offences would have been committed as public crimes, the authorities would give the opportunity for reconciliation and compensation to the victims, if they are willing.

Overall, then, the punishment for brigandage is complementary to that for murder, but concerning acts committed by hostile outsiders, or belligerent apostates, rather than people internal to the community. Both punishments act to restore the natural justice shared by all members of the society envisaged by the Qur'an. The best way that this is done is through forgiveness and reconciliation, which must take place openly, just as the crimes did. If this is not possible, then punishment is used to recalibrate society to once again match the Scale.

13

Private Crimes

Not all crimes identified by the Qur'an must occur within the public sphere. There is a second class of prohibited actions that, although legislated with a distinct punishment if exposed openly, are first and foremost a matter for private morality: thievery (*sariqa*), fornication (*zinā*), and slander (*qadhf*). All three of these form key parts of the first pledge made by members of the Anṣār at ʿAqaba one year before the hijra.[1] This became later known as the Pledge of Women, in order to distinguish it from the commitment to fighting required from men at the subsequent ʿAqaba meeting and thereafter. Within the Qur'an, it is quoted in the context of women wishing to enter into Islam in the latter years of Medina, after the treaty of Ḥudaybiya in 6/628, which is the background for Sūrat al-Mumtaḥana as a whole. The verse reads:

> Prophet, when believing women come and pledge to you that they will not ascribe any partner to God, nor steal, nor fornicate, nor kill their children, nor spread calumny all around (*lā yaʾtīna bi-buhtānin yaftarīnahu bayna aydīhinna wa-arjulihinna*),[2] nor disobey you in any righteous thing, then you should accept their pledge of allegiance and pray to God to forgive them: God is most forgiving and merciful.

Reports also record the Prophet requiring these statements from the women of the Anṣār after first arriving in Medina and also from those entering into Islam following the conquest of Mecca.[3] The prohibition of killing one's own children is directed to a specific custom of Arabians at the time,[4] while the impermissibility of murder should be assumed within the pledge. That the community of Muslims in Medina were to treat the injunctions not just as a moral code, but as a legally enforced one, too, is clear from prophetic commentary tied to the pledge itself.[5]

The name given to these offences and their punishments within early Hadith and jurisprudence is the *ḥudūd* (sing. *ḥadd*; boundaries), a word that is not used to describe them within the Qur'an, although it is found in the related general expression of 'God's moral boundaries'.[6] From a variety of hadiths, this category of offence is understood as characterised by a definite, prescribed punishment that cannot be waived by the authorities once it is brought to them with sufficient evidence.[7]

In the juristic tradition, a curious conceptual amalgamation seems to have taken place between the meaning of the *ḥadd* (boundary) of God and His *ḥaqq* (right), based on the idea that a *ḥadd* cannot be waived, because it is a special boundary set by God as His right. The problem with this idea is that there is no satisfactory explanation for why murder, acknowledged by the Qur'an as the most serious offence against a human being, should not contravene the 'right of God' according to this conception. Moreover, it would seem that there should be a justification for why some disruptions of the moral order transgress His right and others do not. Some commentators have recognised this problem and have tried to retain the distinction by associating God's rights with the rights of the community in general, while treating *qiṣāṣ* for murder as the right of the specific parties involved.[8] However, arguably this does not solve the problem, as what could be more a right of the community than punishing the violation of human life in its midst?

It would seem that any failure to meet a moral obligation impinges upon God's right to be obeyed. The distinctive aspect of the three crimes under consideration is rather that they transgress the private sphere of other individuals with respect to their property, chastity, and chaste reputation.[9] Within the Qur'anic system of corrective justice, the perpetrator of these crimes is called upon to repent, and, where possible, to make restitution, while the victim is called upon to forgive. Punishment is legislated only if such a resolution is not possible because the victim is not able to absolve the crime, or the perpetrator confesses wishing to demonstrate the extent of his or her repentance.[10]

Before analysing the three main prohibitions within the pledge for entry into the community of Muslims, it is worth mentioning that classical scholarship sometimes considers other crimes as *ḥudūd*. I have already discussed the Qur'anic discourse on *baghy* and *ḥirāba* in the previous chapter and have shown how a certain form of belligerent apostasy (*irtidād*) could be read as coming under the same heading. The only remaining topic would be the drinking of alcohol (*sharb*). However, this will be left aside, as the Qur'an does not legislate a punishment for it.

I. Thievery

The earliest reference to thievery (*sariqa*) within the Qur'an is found in the Meccan Sūrat Yūsuf. The passage Q. 12:69–87 deals with the events following the second of the four times that the Prophet Joseph's brothers present themselves before him (*dakhalū 'alayhi*). In this episode, Joseph plants the king's drinking cup within the bag of his brother Benjamin (who is not named within the Qur'an), so that he is able to keep him in Egypt. With the cup found and the brothers accused, events unfold as follows in Q. 12:73–6:

> They said, 'By God! You must know that we did not come to make mischief in your land: we are no thieves.' They asked them, 'And if we find that you are lying, what penalty shall we apply to you?' and they answered, 'The penalty will be [the enslavement of] the person in whose bag the cup is found: this is how we punish wrongdoers.' [Joseph] began by searching their bags, then his brother's, and he pulled it out from his brother's bag.

> In this way We devised a plan for Joseph – he could not have detained his brother as a penalty under the king's law, but rather God willed [him to be detained] (*mā kāna li-ya'khudha akhāhu fī dīni al-maliki illā an yashā'a allāh*).

The exchange between the officials and the brothers – in which the latter specify the punishment – as well as the divine commentary that follows, suggests that it was actually the *sharīʿa* followed by Jacob and his sons that mandated enslavement for the crime of theft, not the king's law.[11] This interpretation requires the grammatical restriction (*al-istithnā'*) in Q. 12:76 to be read as *munqaṭiʿ* (nullified), which means that it does not provide an exception to what precedes, but negates it entirely and provides an alternative: 'but rather God willed [him to be detained] (*illā an yashā'a allāh*)'.[12]

This is an instance of the principle of the 'personality of the law', common in antiquity, in which a person would be judged by their own law, based on tribe or religion, rather than one adhering to a particular territory.[13] Only by the divine wish did the officials invoke this principle, and the brothers reveal the appropriate penalty, making Benjamin's detainment possible.

This is also consistent with the retention of a similar punishment within the Torah, in Exodus 22:1–2:

> If the thief is discovered while tunnelling in [to the home], and he is struck and dies, there is no blood-guilt on his account. If the sun shone upon him [that is, it is clear he meant no physical harm], there is blood-guilt on his account. He shall make restitution; if he has nothing, he shall be sold for his theft.

After the cup is discovered, the brothers, mindful of their promise to their father Jacob not to lose Benjamin, implore Joseph to take one of them as a replacement in Q. 12:78. Joseph replies, 'God forbid that we should take anyone other than the person on whom we found our property (*illā man wajadnā matāʿanā*): that would be unjust of us' (Q. 12: 79).

Although the punishment of enslavement for theft is abrogated by the Qur'an, there is no reason to think that such is the case for the principle interdicting the transferral of liability for punishment, even if the other party is willing to do so. It can also be noted that Joseph uses very precise language in his answer, saying that it would be wrong to take other than the one on whom the property was found, rather than the one who stole. This is because the entire incident is a kind of legal stratagem in which the outward conditions of the law are met, in order to obtain a favoured outcome.[14]

Apart from within the story of Joseph, the crime of theft is only explicitly mentioned in the Qur'an twice. It occurs once in Q. 60:12, as quoted above, presumably with a discretionary punishment, and again in Q. 5:38 with the legislation of amputation. Although a hadith indicates that this latter penalty was applied by at least the Conquest of Mecca in 8/630, this may not be its earliest appearance.[15] A report from al-Kalbī mentions that the first person to have their hand amputated was a member of the Anṣār named (Abū) Ṭuʿma b. Ubayriq,[16] in an incident that possibly occurred between 6/627 and 7/628.[17]

Jurists have discussed the conditions required for a person to be considered a *sāriq* (thief) in the legal sense. They generally act to circumscribe the concept to the minimum number of possible offenders by requiring the stolen item to have been guarded and specifying a minimum value for it, treating these as ambiguous (*mujmal*) aspects requiring further explanation (*bayān*).[18] Abū Zahra provides an alternative to the classical view by arguing that the fact that the verse mentions 'the thief' is an indication that the punishment is only to be applied to the repeat offender who truly deserves this epithet.[19]

The rationale of the punishment, from the Qur'anic perspective, is reflected in the language of Q. 5:38:

> The male thief and the female thief, cut off their hands as a punishment for what they have earned – a deterrent from God: God is almighty and wise (*wa-l-sāriqu wa-l-sāriqatu fa-qṭaʿū aydiyahumā jazāʾan bi-mā kasabā nakālan min allāhi wa-llāhu ʿazīzun ḥakīm*).

The original signification of the verb *kasaba* is to collect something, especially wealth, from which the sense of earning a wage, and in the spiritual realm, a reward or punishment, is derived.[20] The verse plays on this meaning, so the thief is both punished for taking wealth, and requited for earning sin.

Grammatically, *jazāʾan* (as a punishment) is *manṣūb* (accusative) as *mafʿūl min ajli fa-qṭaʿū* (the object that occasions the command 'cut off').[21] Amputation of the hand is thus explained as mandated by the need to give an appropriate punishment for the crime. However, the *ḥikma* is provided by *nakālan*, which stands in an analogous relation to *jazāʾan*.[22] In other words, the specific punishment is in turn predicated, at least in its social dimension, on the existence of a deterrent function.

Q. 5:39 complements Q. 5:38, in characteristic Qur'anic fashion, by transcending strict punishment with the possibility of repentance to God. Some modern authors on this subject criticise their classical counterparts for ignoring this element of forgiveness in their interpretations of Qur'anic penalties[23] and argue that repentance implies the waiving of punishment.[24] However, divine forgiveness and moral rectification do not automatically imply social clemency for open theft. The point is that it is always possible, and indeed necessary, for an individual to repent to God after wrongdoing, and to reform. This is true for the one who hides their transgression, all the way to the other extreme of the one who hopes for expiation via punishment.

That Q. 5:39 concerns repentance prepared for the court of the Hereafter, rather than worldly leniency, is arguably supported by the next verse, Q. 5:40, 'Do you [Prophet] not know that control of the heavens and earth belongs solely to God? He punishes whoever He wills and forgives whoever He wills: God has power over everything.' There is also a hadith in which the Prophet prayed for the acceptance of a thief's repentance after the punishment was applied.[25]

If the import of Q. 5:38–9 within the life of the Medinan Muslim community is not that a person who genuinely regrets and seeks forgiveness after detention by the authorities is absolved from worldly punishment, then it highlights the concern for the criminal to repent sincerely to avoid the far more severe sanction of the Hereafter. This is based on the principle of *iḥsān* and internal *tazkiya*. In terms of justice, the word *nakālan* in Q. 5:38 highlights deterrance, while the use of *aslaḥa* in Q. 5:39 may also allude to compensation due to the victim.

In sum, the Qur'an encourages mutual reconciliation between members of society for private appropriation of wealth between them, as regulated by natural law. It is only when the issue cannot be resolved at this level that the punishment legislated within divine law is enacted. Thus, the underlying ethics, in which a victim has the choice to prosecute an infringement, or overlook it, is the same as in Chapter 12, although originating within the private rather than public sphere.

II. Fornication

The Qur'an's focus on marriage leads to moral, and eventually legal, penalties for illegitimate sexual relations. In the Meccan period, there are a number of verses that establish the basic principle, 'Stay well away from committing obscenities (*lā taqrabū al-fawāḥish*), whether openly or in secret' (Q. 6:151); 'Say, "My Lord only forbids disgraceful deeds (*al-fawāḥish*) – whether they be open or hidden"' (Q. 7:33); 'And do not go anywhere near adultery: it is an outrage, and an evil path (*lā taqrabū al-zinā innahu kāna fāḥishan wa-sā'a sabīlan*)' (Q. 17:32).

These verses, selected from three major Meccan lists of moral prohibitions, establish that *zinā* (fornication, or adultery within a marriage) is a particularly grave type of *fāḥisha* (pl. *fawāḥish*; lewd act, or obscenity). As expected in the earlier stage of revelation, the Qur'an couches the warning in terms of its otherworldly consequences, rather than any immediate societal sanction.

The Medinan phase was inaugurated with the pledges made at ʿAqaba, which included a commitment to refrain from *zinā*, carrying with it the acknowledgement of legislative force to come. The first substantive verses confirming this intention are Q. 4:15–16, which are associated with the period after Uḥud in 3–4/625–6:[26]

> If any of your women commit a lewd act (*fāḥisha*), call four witnesses from among you, then, if they testify to their guilt, keep the women at home until death comes to them or until God shows them another way. If two [men] commit a lewd act, punish them both (*fa-ādhūhumā*); if they repent and mend their ways, leave them alone – God is always ready to accept repentance, He is full of mercy.

There are are a number of ambiguities to be resolved in this passage: identification of who is referred to by 'your women (*nisā'ikum*)' in Q. 4:15 and by 'two [men] (*alladhāni*)' in Q. 4:16; the precise meaning of the offence, *fāḥisha*; and the nature of the punishment in both cases.

Contextually, it seems safe to assume that the provisions made in these verses represent an early stage of legislation with respect to matters of sexual conduct, to be supplemented by the more explicit provision of Q. 24:2–3. There is a textual indication to this in Q. 4:15, 'Or until God shows them another way (*aw yaj'ala allāḥu lahunna sabīlan*)', which indicates a future revision.[27] Although it is possible that 'your women' refers specifically to married women, it is perhaps more likely that the expression refers to the adult females of the community as a whole.

The fact that legislation is introduced at all, the requirement of four witnesses, and the severity of being kept 'at home until death comes', all point to *fāḥisha* in this passage as referring to *zinā*. The *ḥikma* of this injunction is then to prevent the harmful social consequences of extramarital sexual relations by restricting the physical movement of the women who were indulging in this for a temporary period of time, and effecting a change in their character, before a definitive punishment is introduced.

If Q. 4:15 gives an instruction to prevent all fornication within the community involving a woman, then Q. 4:16, with the relative pronoun *alladhāni*, is perhaps most coherently read as dealing with the only remaining possibility, that between two men. The requirement for four witnesses given in the previous verse can be treated as assumed, with the focus turning to the expression used for the sanction applied to the two men, *fa-ādhūhumā*, which could refer to verbal condemnation, or some kind of discretionary physical punishment.[28]

The place of repentance within these verses is consistent with the general Qur'anic pattern. In Q. 4:16, the possibility of repentance and reform is encapsulated in the phrase, 'If they repent and mend their ways, leave them alone (*fa-in tābā wa-aṣlaḥā fa-a'riḍū 'anhumā*).' The repeated use of the particle *fā'* indicates order, so the punishment is intended to trigger moral and spiritual rectification. If this occurs, then the perpetrators are to be left alone.[29] The verses Q. 4:17–18 emphasise the importance of swiftly seeking absolution from sin, while making clear that forgiveness remains open for all until right before death.

The fully developed stage of Qur'anic legislation on *zinā* is found in Q. 24:2. It is likely that this verse was revealed in 5/626–7, due to its connection with the calumny against the Prophet's wife 'Ā'isha after the raid on Banū Muṣṭaliq at al-Muraysī'.[30] This would perhaps date it to about two years after the previous provisions in Q. 4:15–16. Precise language is used to specify that the number of lashes is for both parties and not shared between them, 'Strike the fornicator and fornicatress one hundred times.'

There are two additional commands, both unusual in the context of Qur'anic sanction, 'Do not let compassion for them keep you from carrying out God's law – if you believe in God and the Last Day – and ensure that a group of believers witnesses the punishment.' The first of these could be explained as a response to any perception that *zinā*, at least in the case of an unmarried couple, is a victimless crime. The Qur'an strongly emphasises a moral code in which marriage between a man and woman is essential to regulate sexual relationships, especially in light of the interests of potential children.[31]

The second, a procedural element, adds social censure to the physical reprimand. Asad comments, 'The number of those to be present has been deliberately left unspecified, thus indicating that while the punishment must be given publicity, it need not be made a "public spectacle".'[32] On the contrary, it would seem that the fact that the crime is to be punished at all reflects it gaining a public status (or the culprits choosing to give it one through their confession). That the witnessing of a group of believers is specifically mentioned highlights the deterrent quality of such a spectacle.

Q. 24:3, in stating that 'the fornicator is only [fit] to marry a fornicatress or an idolatress' and vice versa, can be interpreted as a descriptive condemnation of the moral state of the male and female fornicators, rather than a prescriptive condition for the validity of their marriages.[33] Another opinion is that it is to be taken in its manifest sense, but represents a stage of legislation later abrogated by Q. 24:32, 'Marry off the single among you and those of your male and female slaves who are fit [for marriage].'[34]

There is no mention in the Qur'an of punishing married male and female adulterers by stoning them, although one hadith, on the authority of ʿUmar b. al-Khaṭṭāb, suggests that there was a Qur'anic verse legislating this punishment that was later abrogated in terms of recitation, but not practice.[35] Another possibility is to see this punishment, which is found in some hadiths,[36] as a remnant of the law of the Torah that was initially implemented by the Prophet Muḥammad before its abrogation by 100 lashes in Q. 24:2. Accordingly, a report indicates that early Muslim figures were unsure if the Prophet Muḥammad continued to carry out this punishment after the revelation of Sūrat al-Nūr.[37] Abū Zahra mentions that this view accords with some scholars from among the Khawārij, Shi'a, and Muʿtazila.[38]

Abū Zahra also makes his own argument for this position, based on part of Q. 4:25, that may be read as, 'Once [the bondswomen] are married (*fa-idhā uḥṣinna*), if they fornicate, their punishment (*ʿadhāb*) will be half that of a chaste [free] woman.' He proposes that it is not possible for stoning to be halved and therefore this verse implies that a married free woman who fornicates receives lashes.[39] I follow the canonical reciter al-Kisāʾī in suggesting that the more consistent rendering of this verse is, 'Once [the bondswomen] become chaste (*fa-idhā aḥṣanna*)', which reads both the verb *aḥṣanna* and the participle *al-muḥṣināt* (chaste women) in this verse as active, rather than passive constructions.[40] Such a reading, which leaves the question of stoning undecided, emphasises the importance of gradually socialising bondswomen into the sexual norms of the community by legislating a lighter punishment if they fail to meet this standard.[41] This process of 'becoming chaste' reflects the *ḥikma* of the punishment for *zinā* in the Qur'an, which is based in part on preserving knowledge of the child's paternity and lineage, as was repeatedly found in connection to the wife's *ʿidda* in Chapter 10.[42]

The punishment for fornication within the Qur'an is thus intended to prevent society becoming destabilised through the breakdown, or abandonment, of marriage leading to harm for future generations through the neglect of children. Furthermore, the embodiment of social rules within the community according to the Scale is conceived as existing in tandem with healthy souls. The just society is then achieved by the curb on the lustful tendencies within the self that the mere threat, or rare exemplary case, of punishment brings about, rather than by repressive force.

III. Slander

The final crime with a mandated Qur'anic punishment is that of a particular type of slander. The Qur'an, throughout its period of revelation, prohibits the spreading of injurious falsehoods. Thus, Q. 104:1, 'Woe to every slanderous fault-finder!' is held to be early to mid-Meccan,[43] while Q. 49:11–12, which includes a number of related cases, is very late Medinan, possibly dating to 9/630.[44] The slander in question, accusing chaste women of *zinā*, is known as *qadhf* within the juristic literature, although that name is not used in the Qur'an. It thus has an obvious connection with the discussion in the previous section. In fact, the need for this sanction comes precisely because of the severe consequences for someone who is convicted of *zinā*.

As the first part of Sūrat al-Nūr is devoted to this subject, it is appropriate to make some consideration of its *niẓām*. The first verse begins, '[This is] a sura We have sent down and made obligatory (*faraḍnāhā*): We have sent down clear revelations in it, so that you may take heed.' The phrase *faraḍnāhā* alludes to the focus on diverse obligations of social life, including the discussion of slander in Q. 24:4–26.

This sequence is split into three distinct passages, each with linguistic markers: the initial legislative section of Q. 24:4–9 is completed by the elided comment in Q. 24:10, 'If it were not for God's bounty and mercy towards you, if it were not that God accepts repentance and is wise!'[45] The next passage, Q. 24:11–20, is concerned with a moral commentary on the events surrounding the formulation and spread of the slander against the Prophet's wife ʿĀʾisha, providing a social context to the legislation of the first passage.[46] This concludes in Q. 24:20 with a second instance of ellipsis, 'If it were not for God's bounty and mercy and the fact that He is compassionate and merciful!' The third passage, Q. 24:21–6, starts with an address to believers as a whole and proceeds to summarise the general lessons to be learned from the incident, indicating the possibility of closure to the affair. Q. 24:26 concludes the sequence with a comment echoing the moral condemnation of *zinā* in Q. 24:3, which immediately preceded the discussion of slander.

Q. 24:4 legislates eighty lashes for accusing *muḥṣināt* (see comments above) of fornication without the proof of four witnesses. Joined to the physical punishment is the command to the community, 'you shall never accept their testimony again; such are the lawbreakers (*lā taqbalū lahum shahādatan abadan wa-ūlāʾika hum al-fāsiqūn*)'. The main controversy in interpretation is the subject of the exception made in the following verse, Q. 24:5, 'Except for those who repent later and make amends – God is most forgiving and merciful (*illā alladhīna tābū min baʿdi dhālika wa-aṣlaḥū fa-inna allāha ghafūrun raḥīmun*).' Shāfiʿīs argue that repentance allows the future acceptance of a person's testimony by treating the exception as grammatically applying to the order to reject the person's testimony. Contrary to this, Ḥanafīs understand it to operate only upon 'they are the lawbreakers', which they treat as a new grammatical sentence.[47]

Considering the system of punishment as a whole, there do not seem to be strong reasons for waiving these penalties for the credibility of witness. In the case of the punishment for *ḥirāba*, it will be recalled, there was an indication in the phrasing of Q. 5:34 that repentance has some bearing on the punishment inflicted, 'unless they repent before you overpower them – in that case bear in mind that God is forgiving and merciful'. This was related to the public nature of the crime and the opportunity for mutual reconciliation within society.[48]

Slander, like thievery and fornication, occurs at first behind closed doors within the close-knit society that the Qur'an immediately addresses. Only when necessary does it require the intervention of authorities; cases that reach this public level have already exhausted the route of personal forgiveness. Q. 24:5, in mentioning 'repenting later and making amends', closely mirrors the language used in relation to thievery in Q. 5:39 and fornication in Q. 4:16. As in both of these cases, repentance after public prosecution arguably does not waive any part of a culprit's worldly punishment.

Turning to the question of the punishment's *ḥikma*, the reference to *al-muḥṣināt* indicates the primary reason that this particular type of slander has a legal sanction beyond its moral repugnance. This is to ultimately protect the paternity of children through preservation of the reputation of chaste women, potentially present or future mothers, from claims not supported by undeniable evidence.

Q. 24:6–9 excuses the normally strict evidentiary requirements of four witnesses in cases of accusations of adultery by a husband against his wife. Instead, it is possible for the accuser to avoid receiving the punishment for slander if he is to take five oaths as mentioned in the verses, while his wife can avoid the punishment for adultery if she takes five oaths swearing to her innocence and her husband's dishonesty. The *ḥikma* of the legislation within these verses, usually known as *liʿān*, again returns primarily to the question of paternity and lineage. If a husband has good reason to believe that a child is not his, but is unable to provide corroborating evidence, he should not have to resign himself to becoming a cuckold. Instead, it is assumed that a spouse has intimate knowledge of his wife's behaviour and should be able to testify accordingly. Although this applies to adultery even in cases where there is no child involved, the underlying rationale is the rejection of present or future paternity in front of the community and relevant authorities.

However, as the consequences of adultery are very grave for the accused *muḥṣina*, she can declare her husband a liar, and, if she does so, then the one who has lied willingly faces punishment in the Hereafter, although the doubt waives any worldly sanction. At root, this procedure can be considered a mechanism for a husband to publicly express his concerns about paternity within marriage without necessarily exposing either spouse to punishment. Rather, the marriage would be dissolved as irreconcilable (the position of jurists being to mandate divorce in such a situation)[49] and the matter of fidelity left to God's perfect knowledge.

Finally, the eschatological justice experienced by those who participate in the type of slander discussed in this sequence is described with particular appropriateness by self-incrimination with their body parts in Q. 24:24, 'the Day when their own tongues, hands, and feet will testify against them about what they have done'.

In sum, with its primary focus on repentance and conciliation, Qur'anic corrective justice in its worldly manifestation is meant to restore a corrupted society back to the natural Scale of morality in this world and lead to God sparing the human being from stricture in His judgement. Where such a high objective cannot be met, then at least further transgressions can be prevented through the deterrence engendered by the Qur'an's specific punishments. Although the penalties involved are severe, they are embedded within a matrix of specific *ḥikma*s from which they derive their social and moral meaning.

Conclusion

In this book, I have sought to build up a picture of the scripture's moral vision by organising the substantial Qur'anic material relating to the just society according to theme and interpreting it consistently. I have utilised a distinctive theological frame for this thematic reading, one that I argue can be justified from within the Qur'an's own world view. I intend this concluding statement to serve two functions. The first is to present a summary of the key findings in each of the main thematic areas of social justice, insofar as they fit within the underlying moral framework that I have identified and cohere as a single system of ethics. The second is to forward some exploratory reflections about future directions.

The Qur'an sets the establishment of justice within society as a central goal of human life, yet inextricably links it with the inward quest to be true to the spiritual covenant with one's Creator. Here, then, is a moral teleology to which the normative function of the *sharīʿa*, the divine law and moral code, is directed. If human beings, by virtue of their intelligence and free will, are able to despoil the world, so too are they called to act as its stewards. The guidance delivered through revelation, whether in the form of commandments, prohibitions, or recommendations, is not merely to test the obedience of moral agents, but to embed wise purposes (*ḥikma*s) within the life of the wider community. Based on this understanding, societal justice (*qisṭ*) is the condition of society realised by the Wisdom (*ḥikma*) of God's Writ (*kitāb*), which matches the Scale (*mīzān*) of moral value.

This supports a neo-Māturīdī natural law reading of the Qur'an, in which a moral realist position is derived from God's eternal wisdom. Within this framework, the human *fiṭra* can access basic norms of morality through reflection upon experience. A conclusion is that belief in God and natural justice are incumbent upon those who may lack, or reject, a specific scripture, as well as those who accept it and are additionally bound by its injunctions. God's wisdom to create goodness within the world in the form of *ḥikma*s, therefore, acts as the cause for the binding obligation of moral rules, some of which are further socially enforced by human communities as law. Justice in this broad sense emerges as the worldly target that all ethical action aims towards, even as those same practices have a corresponding internal purpose of self-purification.

In my attempt to characterise the macro-structure of societal justice in the Qur'an, I have fallen back on the classical model of three interrelated spheres: political, distributive, and corrective. Thus, political justice, concerned primarily with the legitimisation of authority and the power relationships between individuals and groups, has significant bearing on both the distribution of society's resources and roles, as well as the regulation of its judicial function.

I have argued that the Qur'anic conception of legitimate political authority is predicated on the idea of the morally responsible human being as a *khalīfa*, or steward, within the world. The Qur'an calls for not only leaders, but human beings at all levels of social power and influence to play their individual part in establishing justice. At the collective level, this ideally leads to a political order in which justice is established on the basis of the natural law – revealed legislation represents the means by which God provides additional help to humanity. On this reading of the Qur'anic view, the assumed initial state of nature was not inevitably lawless, but at least potentially harmonious, with human *fiṭra* allowing political actors to govern, and be governed, according to the dictates of the Scale.

Thus, within and beyond the voluntary and intentional community of Muslims, the Qur'an acknowledges the existential choice to believe and to belong accordingly. The Qur'an tells us that humanity was once a single community – its fracture part of God's trials. Perhaps we may add that as the fragments come back together, they may complement one another like a mosaic, or clash like an assortment of broken glass. Understanding the scripture as affirming real moral values within the world means that a vision of justice based upon natural law can be held in common between those who believe in its message and those who do not. When either party transgresses the standards of this natural justice, they are to be corrected.

The Qur'an acknowledges that God does not share out power between nations equally and these differentials, combined with human imperfection and frequent corruption, account for the messy variety of political life. Based on the above comments about the state of nature, I have argued that, for the Muslim community, peace is to be the initial basis for the relationship with other communities and a refuge from conflict. Therefore, the duty of stewardship never implies domination and tyranny over those who differ in belief and commitments, although it may well require courage in standing against those who do not tolerate difference and choose to despoil the earth. Repurposing a famous apocryphal hadith, one can suggest that although the greatest jihad is to plant *ʿadl*, and above that *iḥsān*, within the inner heart, the fruit of these qualities is establishing *qisṭ* within society.

A corollary to this is that the moral logic of political strength is to provide security to those who need it, just as weakness obliges one to seek protection. The defence of those places where God is praised, such as monastery, church, synagogue, or mosque, as well as the fight for freedom of religion and justice itself, also means standing in alliance with those of other traditions when they are in common cause. Moreover, stewardship of the earth must be understood in the sense of keeping the relationship between human beings and the rest of creation balanced on the Scale. Although human beings may feel that they have a power at their disposal akin to Solomon, they must make sure not to tread upon the ants.

Even with an idealised political order, let alone without, society is never static. Any just society must regulate the reciprocal networks of people and their shifting wealth and relationships throughout their lifespans as they transact, give, receive, marry, have children, divorce, widow, bequeath, and inherit.

It is not hidden from the observer of human society that there is a basic conflict between the principle of distributing goods according to individual merit and doing so to reduce inequality among all social actors. In fact, these two divergent conceptions also embody, at their extremes, opposing philosophies of political economy. The first privileges personal, or collective, profit at the expense of other members of society, or the natural world. The second manages the economy with the intention of providing equal wealth, or goods, to all. The Qur'an aims to resolve this tension by affirming the right to individual wealth and its acquisition through voluntary contracts, while restricting the kind of profit that may be accrued through them. Natural law mandates a responsibility to not only trade fairly, but to treat wealth as a trust to be redistributed to those in need. Just as the prohibition of *ribā* intends to prevent the increase of inequality through unearned gain, the institution of *zakāt* as a tax on wealth, not earnings, works to actively decrease it. This means that, like the power often emerging from it, wealth is to ebb and flow fairly around the social world and between generations. Within the world view of the Qur'an, today's slave is tomorrow's sultan.

Human beings continue their civilisations beyond the lifetime of any single person through their children. Marriage regulates reproduction and is meant to provide an ideal environment for love, caring, and growth, both inward and outward. The Qur'an recognises gender differences, enshrining motherhood and fatherhood as the most important purposes of marriage upon which its laws are founded. In this arena, the Qur'an places particular emphasis on the ability of human beings to intuitively realise appropriate moral behaviour within the context of their own situations and societies. Likewise, inheritance and the idea of generational justice are also dependent on the family structure and the particular characteristics of the roles and responsibilities therein.

There is a tension between punishment and reform within any system of law. The Qur'an situates its understanding of the worldly enforcement of fundamental social norms in such a way that the eternal consequences of the Day of Judgement cannot be ignored. Human beings, called upon to act as responsible stewards of God within the world, are given the chance to repent for their wrongdoings and seek forgiveness from the victims of their crimes, before being held to account in the court of the Hereafter. Disruptions to the Scale can be corrected, if not through forgiveness and repentance, then deterrence and compensation.

In the Qur'an, every crime for which a punishment is stipulated allows the perpetrator an opportunity to reform – not after punishment, but before it so that punitive action can be waived entirely if the crime's victims are satisfied that the repentance was sincere. Procedurally, crimes within the public sphere that threaten the lives of members of the community are not the same as those that transgress private boundaries. This distinction, rather than a divvying up of rights between humanity and the divine, intends to ensure that principles of mercy are balanced with those of justice.

If the above comments summarise some of the major synchronic aspects of Qur'anic societal justice as a coherent theme, what can be said of its development over the period of revelation? The answer is a pattern that is not entirely unexpected, although remarkably consistent, within all three major spheres of justice. Strictly moral injunctions in Mecca, often framed within narratives, are given more detailed forms within Medina and in many cases become enforceable through communal authority structures, rather than individual conscience alone. In a smaller number of cases, earlier rules seem to replace rather than specify later ones, such that the theory of *naskh* can be fruitfully invoked.

At an earlier juncture in this book, the question of setting the boundary line to distinguish between natural and divine law was deferred.[1] It is clear that Meccan moral injunctions are typically addressed to a broad audience, including those who do not accept the prophethood of Muḥammad, and that more detailed aspects of the Law are not revealed until the community of believers is constituted in Medina. This leads to the conclusion that, with the possible exception of certain ritual devotions, the message of the Meccan Qur'an can be read as pointing its audience to follow natural law – a morality of which they are expected to be aware – while the Medinan Qur'an provides the further elements of divine law.

Exploring the Qur'an and attempting to understand its deep ethical structure sends me back full circle to the initial hermeneutic question concerning what constitutes a genuine interpretation of a scripture revealed more than 1,400 years ago. Even as I attempt to reconstruct the principles of societal justice in the lives of the Qur'an's first recipients, I do not think of my interpretation as ultimately more than a conceptual model. Thus, I am not sure that we can draw a concrete distinction between a recoverable 'original' meaning and our 'contemporary' one. What is the exegetical tradition except a succession of scholars reinterpreting the meanings of scripture in light of their own horizons? As we move upon the timeline of history, we fuse previous understandings within our current moment.[2] In practical terms, this is reflected in the endless borrowings of the *tafsīr* genre. Again, this is not to relativise all interpretations as equally valid. Faced with multiple exegetical possibilities, I incline towards a fallibilist position: although perhaps only a single view may be true, we are limited in our ability to identify it, let alone to justify it to others on rational grounds.[3]

This observation leads to the point that exegesis, just like any systematic intellectual enquiry according to Alasdair MacIntyre, must take place within the framework of a tradition of thought.[4] I use the term neo-Māturīdism to describe the particular perspective within which I have attempted to work. In this, I draw heavily on foundational principles from the system of al-Māturīdī and to a lesser extent the school tradition that takes his name, while constructively blending this with numerous other sources. For this project, I have borrowed from an eclectic range of classical Islamic texts, as well as thoroughly situating my work within various domains of contemporary thought, centred on the academic discipline of Islamic studies.

As has been suggested in Chapter 2, the idea of neo-Māturīdism requires further work to emerge as a contemporary perspective. The main lines of research can be sketched as follows: a deeper meta-theory characterising it as a tradition of enquiry in the MacIntyrean sense, engagement with modern work in metaphysics and epistemology, a full philosophical treatment of the natural law ethical theory proposed within the present book and an attendant exploration of political philosophy and legal theory. Finally, it may be possible to attempt a practical application of this perspective to concrete modern theological and ethico-legal questions. It is my hope that through sustained careful work of this kind, a distinctive Qur'anic vision of the just society can be adequately represented in the complexity of the contemporary world.

Notes

Epigraph and Introduction

i. Q. 55:9.
ii. Bloom, *The Republic*, p. 45.
1. Bloom, *The Republic*.
2. Aristotle, *The Nicomachean Ethics*, p. 69; Sherif, *Ghazali's Theory of Virtue*, p. 72.
3. See page 19.
4. Khadduri, *The Islamic Conception of Justice*, pp. 8–10.
5. Fakhry, *Ethical Theories*, pp. 11–21.
6. For example, see Donaldson, *Studies in Muslim Ethics*, pp. 23–4.
7. Izutsu, *Ethico-Religious Concepts in the Qur'an*, pp. 209–11. Cf. Al-Shamma, *The Ethical System Underlying the Qur'an*, pp. 121–7.
8. Rahman, *Major Themes of the Qur'an*, pp. 25–44.
9. Hallaq, 'Qur'ānic Constitutionalism and Moral Governmentality', p. 48.
10. Kamali, *Freedom, Equality and Justice*, p. 103.
11. Khadduri, *The Islamic Conception of Justice*, p. 1.
12. Gericke, 'Platonic Justice for the New Millenium?', p. 132.
13. Neuwirth, *Scripture, Poetry and the Making of Community*, p. xxiv.
14. Fakhry, *Ethical Theories*, p. 1.
15. I note that some recent scholarship argues that it is more meaningful to understand the early followers of the Prophet Muḥammad as a loose group of 'believers' rather than Muslims, although I do not find this position compelling and, in any case, the theological nature of my project provides leeway to bypass it. See Donner, *Muhammad and the Believers*, pp. 57–8; Al-Azmeh, *Emergence*, pp. 361–5.
16. Hallaq, 'Groundwork of the Moral Law', p. 259.
17. See Hallaq, 'Groundwork of the Moral Law', pp. 270–1. Despite his reservations, Hallaq concedes that our discussion of the Qur'an in terms of a moral–legal dichotomy is unavoidable. Hallaq, 'Groundwork of the Moral Law', p. 259.
18. Rahman, *Islam and Modernity*, pp. 6–7.
19. Saeed, 'Fazlur Rahman', p. 53.
20. Saeed, *Interpreting the Qur'an*, pp. 150–2.
21. Gadamer, *Truth and Method*, pp. 313–15.
22. Auda, *Maqāṣid al-Sharī'ah*, pp. 45–6.
23. See MacIntyre, 'A Partial Response to My Critics', p. 295; MacIntyre, *The Tasks of Philosophy*, pp. 52–73.
24. Smith, 'The True Meaning of Scripture', p. 504.
25. See the use of this narrative by al-Jaṣṣāṣ, *Al-Fuṣūl*, vol. 4, pp. 140–1.
26. Al-Khālidī, *Al-Tafsīr al-mawḍū'ī*, pp. 54–6. Hassan Hanafi's article on thematic exegesis, although having some useful observations, circumscribes the genre to a narrower ambit than it deserves. Hanafi, 'Method of Thematic Interpretation', pp. 195–211.
27. Audi (ed.), *The Cambridge Dictionary of Philosophy*, pp. 377–8.
28. Kamali, *Freedom, Equality and Justice*, pp. 105–6.

Chapter 1

1. ʿAbd al-Bāqī, *Al-Muʿjam al-mufahras*, pp. 262–4. See page 24.
2. Ibn Manẓūr, *Lisān*, vol. 2, p. 951.
3. Ibn Manẓūr, *Lisān*, vol. 2, p. 953.
4. Al-Iṣfahānī, *Mufradāt*, p. 175.
5. Al-Alūsī, *Rūḥ al-maʿānī*, vol. 27, p. 21.
6. See Wolterstorff, *Justice*, p. 282.
7. This reading is close to the Māturīdī view of the inconceivability of ascribing certain actions to God on the grounds of their conflict with His eternal wisdom. The Ashʿarīs, highlighting God's attribute of will ahead of that of wisdom, argue that nothing constrains the decision of God, although He has no need to change from the commitments He chooses to make. See the discussion in Chapter 2.
8. See pages 24–5.
9. Cf. Q. 6:12.
10. An oft-quoted hadith makes clear that although justice is guaranteed, it is only God's mercy that allows the ultimate success of entering Paradise. Al-Bukhārī, *Ṣaḥīḥ*, vol. 3, p. 1,177.
11. Cf. 16:90 and see pages 2 and 17.
12. Klein, 'Call, Covenant, and Community', p. 125.
13. This is possibly a better translation than the alternative rendering 'about their souls', as the word *ẓuhūr* (loins, lit. backs) seems to indicate physical bodies. In any case, the implication is that they possessed intellect. Al-Suyūṭī and al-Maḥallī, *Tafsīr*, p. 173.
14. Al-Qāḍī, 'The Primordial Covenant', p. 336.
15. The Qur'an does not explicitly mention the place of the Prophet Muḥammad in this context, yet there is a significant strand of Islamic tradition that asserts that his soul was the primordial light and first creation, based on Hadith and *sīra* literature. Ernst, 'Muḥammad as the Pole of Existence', pp. 123–4. Qur'anic verses are sometimes interpreted in this regard, for instance, Q. 21:107, 'We did not send you except as a mercy for all the worlds (*raḥmatan li-l-ʿālamīn*).' Al-Alūsī, *Rūḥ al-maʿānī*, vol. 17, p. 105.
16. Al-Māturīdī, *Taʾwīlāt*, vol. 6, pp. 106–7. For more discussion of this concept, see page 14.
17. See al-Attas, *Prolegomena*, p. 46. Cf. Al-Iṣfahānī, *Mufradāt*, p. 335.
18. This kind of *muqaddam* (preposition) and *muʾakkhar* (postposition) of words in the Qur'an is discussed by al-Suyūṭī, *Al-Itqān*, vol. 3, p. 36. See page 90. There is an alternative reading of *khalīqatan* (creation) instead of *khalīfatan* on the authority of Zayd b. ʿAlī and Abū Ibrāhīm. Al-Ḥalabī, *Al-Durr*, vol. 1, p. 253. This is not a well-known reading and is precluded by the similar wording of Q. 38:26, where it would make little sense.
19. Abū Suʿūd, *Irshād*, vol. 1, p. 142.
20. See Al-Qāḍī, 'The Term "Khalīfa"', pp. 398–404.
21. Al-Iṣfahānī, *Mufradāt*, p. 212.
22. Al-Rāzī, *Al-Tafsīr al-kabīr*, vol. 2, p. 165.
23. Abū Suʿūd, *Irshād*, vol. 1, p. 142.
24. For discussion of the political implications of stewardship, see Chapter 5.
25. Some early exegetes suggest that jinn had previously been placed upon the earth and that the angels' judgement is based on their conduct. Al-Ṭabarī, *Tafsīr*, vol. 1, p. 500.
26. Cf. Al-Rāzī, *Al-Tafsīr al-kabīr*, vol. 2, p. 166–74.
27. Al-Nasafī, *Madārik*, p. 45. See Q. 2:38.
28. Early Muslims differed over whether the Devil, mentioned as a jinn, belonged to a specific category of angel, or a separate class of creation altogether. Al-Ṭabarī, *Tafsīr*, vol. 1, pp. 535–41.
29. Al-Māturīdī, *Taʾwīlāt*, vol. 1, p. 107.
30. This was also the conclusion reached by al-Māturīdī who interprets Q. 54:49, 'We have created all things in due measure (*bi-qadar*)', as first and foremost their value of either good (*khayr*) or evil (*sharr*). Al-Māturīdī, *Kitāb al-tawḥīd*, p. 396. Cf. Frank, 'Notes and Remarks on the Ṭabāʾiʿ', pp. 143–5. A number of modern commentators concur with this assessment of the Qur'an's metaethical view. See Hourani, *Reason and Tradition*, pp. 30–1; Nasr, *Religion and the Order of Nature*, pp. 60–1; Hallaq, 'Groundwork of the Moral Law', pp. 259–62; Reinhart, *Before Revelation*, p. 38. Cf. Al-Ashʿarī, *Kitāb al-lumaʿ*, p. 117.
31. Al-Māturīdī, *Taʾwīlāt*, vol. 4, p. 257.

32. Al-Iṣfahānī, *Mufradāt*, pp. 675-6.
33. See Reinhart, 'Ethics and the Qur'ān'.
34. See Daiber, *The Islamic Concept of Belief*, p. 169; Al-Māturīdī, *Kitāb al-tawḥīd*, p. 301. Cf. Al-Bayḍāwī, *Anwār*, vol. 2, p. 221.
35. Lumbard, 'Covenant and Covenants', p. 11.
36. David Burrell has argued that the state of Arabia before the arrival of the Qur'an can be considered an analogue to the fallen condition before Christ. Burrell, 'A Philosophical-Theologian's Journey', pp. 60–1. This point ignores the acceptance of Adam's repentance in Q. 2:37. It is also difficult to square with either the natural law interpretation of ethics favoured in this book, in which human beings are contingently, not necessarily, in a fallen state before revelation, or a voluntaristic one in which they are not liable for punishment until receiving a new message.
37. Cf. Al-Qāḍī, 'The Primordial Covenant', p. 336.
38. Hourani, *Reason and Tradition*, p. 45.
39. Reinhart, *Before Revelation*, pp. 7–8.
40. For a summary of the former view, see al-Ṭūfī, *Dar'*, pp. 82–3. The latter is expressed in al-Māturīdī, *Ta'wīlāt*, vol. 8, pp. 243–4.
41. Hourani, *Reason and Tradition*, p. 26.
42. Another verse that possibly suggests an internal ability to determine some aspects of right and wrong is Q. 91:7–8, 'The soul and what shaped it: so he inspired it with its disobedience and its piety (*fa-alhamahā fujūrahā wa-taqwāhā*).' Draz, *The Moral World of the Qur'an*, p. 245. See page 37.
43. This seems to directly contrast with a group mentioned in Q. 3:21, 'Those who disbelieve in the signs of God, kill the prophets without right, and kill those among humanity who command justice (*qisṭ*).' Based on the characteristics mentioned in the verse, as well as the surrounding passage, the reference is almost certainly to members of the Children of Israel.
44. See page 142.
45. A word used almost synonymously with *sharī'a* is *shir'a*, which is found in Q. 5:48.
46. Lane, *Lexicon*, vol. 2, p. 1,535.
47. Hallaq, 'Groundwork of the Moral Law', pp. 256–9.
48. This is in response to the prayer of the Prophet Abraham in the earlier verse Q. 2:129, 'Our Lord, raise up amongst them a messenger from them.' Cf. Q. 62:2, 3:164, and 4:113.
49. See the *taḥaddī* (challenging) verses, which Boullata argues can be placed in chronological order, as follows: Q. 52:33–4, 11:13, 10:38, 17:88, 2:23–4. Boullata, 'Rhetorical Interpretation', p. 140.
50. Cf. Q. 13:11, 8:53, and 91:9–10.
51. Madigan, *The Qur'ān's Self-Image*, p. 213.
52. See Cragg, *A Certain Sympathy of Scriptures*, p. 124.
53. Cf. Q. 2:178 and 2:216.
54. Ibn Manẓūr, *Lisān*, vol. 5, p. 3,817.
55. See page 157.
56. Madigan, *The Qur'ān's Self-Image*, p. 177.
57. See page 148.
58. Madigan, *The Qur'ān's Self-Image*, p. 173.
59. Madigan, *The Qur'ān's Self-Image*, pp. 177–8.
60. Al-Suyūṭī and al-Maḥallī, *Tafsīr*, p. 23.
61. Al-Nasafī, *Madārik*, p. 87.
62. Cf. Q. 33:34.
63. Al-Ḥalabī counts twenty-four points to which it refers. Al-Ḥalabī, *Al-Durr*, vol. 7, p. 357.
64. See page 172.
65. Hallaq, 'Qur'ānic Constitutionalism and Moral Governmentality', p. 16.
66. Al-Farāhī, *Mufradāt*, p. 175.
67. Al-Shāfi'ī, *Al-Risāla*, p. 78; Lowry, 'Early Islamic Exegesis', pp. 143–5.
68. MacIntyre, *After Virtue*, pp. 150–2. *Ḥikma* as it relates to the link between rules and their virtuous application can be compared to the Greek ethical concept of *phronesis* (practical wisdom). Taylor, 'Justice after Virtue', pp. 28–9. There is also a communal dimension to this idea, see Denny, 'Ethics and the Qur'ān', pp. 108–9.

69. Equity has a root in the word *aequus*, of unknown origin, meaning 'even', 'just', 'equal'. Barnhart (ed.), *Chambers Dictionary of Etymology*, p. 338. See also Khadduri, *The Islamic Conception of Justice*, p. 7.
70. Lane, *Lexicon*, vol. 2, p. 1,972. See Q. 4:3 and 4:128.
71. Ibn Manẓūr, *Lisān*, vol. 4, p. 2,838. See Q. 4:58.
72. Ibn Manẓūr, *Lisān*, vol. 4, p. 2,838. See Q. 6:152.
73. Badawi and Abdel Haleem, *Dictionary*, p. 605. See Q. 82:7, in which the reading *ʿadalaka* reflects the definition given above, but *ʿadallaka* means, 'He straightened you and made you proportionate, balanced in creation.' Ibn Manẓūr, *Lisān*, vol. 4, p. 2,840.
74. Badawi and Abdel Haleem, *Dictionary*, p. 605; Lane, *Lexicon*, vol. 2, p. 1,972. See Q. 6:70.
75. Badawi and Abdel Haleem, *Dictionary*, p. 605; Lane, *Lexicon*, vol. 2, p. 1,972. See Q. 27:60.
76. Ibn Manẓūr, *Lisān*, vol. 4, p. 2,839; Lane, *Lexicon*, vol. 2, p. 1,973. See Q. 6:18.
77. Lane, *Lexicon*, vol. 2, p. 1,974.
78. Al-Attas, *Islām and Secularism*, p. 76.
79. Al-Rāzī, *Mukhtār al-ṣiḥāḥ*, pp. 176, 223.
80. Al-Aṣfahānī, *Mufradāt*, pp. 401–2; Ibn Manẓūr, *Lisān*, vol. 4, p. 2,756.
81. Although technically *iṣlāḥ* is the proper antonym of *fasād*. See page 9.
82. Lane, *Lexicon*, vol. 2, p. 2,522.
83. Ibn Manẓūr, *Lisān*, vol. 5, p. 3,626.
84. Al-Iṣfahānī, *Mufradāt*, p. 511.
85. Lane, *Lexicon*, vol. 2, p. 2,523.
86. The word *qisṭās*, meaning 'scale' or 'balance', is found in Q. 17:35 and 26:182. The weight of scholarly opinion, classical and modern, is that it is a foreign loan word, rather than a derivation from *qisṭ*. Jeffery, *Foreign Vocabulary*, pp. 238–9.
87. Dāwūd, *Muʿjam*, p. 341.
88. Ibn Manẓūr, *Lisān*, vol. 5, pp. 3,626–7.
89. This construction showcases the polysemy of the verb *ʿadala*, as it can also be interpreted as 'Refrain from following your own desire and thereby deviating from the truth'. Al-Zamakhsharī, *Al-Kashshāf*, p. 265.
90. Also see Q. 3:18, 'God bears witness that there is no god but He, as do the angels and people of knowledge, upholding justice (*shahida allāhu annahu lā ilāha illa huwa wa-l-malāʾikatu wa-ūlū al-ʿilmi qāʾiman bi-l-qisṭ*).' This verse can be read in several ways, including that, for people of knowledge, witnessing the unicity of God carries with it a duty to uphold justice among His creation.
91. The two terms are also used in Q. 4:3 and 4:127. See pages 162–4.
92. Al-Rāzī, *Al-Tafsīr al-kabīr*, vol. 28, p. 129.
93. Ibn al-ʿArabī, *Aḥkām*, vol. 4, p. 1785. See page 105.
94. Al-Attas, *Prolegomena*, pp. 42–4.
95. Al-Attas, *Prolegomena*, p. 44.
96. Q. 2:143, 16:89, 22:78, and 10:47.
97. Al-Alūsī, *Rūḥ al-maʿānī*, vol. 1, p. 218.
98. Cf. Q. 60:4, 'You have a good example (*uswatun ḥasanatun*) in Abraham and his companions.'
99. Al-Ṭabarī, *Tafsīr*, vol. 11, p. 423.
100. See Sayyid Quṭb, *Fī ẓilāl al-qurʾān*, vol. 3, p. 1,644; Al-Mehri (ed.), *The Qurʾān*, p. 160; Al-Hilālī and Khan, *The Noble Qurʾan*, p. 249. It is also present as an opinion in classical works, see al-Suyūṭī and al-Maḥallī, *Tafsīr*, p. 192; Al-Māturīdī, *Taʾwīlāt*, vol. 6, p. 350.
101. There is a fairly tenuous attempt at a explanation of this in al-Māturīdī, *Taʾwīlāt*, vol. 6, p. 350.
102. See page 151.
103. Al-Ghazālī, *The Remembrance of Death*, pp. 124–5. Cf. Q. 50:22.
104. See earlier in the same sura, Q. 10:4, '[God] originates creation, then repeats it to reward with justice (*bi-l-qisṭ*) those who believe and do good deeds.'
105. Fakhry, *Ethical Theories*, pp. 14–17. Cf. O'Shaughnessy, 'Creation with Wisdom', p. 208.
106. Cf. Q. 11:45. Note that the name al-Ḥakam is found in the familiar list of ninety-nine names, along with al-Ḥakīm, al-ʿAdl and al-Muqsiṭ. Al-Tirmidhī expresses doubts about the authenticity of the list, although not the first part of the hadith encouraging learning God's Names. Al-Tirmidhī, *Sunan*, vol. 2, pp. 899–900.

107. M. A. S. Abdel Haleem, 'The Qur'an: Language, Style and Translation into English' (Lecture, School of Oriental and African Studies, London, 6 January 2009). See Q. 31:8–9, 40:8, 5:117–18, 4:56, and 4:111.
108. Rahbar, *God of Justice*, pp. 22–4.
109. Izutsu, *Ethico-Religious Concepts*, p. 165.
110. Hallaq, 'Qur'ānic Constitutionalism and Moral Governmentality', p. 15.
111. Izutsu, *Ethico-Religious Concepts*, p. 165.
112. Al-Māturīdī, *Ta'wīlāt*, vol 9, p. 288.
113. Cf. Al-Samarqandī, *Al-'Ālim wa-l-muta'allim*, pp. 16–18.
114. Al-Māturīdī, *Kitāb al-tawḥīd*, pp. 419–20.

Chapter 2

1. Heidegger, *An Introduction to Metaphysics*, pp. 7–8.
2. Ward, *Religion and Creation*, p. 196. The argument from necessity for the existence of God is most famously put by Ibn Sīnā. Lizzini, 'Ibn Sina's Metaphysics'.
3. See page 9.
4. Milton, *Paradise Lost*, p. 4.
5. Interestingly, H. M. al-Shāfi'ī also puts the Māturīdīs closer than any of the other major theological schools of Islam to the 'Qur'anic position'. Abdel Haleem, 'Early *Kalām*', p. 83.
6. Gerson, 'Plotinus'.
7. Germann, 'Al-Farabi's Philosophy of Society and Religion'.
8. Torchia, Creatio ex nihilo, pp. xiii–xiv; Wildberg, 'John Philoponus'.
9. Gimaret, 'Mu'tazila'.
10. Hinds, 'Miḥna'.
11. Gimaret, 'Mu'tazila'.
12. Al-Juwaynī, *Al-Shāmil*, pp. 134–5.
13. Frank, 'Notes and Remarks on the Ṭabā'i'', p. 145; Rozenthal, *Knowledge Triumphant*, pp. 35–40.
14. He uses the term *dalālat al-shāhid 'alā al-ghā'ib*. Al-Māturīdī, *Kitāb al-tawḥīd*, p. 92. See Rudolph, *Al-Māturīdī and the Development of Sunnī Theology*, pp. 281–2. However, he rejects using this principle to arrive at the eternality of the world, or the modality (*kayfiyya*) and quiddity (*mā'iyya*) of God. Al-Māturīdī, *Kitāb al-tawḥīd*, p. 93. Cerić, *Roots of Synthetic Theology in Islam*, pp. 102–5.
15. Al-Māturīdī, *Kitāb al-tawḥīd*, p. 167.
16. Al-Māturīdī, *Kitāb al-tawḥīd*, pp. 192–3; Shaykhzāde, *Kitāb naẓm al-farā'id*, p. 28; Al-Bayāḍī, *Ishārāt*, p. 37.
17. Pessagno, 'Uses of Evil', p. 63.
18. Al-Māturīdī, *Kitāb al-tawḥīd*, p. 110. Erkan M. Kurt argues that al-Māturīdī's understanding of *takwīn* as an eternal attribute is incoherent, because it denies temporality to God's acts of creation. He thus sides in his reckoning with the Karrāmiyya, Ibn Taymiyya, and some Sufis by introducing temporality into the divine will and creativity. Kurt, *Creation: The Principle of Nature in Islamic Metaphysics*, pp. 59–60, 69–71. For a statement about al-Māturīdī's understanding of God's absolute eternality, see Rudolph, *Al-Māturīdī and the Development of Sunnī Theology*, p. 287.
19. Arguably the closest that any of the Mu'tazila came to formally acknowledging attributes was Abū Hāshim and his doctrine of modes (*aḥwāl*). According to this theory, which can be considered a development of standard Mu'tazilī doctrine, God's knowledge, for instance, merely refers to God's essence when in the 'mode' of knowing. This mode, however, was something imputed by the human mind and not a genuine property, or individuation of the divine essence. Gardet, 'Al-Djubbā'ī'. See Thiele, 'Abū Hāshim al-Jubbā'ī's (d. 321/933) Theory of "States" (aḥwāl)'.
20. Al-Māturīdī, *Kitāb al-tawḥīd*, p. 193.
21. Al-Māturīdī, *Kitāb al-tawḥīd*, p. 297.
22. This is a technical term for al-Māturīdī, implying giving one or more non-definitive interpretive meanings to higher realities. See Galli, 'Some Aspects', pp. 4–5.
23. Al-Māturīdī, *Kitāb al-tawḥīd*, p. 164. Cf. pp. 108, 192; Al-Māturīdī, *Ta'wīlāt*, vol. 5, p. 107.
24. See page 20.

25. Rudolph, *Al-Māturīdī and the Development of Sunnī Theology*, p. 299; Jackson, *Islam and the Problem of Black Suffering*, p. 112.
26. Al-Māturīdī, *Kitāb al-tawḥīd*, p. 395.
27. Al-Māturīdī, *Kitāb al-tawḥīd*, p. 395.
28. Al-Māturīdī, *Kitāb al-tawḥīd*, p. 113. Cf. Q. 36:82.
29. A comparison can be made to Augustine's idea of divine wisdom (*divina sapientia*). Crowe, *The Changing Profile of the Natural Law*, p. 64.
30. Jackson, *Islam and the Problem of Black Suffering*, p. 113.
31. Al-Bāqillānī, *Kitāb al-tamhīd*, pp. 262–3.
32. Frank, 'Currents and Countercurrents', p. 122. See page 34.
33. Al-Rāzī, *Muḥaṣṣal*, p. 186.
34. Shaykhzāde, *Kitāb naẓm al-farā'id*, p. 28.
35. Al-Bazdawī, *Uṣūl al-dīn*, p. 76.
36. Al-Bazdawī, *Uṣūl al-dīn*, pp. 43–82.
37. Al-Nasafī, *Tabṣirat al-adilla*, p. 587.
38. Al-Nasafī, *Tabṣirat al-adilla*, p. 588.
39. Al-Nasafī, *Sharḥ al-'umda*, p. 212; Shaykhzāde, *Kitāb naẓm al-farā'id*, p. 28.
40. Shaykhzāde, *Kitāb naẓm al-farā'id*, p. 28.
41. For identification of the Baghdad school with the doctrine of *aṣlaḥ*, see Frank, '*Kalām* and Philosophy', p. 93.
42. Frank, '*Kalām* and Philosophy', pp. 76–7.
43. Also known as Abū al-Qāsim al-Balkhī, he spent a long time in Baghdad under the tutelage of Abū al-Ḥusayn al-Khayyāt. He was, however, a native of Balkh and apparently travelled back eastwards later in life, founding a school in Nasaf, less than 100 miles from al-Māturīdī's city of Samarqand and becoming the chief representative of the Mu'tazila in the region. Nader, 'al-Balkhī'; Madelung, 'al-Māturīdī'.
44. Al-Māturīdī, *Kitāb al-tawḥīd*, p. 296. See Cerić, *Roots of Synthetic Theology in Islam*, p. 217. For a comparison of Zoroastrian views with that of the Mu'tazila, see Hourani, *Reason and Tradition*, pp. 74–7.
45. The Basran Mu'tazila developed their theological system in response to the criticism offered by their opponents, such that by the time of Qāḍī 'Abd al-Jabbār (d. 415/1025) it had reached a considerable level of complexity. Thus, he does not accept the concept of *'illa* as a necessitating cause (*al-sabab al-mujīb*) applying to God. Frank, '*Kalām* and Philosophy', p. 82. Furthermore, he takes the position that it is neither impossible for God to do less than the best for a human agent, nor admissible to think that He does. Hourani, *Reason and Tradition*, p. 105. Here he contrasts with al-Māturīdī, who we shall see has no problem with arguing that humans sometimes experience what is not for their personal best, but has some other underlying wisdom.
46. Al-Māturīdī, *Kitāb al-tawḥīd*, p. 296. Al-Māturīdī uses the phrase '*lā 'an shay*'' (lit. not based upon a thing) as a technical term to denote the negation of an *'illa* for God.
47. In his *tafsīr* for this verse he states that it has two aspects, the bringing into being of the creation, and God's absolute control over it. Al-Māturīdī, *Ta'wīlāt*, vol. 5, p. 385.
48. Al-Māturīdī, *Kitāb al-tawḥīd*, p. 297.
49. 'Abd al-Jabbār, *Sharḥ al-uṣūl al-khamsa*, p. 313.
50. Frank, 'Can God Do What is Wrong?', pp. 73–6.
51. See Pessagno, 'Uses of Evil', pp. 77–9.
52. Al-Ash'arī, *Kitāb al-luma'*, p. 117.
53. Al-Māturīdī, *Kitāb al-tawḥīd*, p. 297.
54. Al-Māturīdī, *Kitāb al-tawḥīd*, p. 297.
55. Al-Māturīdī, *Kitāb al-tawḥīd*, pp. 297–8.
56. Al-Māturīdī, *Kitāb al-tawḥīd*, p. 298.
57. Cerić, *Roots of Synthetic Theology in Islam*, p. 219; Frank, 'Notes and Remarks on the Ṭabā'i'', p. 145; Abū Zahra, *Al-Aqīda*, pp. 62–3.
58. Al-Māturīdī, *Kitāb al-tawḥīd*, p. 301.
59. See page 37.
60. Al-Māturīdī, *Kitāb al-tawḥīd*, p. 307.

61. Cerić, *Roots of Synthetic Theology in Islam*, p. 217.
62. Similar was affirmed by Abū Jaʿfar al-Ṭaḥāwī (d. 321/933), a contemporaneous Egyptian Ḥanafī scholar, who is credited with the development of catechisms acceptable to all strands of Sunnī theological thought. Al-Ṭaḥāwī, *Matn al-ʿaqīdat al-Ṭaḥāwiyya*, pp. 16–17.
63. Jackson, *Islam and the Problem of Black Suffering*, p. 89.
64. Jackson argues that overwhelming focus on the question of human free will reflects modern theological sensibilities; the Ashʿarīs were far more concerned with attributing actions entirely to God. Jackson, *Islam and the Problem of Black Suffering*, pp. 88–9.
65. Rudolph, *Al-Māturīdī and the Development of Sunnī Theology*, p. 305.
66. Al-Nasafī, *Sharḥ al-ʿumda*, p. 356; Al-Nasafī, *Tabṣirat al-adilla*, pp. 786–7.
67. Shaykhzāde, *Kitāb naẓm al-farāʾid*, p. 30.
68. Al-Māturīdī, *Kitāb al-tawḥīd*, p. 295.
69. Cf. Reinhart, 'Ethics and the Qurʾān'.
70. Al-Māturīdī, *Kitāb al-tawḥīd*, p. 105.
71. Rudolph, *Al-Māturīdī and the Development of Sunnī Theology*, p. 259.
72. Rudolph connects the *ṭabāʾiʿ* with the four elements of antique philosophy. Rudolph, *Al-Māturīdī and the Development of Sunnī Theology*, p. 255. Frank argues that they are rather 'the natural action of the material constituents of bodies, i.e., their specific behavior, active and passive, as is determined by and flows directly from the nature of their materiality'. Frank, 'Notes and Remarks on the Ṭabāʾiʿ', p. 138.
73. See Rudolph, *Al-Māturīdī and the Development of Sunnī Theology*, pp. 255–60.
74. Dhanani suggests that al-Māturīdī juxtaposed his theory of *ṭabāʾiʿ* with *kalām* atomism. Dhanani, 'Al-Māturīdī and al-Nasafī on Atomism and the Ṭabāʾiʿ', p. 72. However, Rudolph argues that his mere use of the language of accidents and bodies does not necessarily mean that he understood the latter to be composed of atoms. Rudolph, *Al-Māturīdī and the Development of Sunnī Theology*, pp. 245–7.
75. Al-Ashʿarī, *Maqālāt al-islāmiyyīn*, vol. 1, p. 313.
76. Sorabji, *Matter, Space and Motion*, p. 57.
77. See Bacon, *Universals*, pp. 2–4; Ehring, *Tropes*, p. 98. A proposal for future research is to explore which contemporary metaphysical theories could best advance a neo-Māturīdī theological perspective.
78. Al-Juwaynī, *Al-Shāmil*, p. 160.
79. Rudolph, *Al-Māturīdī and the Development of Sunnī Theology*, p. 260.
80. McGinnis, 'Arabic and Islamic Natural Philosophy'.
81. Al-Māturīdī, *Kitāb al-tawḥīd*, pp. 83–5; Rudolph, *Al-Māturīdī and the Development of Sunnī Theology*, pp. 259–60. See also Schöck, 'Jahm b. Ṣafwān (d. 128/745–6) and the "Jahmiyya" and Ḍirār b. ʿAmr (d. 200/815)', pp. 75–6. Dorroll provides further analysis of this notion of constant worldly flux (*taqallub*) in al-Māturīdī's thought. Dorroll, 'The Universe in Flux', p. 132.
82. Hourani, *Reason and Tradition*, p. 23. Cf. Garner and Rosen, *Moral Philosophy*, p. 215.
83. Al-Māturīdī, *Kitāb al-tawḥīd*, p. 167.
84. Reinhart, *Before Revelation*, p. 38. Also, it is important to note that while virtually all Ḥanafīs and Muʿtazilīs can be presumed moral realists in the early period, there was greater variance within the Shāfiʿī and Ḥanbalī schools before later adoption of the Ashʿarī perspective. Reinhart has compiled a list of thirteen Shāfiʿīs who lived in the fourth/tenth and fifth/eleventh centuries, that is contemporaneous or later than al-Māturīdī and al-Ashʿarī. Nine of these figures held a position that before revelation the use of beneficial things within the world is 'permitted', a view closely associated with moral realism, while the other four are said to have held that these things are 'proscribed', for the reason that they are the property of God. This latter opinion, which was to become rare in later centuries, nonetheless also has a realist basis. Reinhart, *Before Revelation*, p. 22.
85. It seems that al-Ashʿarī is the first individual to whom is ascribed a position of allowing 'no assessment' at all of morality before the coming of revelation. Reinhart, *Before Revelation*, p. 25. However, there is an indication to this idea already in al-Shāfiʿī. For instance, he comments, 'Justice is that he acts in obedience to God, as He for them is the way to knowledge of justice and what contravenes it (*al-ʿadlu an yaʿmala bi-ṭāʿati allāhi fa-kāna lahum sabīlu ilā ʿilmi al-ʿadli wa-lladhī yukhālifuhu*).' Al-Shāfiʿī, *Al-Risāla*, p. 25. Also, see Kelsay, 'Divine Command Ethics', pp. 116–18. Cf. Hourani, *Reason and Tradition*, p. 46.

86. Al-Zuhaylī, *Uṣūl*, vol. 1, pp. 116–20; Shihadeh, 'Theories of Ethical Value', pp. 401– 2.
87. Al-Ash'arī, *Kitāb al-luma'*, p. 117.
88. See Al-Ghazālī, *Al-Mustaṣfā*, vol. 1, p. 62; Shihadeh, 'Theories of Ethical Value', pp. 396–404.
89. Reinhart, *Before Revelation*, p. 175.
90. Vasalou, *Moral Agents*, p. 5; Vasalou, *Moral Agents*, pp. 22–3.
91. For a general defence of philosophical realism, see Miller, 'Realism, Antirealism, and Common Sense'.
92. Cf. Vasalou, *Ibn Taymiyya's Theological Ethics*, pp. 141–2.
93. Al-Māturīdī, *Kitāb al-tawḥīd*, p. 396.
94. He also mentions truth (*ḥaqq*) and falsehood (*bāṭil*). Al-Māturīdī, *Kitāb al-tawḥīd*, p. 396. See also Pessagno, 'Uses of Evil', p. 71.
95. Jackson, *Islam and the Problem of Black Suffering*, p. 115.
96. Schaffer, 'The Individuation of Tropes', pp. 247–9.
97. Shihadeh, 'Theories of Ethical Value', p. 398.
98. Hourani, *Reason and Tradition*, p. 104.
99. Emon, *Islamic Natural Law Theories*, p. 40. Considerable additional nuance can be added to this picture. See Vasalou, *Ibn Taymiyya's Theological Ethics*, pp. 148–56.
100. Hourani, *Reason and Tradition*, p. 47.
101. The debate between the two positions can be related to that over moral cognivitism in contemporary philosophy. See van Roojen, 'Moral Cognitivism vs. Non-Cognitivism'. A position that can suffice with revelation entirely is discussed by Hourani as probably the assumption of the Muslim philosophers, although not vocalised for reasons of 'prudence or genuine religious conviction'. Hourani, *Reason and Tradition*, pp. 24–5.
102. Hourani, *Reason and Tradition*, p. 46.
103. Shaykhzāde, *Kitāb naẓm al-farā'id*, p. 32.
104. Al-Ghazālī, *Al-Mustaṣfā*, vol. 1, p. 62.
105. Shihadeh, 'Theories of Ethical Value', p. 404.
106. Weiss, *The Search for God's Law*, p. 87.
107. Al-Māturīdī, *Ta'wīlāt*, vol. 8, p. 243.
108. Al-Māturīdī, *Kitāb al-tawḥīd*, pp. 72–4.
109. Al-Nasafī, *Tabṣirat al-adilla*, p. 145.
110. Al-Māturīdī, *Ta'wīlāt*, vol. 17, p. 222.
111. Al-Māturīdī, *Ta'wīlāt*, vol. 17, p. 222. This moral core is comprised of rules that are rationally known to be not subject to abrogation. See al-Māturīdī, *Ta'wīlāt*, vol. 6, p. 465. Cf. Kamali, *Principles*, pp. 206–7.
112. Al-Māturīdī, *Ta'wīlāt*, vol. 11, pp. 185–6. He references the well-known hadith, 'Every child is born in a state of *fiṭra* and his parents make him a Jew or a Christian.' Al-Bukhārī, *Ṣaḥīḥ*, vol. 3, p. 1,335.
113. Al-Māturīdī, *Ta'wīlāt*, vol. 17, p. 222.
114. Hourani, *Reason and Tradition*, p. 103.
115. Vasalou, *Moral Agents*, pp. 22–3.
116. Al-Māturīdī, *Kitāb al-tawḥīd*, p. 252. Cf. Thomas Aquinas who makes a similar argument about the indispensibility of a revealed Law despite the light of natural reason. Aquinas, 'Summa Theologica', vol. 1, p. 2.
117. Al-Māturīdī, *Kitāb al-tawḥīd*, p. 252. Al-Māturīdī is close to the position of the Basran Mu'azila on this point. Frank, 'Moral Obligation', p. 206. An opposing view is discussed by Reinhart, *Before Revelation*, pp. 173–5.
118. Al-Māturīdī, *Kitāb al-tawḥīd*, p. 72.
119. Al-Māturīdī, *Kitāb al-tawḥīd*, p. 74. Al-Māturīdī provides a classification of the different weights of reports as well as affirming the absolute certainty of the Qur'an. See also Cerić, *Roots of Synthetic Theology in Islam*, p. 93.
120. Al-Māturīdī, *Kitāb al-tawḥīd*, p. 167. Cf. Hourani, *Reason and Tradition*, p. 45.
121. Al-Shāshī, *Uṣūl al-Shāshī*, p. 104.
122. Al-Zarkashī, *Al-Baḥr al-muḥīṭ*, p. 142.
123. Reinhart, *Before Revelation*, p. 56.
124. Al-Bayāḍī, *Ishārāt*, pp. 62–4; Al-Zuhaylī, *Uṣūl*, vol. 1, p. 120; Reinhart, *Before Revelation*, pp. 53–4.

125. Reinhart, *Before Revelation*, p. 48. For an early discussion of this idea, see al-Jaṣṣāṣ, *Al-Fuṣūl*, vol. 3, p. 249. Cf. Ramadan, *Radical Reform*, pp. 87–90.
126. Draz, *The Moral World of the Qur'an*, p. 19.
127. Reinhart, 'Islamic Law as Islamic Ethics', p. 186.
128. Al-Ghazālī, *Al-Mustaṣfā*, vol. 1, p. 55. Many jurists utilised a comprehensive definition that also included the *ḥukm waḍ'ī* (contextual ruling), which regulates the implementation of the *ḥukm taklīfī*. Al-Ghazālī, and others who followed him, such as Ibn al-Subkī, saw this situational element of the Divine address as necessary for the *aḥkām*, but not to be included within them. Zaydān, *Al-Ḥukm*, pp. 17–18.
129. Kamali, *Principles*, pp. 413–31; Reinhart, '"Like the Difference between Heaven and Earth"', pp. 207–9.
130. Zysow, *Economy*, pp. 63–4. Cf. Reinhart, '"Like the Difference between Heaven and Earth"', pp. 220–5.
131. Reinhart, *Before Revelation*, pp. 31, 38–9.
132. Zysow, *Economy*, pp. 222–3; Weiss, *The Search for God's Law*, p. 581. See also pp. 571–82.
133. Zysow, *Economy*, pp. 222–3; Weiss, *The Search for God's Law*, p. 593.
134. El Shamsy, 'Wisdom', pp. 24–5.
135. El Shamsy, 'Wisdom', pp. 22, 28.
136. Al-Jaṣṣāṣ, *Al-Fuṣūl*, vol. 4, pp. 140–1; Shehaby, ''Illa and Qiyās', p. 40. Cf. Weiss, *The Search for God's Law*, pp. 594–6.
137. Al-Dabūsī and al-Karkhī, *Ta'sīs al-naẓar*, p. 172.
138. Zysow, *Economy*, pp. 208–10.
139. Emon, *Islamic Natural Law Theories*, p. 130.
140. El Shamsy, 'Wisdom', p. 31; Weiss, *The Search for God's Law*, pp. 581–2.
141. El Shamsy, 'Wisdom', pp. 33–4. See al-Raysūnī, *Imām Al-Shāṭibī's Theory*, pp. 12–24. There is some discussion over how closely this idea should be connected to the earlier Mālikī idea of *maṣlaḥa mursala* (unregulated benefit). Nyazee, *Islamic Jurisprudence*, p. 201.
142. Emon, *Islamic Natural Law Theories*, p. 139.
143. Al-Shāṭibī, *Al-Muwāfaqāt*, vol. 1, pp. 265–8. There is not space here to discuss the details of the various *maqāṣid* theories, nor to catalogue the historical development of the discipline. See al-Raysūnī, *Imām Al-Shāṭibī's Theory*, pp. 1–37.
144. This is the order given in al-Ghazālī, *Al-Mustaṣfā*, vol. 1, p. 287. Al-Āmidī argued for the order as follows: religion, life, progeny, reason, and wealth. Al-Āmidī, *Al-Iḥkām*, vol. 4, p. 340. Al-Qarāfī mentions that some added a sixth necessity: honour (*'irḍ*). Al-Qarāfī, *Sharḥ tanqīh*, p. 350. For a modern attempt, see Gomaa, *Wa-qāla al-imām*, pp. 98–9.
145. Al-Juwaynī, *Al-Burhān*, vol. 2, p. 1,151.
146. Emon, *Islamic Natural Law Theories*, p. 135.
147. Al-Ghazālī, *Al-Mustaṣfā*, vol. 1, p. 285.
148. Vasalou, *Ibn Taymiyya's Theological Ethics*, p. 165.
149. Hallaq, *History*, pp. 214–20; Zaman, *Modern Islamic Thought*, pp. 109–19.
150. Auda, *Maqāṣid al-Sharī'ah*, p. 4.
151. Ramadan, *Radical Reform*, p. 141; Auda, *Maqāṣid al-Sharī'ah*, pp. 6–9.
152. Al-Raysūnī, *Imām Al-Shāṭibī's Theory*, p. 364.
153. Nyazee, *Islamic Jurisprudence*, pp. 203–4.
154. Nyazee, *Islamic Jurisprudence*, p. 207.
155. Zysow, *Economy*, pp. 223–4.
156. Al-Samarqandī, *Mīzān*, vol. 2, p. 863.
157. See Frank, '*Al-Ma'nā*', p. 250.
158. Al-Samarqandī, *Mīzān*, pp. 863–4.
159. Al-Māturīdī, *Ta'wīlāt*, vol. 6, p. 392.
160. Defence of taking this reading, rather than *ma'khadh*, is given in Zysow, 'Mu'tazilism and Māturīdism', pp. 238–9.
161. Al-Samarqandī, *Mīzān*, vol. 2, p. 1,049.
162. Al-Māturīdī, *Ta'wīlāt*, vol. 1, p. 199.
163. Cf. Weiss, *The Search for God's Law*, pp. 529–30.
164. Neuwirth, *Scripture, Poetry and the Making of Community*, p. xxviii.

165. See page 22.
166. Cf. Al-Attas, *Prolegomena*, p. 17; Smirnov, 'Understanding Justice', p. 347.
167. Kamali, *Freedom, Equality and Justice*, p. 113.

Chapter 3

1. Esack, 'Qur'anic Hermeneutics', pp. 394–6.
2. Johns, 'A Humanistic Approach', p. 80.
3. Neuwirth, 'Structure and the Emergence of Community', p. 146.
4. Ibn Taymiyya, *Muqaddima*, p. 93.
5. Galli, 'Some Aspects', p. 5.
6. See note 5 on page 199.
7. Al-Shinqīṭī, *Aḍwā' al-bayān*, pp. 7–16.
8. Abdel Haleem, 'Grammatical Shift', p. 160.
9. Al-Suyūṭī, *Al-Itqān*, vol. 1, p. 445.
10. Al-Bazdawī, *Kanz*, p. 98.
11. Izutsu, *Ethical Terms*, pp. 10–11.
12. Izutsu, *Ethical Terms*, pp. 33–8.
13. See al-Khālidī, *Al-Tafsīr al-mawḍū'ī*, p. 63.
14. Ibn 'Āshūr, *Al-Tafsīr wa-rijāluhu*, pp. 80–1.
15. Abdul-Raof, *Arabic Rhetoric*, p. 97.
16. Ḍayf, *Al-Mu'jam*, p. 972.
17. Al-Jāḥiẓ, *Naẓm al-qur'ān*, pp. 46-8.
18. Cf. Ibn Khaldūn, *Muqaddima*, p. 661.
19. Abdel Haleem, *Understanding the Qur'an*, p. 159.
20. Jenssen, *Subtleties and Secrets*, p. 36.
21. Jenssen, *Subtleties and Secrets*, p. 40.
22. Al-Suyūṭī, *Al-Itqān*, vol. 3, pp. 86–90; Al-Zarkashī, *Al-Burhān*, pp. 455–73.
23. Abdel Haleem, 'Grammatical Shift', p. 430.
24. Ali, *Medieval Islamic Pragmatics*, p. 66.
25. Al-Qazwīnī, *Al-Talkhīṣ*, pp. 37–8.
26. Here *ḥukm* denotes a fact borne by the sentence and is a distinct concept from the ethical assessment of a particular act discussed on pages 38–9.
27. Jenssen, *Subtleties and Secrets*, pp. 63–4.
28. Al-Qazwīnī, *Al-Talkhīṣ*, p. 38. Cf. Owens (ed.), *The Oxford Handbook of Arabic Linguistics*, pp. 189–95.
29. Al-Jārim and Amīn, *Al-Balāghat al-wāḍiḥa*, pp. 146–7.
30. Al-Qazwīnī, *Al-Talkhīṣ*, p. 41.
31. Muslim scholars within the genre of *uṣūl al-fiqh* identified verbal, or text-based, and non-verbal or situational contexts. Ali, *Medieval Islamic Pragmatics*, p. 55. Within the hermeneutic model of this study, intra-textuality and *niẓām* are two aspects of the former, while socio-historical context comprises the various aspects of the latter.
32. Al-Jārim and Amīn, *Al-Balāghat al-wāḍiḥa*, p. 170.
33. Abdel Haleem, *Understanding the Qur'an*, p. 212.
34. Mohammad Akram Nadwi, 'Coherence in the Qur'an' (Lecture, Birkbeck, London, 22 July 2012).
35. Ali, *Medieval Islamic Pragmatics*, p. 35.
36. Al-Qazwīnī, *Al-Talkhīṣ*, pp. 429–35.
37. Al-Qazwīnī, *Al-Talkhīṣ*, p. 435.
38. Al-Suyūṭī, *Al-Itqān*, vol. 3, pp. 279–81.
39. Al-Farāhī, *Dalā'il al-niẓām*, p. 4.
40. Mir, 'The Sūra as a Unity', p. 212. Also, see the following works by academics Cuypers, *The Banquet*; Cuypers, *The Composition of the Qur'an*; Robinson, *Discovering the Qur'an*; Zahniser, 'Major Transitions', pp. 26–55.
41. Badawī, *Usus al-naqd*, p. 322.

42. Quṭb's terminology is *miḥwar* (pivot), which performs a similar role. Mir, 'The Sūra as a Unity', p. 213.
43. Al-Farāhī, *Dalā'il al-niẓām*, p. 73.
44. Mir, *Coherence in the Qur'an*, p. 85.
45. Mir, 'The Sūra as a Unity', p. 219.
46. El-Awa, *Textual Relations*, pp. 39–40. Cf. Iser, 'The Reading Process', pp. 1–2.
47. A. H. Johns, review of *Textual Relations in the Qur'an: Relevance, Coherence and Structure*, by Salwa M. S. El-Awa. *Journal of Qur'anic Studies* 8/1 (2006), p. 130.
48. For further literature, see Locate, *Makkan and Madinan Revelations*, p. 14.
49. Zebiri, *Maḥmūd Shaltūt*, p. 169.
50. Discussion of Sūrat al-Aʿraf in Chapter 5, al-Mumtaḥana in Chapter 6, and Quraysh in Chapter 8 are the closest that this book comes to such engagement with macrostructure.
51. El-Awa, *Textual Relations*, pp. 46–53. Johns is positive of this aspect of El-Awa's thesis and sees it as a hypothesis that deserves testing. A. H. Johns, review of *Textual Relations in the Qur'an: Relevance, Coherence and Structure*, by Salwa M. S. El-Awa, p. 130. For an opposing view, see Andrew Rippin, *Reading the Qur'ān with Richard Bell*, review of *A Commentary on the Qur'ān*, by Richard Bell. *Journal of the American Oriental Society* 112/4 (1992), p. 641.
52. El-Awa, *Textual Relations*, p. 24.
53. Maḥmūd, *Dirāsāt*, p. 39.
54. See page 49.
55. Reinhart, 'Jurisprudence', p. 447.
56. See Iṣlāḥī, *Tadabbur-e-Qur'ān*, vol. 1, p. 35.
57. Cragg, *The Event of the Qur'an*, pp. 16–17.
58. Saeed, 'Fazlur Rahman', p. 47.
59. Cf. Taylor, 'Justice after Virtue', p. 35.
60. Reinhart, 'Ethics and the Qur'ān'.
61. See Alasdair MacIntyre's defence of a related point in MacIntyre, 'A Partial Response to My Critics', p. 295.
62. Sadeghi and Bergmann, 'The Codex of a Companion', pp. 348–54. There has also been recent interest in early manuscripts in Birmingham and Tübingen. See also Sinai, 'Consonantal Skeleton … Part I' and Sinai, 'Consonantal Skeleton … Part II'.
63. See Schoeler, *The Oral and Written*.
64. See Berg, *The Development of Exegesis in Early Islam*, pp. 6–64. Motzki responds to Berg's characterisation of the positions in Motzki, 'Authenticity of Muslim Traditions Reconsidered', pp. 211–57. Also useful is Motzki, 'Dating Muslim Traditions'.
65. Wansbrough, *Quranic Studies*, p. 144.
66. Lüling, *Über den Ur-Qur'an*. See Lüling, *A Challenge*, pp. 17–18.
67. Luxenberg, *Die Syro-Aramäische Lesart*. See Donner, 'The Qur'an in Recent Scholarship', p. 33.
68. Sinai and Neuwirth, 'Introduction', p. 10. For Wansbrough's own reflections on his influence, see Wansbrough, 'Res Ipsa Loquitur', p. 10.
69. Such a view has been implicitly or explicitly mentioned in critique of Wansbrough's assumptions. See Donner, *Narratives of Islamic Origins*, pp. 25–31.
70. See Zysow, *Economy*, pp. 7-17.
71. Motzki, 'Introduction', pp. xiv–v; Berg, 'Competing Paradigms', p. 284.
72. Sinai and Neuwirth, 'Introduction', p. 13. Such a diachronic analysis must be balanced with sensitivity to synchronic textual structure, as Neuwirth observes herself. Neuwirth, 'Structure and the Emergence of Community', p. 147.
73. Wansbrough's idea of displacing the Qur'an outside of the Arabian Peninsula, despite the interest it received, has rarely been accepted. It was continued by his student G. F. Hawting. See Hawting, *The Idea of Idolatry*, pp. 16–18.
74. Cf. Saleh, 'The Etymological Fallacy', pp. 652–3.
75. Schoeler, *The Biography of Muḥammad*, pp. 114–16; Motzki, 'The Origins of Muslim Exegesis', p. 290.
76. Brown, *Hadith*, pp. 92–6; Brown, *Canonization*, p. 116.
77. Jonathan A. C. Brown, review of *Encyclopedia of Canonical Ḥadīth*, by G. H. A. Juynboll, *Journal of Islamic Studies* 19/3 (2008), p. 396.

78. For instance, see Juynboll, *Muslim Tradition*, pp. 161–2, following Goldziher, *Muslim Studies*, vol. 2, p. 141.
79. Brown, *Hadith*, p. 96.
80. Brown, '*Matn* Criticism', pp. 164–73.
81. Al-Jaṣṣāṣ, *Al-Fuṣūl*, vol. 3, pp. 113–19. Also see Bedir, 'An Early Response', pp. 301–5.
82. Brown, review of *Encyclopedia of Canonical Ḥadīth*, by G. H. A. Juynboll, p. 396.
83. Al-Tirmidhī, *Sunan*, vol. 2, p. 1,007; Ali, *Al-Tirmidhī*, p. 172.
84. Al-Ḥanbalī, *Sharḥ ʿilal*, vol. 1, p. 411.
85. Al-Tirmidhī, *Sunan*, vol. 2, pp. 1,006–9; Al-Ḥanbalī, *Sharḥ ʿilal*, vol. 1, pp. 413–17.
86. Reinhart, 'Juynbolliania', pp. 440–1.
87. Motzki, '*Al-Radd*', pp. 211–12.
88. Motzki, 'The Origins of Muslim Exegesis', pp. 240–1.
89. Motzki, 'Whither *Ḥadīth* Studies?', pp. 55–8.
90. Motzki, 'Whither *Ḥadīth* Studies?', pp. 51–2.
91. Al-Sibāʿī, *Al-Sunna*, p. 274.
92. Al-Sibāʿī, *Al-Sunna*, p. 275.
93. Motzki, 'The Murder of Ibn Abi 'l-Huqayq', pp. 233–4.
94. Hallaq, 'The Authenticity of Prophetic Hadith', pp. 75–90.
95. Brown, 'Did the Prophet Say It or Not?', p. 285.
96. Cf. Calder, 'History and Nostalgia', p. 58.
97. The practice of using the Hebrew Bible in translation as a source for Qur'anic exegesis has particular precedent in the work of the scholar al-Biqāʿī. See Saleh and Casey, 'An Islamic Diatessaron'.
98. For the difficulty in providing any precise order, see Stefanidis, 'The Qur'an Made Linear', pp. 13–15. A new stylometric approach is attempted in Sadeghi, 'The Chronology of the Qurʾān'.
99. Powers, 'The Exegetical Genre', pp. 122–3; Qadhi, *An Introduction to the Sciences of the Qur'aan*, p. 251.
100. Shāh Walī Allāh, *Al-Fawz al-kabīr*, pp. 53–60.
101. Powers, 'On the Abrogation of the Bequest Verses', pp. 246–7.
102. Al-Māturīdī, *Taʾwīlāt*, vol. 1, pp. 257–8.
103. Al-Farāhī, *Rasāʾil*, p. 157.
104. Al-Samarqandī, *Al-ʿĀlim wa-l-mutaʿallim*, p. 11; Kamali, *Principles*, pp. 206–7.
105. See pages 148 and 166.
106. Rippin, 'The Function of *asbāb al-nuzūl*', p. 1; Rubin, *The Eye of the Beholder*, pp. 226–8.
107. Qadhi, *An Introduction to the Sciences of the Qur'aan*, pp. 111–15.
108. Al-Suyūṭī, *Al-Itqān*, vol. 1, p. 115
109. Rippin, 'The Exegetical Genre *asbāb al-nuzūl*', p. 15.
110. Al-Suyūṭī, *Al-Itqān*, vol. 1, p. 112. Cf. Rippin, 'Al-Zarkashī and al-Suyūṭī', p. 253.
111. The other main use of *hattā* is to express the meaning 'so that …'
112. These categories with examples are given by Qaṭṭān, *Mabāḥith*, pp. 192–3.
113. Al-Bukhārī, *Kashf al-asrār*, vol. 2, p. 266. It is defended vigorously by al-Zurqānī, *Manāhil al-ʿirfān*, vol. 1, pp. 120–2.
114. Al-Zurqānī, *Manāhil al-ʿirfān*, vol. 1, p. 119; Zalaṭ, *Mabāḥith*, p. 70.
115. Qaṭṭān, *Mabāḥith*, p. 191.
116. For a famous example of the Prophet Muḥammad specifying one verse by another, see al-Bukhārī, *Ṣaḥīḥ*, vol. 2, p. 931.
117. Al-Suyūṭī, *Al-Itqān*, vol. 1, pp. 109, 111; Cf. Zalaṭ, *Mabāḥith*, p. 74.
118. Ibn Taymiyya, *Muqaddima*, p. 47.
119. Al-Zurqānī, *Manāhil al-ʿirfān*, vol. 1, pp. 118–19. Another point that is often mentioned in this context is that an *ʿāmm* expression with a known *sabab* can only be specified with respect to the members beyond this *sabab*. This is because the 'entry of the form of the *sabab* in the *āmm* expression is *qaṭʿī* (definitive), so the removal of it by *ijtihād* (exhaustive legal enquiry) is not permissible'. Al-Suyūṭī, *Al-Itqān*, vol. 1, p. 108; Zalaṭ, *Mabāḥith*, pp. 62–3.
120. Al-Suyūṭī, *Al-Itqān*, vol. 1, p. 113.
121. Al-Suyūṭī, *Al-Itqān*, vol. 1, p. 113.
122. Rippin, 'Al-Zarkashī and al-Suyūṭī', p. 254.

123. See pages 125 and 159.
124. Al-Suyūṭī, *Al-Itqān,* vol. 1, p. 113.
125. Jackson, 'Fiction and Formalism', pp. 195-200.
126. Zysow, *Economy*, p. 50.
127. Vishanoff, *Formation*, pp. 63–5. Cf. Hallaq, 'Was al-Shafiʿi the Master Architect', pp. 600–1; Jackson, 'Fiction and Formalism', pp. 187–90.
128. Al-Shāfiʿī, *Al-Risāla*, pp. 21–2; Ali, *Medieval Islamic Pragmatics*, pp. 52–3; Reinhart, 'Jurisprudence', p. 441.
129. See pages 41–2.
130. Al-Nasafī, *Al-Manār*, p. 13; Al-Bukhārī, *Kashf al-asrār*, vol. 2, p. 253. See Zysow, *Economy*, p. 103.
131. Zysow, *Economy*, p. 103.
132. Scholars who accepted *mafhūm al-mukhālafa* divided it into five types. As I am not going to make use of the principle, I have omitted discussion of these. See Auda, *Maqāṣid al-Sharīʿah*, pp. 98–100.
133. Al-Suyūṭī, *Al-Itqān*, vol. 3, pp. 127–8.
134. See page 41.
135. Al-Zuhaylī, *Uṣūl*, vol. 1, pp. 665–8.
136. Douglas Hofstadter, review of *Mental Leaps: Analogy in Creative Thought*, by Keith Holyoak and Paul Thagard. *AI Magazine* 16/3 (1995), p. 76.
137. Nyazee, *Islamic Jurisprudence*, pp. 28–9.
138. Schleiermacher, *Hermeneutics*, p. 229.

Chapter 4

1. For ease of expression, the name Medina shall be used for pre-Islamic references to the settlement known as Yathrib, which is also the name of an area in its northern quarter. Lecker, 'On the Markets of Medina', p. 193.
2. Use of the word political should not be taken as an assumption of particular features of the 'state', but rather taken in the sense 'of or pertaining to public life and affairs as involving authority and government'. Stevenson (ed.), *Shorter Oxford English Dictionary*, vol. 2, p. 2,269. Cf. Hallaq, *The Impossible State*, pp. 1–3.
3. Maine, *Ancient Law*, p. 115.
4. Hoyland, *Arabia and the Arabs*, p. 119.
5. Meeker, *Literature and Violence*, pp. 8–9.
6. Hoyland, *Arabia and the Arabs*, pp. 78–83; Shahid, 'Ghassān'; Shahid, 'Lakhmids'.
7. Bowersock, *Roman Arabia*, pp. 156-8.
8. Watt, *Muḥammad at Mecca*, p. 5; Shahid, *Byzantium and the Arabs in the Fifth Century*, pp. 350–60. For a revisionist account, treating the story of Quṣayy as a foundation myth, see Retsö, *The Arabs in Antiquity*, pp. 614–15.
9. The first five members of this list are mentioned in Ibn Hishām, *Al-Sīra*, vol. 1, p. 88. All six are found in Al-Ḥalabī, *Al-Sīra*, vol. 1, p. 22.
10. Nuʿmānī, *Sīrat al-nabī*, vol. 1, pp. 154–5.
11. This name is mentioned in Q. 6:92.
12. Shahid, *Byzantium and the Arabs in the Fifth Century*, p. 355; Kister, 'Mecca and Tamīm (Aspects of Their Relations)', p. 138.
13. Shahid, 'Ghassān'; Lecker, 'The Levying of Taxes', p. 115.
14. Al-Ḥalabī, *Al-Sīra*, vol. 1, p. 25.
15. Watt, *Muḥammad at Mecca*, p. 8. Note that the word *malaʾ* is used in the Qur'an to denote the chiefs of the Children of Israel in Q. 2:246 and the Meccan clan leaders themselves in Q. 38:6. See pages 86–7 and 89.
16. Al-Ṭaḥāwī, *Sharḥ mushkil*, vol. 15, p. 221.
17. The principle clans of the Aḥlāf were as follows: ʿAbd al-Dār, Makhzūm, Sahm, Jumaḥ, and ʿAdī. A couple of the outlying clans (Quraysh al-Ẓawāhir), ʿĀmir b. Luʾayy and Muḥārib, stayed neutral. Watt,

Muḥammad at Mecca, pp. 5–6. There is evidence for the sustained relevance of these two groups, including Qurashī Muslims fighting the Battle of Uḥud under their banners. Kister, 'Some Reports Concerning Mecca', p. 83. Also see pp. 81–4.

18. Al-Ḥalabī, *Al-Sīra*, vol. 1, p. 188.
19. Ibn Hishām, *Al-Sīra*, vol. 1, p. 124.
20. Fück, 'Fidjār'; Kister, 'Al-Ḥīra', p. 154.
21. Watt, *Muḥammad at Mecca*, p. 31; Ibn Ḥabīb, *Kitāb al-munammaq*, pp. 90–4.
22. Kister, 'Some Reports Concerning Mecca', p. 75. Hawting expresses surprise about the lack of importance of the *ḥijāba* office in key parts of the *sīra* literature. Hawting, 'The "Sacred Offices" of Mecca', pp. 69–70. This could perhaps be explained by the above discussion about its primarily ceremonial significance, as well as focus by Muslim historians on the offices connected to the family of the Prophet.
23. Ibn Ḥabīb, *Kitāb al-munammaq*, pp. 127–8; Al-Bukhārī, *Ṣaḥīḥ*, vol. 2, p. 904.
24. Ibn Ḥabīb, *Kitāb al-munammaq*, p. 128.
25. Al-Azraqī, *Akhbār makka*, pp. 180, 183. There is also a report to the effect that Abū Ṭālib originally held both offices, but was forced to cede them to his brother ʿAbbās upon failure to repay him a loan. Ibrahim, *Merchant Capital*, p. 61. However, see the reservations expressed in Al-Azmeh, *Emergence*, p. 203.
26. Ibrahim, *Merchant Capital*, pp. 62–70.
27. Newby, *Jews of Arabia*, p. 114.
28. Al-Azraqī, *Akhbār makka*, p. 185.
29. Ibn Hishām, *Al-Sīra*, vol. 2, p. 212.
30. Ibn ʿAbd Rabbih, *Al-ʿIqd*, vol. 3, p. 267.
31. Watt, *Muḥammad at Medina*, p. 56. Watt here implicitly corrects his earlier statement that '[t]he domination of Mecca by Abū Sufyān during Muḥammad's prime was not due to the holding of any office carrying authority'. Watt, *Muḥammad at Mecca*, p. 9.
32. Newby, *Jews of Arabia*, pp. 49–51. Also, see Lecker, 'A Jew with Two Sidelocks'.
33. Watt, *Muḥammad at Mecca*, p. 142.
34. Al-Samhūdī, *Wafāʾ*, vol. 1, pp. 125–6.
35. Vajda, 'ʿAmālīḳ'.
36. Lecker, 'The Levying of Taxes', p. 123.
37. Al-Samhūdī, *Wafāʾ*, vol. 1, pp. 142–4.
38. Lecker, 'Glimpses of Muḥammad's Medinan Decade', p. 69.
39. Al-Bayhaqī, *Al-Sunan al-kubrā*, vol. 9, p. 308.
40. Lecker, 'King Ibn Ubayy', p. 46. Lecker revises his previous conclusion that this demonstrates the Jewish tribes were actually the dominant group in Medina at the time of the hijra. Cf. Lecker, 'Wāqidī's Account', p. 17.
41. Kister, 'Al-Ḥīra', pp. 147–8.
42. Bosworth, 'Buʿāth'.
43. The Pledge of Women seems to have been retrospectively named as such despite no women being present at the meeting, because, not requiring a commitment to fight, it remained the pledge made by believing women who wished to enter the community throughout the prophetic period. See page 181.
44. Watt, *Muḥammad at Mecca*, pp. 144–5.
45. Ibn Hishām, *Al-Sīra*, vol. 2, p. 58.
46. Lecker, 'King Ibn Ubayy', p. 44.
47. Lecker, 'King Ibn Ubayy', p. 47.
48. See Bowersock, *Crucible*, pp. 108–12.
49. Meeker, *Literature and Violence*, p. 7.
50. Ibn Khaldūn, *Muqaddima*, pp. 139–40.
51. Hoyland, *Arabia and the Arabs*, pp. 99–101.
52. Kister, 'Some Reports Concerning Mecca', pp. 76–7.
53. Bukharin, 'Mecca on the Caravan Routes', p. 131. Bukharin convincingly explains why the existence of sea transit via the Red Sea did not obviate the importance of caravan trading through the peninsula.
54. Ibrahim, *Merchant Capital*, p. 40.
55. Heck, 'Alternate Hypothesis', p. 558.

56. Heck, 'Alternate Hypothesis', pp. 558–86. There was also a concentration of gold mines in the area known as al-Yamāma, a plateau due east of the Ḥijāz, and numerous other gold, silver, and precious stone mines scattered around the peninsula. Al-Hamdānī, *Ṣifa*, pp. 267, 321. Meccan traders were involved in financing mining operations, or, at the very least, using gold and particularly silver for transactions.
57. Heck, 'Alternate Hypothesis', pp. 564–71.
58. Heck, 'Alternate Hypothesis', p. 572. Heck mentions the production of 'natural bilateral commercial flows', the importing and exporting of the same basic type of goods, although differing in price, quality, and exact specification.
59. Serjeant, 'Meccan Trade', pp. 478–9.
60. Serjeant, 'Meccan Trade', p. 479.
61. Nuʿmānī, *Sīrat al-nabī*, vol. 1, p. 156.
62. Serjeant, 'Meccan Trade', p. 479.
63. Heck, 'Alternate Hypothesis', p. 559.
64. Kister, 'Some Reports Concerning Mecca', pp. 61–2.
65. Kister, 'Mecca and Tamīm (Aspects of Their Relations)', pp. 116–17.
66. Serjeant, 'Meccan Trade', p. 480.
67. Kister, 'Some Reports Concerning Mecca', pp. 75–6. Also see Bowersock, *Crucible*, pp. 25–7.
68. Kister, 'Some Reports Concerning Mecca', pp. 75–6.
69. Al-Ḥalabī, *Al-Sīra*, vol. 1, pp. 185–6.
70. See page 67.
71. Bonner, 'The Arabian Silent Trade', pp. 41–2, 45.
72. Bonner, 'The Arabian Silent Trade', pp. 42–5.
73. Ibrahim, *Merchant Capital*, pp. 57–8, 62; Watt, *Muḥammad at Mecca*, p. 19.
74. Gül, 'Ribā (Usury) Prohibition', pp. 4–6.
75. Al-Bukhārī, *Ṣaḥīḥ*, vol. 1, p. 434.
76. Mālik, *Al-Muwaṭṭaʾ*, p. 35.
77. Al-Bukhārī, *Ṣaḥīḥ*, vol. 1, p. 437.
78. Al-Bukhārī, *Ṣaḥīḥ*, vol. 1, p. 439.
79. Watt, *Muḥammad at Mecca*, p. 142.
80. Newby, *Jews of Arabia*, p. 75.
81. Newby, *Jews of Arabia*, p. 77.
82. See page 69.
83. Lecker, 'Muḥammad at Medina', p. 42.
84. For a different interpretation of Qaynuqāʿ's time of expulsion, see page 109.
85. Al-Ḥalabī, *Al-Sīra*, vol. 2, p. 287.
86. Lecker, 'On the Markets of Medina', p. 187.
87. Lecker, 'On the Markets of Medina', p. 186.
88. Lecker, 'On the Markets of Medina', p. 194.
89. Ibn Hishām, *Al-Sīra*, vol. 2, p. 108.
90. See the map in Lecker, 'On the Markets of Medina', p. 193.
91. Kister, 'The Market of the Prophet', pp. 274–5.
92. Al-Bukhārī, *Ṣaḥīḥ*, vol. 1, p. 386.
93. See page 71.
94. Hoyland, *Arabia and the Arabs*, pp. 129–30.
95. Watt, *Muḥammad at Medina*, p. 378.
96. Al-Bukhārī, *Ṣaḥīḥ*, vol. 3, p. 1,075.
97. Al-Bukhārī, *Ṣaḥīḥ*, vol. 3, p. 1,075; ʿAlī, *Al-Mufaṣṣal*, vol. 5, pp. 538–9.
98. Al-Bukhārī, *Ṣaḥīḥ*, vol. 3, p. 1,075.
99. Brunschvig, 'ʿAbd'.
100. Watt, *Muhammad at Medina*, pp. 293–4.
101. Watt, *Muḥammad at Mecca*, pp. 154–7.
102. Crone, *Roman, Provincial and Islamic Law*, p. 58.
103. Crone, *Roman, Provincial and Islamic Law*, p. 60.
104. ʿAlī, *Al-Mufaṣṣal*, vol. 5, p. 638.

105. Nicholson, *A Literary History*, p. 83. Durayd belonged to the Hawāzin tribal grouping and the raid in question was against the Ghaṭafān. He was later a commander at the battle of Ḥunayn in 8/630 and was killed immediately after this by the Muslim army in an encounter at Awṭās. Al-Bukhārī, *Ṣaḥīḥ*, vol. 2, pp. 859–60; Petráček, 'Durayd b. al-Ṣimma'.
106. Al-Ṭā'ī, *Dīwan al-Ḥimāsa*, p. 145. The first and second lines have been swapped with the third and fourth, which matches the well-known version in *Kitāb al-aghānī* and has a more coherent meaning. See Stetkevych, *The Poetics of Islamic Legitimacy*, pp. 52–3.
107. See page 66.
108. See Farès and eds, 'Murū'a'.
109. This issue comes to the fore in the matter of *qiṣāṣ* for murder. See page 173.
110. ʿAlī, *Al-Mufaṣṣal*, vol. 5, p. 638.
111. Surty, *Studies*, p. 54.
112. Surty lists only two prominent *kāhins* by name, as opposed to more than twenty *ḥakams*. Surty, *Studies*, pp. 55–7. However, it is clear that much *kāhin* material has been lost, so this may not be an entirely accurate comparison. Jones, 'The Language of the Qur'an', p. 32.
113. Jones, 'The Language of the Qur'an', p. 33.
114. Jones, 'The Language of the Qur'an', p. 63.
115. Al-Ḥalabī, *Al-Sīra*, vol. 1, pp. 54–5.
116. See page 66.
117. Kister, 'Mecca and the Tribes of Arabia', p. 53. There is obviously here a blurring of political and judicial arbitration. See page 94.
118. ʿAlī, *Al-Mufaṣṣal*, vol. 5, p. 638.
119. Ibn ʿAbd Rabbih, *Al-ʿIqd*, vol. 3, pp. 267–8.
120. Surty, *Studies*, p. 65.
121. Ibn Ḥabīb, *Kitāb al-munammaq*, p. 87.
122. Surty, *Studies*, p. 64; Shahid, 'ʿUkāẓ'. However, see comments on page 72.
123. Finster, 'Arabia in Late Antiquity', p. 71. Cf. Lecker, *People, Tribes and Society*, p. ix; Watt, 'Hawāzin'.
124. Fück, 'Fidjār'. See pages 67 and 72.
125. Newby, *Jews of Arabia*, p. 54.
126. Abū Dāwūd, *Sunan*, vol. 2, p. 753. See pages 103 and 175–6.
127. Iṣlāḥī, *Tadabbur-e-Qur'ān*, vol. 1, p. 443.
128. Mair, *Primitive Government*, pp. 36–7.
129. Hoyland, *Arabia and the Arabs*, p. 122.
130. Bravmann argues that the communal duty to deliver up a criminal has a Bedouin origin. See Bravmann, *The Spiritual Background of Early Islam*, pp. 315–34.
131. Lecker, *The 'Constitution of Medina'*, pp. 123–4.
132. Nicholson, *A Literary History*, p. 93.
133. Hoyland, *Arabia and the Arabs*, pp. 122–3.
134. See pages 69 and 72.
135. Meeker, *Literature and Violence*, p. 18.
136. Kennedy, *On Fiction and* Adab, pp. 252–3.
137. Watt, *Muḥammad at Mecca*, p. 142.
138. ʿAlī, *Al-Mufaṣṣal*, vol. 5, pp. 559–60.

Chapter 5

1. For a discussion of the importance of paradigmatic figures and narratives for imparting an insightful understanding of virtuous action in varying circumstances, see Taylor, 'Justice after Virtue', p. 28.
2. Black, *Islamic Political Thought*, p. 13; Donner, *Narratives of Islamic Origins*, p. 44.
3. Rosenthal, *Political Thought*, p. 23.
4. Asad, *State and Government*, p. 15.
5. The plurals *khalā'if* and *khulafā'* are also prominent in the Qur'an, while the linguistic parallel to *mulk*, the *maṣdar* (infinitive noun) *khilāfa* (stewardship, or successorship), is not used, but is implied.

6. Al-Iṣfahānī, *Mufradāt*, p. 597.
7. Al-Iṣfahānī, *Mufradāt*, p. 597.
8. Ibn Khaldūn, *Muqaddima*, p. 173; Abdesselem, *Dirāsāt*, pp. 46–7.
9. Rosenthal, *Political Thought*, pp. 84–5.
10. Ibn Khaldūn, *Muqaddima*, pp. 212–13.
11. Khadduri, *War and Peace*, p. 16.
12. Khan, *Political Concepts*, p. 7.
13. See page 12. Cf. Lane, *Lexicon*, vol. 1, p. 792.
14. Crone and Hinds, *God's Caliph*, pp. 6–11.
15. Al-Zabīdī gives the primary meaning of *khalīfa* as *al-sulṭān al-aʿẓam* (the greatest authority). Al-Zabīdī, *Tāj al-ʿarūs*, vol. 23, p. 264. This meaning is also found in Al-Rāzī, *Mukhtār al-ṣiḥāḥ*, p. 78.
16. Technically *khulafāʾ* is the plural of *khalīf*, but it is allowed due to *khalīfa* usually taking the masculine grammatical form. Al-Zabīdī, *Tāj al-ʿarūs*, vol. 23, p. 264. See Q. 7:69, 7:74, and 27:62. The word *khalāʾif* is used in Q. 6:165, 10:73, 10:14, and 35:39.
17. Cf. Al-Fārābī, *Kitāb ārāʾ*, pp. 117–30.
18. Hamid, *The Qurʾan & Politics*, p. 65.
19. See Pangle and Burns, *The Key Texts of Political Philosophy*, pp. 259–72, 280–8, 300–1.
20. See page 16.
21. The Prophet is directly or implicitly addressed in the following relevant verses: Q. 2:30, 2:246–52, 2:258, 11:59, 18:83–98, 38:26, 43:51–6, 3:26, 3:65, 48:10, and 48:18; while the believers are addressed in Q. 4:59, 4:65, and 4:80. On the same topic, there is also the narration of a historical address to the Children of Israel in Q. 5:12–13 and 5:20.
22. Abdel Haleem, 'Qur'anic Employment', p. 55.
23. For the argument that Q. 42:13–15 are a command to establish political control over the Quraysh while still in Mecca, see Hamid, *The Qurʾan & Politics*, p. 75.
24. Watt, *Muḥammad at Mecca*, p. 126.
25. Cf. Wolf, 'Social Organization', pp. 344–52.
26. This is the case for the ʿUthmanī text and that attributed to Ubayy b. Kaʿb. The *muṣḥaf* of Ibn Masʿūd reverses the order of the two suras. See Ibn Nadīm, *Kitāb al-fihrist*, p. 29. For further discussion on Ibn Masʿūd's reading of the Qur'an, see Harvey, 'The Legal Epistemology of Qur'anic Variants'.
27. See pages 123–4.
28. See page 188. For further discussion of the relationship of the stories of these various prophets within the sura's *niẓām*, see Johns, 'Shuʿayb, Orator of the Prophets', pp. 137–43.
29. Cf. Q. 11:116–17.
30. The context here is the failure to use their power to establish justice based on faith. Cf. Q. 6:6.
31. *ʿAhd* may also foreshadow the 'primordial covenant' to be mentioned later in the same sura in Q. 7:172. See pages 10–11. For the political connotations of the word, see page 101.
32. Cf. Q. 70:40.
33. See page 60.
34. Ibn ʿĀshūr, *Tafsīr al-taḥrīr*, vol. 6, p. 161. Qur'anic usage of the past tense to express the future has been commented on since at least the time of Muqātil b. Sulaymān (d. 150/767). Muqātil b. Sulaymān, *Tafsīr Muqātil*, vol. 1, p. 520.
35. See 1 Samuel 10:17–25.
36. This category corresponds to Ibn Khaldūn's wider *siyāsa dīniyya*, which allows him to include the imperfect religious basis of the historical Islamic caliphate. See page 82.
37. Compare with the hadith on the authority of Ḥudhayfa b. al-Yamān that mentions a number of post-prophetic stages: stewardship in the manner of prophecy (*khilāfa ʿalā minhāj al-nubuwwa*), bitingly unjust rule (*mulk ʿāḍḍ*), tyrannical rule (*mulk jabriyya*), and, finally, a return to stewardship. Ibn Ḥanbal, *Musnad*, vol. 30, pp. 355–6. The editor, Shuʿayb Arnāʾūṭ, declares it *ḥasan*. Other hadiths merely indicate two periods: thirty years of *khilāfa* followed by *mulk*. See Abū Dāwūd, *Sunan*, vol. 2, p. 781; Al-Tirmidhī, *Sunan*, vol. 2, p. 573.
38. Lace, *Understanding the Old Testament*, pp. 77–8.
39. Mir, *Understanding the Islamic Scripture*, p. 42.

40. Iṣlāḥī, *Tadabbur-e-Qur'ān*, vol. 1, p. 579. Cf. Exodus 25:10–22. '[The] Tabernacle [housing the Ark of the Covenant], and later the Temple in Jerusalem, was intended to be the central rallying point of the nation, ringed by the tribes, topped by the cloud of God's Presence, and the place to which every Jew would bring his offerings.' Scherman, *Tanach*, p. 196.
41. See Q. 27:23–44.
42. Scherman, *Tanach*, pp. 684–5.
43. In the Hebrew Bible, this test is given by the Judge Gideon some 200 years prior to the time of Saul. Judges 7:5–7; Scherman, *Tanach*, pp. 2,025–6.
44. Al-Suyūṭī and al-Maḥallī, *Tafsīr*, p. 41.
45. Al-Nasafī, *Madārik*, p. 130.
46. See 2 Samuel 22:1–23:7. Sosevsky, *Samuel II*, p. 431.
47. Al-Rāzī, *Al-Tafsīr al-kabīr*, vol. 6, p. 202.
48. Al-Suyūṭī and al-Maḥallī, *Tafsīr*, p. 41.
49. See page 108.
50. The same wording occurs in Q. 22:40. See page 90 and compare with pages 111–12.
51. Nöldeke, *Geschichte des Qorāns*, vol. 1, p. 184.
52. Iṣlāḥī, *Tadabbur-e-Qur'ān*, vol. 1, p. 584.
53. This is mirrored in the outnumbered believers present at Badr – also about 310 – as explicitly mentioned within hadiths in the collection of al-Bukhārī on the authority of al-Barā' b. 'Āzib. Al-Bukhārī, *Ṣaḥīḥ*, vol. 2, p. 784.
54. Iṣlāḥī, *Tadabbur-e-Qur'ān*, vol. 1, p. 566.
55. Al-Suyūṭī, *Al-Itqān*, vol. 3, p. 90.
56. Al-Nasafī, *Madārik*, p. 1,015.
57. Al-Bukhārī, *Ṣaḥīḥ*, vol. 3, p. 1,418.
58. Al-Ghazālī, *Nahw tafsīr mawḍū'ī*, p. 351.
59. Cf. 2 Samuel 11–12:24 and the discussion in al-Rāzī, *Al-Tafsīr al-kabīr*, vol. 26, pp. 189–94.
60. The reversal of sentence order in this way is mentioned by al-Suyūṭī, *Al-Itqān*, vol. 3, p. 39. See page 12.
61. Al-Ṣāwī, *Hāshiya*, vol. 3, p. 296.
62. Nöldeke puts this verse prior to 5/627 due to reference to Banū Qurayẓa whom traditional reports state were executed following the Battle of Khandaq. Nöldeke, *Geschichte des Qorāns*, vol. 1, pp. 230–1. See pages 9–10.
63. Cf. Q. 27:15.
64. See Q. 21:79, 34:10, and 38:18–19.
65. See Q. 4:163 and 17:55.
66. See Q. 21:81–2, 27:16–44, and 34:12–14.
67. *Ṣafana* in relation to horses refers to a position with three legs on the ground and the fourth resting on the edge of the hoof. Ḍayf, *Al-Mu'jam*, p. 537. Al-Rāzī views the whole expression as representing perfection in stillness (*ṣāfināt*) and motion (*jiyād*). Al-Rāzī, *Al-Tafsīr al-kabīr*, vol. 26, p. 204.
68. Al-Rāzī, *Al-Tafsīr al-kabīr*, vol. 26, p. 204.
69. Al-Rāzī, *Al-Tafsīr al-kabīr*, vol. 26, p. 206.
70. Al-Rāzī, *Al-Tafsīr al-kabīr*, vol. 26, p. 206. Anthony Johns discusses al-Rāzī's reasoning for his interpretation of this passage and, despite critiquing some of his argumentative rhetoric, admits the cogency of his explanation of the story. Johns, 'Solomon and the Horses', pp. 20–1.
71. Al-Ṭabarī, *Tafsīr*, vol. 20, pp. 87–92.
72. Al-Rāzī, *Al-Tafsīr al-kabīr*, vol. 26, p. 209. The latter translation is found in Abdel Haleem, *The Qur'an*, p. 456.
73. Lane, *Lexicon*, vol. 2, p. 2,862.
74. Cf. Q. 34:12.
75. Lane, *Lexicon*, vol. 2, p. 1,616.
76. Cf. Q. 42:36–8.
77. M. A. S. Abdel Haleem, 'The Qur'an: Language, Style and Translation into English' (Lecture, School of Oriental and African Studies (SOAS), London, 6 January 2009).
78. Asad, *Message*, p. 498.

79. Stenton, *Anglo-Saxon England*, p. 492.
80. Al-Qurṭubī, *Al-Jāmi'*, vol. 13, p. 373.
81. Al-Suyūṭī, and al-Maḥallī, *Tafsīr*, p. 43.
82. See pages 182–3 below.
83. See Chapter 2.
84. Cf. Khadduri, *War and Peace*, p. 10.
85. Khadduri, *War and Peace*, pp. 10–11.
86. Ibn Khaldūn, *Muqaddima*, pp. 216–17.
87. Zayd b 'Alī, *Al-Ṣafwa*, pp. 30–1, 94, 101; Madelung, *Succession*, pp. 6–18.
88. The Qur'an also mentions what is to be done if a group from the community is disloyal. The main verses cited are Q. 49:9–10 (see page 21). Also see the discussion of the verses of *hirāba* on pages 178–80.
89. Asad, *Message*, p. 100. More specifically, linking Q. 4:60 to Ka'b b. Ashraf who died just before the siege of Banū al-Naḍīr in 4/625 gives a more precise dating. Watt, 'Ka'b b. Ashraf'.
90. See page 109.
91. Ibn Taymiyya, *Siyāsa*, p. 4.
92. Zamakhsharī, *Al-Kashshāf*, p. 242.
93. Al-Suyūṭī, *Lubāb*, p. 83; Al-Bukhārī, *Ṣaḥīḥ*, vol. 2, p. 921.
94. Al-Qurṭubī, *Al-Jāmi'*, vol. 6, pp. 429–30. See page 97.
95. Al-Ghazālī, *Nahw tafsīr mawḍū'ī*, pp. 55–7.
96. Badawi and Abdel Haleem, *Dictionary*, p. 567; Al-Iṣfahānī, *Mufradāt*, p. 389.
97. The singular form can be read in Q. 4:60 and 4:76, the plural form in Q. 2:256–7 and 39:17. Either can be read in Q. 4:51, 5:60, and 16:36.
98. Al-Zabīdī, *Tāj al-'arūs*, vol. 16, p. 522.
99. Al-Ṭabarī, *Tafsīr*, vol. 7, pp. 193–5.
100. Al-Qurṭubī, *Al-Jāmi'*, vol. 6, pp. 440–1; Al-Bukhārī, *Ṣaḥīḥ*, vol. 2, pp. 921–2.
101. Al-Ṭabarī, *Tafsīr*, vol. 7, pp. 204–5.
102. Al-Qurṭubī, *Al-Jāmi'*, vol. 6, p. 440.
103. Abū Su'ūd, *Irshād*, vol. 1, p. 728.
104. See page 49.
105. Cf. Q. 2:249. See page 88.
106. 'Alī, *The Holy Qur-ān*, vol. 1, p. 205.
107. Al-Qurṭubī, *Al-Jāmi'*, vol. 6, p. 479.
108. Al-Tirmidhī, *Sunan*, vol. 1, p. 358.
109. Al-Māwardī, *Al-Aḥkām*, p. 4; Asad, *State and Government*, p. 34.
110. Al-Ṭaḥāwī, *Matn al-aqīdat al-Ṭaḥawiyya*, p. 14.
111. Cf. al-Juwaynī who argues that it is obligatory to remove an unjust ruler, just as it is impermissible to pledge allegiance to one. Al-Juwaynī, *Al-Ghiyāthī*, p. 271.

Chapter 6

1. See Khadduri, *The Islamic Law of Nations*, pp. 8–9; Kelsay, *Arguing the Just War in Islam*, pp. 99–100.
2. This assumption of consistency in Qur'anic statements relating to conflict has been challenged in Firestone, 'Disparity and Resolution', pp. 17–19. It is defended in Abdel Haleem, 'Qur'anic '*jihād*'', pp. 160–1.
3. See Ibn Juzayy, *Al-Tashīl*, pp. 13–15.
4. Ibn Hishām, *Al-Sīra*, vol. 1, p. 206.
5. See page 87.
6. Al-Bukhārī, *Ṣaḥīḥ*, vol. 2, p. 915–16.
7. Lecker, *Muslims, Jews and Pagans*, pp. 19–20.
8. Al-Kāndahlawī, *Awjaz*, vol. 6, p. 188.
9. Cf. Q. 5:44.
10. See Griffith, 'Christians and Christianity'.
11. Fiey, 'Naṣārā'.

12. Blois, 'Sabians'. This corresponds with the view of the early exegete Mujāhid. Al-Kāndahlawī, *Awjaz*, vol. 6, p. 188.
13. See pages 68–70.
14. Bukharin, 'Mecca on the Caravan Routes', p. 130.
15. Nebes, 'The Martyrs of Najrān', p. 48; Finster, 'Arabia in Late Antiquity', pp. 71–2; Shahid, *Byzantium and the Arabs in the Fifth Century*, pp. 294–5. Also see Al-Azmeh, *Emergence*, pp. 263–6.
16. Munt, '"No Two Religions"', pp. 252–4.
17. Asad argues that it belongs to the last year before the Prophet made hijra. Asad, *Message*, p. 202.
18. Ibn Hishām, *Al-Sīra*, vol. 2, pp. 105–7.
19. See pages 10–11.
20. Al-Iṣfahānī, *Mufradāt*, p. 446.
21. Ibn Manẓūr, *Lisān*, vol. 6, p. 4,764.
22. For discussion of Q. 49:9, see page 21. For discussion of Q. 4:128, see pages 149–50.
23. This is the view of Qatāda and ʿIkrima who also mention Q. 9:36 and Sūrat Barāʾa (al-Tawba) in general, while their teacher Ibn ʿAbbās says that Q. 44:35 is the abrogating verse. Al-Qurṭubī, *Al-Jāmiʿ*, vol. 10, p. 63.
24. See pages 111–12.
25. Al-Jaṣṣāṣ, *Aḥkām*, vol. 4, pp. 254–5. See the discussion on pages 58–9.
26. Other views on the length agreed for the treaty include three and four years. Al-Qurṭubī, *Al-Jāmiʿ*, vol. 10, p. 65.
27. Ibn Hishām, *Al-Sīra*, vol. 2, pp. 112–15. Ibn Hishām, following Ibn Isḥāq, redacts the text of the Covenant without an *isnād*, although one is supplied by Ibn Abī Khaythama, and also by Aḥmad b. Ḥanbal. Al-Būṭī, *Fiqh al-sīra*, p. 150. There are hadiths recorded by Ibn Ḥanbal that mention the Covenant without quoting its text, but these are considered weak by al-Arnāʾūṭ. Ibn Ḥanbal, *Musnad*, vol. 4, p. 258; vol. 11, pp. 504–5. Another redaction of Ibn Isḥāq can be found in Abū ʿUbayd al-Qāsim b. Sallām. Munt, *The Holy City of Medina*, p. 55. There are also reports about the physical preservation of the written document by the descendants of the Caliph ʿUmar b. al-Khaṭṭāb along with other letters relating to taxation. See Lecker, *The 'Constitution of Medina'*, pp. 196–200.
28. Watt, *Muḥammad at Medina*, pp. 227–8.
29. Lecker, 'Did Muḥammad Conclude Treaties', pp. 35–6.
30. Ibn Hishām, *Al-Sīra*, vol. 2, p. 114.
31. Asad, *Message*, p. 139.
32. Abū Dāwūd, *Sunan*, vol. 2, pp. 611, 753; Al-Nasāʾī, *Sunan*, vol. 2, p. 771. The date of 4/625 for al-Naḍīr's expulsion is argued in Jones, 'The Chronology of the Maghāzī', pp. 268–9. The content of these reports is summarised on pages 175–6.
33. Al-Ṭabarī, *Tafsīr*, vol. 8, pp. 414–17. See page 187.
34. Cf. Q. 7:156–8.
35. For a nuanced discussion of the classical theological position that the Qur'an supersedes previous revealed dispensations, the implications for salvation and various challenges by modern Muslim thinkers, see Winter, 'Last Trump Card'.
36. Al-Bayḍāwī, *Anwār*, vol. 1, p. 278.
37. See pages 175–6.
38. Al-Iṣfahānī, *Mufradāt*, p. 689.
39. Al-Ṭabarī, *Tafsīr*, vol. 22, pp. 559–64.
40. See page 111.
41. Lane, *Lexicon*, vol. 1, p. 175.
42. Al-Qurṭubī, *Al-Jāmiʿ*, vol. 20, pp. 407–8.
43. Ibn Hishām, *Al-Sīra*, vol. 3, p. 207; vol. 4, pp. 17–18; Kister, 'Khuzāʿa'.
44. See page 21.
45. Ibn Hishām, *Al-Sīra*, vol. 4, p. 17.
46. Ibn Hishām, *Al-Sīra*, vol. 4, p. 20. Also see Al-Azmeh, *Emergence*, pp. 367–8.
47. MacIntyre, *Whose Justice? Which Rationality?*, p. 146.
48. Izutsu, *Ethico-Religious Concepts*, pp. 105–6.
49. Izutsu, *Ethical Terms*, p. 212.

Chapter 7

1. See the comments about Q. 2:251 on page 89 and Q. 22:40 on page 108. For a general analysis of the term jihad in the Qur'an, see Abdel Haleem, 'Qur'anic '*jihād*'', pp. 147–8.
2. See page 83.
3. For instance, Ibn Juzayy al-Kalbī quotes 114 verses in fifty-four suras, which he says are all abrogated by Q. 9:5 and Q. 2:216. Ibn Juzayy, *Al-Tashīl*, pp. 13–15.
4. Al-Māturīdī, *Ta'wīlāt*, vol. 6, p. 330.
5. Al-Māturīdī, *Ta'wīlāt*, vol. 6, p. 331.
6. Al-Māturīdī, *Ta'wīlāt*, vol. 6, p. 330.
7. Al-Qaraḍāwī claims that the Ḥanafīs made fighting non-Muslims conditional on their belligerence towards the Muslim community, in which he quotes the Ḥanafī *fiqh* manual *al-Ḥidāya* by al-Marghīnānī and its commentary *al-ʿInāya* by al-Bābartī. Al-Qaraḍāwī, *Fiqh al-jihād*, vol. 1, p. 373. However, the section that he refers to only discusses whether jihad is a personal or community obligation, while the clear rule in the former text is that they are to be fought even if they do not initiate aggression due to the general wording of the Qur'an. Al-Marghīnānī, *Al-Hidāya*, vol. 4, pp. 217–19. Al-Bābartī adds that the defensive rule in Q. 2:191 is abrogated. Al-Bābartī, *Sharḥ al-ʿināya*, vol. 4, p. 282. Although it is not the position of the Ḥanafīs, the interpretation of jihad as a response to the attacks of others is mentioned as the view of al-Thawrī. Al-ʿAynī, *Al-Bināya sharḥ al-hidāya*, vol. 7, pp. 97–8.
8. See page 23.
9. See Sayyid Quṭb, *Fī ẓilāl al-qur'ān*, vol. 3, p. 1,644. There is a response to the position of Quṭb in al-Qaradāwī, *Fiqh al-jihād*, vol. 1, pp. 395–404.
10. Al-Suyūṭī mentions that verses in Sūrat al-Ḥajj are considered Medinan if the text indicates it, even if there is a lack of extra-Qur'anic support. Al-Suyūṭī, *Al-Itqān*, vol. 1, p. 58.
11. Al-Bukhārī, *Ṣaḥīḥ*, vol. 2, p. 1,015.
12. Abdel Haleem, *The Qur'an*, p. 546.
13. Ibn Hishām, *Al-Sīra*, vol. 3, pp. 114–15 and see pages 102–3. Note that distribution of the spoils of al-Naḍīr within Q. 59:7 is discussed on pages 135–6.
14. Jones, 'The Chronology of the Maghāzī', p. 195.
15. Al-Bukhārī, *Ṣaḥīḥ*, vol. 2, p. 798; Muslim, *Ṣaḥīḥ*, vol. 2, p. 768.
16. Abdel Haleem suggests that Q. 59:15, 'Like those who went just before them (*ka-mithli alladhīna min qablihim qarīban*)' may allude to Qaynuqāʿ. Abdel Haleem, *The Qur'an*, p. 548. Another view is that it refers to the pagans of Badr. Al-Suyūṭī and al-Maḥallī, *Tafsīr*, p. 547.
17. Ibn Hishām, *Al-Sīra*, vol. 3, pp. 140–2.
18. Al-Ṭabarī, *Tafsīr*, vol. 19, p. 72.
19. Al-Ṭabarī, *Tafsīr*, vol. 19, p. 72; Ibn Hishām, *Al-Sīra*, vol. 3, pp. 148–9. Al-Bukhārī reports execution of the male combatants and captivity of their children (in a second hadith: women and children, as well as division of their wealth). Al-Bukhārī, *Ṣaḥīḥ*, vol. 2, p. 820.
20. Ibn Hishām, *Al-Sīra*, vol. 3, p. 149. See pages 103–4 and 183.
21. Ahmad, *Muḥammad and the Jews*, pp. 73–94.
22. Ahmad, *Muḥammad and the Jews*, pp. 90–1.
23. Al-Ṭabarī, *Tafsīr*, vol. 19, pp. 82–3.
24. It is reported that the *muṣḥaf* of Ibn Masʿūd did have a *basmala* at the beginning of this sura. Jeffery, *Materials*, p. 44.
25. Al-Rāzī, *Al-Tafsīr al-kabīr*, vol. 15, pp. 215–17. Cf. Al-Tirmidhī, *Sunan*, vol. 2, pp. 780–1.
26. The link between *yawm al-naḥr*, the hajj's Day of Sacrifice, and *yawm al-ḥajj al-akbar* is explicit in al-Bukhārī, *Ṣaḥīḥ*, vol. 2, p. 939.
27. Jones, 'The Chronology of the Maghāzī', p. 206.
28. Al-Bukhārī, *Ṣaḥīḥ*, vol. 2, p. 939. This is recorded with a different *isnād* on the same page.
29. This accords with the view of al-Zuhrī. Al-Ṭabarī, *Tafsīr*, vol. 11, pp. 310–11.
30. Al-Rāzī, *Al-Tafsīr al-kabīr*, vol. 15, p. 220.
31. Ibn Hishām, *Al-Sīra*, vol. 4, p. 173. Cf. Q. 9:36.
32. Al-Ṭabarī, *Tafsīr*, vol. 11, p. 317.

33. Al-Jaṣṣāṣ, *Aḥkām*, vol. 4, pp. 269–70; Al-Qurṭubī, *Al-Jāmiʿ*, vol. 10, p. 109.
34. Abdel Haleem, 'Qur'anic '*jihād*'', p. 155; Abdel Haleem, *The Qur'an*, p. 188.
35. Al-Qurṭubī, *Al-Jāmiʿ*, vol. 10, p. 115.
36. Al-Zamakhsharī, *Al-Kashshāf*, p. 424.
37. Al-Ṭabarī, *Tafsīr*, vol. 11, pp. 350–1, 353.
38. Abdel Haleem, 'Qur'anic '*jihād*'', p. 154.
39. Munt, '"No Two Religions"', p. 255.
40. See the discussion on pages 68–9. Also see Al-Azmeh, *Emergence*, pp. 391–2.
41. Watt, *Muḥammad at Medina*, p. 115.
42. Asad, *Message*, p. 254. Nöldeke proposes that this verse could be connected with the battle of Muʿta, which took place against a Christian Byzantine army in 8/629. Nöldeke, *Geschichte des Qorāns*, vol. 1, p. 224.
43. For an argument based on stylistic considerations, see Abdel Haleem, 'The *Jizya* Verse', p. 79.
44. Abdel Haleem, 'The *Jizya* Verse', p. 74.
45. See page 11.
46. Al-Ṭabarī, *Tafsīr*, vol. 11, pp. 407–8.
47. Asad, *Message*, p. 262.
48. See page 22–3.
49. See al-Ṭabarī, *Tārīkh*, vol. 3, pp. 378–80.
50. Abū Dāwūd, *Sunan*, vol. 2, p. 528. Another hadith on the same page makes Yemenī garments from the Maʿāfirī tribe equivalent to one dinar for the purpose of jizya. The agreement is usually understood to have been concluded following the Najran delegation's withdrawal from the mutual cursing (*mubāhala*) mentioned in Q. 3:61. Al-Suyūṭī and al-Maḥallī, *Tafsīr*, pp. 57–8.
51. See pages 103–4.
52. Of the major schools of jurisprudence, this is closest to the view of Mālik, who deems jizya applicable to all non-Muslims bar apostates (Abū Ḥanīfa accepts it from Scriptuaries and all non-Arabians, while al-Shāfiʿī restricts it to the Scriptuaries of non-Arabians). Al-ʿAynī, *ʿUmdat al-qārī*, vol. 15, p. 78.
53. Al-Bukhārī, *Ṣaḥīḥ*, vol. 2, p. 616; Mālik, *Al-Muwaṭṭaʾ*, p. 96.
54. See the hadith of Burayda that explicitly mandates the taking of jizya and *dhimma* from pagans. Muslim, *Ṣaḥīḥ*, vol. 2, pp. 753–4. The same tradition is found in the *Kitāb al-āthār* of Abū Yūsuf, in which the narration branches to be narrated via Abū Ḥanīfa rather than Sufyān al-Thawrī. Another chain is given by Abū Yūsuf going instead through Yaḥyā b. Saʿīd, as well as a version going to a different companion, al-Nuʿmān b. al-Muqarrin al-Muzanī, through a less reliable path of transmission. Abū Yūsuf, *Kitāb al-āthār*, pp. 192–3. A shortened version of the same basic tradition on the authority of Abū Ḥanīfa can be found in al-Shaybānī, *Kitāb al-āthār*, vol. 2, p. 728. In this version, *dār al-muhājirīn* (Abode of the Emigrants) is glossed as *dār al-islām* (Abode of Islam). This possibly reflects the shift to the later juristic classification of 'the two abodes'.
55. Muslim, *Ṣaḥīḥ*, vol. 2, p. 769; Al-Tirmidhī, *Sunan*, vol. 1, p. 434; Abū Dāwūd, *Sunan*, vol. 2, p. 527.
56. Al-Mizzī, *Tuḥfat al-ashrāf*, vol. 7, p. 189; Al-Mizzī, *Tahdhīb al-kamāl*, vol. 26, p. 411.
57. Al-Bukhārī, *Ṣaḥīḥ*, vol. 2, pp. 618–19. Cf. Muslim, *Ṣaḥīḥ*, vol. 2, p. 768.
58. Al-ʿAsqalānī, *Fatḥ al-bārī*, vol. 6, p. 313.
59. Al-Bukhārī, *Ṣaḥīḥ*, vol. 2, p. 615; Mālik, *Al-Muwaṭṭaʾ*, p. 352; Abū Dāwūd, *Sunan*, vol. 2, p. 527.
60. Munt, '"No Two Religions"', pp. 264-6.
61. See page 146.
62. Al-Bukhārī, *Ṣaḥīḥ*, vol. 2, pp. 619; Al-Mizzī, *Tuḥfat al-ashrāf*, vol. 4, p. 326.

Chapter 8

1. Ghānim, *Al-Qurʾān wa-l-iqtiṣād al-siyāsī*, p. 97. Cf. Q. 24:33 and 57:7.
2. See Quṭb, *Social Justice in Islam*, pp. 46–7.
3. The importance of trade in the socio-economic makeup of seventh-century Arabia is discussed on pages 70–3.
4. Al-Rāzī, *Al-Tafsīr al-kabīr*, vol. 32, p. 103.

5. See page 71.
6. Lane, *Lexicon*, vol. 2, p. 3,057.
7. See note 86 on page 198.
8. Al-Rāzī, *Al-Tafsīr al-kabīr*, vol. 20, p. 206.
9. Cf. Q. 12:58–9.
10. Johns, 'Shu'ayb', p. 137.
11. See pages 84–6.
12. Abū Su'ūd, *Irshād*, vol. 2, p. 370.
13. Johns, 'Shu'ayb', p. 145.
14. This may be connected to the concept of *ḥirāba* (brigandage). See page 180.
15. Al-Bayḍāwī, *Anwār*, vol. 1, p. 477.
16. Cf. Al-'Iwaḍī, '*I'jāz al-qur'ān al-karīm*', pp. 195–6.
17. Abū Su'ūd, *Irshād*, vol. 3, p. 81. He relates this to Q. 44:49 in which the guards of Hell punish a sinful person, proclaiming '*dhuq innaka anta al-'azīzu al-karīm* (Taste this, you powerful, respected man!)'. Both cases are instances of *tahakkum* (mocking address). Al-Suyūṭī, *Al-Itqān*, vol. 3, p. 87.
18. There is a parallel expression with respect to the fate of Shu'ayb's people in Q. 7:92 and 11:95, as well as one about Thamūd in Q. 11:68.
19. Al-Jamal, *Al-Futūḥāt*, vol. 4, pp. 522–3.
20. See page 73.
21. Cf. page 104.
22. See page 129 and pages 162, 165.
23. See page 161.
24. See pages 60–1.
25. Abū Su'ūd, *Irshād*, vol. 1, p. 686.
26. Al-Rāzī, *Al-Tafsīr al-kabīr*, vol. 10, p. 69.
27. In later works, al-Rāzī leaves classical Ash'arī voluntarism for a form of consequentialism. See Shihadeh, *The Teleological Ethics of Fakhr al-Dīn al-Rāzī*, pp. 64–6.
28. Al-Rāzī, *Al-Tafsīr al-kabīr*, vol. 10, p. 70.
29. Al-Qazwīnī, *Al-Talkhīṣ*, p. 381.
30. Al-Zamakhsharī, *Al-Kashshāf*, p. 233.
31. Al-Qurṭubī, *Al-Jāmi'*, vol. 4, pp. 423–64.
32. Ḍayf, *Al-Mu'jam*, p. 318.
33. Al-Rāzī, *Al-Tafsīr al-kabīr*, vol. 7, p. 116.
34. Al-Qurṭubī, *Al-Jāmi'*, vol. 4, p. 431.
35. Asad, *Message*, p. 63.
36. Na'im, *Toward an Islamic Reformation*, p. 116.
37. Asad, *Message*, p. 63; Watt, *Muḥammad at Medina*, pp. 289–90.
38. See pages 19–21.
39. Iṣlāḥī, *Tadabbur-e-Qur'ān*, vol. 1, pp. 651–2.
40. Al-Rāzī, *Al-Tafsīr al-kabīr*, vol. 7, p. 127.
41. Ibn Manẓūr, *Lisān*, vol. 3, p. 1,572.
42. Usmani, *The Historic Judgement on Interest*, pp. 32–6, 40–2.
43. Stevenson (ed.), *Shorter Oxford English Dictionary*, vol. 1, p. 1,057. See Muslim, *Ṣaḥīḥ*, vol. 2, p. 676. Jurists came to different conclusions about the *'illa* shared by these six items and their extension to other cases. Al-Zuhaylī, 'The Juridical Meaning of Riba', pp. 30–41. A compelling explanation of *ribā al-faḍl*, although not adopted in its entirety by any of the traditional schools, is based on the possibility that the commodities are liable to be used as money. As soon as they come into use as a medium of exchange, they become exchangeable in kind according to their measure and not their grade, which represents an unjustified increase for those who previously bought a greater volume of the cheaper type. See Usmani, *The Historic Judgement on Interest*, p. 41.
44. Rahman, 'Riba and Interest', p. 32.
45. Al-Ṣabbāḥ, *Mabāḥith*, p. 59. See pages 162 and 185.
46. Gül, 'Ribā (Usury) Prohibition', pp. 9–10.
47. See page 37.

48. Fazlur Rahman argues for the fourth, or fifth year of prophecy, or even earlier based on its reference to the defeat of the Byzantine army. Rahman, 'Riba and Interest', p. 3. Asad prefers a slightly later date of the sixth or seventh year. Asad, *Message*, p. 617. Nöldeke puts it in his third Meccan period. Nöldeke, *Geschichte des Qorāns*, vol. 1, p. 149.
49. Asad, *Message*, p. 623.
50. Rosen, *The Justice of Islam*, p. 169.
51. Al-Qurṭubī, *Al-Jāmi'*, vol. 16, p. 437. The verse's reference to usury is upheld by al-Ḥasan al-Baṣrī and others. Al-Qurṭubī, *Al-Jāmi'*, vol. 16, p. 438.
52. Rahman, 'Riba and Interest', p. 3.
53. See pages 123–4.
54. Asad, *Message*, p. 65.
55. Abū Dāwūd, *Sunan*, vol. 2, p. 435.
56. Rahman, 'Riba and Interest', pp. 6–7.
57. See page 93. M. A. Choudhury gives a technical economic argument with a similar result: a prohibition of compound rates implies prohibition of simple rates, as the former can be expressed as equivalent to the latter. Choudhury, 'Usury'.
58. See Deuteronomy 23:20–1 and Cornell, 'In the Shadow of Deuteronomy'.
59. This is on the authority of Ibn 'Abbās and although it is part of the same passage does not, strictly speaking, concern *ribā*, but rather the return to God for judgement. Al-Bukhārī, *Ṣaḥīḥ*, vol. 2, p. 909.
60. Al-Rāzī, *Al-Tafsīr al-kabīr*, vol. 7, p. 106. Cf. Al-Zuhaylī, 'The Juridical Meaning of Riba', p. 26.
61. Al-Ṭabarī, *Tafsīr*, vol. 5, pp. 43–4.
62. Riḍā, *Tafsīr al-manār*, vol. 3, p. 97.
63. Sherman Jackson, 'Western Muslims and Human Rights: An Alternative Framework' (Lecture, Human Rights in Islam: The Politics of Cultural Transformation, Duke University, Durham, NC, USA, 24 February 2011).
64. See pages 34–7.
65. The theme emerges in the *khuṭbat al-wadā'* on the Prophet's final pilgrimage. Ibn Hishām, *Al-Sīra*, vol. 4, p. 173.

Chapter 9

1. See page 72.
2. This is likely to refer to the usurpation of the inheritance of orphans; see page 160.
3. Cf. Korah's fate in Q. 28:76–82.
4. Al-Ḥaddād, *Worship*, p. x.
5. Al-Qurṭubī, *Al-Jāmi'*, vol. 10, p. 356.
6. See Q. 17:26–9, 25:63–7, 30:38–9, 70:24-5, and 76:8–9.
7. Al-Qaraḍāwī, *Fiqh al-zakāt*, vol. 1, p. 61.
8. Ibrāhīm al-Nakha'ī argues that Q. 6:141 was abrogated by the land taxes of *'ushr* and *niṣf al-'ushr* in the Medinan period. Al-Ṭabarī, *Tafsīr*, vol. 9, p. 610. Al-Jaṣṣāṣ rejects this inference, countering that the expression includes both the meaning of an informal harvest tithe and the later formal kind. Al-Jaṣṣāṣ, *Aḥkām*, vol. 4, p. 177.
9. See Avery-Peck, 'Charity in Judaism'.
10. Al-Qurṭubī, *Al-Jāmi*, vol. 2, p. 24.
11. Lane, *Lexicon*, vol. 1, p. 1,133.
12. Lane, *Lexicon*, vol. 1, p. 2,426. Cf. Lane, *Lexicon*, vol. 1, p. 1,395.
13. Lane, *Lexicon*, vol. 1, p. 2,427.
14. Al-Ṭabarī, *Tafsīr*, vol. 5, p. 26.
15. Abū al-Su'ūd, *Irshād*, vol. 1, p. 410.
16. Al-Zamakhsharī, *Al-Kashshāf*, p. 152.
17. Al-Ṭabarī, *Tafsīr*, vol. 11, pp. 512–13.
18. Al-Jaṣṣāṣ, *Aḥkām*, vol. 4, p. 323.
19. Al-Bukhārī, *Ṣaḥīḥ*, vol. 2, p. 908.

20. Al-Suyūṭī and al-Maḥallī, *Tafsīr*, p. 546.
21. Al-Ṭūsī, *Al-Tibyān*, vol. 9, p. 564. See also Q. 8:41.
22. Cf. Ibn Taymiyya, *Siyāsa*, p. 45.
23. Cf. Bonner, 'Poverty and Economics in the Qur'an', pp. 392, 397–8, 403.
24. Quṭb, *Social Justice in Islam*, p. 136.
25. Ibn ʿĀbidīn, *Radd al-muḥtār*, vol. 3, p. 170.
26. Al-Qaraḍāwī, *Fiqh al-zakāt*, vol. 1, p. 72.
27. Also see Q. 61:10–11 and 8:60.
28. Al-Qaraḍāwī, *Fiqh al-zakāt*, vol. 1, p. 71.
29. Al-Ṭabarī, *Tafsīr*, vol. 11, pp. 507–8; Al-Suyūṭī, *Lubāb*, pp. 140–1. Al-Qurṭubī gives the name Ḥurqūṣ b. Zuhayr. Al-Qurṭubī, *Al-Jāmiʿ*, vol. 10, pp. 243–4. The incident is reported without reference to the verse in al-Bukhārī, *Ṣaḥīḥ*, vol. 3, pp. 1,256–7; Muslim, *Ṣaḥīḥ*, vol. 1, p. 418.
30. Mir, *Understanding the Islamic Scripture*, pp. 137–8.
31. Al-Qurṭubī gives nine different explanations. Al-Qurṭubī, *Al-Jāmiʿ*, vol. 10, pp. 246–50.
32. Maimonides discusses eight levels of giving, in which the highest puts a poor person in the position where he can dispense with other people's aid. Avery-Peck, 'Charity in Judaism'.
33. Al-Shaybānī, *Muwaṭṭaʾ al-imām Mālik*, p. 114.
34. Ibn al-Mundhir, *Al-Ishrāf*, vol. 3, p. 90.
35. Al-Jaṣṣāṣ, *Aḥkām*, vol. 4, p. 324.
36. Al-Jaṣṣāṣ, *Aḥkām*, vol. 4, p. 324. Cf. Abū Suʿūd, *Irshād*, vol. 2, pp. 566–7.
37. Ibn al-ʿArabī, *Aḥkām*, vol. 2, p. 966; Al-Shaybānī, *Al-Aṣl*, vol. 2, p. 142. See page 41.
38. Ibn al-Mundhir, *Al-Ishrāf*, vol. 3, p. 93.
39. Ibn al-ʿArabī, *Aḥkām*, vol. 2, p. 967.
40. Al-Ṭaḥāwī, *Aḥkām*, vol. 1, p. 367.
41. Al-Māturīdī, *Taʾwīlāt*, vol. 10, p. 157.
42. Crone, 'Two Legal Problems', pp. 3–4.
43. Crone, 'Two Legal Problems', p. 4.
44. Cuypers, *The Composition of the Qur'an*, pp. 110–11.
45. Al-Ṭabarī, *Tafsīr*, vol. 17, pp. 278–81.
46. Al-Māturīdī, *Taʾwīlāt*, vol. 10, pp. 157–8.
47. Al-Ṭabarī, *Tafsīr*, vol. 17, p. 277.
48. Al-Māturīdī, *Taʾwīlāt*, vol. 10, p. 157.
49. Al-Ṭabarī, *Tafsīr*, vol. 17, pp. 276–8. The view of obligation, although not an opinion of the surviving Sunnī schools of law, is transmitted within second-/eighth-century Ibāḍī jurisprudence. Abū al-Ghānim al-Khurāsānī, *Al-Mudawwana al-kubrā*, vol. 3, p. 60.
50. Al-Ṭabarī, *Tafsīr*, vol. 17, p. 287.
51. See the narration of Saʿīd b. Jubayr in al-Jaṣṣāṣ, *Aḥkām*, vol. 4, p. 326.
52. Al-Ṭabarī, *Tafsīr*, vol. 17, pp. 290–4.
53. Mālik, *Al-Muwaṭṭaʾ*, p. 381.
54. Al-Jaṣṣāṣ, *Aḥkām*, vol. 4, pp. 329–30.
55. See Abdel Haleem, 'Qur'anic '*jihād*', p. 156.
56. Ibn al-ʿArabī, *Aḥkām*, vol. 2, p. 969.
57. Al-Kāsānī, *Badāʾiʿ*, vol. 2, p. 465; Al-Jaṣṣāṣ, *Aḥkām*, vol. 4, p. 330.
58. Al-Ṭaḥāwī, *Aḥkām*, vol. 1, p. 370; Al-Jaṣṣāṣ, *Aḥkām*, vol. 4, p. 329.
59. Al-Rāzī, *Al-Tafsīr al-kabīr*, vol. 16, p. 113.
60. Al-Jaṣṣāṣ, *Aḥkām*, vol. 4, p. 330; Ibn al-ʿArabī, *Aḥkām*, vol. 2, p. 970.
61. Ibn al-Mundhir, *Al-Ishrāf*, vol. 3, p. 95.

Chapter 10

1. Blackburn (ed.), 'Society', in *The Oxford Dictionary of Philosophy*.
2. Al-Naḥḥās, *Iʿrāb*, p. 231.
3. See Giladi, 'Family'.

4. Ibn Manẓūr, *Lisān*, vol. 6, p. 4,537.
5. Buchholz, 'Marriage'.
6. See al-Māturīdī, *Ta'wīlāt*, vol. 11, pp. 170–1.
7. Al-Zamakhsharī, *Al-Kashshāf*, p. 827. See pages 147–8 and 156–7.
8. See pages 154 and 187.
9. Al-Iṣfahānī, *Mufradāt*, p. 472.
10. See page 10.
11. See pages 14, 22, 25.
12. ʿAlī, *Al-Mufaṣṣal*, vol. 5, p. 533.
13. ʿAlī, *Al-Mufaṣṣal*, vol. 5, p. 547.
14. Al-Tirmidhī, *Sunan*, vol. 1, pp. 303–4. The Prophet is given permission for more than four wives in Q. 33:50 and later restricted from additional marriage or divorce with free women in Q. 33:52.
15. See pages 162–3.
16. Gomaa, *Al-Bayān*, pp. 45–6.
17. Al-Ṭabarī, *Tafsīr*, vol. 7, pp. 573–5.
18. Barlas, *'Believing Women'*, p. 191. Cf. Wadud, *Qur'an and Woman*, p. 83.
19. See pages 73–4.
20. An example is found in reports that the Prophet Muḥammad set Ṣafiyya bint Ḥuyayy free following the Battle of Khaybar and then treated her manumission as dower for their marriage. Al-Bukhārī, *Ṣaḥīḥ*, vol. 3, p. 1,066. Cf. Ibn Hishām, *Al-Sīra*, vol. 3, p. 222.
21. Al-Jaṣṣāṣ, *Aḥkām*, vol. 2, p. 349.
22. Harvey, 'The Preferences of al-Kisāʾī', pp. 325–7. Note: rendering *ahl* here as 'masters' seems preferable to 'families', which was used in the article.
23. Al-Bukhārī, *Ṣaḥīḥ*, vol 3, p. 1,403; Abū Dāwūd, *Sunan*, vol. 1, pp. 353–4; ʿAlī, *Al-Mufaṣṣal*, vol. 5, p. 533.
24. Ibn Manẓūr, *Lisān*, vol. 6, p. 4,242.
25. ʿAlī, *Al-Mufaṣṣal*, vol. 5, p. 534.
26. ʿAlī, *Al-Mufaṣṣal*, vol. 5, p. 531.
27. Al-Māturīdī, *Ta'wīlāt*, vol. 2, pp. 117–8.
28. Ibn Manẓūr, *Lisān*, vol. 6, p. 4,369.
29. See page 155.
30. Al-Jaṣṣāṣ, *Aḥkām*, vol. 2, p. 100; Al-Māturīdī, *Ta'wīlāt*, vol. 2, p. 80.
31. This is similar to Abdel Haleem's translation. In an earlier work, he renders *bi-mā faḍḍala allāhu baʿḍahum ʿalā baʿḍ* as 'because God has assigned this extra role to them', reading *mā* as *maṣdariyya* (gerundial), meaning that it turns the verb into a verbal noun. Abdel Haleem, *Understanding the Qur'an*, pp. 51–2.
32. Chaudhry, *Domestic Violence*, p. 27; Bauer, *Gender Hierarchy*, p. 248.
33. Ibn Hishām, *Al-Sīra*, vol. 1, p. 124.
34. See page 62.
35. Cf. Hidayatullah, *Feminist Edges*, pp. 189–91.
36. Al-Ṭabarī, *Tafsīr*, vol. 6, p. 690.
37. Al-Naḥḥās, *Iʿrāb*, p. 243.
38. See page 182.
39. Al-Rāzī, *Al-Tafsīr al-kabīr*, vol. 10, p. 89.
40. Also see Q. 17:31, 43:17–18 and 81:8–9.
41. Giladi, 'Parents'.
42. Al-Qurṭubī, *Al-Jāmiʿ*, vol. 19, p. 195.
43. See pages 156–8.
44. The phrase *wa-ʿalā al-wārithi mithlu dhālika* (and upon the heir is the like of that) has provoked considerable debate among early Muslims over which heir and responsibility is meant. See al-Ṭabarī, *Tafsīr*, vol. 4, pp. 221–35.
45. Al-Ṭabarī, *Tafsīr*, vol. 4, pp. 243–4.
46. See Al-Azmeh, *Emergence*, p. 379.
47. Al-Māturīdī, *Ta'wīlāt*, vol. 11, p. 309. See the translation of this verse on page 18. Also, Q. 8:75 is a possible candidate for the abrogating verse.

48. Al-Ṭabarī, *Tafsīr*, vol. 19, pp. 114–16.
49. For a radically different interpretation of the verses concerning Zayd and his adoptive status, see Powers, *Muḥammad is Not the Father of Any of Your Men*, pp. 35–71.
50. Abdel Haleem translates *nushūz* as 'high-handedness', which better captures some of the spatial connotations of the word, perhaps at the expense of its severity. Abdel Haleem, *The Qur'an*, p. 85.
51. Al-Ṭabarī, *Tafsīr*, vol. 7, pp. 548–60.
52. Al-Māturīdī, *Ta'wīlāt*, vol. 4, p. 59. See 155.
53. See page 60.
54. See pages 163–4.
55. Al-Ṭabarī, *Tafsīr*, vol. 7, pp. 556, 559.
56. See page 144.
57. The first part of this verse is discussed on pages 146–7.
58. Brown, *Misquoting Muḥammad*, p. 270.
59. Al-Ṭabarī, *Tafsīr*, vol. 6, p. 697.
60. Al-Shāfi'ī, *Aḥkām*, vol. 1, pp. 44–5. See also Abdel Haleem, *Understanding the Qur'an*, p. 55.
61. Al-Jaṣṣāṣ, *Al-Fuṣūl*, vol. 1, pp. 86–7; Al-Sarakhsī, *Uṣūl*, vol. 1, pp. 200–2; Al-Qarāfī, *Sharḥ tanqīh*, p. 95.
62. Muqātil b. Sulaymān, *Tafsīr Muqātil*, vol. 1, p. 371; Al-Māturīdī, *Ta'wīlāt*, vol. 3, p. 208. See also, Abdel Haleem, *Understanding the Qur'an*, pp. 54–5.
63. The verses are critical of two of the Prophet's wives, identified in hadiths as 'Ā'isha and Ḥafṣa. See al-Bukhārī, *Ṣaḥīḥ*, vol. 3, pp. 1,088–9. Some reports suggest that the cause for this strife was the Prophet's bondswoman Māriya al-Qibṭiyya, with whom he would cohabit before they got him to prohibit her for himself. Al-Ṭabarī, *Tafsīr*, vol. 23, pp. 83–6; Al-Suyūṭī, *Lubāb*, p. 265. Another suggestion is that he restricted himself from a permissible drink. Al-Ṭabarī, *Tafsīr*, vol. 23, p. 89.
64. Al-Bukhārī, *Ṣaḥīḥ*, vol. 3, p. 1,089. A summarised version of this report is found in Abū Yūsuf, *Kitāb al-āthār*, p. 180. Al-Shaybānī's version, on the authority of al-Zuhrī, mentions the Prophet 'forswore his wives for a month (*ālā min nisā'ihi shahran*)'. Al-Shaybānī, *Kitāb al-āthār*, vol. 2, p. 477.
65. It appears that this was Q. 65:5. Muslim, *Ṣaḥīḥ*, vol. 1, pp. 616–17.
66. This seems to relate to the more general verses Q. 33:28–9, 'O Prophet, say to your wives, "If you desire the worldly life and its adornment, then come, I will make provision for you and release you with goodness. However, if you desire God, His Messenger and the Hereafter, then (know that) God has prepared great rewards for those of you who are excellent in their conduct."' Muslim, *Ṣaḥīḥ*, vol. 1, pp. 615–16.
67. It can also refer to the act of sexual intercourse, as in the expression, 'the stallion coupled with the she-camel (*ḍaraba al-faḥlu al-nāqata*)'. Lane, *Lexicon*, vol. 2, p. 1,778. Al-Iṣfahānī mentions this usage, connecting it to the figurative expression *ṭaraqahā* (the male knocked upon the female [as if with a hammer]). Al-Iṣfahānī, *Gharīb*, vol. 2, p. 384. This seems to be the basis for Ahmed Ali's translation 'and go to bed with them (when they are willing)'. Ali, *Al-Qur'an: A Contemporary Translation*. See also Chaudhry, *Domestic Violence*, pp. 180–2.
68. Al-Iṣfahānī, *Mufradāt*, p. 377.
69. Abu Dāwūd, *Sunan*, vol. 1, p. 363.
70. Al-Suyūṭī, *Lubāb*, p. 78. For discussion of *qiṣāṣ*, see pages 171–7.
71. Al-Ṭabarī, *Tafsīr*, vol. 6, p. 688. See Chaudhry, '"I Wanted One Thing and God Wanted Another ..."', p. 424; Brown, *Misquoting Muḥammad*, p. 275.
72. Muslim, *Ṣaḥīḥ*, vol. 1, p. 500; Abū Dāwūd, *Sunan*, vol. 1, p. 326; Ibn Mājah, *Sunan*, p. 451.
73. Al-Tirmidhī, *Sunan*, vol. 1, p. 314. He notes that *'awān* should be read as 'prisoners' and includes the same *matn* in a slightly longer version of the *khuṭba* in vol. 2, pp. 781–2; Ibn Mājah, *Sunan*, pp. 269–70. Also see al-Ṭaḥāwī, *Sharḥ mushkil*, vol. 6, p. 344; Ibn Hishām, *Al-Sīra*, vol. 4, p. 173 and the gloss of Q. 4:34 in al-Bukhārī, *Ṣaḥīḥ*, vol. 3, p. 1,091.
74. Al-Ṭabarī, Tafsīr, vol. 6, pp. 711–12. See Chaudhry, *Domestic Violence*, pp. 82–3.
75. Al-Ṭabarī, Tafsīr, vol. 6, pp. 713–15.
76. Ibn Manẓūr, *Lisān*, vol. 4, p. 2,720.
77. Ali, *Sexual Ethics and Islam*, pp. 125–31. For another perspective, see Abdel Haleem, 'Euphemism', pp. 128–30.
78. Ali, *Sexual Ethics and Islam*, pp. 131–2.
79. Hidayatullah, *Feminist Edges*, pp. 150–2.

80. See pages 3–4.
81. ʿAlī, *Al-Mufaṣṣal*, vol. 5, pp. 551–2.
82. ʿAlī, *Al-Mufaṣṣal*, vol. 5, p. 551.
83. This is the view adopted by early Kufan jurists. Al-Shaybānī, *Kitāb al-āthār*, vol. 2, p. 482.
84. ʿAlī, *Al-Mufaṣṣāl*, vol. 5, p. 554.
85. ʿAlī, *Al-Mufaṣṣāl*, vol. 5, p. 553.
86. This name is mentioned by the Companion ʿAbd Allāh b. Masʿūd. Abū Yūsuf, *Kitāb al-āthār*, p. 143; Al-Shaybānī, *Kitāb al-āthār*, p. 437.
87. Al-Ṭabarī, *Tafsīr*, vol. 4, pp. 317–32. Al-Māturīdī argues that the guardian's right to control the dower is abrogated by the Prophet Muḥammad's *sharīʿa*. See page 145.
88. Al-Māturīdī, *Taʾwīlāt*, vol. 11, p. 366.
89. Al-Jaṣṣāṣ, *Aḥkām*, vol. 2, p. 236.
90. See page 144.
91. Also see the use of the phrase *mīthāqan ghalīẓan* in Q. 4:154 and Q. 33:7.
92. Al-Nasafī, *Madārik*, p. 119.
93. See page 146.
94. Al-Jaṣṣāṣ, *Aḥkām*, vol. 2, p. 138.
95. Al-Jaṣṣāṣ, *Aḥkām*, vol. 5, pp. 355–6.
96. Al-Māturīdī, *Taʾwīlāt*, vol. 15, p. 235.
97. Al-Qurṭubī, *Jāmiʿ*, vol. 4, p. 203. See page 167.

Chapter 11

1. Quṭb, *Social Justice in Islam*, pp. 84–5.
2. Ibn Manẓūr, *Lisān*, vol. 6, p. 4,948.
3. Al-Iṣfahānī, *Mufradāt*, p. 694; Ibn Manẓūr, *Lisān*, vol. 6, pp. 6,948–9.
4. See pages 146–7.
5. See page 4. The other Meccan verses are Q. 6:152, 17:34, 86:8, 89:17, 90:15, 93:6, 93:9, and 107:2.
6. This is an instance of the definite article for *maʿhūd li-al-dhiʾn*. The Medinan verses are Q. 2:83, 2:177, 2:215, 2:220, 4:2, 4:3, 4:6, 4:8, 4:10, 4:36, 4:127, 8:41, and 59:7.
7. See the discussion of sura pairs in Mir, *Coherence in the Qurʾan*, p. 76.
8. Abdel Haleem, *The Qurʾan*, p. 36.
9. Asad, *Message*, p. 100.
10. Al-Bukhārī, *Ṣaḥīḥ*, vol. 2, pp. 803–4.
11. Al-Bukhārī, *Ṣaḥīḥ*, vol. 2, p. 805.
12. The word *amwāl* (sing. *māl*), which is used throughout the passage, can refer to wealth or property and is often used specifically for camels. Badawi and Abdel Haleem, *Dictionary*, p. 907.
13. Al-Qurṭubī, *Al-Jāmiʿ*, vol. 6, p. 20. He states it as the opinion of a number of early authorities: Saʿīd b. Musayyab, al-Ẓuhrī, al-Saddī and al-Ḍaḥḥāk.
14. Al-Rāzī, *Al-Tafsīr al-kabīr*, vol. 9, p. 170.
15. This is on the authority of Qatāda. Al-Ṭabarī, *Tafsīr*, vol. 6, p. 357.
16. Lane, *Lexicon*, vol. 1, p. 662.
17. See page 144.
18. Al-Bukhārī, *Ṣaḥīḥ*, vol. 3, p. 1,062.
19. Al-Bukhārī, *Ṣaḥīḥ*, vol. 2, p. 924.
20. See al-Bayḍāwī, *Anwār*, vol. 1, p. 247.
21. See Watt, *Muḥammad at Medina*, p. 273.
22. Mir, *Understanding the Islamic Scripture*, p. 100.
23. See al-Suyūṭī, *Al-Itqān*, vol. 1, p. 112.
24. See the discussion of Q. 4:25 on page 145.
25. Mir, *Understanding the Islamic Scripture*, p. 109.
26. See page 145.
27. Al-Rāzī, *Al-Tafsīr al-kabīr*, vol. 11, p. 63.

28. Al-Naḥḥās, *I'rāb*, p. 265.
29. Cf. Q. 2:174.
30. Maḥmūd, *Fatāwā*, p. 160.
31. See pages 230–2.
32. Al-Naḥḥās, *Al-Nāsikh wa-l-mansūkh*, vol. 1, p. 483.
33. See pages 157–8.
34. Mālik, *Al-Muwaṭṭa'*, p. 295; Al-Naḥḥās, *Al-Nāsikh wa-l-mansūkh*, vol. 1, pp. 482–3; Ibn Hishām, *Al-Sīra*, vol. 4, p. 174. For a discussion of the partial-abrogation position, see Powers, 'On the Abrogation of the Bequest Verses', pp. 260–2.
35. Al-Bukhārī, *Ṣaḥīḥ*, vol. 2, p. 532.
36. Powers, 'On the Abrogation of the Bequest Verses', pp. 259–66.
37. Al-Qurṭubī, *Al-Jāmi'*, vol. 6, p. 93.
38. Al-Bukhārī, *Ṣaḥīḥ*, vol. 3, p. 1,361.
39. Haskafi, *The Durr-ul-Mukhtar*, pp. 441–2.
40. Al-Ṭabarī, *Al-Tafsīr*, vol. 6, pp. 474–5. The word *kalāla* can also be used adverbially for inheriting in this way. Al-Zabīdī, *Tāj al-'arūs*, vol. 30, pp. 342–3.
41. Al-Ṭabarī, *Tafsīr*, vol. 6, p. 483; Al-Tha'labī, *Al-Kashf wa-l-bayān*, vol. 3, p. 270. Later sources also attribute this reading to Ubayy b. Ka'b, which may be an attempt to lend it greater authority. Al-Zamakhsharī, *Al-Kashshāf*, p. 226.
42. See Powers, *The Formation of the Islamic Law of Inheritance*; Powers, *Muḥammad is Not the Father of Any of Your Men*. Also see Cilardo, *The Qur'anic Term* Kalāla; Pavlovitch, *The Formation of the Islamic Understanding of* Kalāla.
43. Powers, *Muḥammad is Not the Father of Any of Your Men*, pp. 228–9.

Chapter 12

1. See page 24.
2. See page 25.
3. Draz, *The Moral World of the Qur'an*, p. 119.
4. Foucault, *Discipline and Punish*, pp. 33–4.
5. Foucault, *Discipline and Punish*, p. 58.
6. Draz, *The Moral World of the Qur'an*, p. 121.
7. The generality of address is despite its use of the singular verb form in Q. 17:22, 'set up no other god beside God (*lā taj'al ma'a allāhi ilāhan ākhara*)'. See Abdel Haleem, *The Qur'an*, p. 285. Al-Farāhī explains that, in these cases, the sentence may be grammatically directed to the Prophet as spokesman for the people, or independently of him as *iltifāt* (change of address for rhetorical purposes). Al-Farāhī, *Asālīb al-qur'ān*, pp. 160–3.
8. See pages 174–6.
9. Lane, *Lexicon*, vol. 2, p. 2,526.
10. Iṣlāḥī, *Tadabbur-e-Qur'ān*, vol. 1, p. 445.
11. Al-Suyūṭī, *Lubāb*, vol. 2, p. 32.
12. Al-Qurṭubī, *Al-Jāmi'*, vol. 3, p. 65. Zalaṭ, *Tafsīr āyāt al-aḥkām*, vol. 1, p. 339. Cf. The regulations concerning *qiṣāṣ* in the Covenant of Medina. Ibn Hishām, *Al-Sīra*, vol. 2, pp. 113–14.
13. Al-Rāzī, *Al-Tafsīr al-kabīr*, vol. 5, pp. 44–5. Cf. Al-Qurṭubī, *Al-Jāmi'*, vol. 3, pp. 66–7.
14. Asad reaches the same position with a linguistic understanding of Qur'anic *ījāz*. Asad, *Message*, p. 37. Also see Zalaṭ, *Tafsīr āyāt al-aḥkām*, vol. 1, p. 345.
15. Cf. Al-Suyūṭī, *Al-Itqān*, vol. 3, pp. 87, 90.
16. Cuypers, *The Banquet*, p. 191.
17. An analogous phrase is used elsewhere in the Qur'an for the Prophet Noah in Q. 10:71 and the Prophet Abraham in Q. 26:69.
18. Al-Zamakhsharī, *Al-Kashshāf*, p. 288.
19. Al-Jārim and Amīn, *Al-Balāghat al-wāḍiḥa*, p. 229.
20. Al-Bārbartī, *Sharḥ al-talkhīṣ*, p. 382.

21. Brown, *A Hebrew and English Lexicon of the Old Testament*, p. 196.
22. Danby, *Tractate Sanhedrin Mishnah and Tosefta*, pp. 78–9.
23. Neusner, 'Midrash and the Oral Torah'.
24. Al-Bukhārī, *Ṣaḥīḥ*, vol. 2, p. 900; Al-Bukhārī, *Ṣaḥīḥ*, vol. 3. p. 1,388.
25. Cf. Q. 5:28–9 and 4:93.
26. Compare with the case of dietary regulations, in which Zellentin argues that the initial laws of the Children of Israel (Q. 6:146) were increased after the incident of the Golden Calf (Q. 3:93). Jesus lifted some of these additional restrictions (Q. 3:50) and the Prophet Muḥammad went even further (Q. 7:157). See Zellentin, *Legal Culture*, pp. 168–9.
27. For a general discussion on the differing of divine laws between prophetic communities on account of their varying characters, see Shāh Walī Allāh, *The Conclusive Argument from God*, p. 263.
28. See page 103.
29. Abū Dāwūd, *Sunan*, vol. 2, p. 753; Al-Nasāʾī, *Sunan*, vol. 2, p. 771.
30. Abū Dāwūd, *Sunan*, vol. 2, p. 611; Al-Nasāʾī, *Sunan*, vol. 2, p. 771.
31. Al-Nasafī, *Madārik*, p. 287.
32. Exodus 21:23–5. Cf. Leviticus 24:19–21; Deuteronomy 19:21.
33. Al-Rāzī, *Al-Tafsīr al-kabīr*, vol. 12, p. 7.
34. See Zalaṭ, *Tafsīr āyāt al-aḥkām*, vol. 1, p. 341; Al-Matroudi, '*Al-Qarīna*', pp. 231–3.
35. See page 106.
36. See Kamali, *Freedom, Equality and Justice in Islam*, p. 112.
37. Al-Suyūṭī, *Al-Itqān*, vol. 1, pp. 70–1.
38. Al-Suyūṭī quotes Q. 42:39–41 in this regard. Al-Suyūṭī, *Al-Itqān*, vol. 1, p. 71. However, Q. 42:42–3 are integrally connected to these verses in meaning, making it implausible that they were revealed in Mecca years before.
39. Muslim narrates the same story in various hadiths, using the names ʿUkl, ʿUrayna, or mentioning both options. Muslim, *Ṣaḥīḥ*, vol. 2, pp. 722–4.
40. Al-Bukhārī, *Ṣaḥīḥ*, vol. 3, p. 1,372. Al-Bukhārī follows this with three more hadiths based on the same event, differing only slightly in wording and incidental details. Al-Bukhārī, *Ṣaḥīḥ*, vol. 3, pp. 1,372–3. Suyūṭī confirms the status of this event as the *sabab al-nuzūl* for Q. 5:33 with other reports. Al-Suyūṭī, *Lubāb*, vol. 2, p. 106. It is widely collected in the books of Hadith, *sīra*, and *maghāzī*. See Anthony, 'Crime and Punishment in Early Medina', pp. 385–90.
41. Al-Shaybānī, *Kitāb al-āthār*, vol. 2, pp. 548–9. Also see the more general hadith mentioning the *hirāba* punishment in Abū Dāwūd, *Sunan*, vol. 2, p. 726; Al-Nasāʾī, *Sunan*, vol. 2, pp. 662–3.
42. Al-Nasāʾī, *Sunan*, vol. 2, p. 665.
43. Anthony, 'Crime and Punishment in Early Medina', pp. 434–5.
44. Al-Ṭabarī, *Tafsīr*, vol. 8, pp. 368–9. See Anthony, 'Crime and Punishment in Early Medina', p. 425.
45. Al-Būṭī, *Fiqh al-sīra*, pp. 167, 190–1 and 224–5.
46. See page 110.
47. See page 21.
48. See Q. 4:18, 'It is not true repentance when people continue to do evil until death confronts them and then say, "Now I repent," nor when they die defiant: We have prepared a painful torment for these.' A hadith mentions, 'God accepts the repentance of His servant until the paroxysms of death.' Al-Tirmidhī, *Sunan*, vol. 2, p. 907.
49. Al-Mawṣalī, *Kitāb al-ikhtiyār*, vol. 4, p. 137.
50. Al-Misrī, *Reliance*, p. 616.

Chapter 13

1. Al-Būṭī, *Fiqh al-sīra*, pp. 116–17.
2. Some commentaries suggest that this refers to a woman concealing the true father of her child. Al-Suyūṭī and al-Maḥallī, *Tafsīr*, p. 551. However, the hadith of ʿUbāda b. Ṣāmit in the collection of Muslim replaces this phrase with *lā yaʿḍaha baʿḍunā baʿḍan* (some of us would not calumniate others). Ibn

Manẓūr mentions the verse and provides 'in every direction' as the meaning of *bayna aydīhinna wa-arjulihinna*, making clear the reference to slander. Ibn Manẓūr, *Lisān*, vol. 6, p. 4,954.

3. Al-Qurṭubī, *Al-Jāmi'*, vol. 20, pp. 423–4.
4. See page 147.
5. Muslim, *Ṣaḥīḥ*, vol. 2, p. 743. Cf. Al-Bukhārī, *Ṣaḥīḥ*, vol. 3, p. 1,369.
6. Note that Fazlur Rahman, reflecting the prevailing academic arguments about the Hadith literature in his time, argues that they do not provide a reliable context for the interpretation of the Qur'anic rules of punishment. Rahman, 'The Concept of Ḥadd', pp. 237–8. Kamali has contended that they do not present the *ḥudūd* as fixed punishments. Kamali, *Punishment in Islamic Law*, p. 68.
7. The Prophet is reported to have said, 'Forgive the prescribed punishments amongst yourselves, as those that are brought to me must be inflicted.' Abū Dāwūd, *Sunan*, vol. 2, p. 731; Al-Nasā'ī, *Sunan*, vol. 2, pp. 794–5. Other narrations stress this point in particular cases of theft. Al-Bukhārī, *Ṣaḥīḥ*, vol. 3, p. 1,370–1; Mālik, *Al-Muwaṭṭa'*, p. 327. However, a man who had committed an unspecified offence, but kept it to himself, was considered forgiven after praying the congregational prayer with the community. Al-Bukhārī, *Ṣaḥīḥ*, vol. 3, pp. 1,376–7.
8. Abū Zahra, *Falsafat al-'uqūba*, pp. 72–3.
9. See the rendering of Q. 4:34 on pages 146–7.
10. See the famous story of Mā'iz b. Mālik who came to the Prophet confessing adultery and asking to be purified through punishment. Muslim, *Ṣaḥīḥ*, vol. 2, pp. 736–7.
11. Al-Rāzī, *Al-Tafsīr al-kabīr*, vol. 18, p. 182. Note that the Biblical account has the brothers declaring death for the thief and slavery for the rest of them, while the official lightens it to slavery for the thief alone. Genesis 44:9–10.
12. See page 125.
13. Liebesny, *The Law*, pp. 8–9.
14. Al-Matroudi, '*Al-Qarīna*', p. 214.
15. Muslim, *Ṣaḥīḥ*, vol. 2, p. 733.
16. Al-Wāḥidī, *Reasons & Occasions*, p. 109.
17. Nöldeke, *Geschichte des Qorāns*, vol. 1, pp. 229–30.
18. Al-Jaṣṣāṣ, *Aḥkām*, vol. 4, p. 62.
19. Abū Zahra, *Falsafat al-'uqūba*, p. 149.
20. Lane, *Lexicon*, vol. 2, pp. 2,608–9.
21. Al-Ḥalabī, *Al-Durr*, vol. 4, p. 265.
22. Al-Ḥalabī, *Al-Durr*, vol. 4, p. 265.
23. Kamali, *Punishment in Islamic Law*, pp. 52–3.
24. Abū Zahra, *Falsafat al-'uqūba*, pp. 149–50.
25. Abū Dawūd, *Sunan*, vol. 2, p. 731.
26. Nöldeke, *Geschichte des Qorāns*, vol. 1, pp. 195–6; Asad, *Message*, p. 100.
27. Exegetes differ on whether this verse is thus abrogated by later revelation of the Qur'an or the prophetic Sunna. Al-Jamal prefers the view that it is elaborated by later legislation, with the word *sabīlan* (a way) taken as a *mujmal* expression. Al-Jamal, *Al-Futūḥāt*, vol. 1, pp. 386–7.
28. Al-Suyūṭī and al-Maḥallī, *Tafsīr*, p. 80.
29. For the argument that repentance waives punishment entirely, see Kamali, *Punishment in Islamic Law*, pp. 58–60.
30. Asad, *Message*, p. 532; Jones, 'The Chronology of the Maghāzī', pp. 220–1.
31. See page 143.
32. Asad, *Message*, p. 532.
33. Al-Nasafī, *Madārik*, p. 769.
34. Al-Bayḍāwī, *Anwār*, vol. 2, p. 118.
35. Mālik, *Al-Muwaṭṭa'*, p. 323.
36. For instance, see al-Bukhārī, *Ṣaḥīḥ*, vol. 3, p. 1,381; Muslim, *Ṣaḥīḥ*, vol. 2, pp. 738–9.
37. Muslim, *Ṣaḥīḥ*, vol. 2, p. 740.
38. Abū Zahra, *Falsafat al-'uqūba*, pp. 113–15.
39. Abū Zahra, *Falsafat al-'uqūba*, pp. 111.

40. Bilfaqīh, *Al-Qirā'āt*, p. 82. Al-Kisā'ī only reads *muḥṣanāt* in the sense of 'married women' once, in Q. 4:24. See Harvey, 'The Preferences of al-Kisā'ī', pp. 325–8. Cf. Wirtzum, 'Q 4:24 Revisited', pp. 3–8.
41. Harvey, 'The Preferences of al-Kisā'ī', p. 327.
42. See pages 154–5.
43. Al-Suyūṭī, *Al-Itqān*, vol. 1, p. 53.
44. Asad, *Message*, p. 792.
45. For a brief note on this feature, see Abdel Haleem, *The Qur'an*, p. 351.
46. This also seems related to the condemnation of hypocrites and the sick at heart in Q. 33:60–2.
47. Al-Ḥalabī, *Al-Durr*, vol. 8, pp. 382–3.
48. See page 180.
49. The ruling of the Shāfi'ī school of law is that they may never remarry. Al-Misrī, *Reliance*, p. 575. The main view of the Ḥanafī school is that remarriage would be possible. Al-Mawṣalī, *Kitāb al-ikhtiyār*, vol. 3, p. 208.

Conclusion

1. See page 42.
2. Gadamer, *Truth and Method*, p. 317.
3. See Zysow, *Economy*, pp. 271–2.
4. MacIntyre, *Whose Justice? Which Rationality?*, p. 350.

Glossary of Arabic Terminology

ʿadl	justice; equity
āḥād	single-authority transmission not continuously mass-transmitted (hadith)
ʿahd (pl. *ʿuhūd*)	covenant; peace treaty
ahl al-kitāb	Scriptuaries
al-amāna	the Trust (of moral responsibility); anything entrusted
ʿāmm	general
ʿaṣabiyya	group identity
asbāb al-nuzūl	occasions of revelation
ʿaṭf	conjunction
āya (pl. *āyāt*)	verse; sign
balāgha	rhetoric
barāʾ	disavowal (of treaties)
basmala	the invocation *bi-sm-illāh al-raḥmān al-raḥīm* (in the Name of God, the Merciful, the Compassionate)
bayān	explanation
bayyināt	proofs, or evidences
al-dhikr	the Reminder (Qur'an); the Torah
dhimma	security
dīn	religion (sense of the Latin *religare*, 'to obligate'); indebtedness to God
diya	blood money
faḍl	generosity, or grace
fāḥisha (pl. *fawāḥish*)	lewd act, or obscenity
fasād	corruption
faṣl	disjunction
fiqh	jurisprudence
fiṭra	natural disposition
gharīb	singly narrated; obscure (hadith)
ghazw	raid (usually Bedouin)
ḥakam (pl. *ḥukkām*)	arbitrator
al-ḥakīm	the Wise, or the Just
ḥakīm	wise, or just
ḥaqq (pl. *ḥuqūq*)	right

ḥaram	sanctuary
ḥasan	good; reliable (hadith)
hijāba	traditional Qurashī office possessing the keys to the Kaʿba
al-ḥikma	the Wisdom (of the Writ)
ḥikma	wisdom; principle, wise benefit, rationale
ḥirāba	brigandage
hudā	guidance
ḥudūd (sing. *ḥadd*)	boundaries; private crimes
ḥukm (pl. *aḥkām*)	ruling; judgement; valuation (of an informative utterance)
ḥukm taklīfī	commissioning, or defining ruling
ḥukm waḍʿī	situational ruling
ʿidda	waiting period of three menstrual cycles (before remarriage)
iḥsān	spiritual excellence, or beneficence
ījāz	brevity, or concision
iʿjāz	inimitability
ijtihād	exhaustive legal enquiry
ikhtiyār	free will, or choice
īlāf	security pacts
īlāʾ	oath by which a husband forswears from sexual relations with his spouse
ʿilla (pl. *ʿilal*)	sign, or legal cause (also, see *ḥikma*); subtle flaw (hadith)
ʿilm	knowledge
ʿilm al-maʿānī	contextual semantics
inshāʾ	performative utterance
iṣlāḥ	rectification
isnād	chain of authorities
isnād-cum-*matn* analysis	study of hadith textual variants by their chains
al-istighrāq	each member within the class
al-istithnāʾ munqaṭiʿ	the exception is not included in the original set
jawr	injustice, or oppression
jihād	just war; striving
jizya	tribute
kāhin	soothsayer
kalām	rational theology; speech
kasb	acquisition
khabar	informative utterance
khalīfa (pl. *khalāʾif*, or *khulafāʾ*)	steward; successor
khāṣṣ	specific
khilāfa	stewardship
khulʿa	compensatory divorce
khuṭbat al-wadāʿ	farewell sermon (of the Prophet Muḥammad)
al-kitāb	the Writ; the Scripture

kitāb (pl. *kutub*)	writing, book; contract of indenture; obligation; law
kulliyyāt	universal considerations
mafhūm al-mukhālafa	contrary implicature; stipulation indicates specification
maʿhūd li-l-dhiʾn	known referent
malaʾ	council of chiefs; chiefs
maʿnā	meaning; cause (see *ḥikma* and *ʿilla*)
maqāṣid al-sharīʿa	the higher objectives of the divine law and moral code
marfūʿ	ascribed to the Prophet (hadith)
maʿrūf	customarily recognised
maṣlaḥa (pl. *maṣāliḥ*)	benefit
matn	textual corpus (hadith)
mawālī (sing. *mawlā*)	clients; freed slaves; protégés
mawqūf	halting at a Companion or Follower (hadith)
milla	prophetic community (see *umma*)
mīthāq	covenant; peace treaty
al-mīzān	the Scale (of moral value); the natural law
muḥṣanāt	married women
muḥṣināt	chaste women
mujmal	ambiguous
mukhātaba	address
mulk	sovereignty; kingdom; political authority; capacity to attain rule
munāsaba (pl. *munāsabāt*)	appropriateness
muṣḥaf	codex (of the Qur'an)
nafaqa	provision
naskh	abrogation
naẓm	syntax-pragmatics; coherence; verse (as opposed to prose); inimitability
niẓām	textual structure
nushūz	enmity
qarīna	indication
qaṣr	restriction (grammatical)
qatl	murder
qibla	prayer direction
qirāʾa (pl. *qirāʾāt*)	variant reading, or recitation (of the Qur'an)
qiṣāṣ	talion, or punishment in kind
qisṭ	justice; societal justice
qiyāda	traditional Qurashī office allowing mounts permission to travel
qiyās	analogy
qiyās al-ghāʾib ʿalā al-shāhid	the hidden is analogous to the manifest
rabb	Lord
ribā	usury; unjust profit

rifāda	traditional Qurashī office hosting pilgrims with food
sabab	cause, or means; occasion (see *asbāb al-nuzūl*)
safah	foolish, or folly
ṣaḥīḥ	sound (hadith)
al-sharīʿa	lit. 'the Path'; the divine law and moral code
shirk	worship of another beside God
shudhūdh	inconsistency (hadith)
shūrā	Consultation
ṣifa (pl. *ṣifāt*)	attribute
siqāya	traditional Qurashī office providing water to pilgrims
sīra	prophetic biography
suknā	housing
ṣulḥ	truce; peaceful settlement
tafsīr	exegesis
tafsīr mawḍūʿī	thematic exegesis
takhsīs al-ʿāmm	specification of the general expression
takwīn	*ex-nihilo* creativity
taʿlīl	attribution of a legal, or semantic, cause
al-tanṣīṣ lā yadillu alā al-takhṣīṣ	stipulation does not indicate specification
taqwā	piety, or consciousness of God
taʿrīf al-jins	definition of the class
tawātur	continuous mass transmission
tawḥīd	unicity
taʾwīl	interpretation; consequence, or place to which something returns; figurative meaning
tazkiya/tazkiyat al-nafs	spiritual purification
ʿulūm al-qurʾān	the Qur'anic disciplines
umma	community; prophetic community
uṣūl al-fiqh	legal theory
walāʾ	alliance
waṣiyya	bequest
waṣl	conjunction
wujūh al-qurʾān	Qur'anic polysemy
yatīm (pl. *yatāmā*)	orphan
zabūr	the Psalms of David
ẓāhir	manifest, or obvious
zakāt	alms; obligatory alms
ẓihār	insulting oath by which a husband forswears from sexual relations with his spouse
zinā	fornication; adultery
zubur	scriptures
ẓulm	injustice, or wrongdoing

Bibliography

I. Primary sources

ʿAbd al-Jabbār b. Aḥmad, *Sharḥ al-uṣūl al-khamsa*, ed. ʿAbd al-Karīm ʿUthmān (Cairo: Maktaba Wahba, 1996).

Abū Dāwūd, Sulaymān b. al-Ashʿath, *Sunan Abī Dāwūd*, 2 vols (Vaduz: Thesaurus Islamicus Foundation, 2000).

Abū Suʿūd b. Muḥammad al-ʿImādī, *Irshād al-ʿaql al-salīm ilā mazāyā al-kitāb al-karīm*, ed. ʿAbd al-Qādir Aḥmad ʿAṭāʾ, 5 vols (Riyadh: Maktabat al-Riyāḍ al-Ḥadīth, n. d.).

Abū Yūsuf, Yaʿqūb b. Ibrāhīm, *Kitāb al-āthār*, ed. Abū al-Wafāʾ al-Afghānī (Hyderabad: Lajna Iḥyāʾ al-Maʿārif al-Nuʿmaniyya, 1938–9).

Al-Alūsī, Shihāb al-Dīn, *Rūḥ al-maʿānī fī tafsīr al-qurʾān al-ʿaẓīm wa-l-sabʿ al-mathānī*, ed. Muḥammad Munīr ʿAbdah Aghā al-Dimashqī, 30 vols (Beirut: Idārat al-Ṭibāʿat al-Munīriyya, n. d.).

Al-Āmidī, ʿAlī b. Muḥammad, *Al-Iḥkām fī uṣūl al-aḥkām*, ed. ʿAbd al-Razzāq ʿAfīfī, 4 vols (Riyadh: Dār al-Ṣamīʿī, 2003).

Al-Ashʿarī, Abū al-Ḥasan, *Maqālāt al-islāmiyyīn wa-ikhtilāf al-muṣallīn*, ed. Muḥammad Muḥyī al-Dīn ʿAbd al-Ḥamīd, 2 vols (Cairo: Maktaba al-Nahda al-Miṣriyya, 1950).

Al-Ashʿarī, Abū al-Ḥasan, *Kitāb al-lumaʿ fī al-radd ʿalā ahl al-zaygh wa-l-bidʿa*, ed. H. Ghurāba (Cairo: Maṭbaʿa Miṣr, 1955).

Al-ʿAsqalānī, Ibn Ḥajar, *Fatḥ al-bārī bi-sharḥ ṣaḥīḥ al-Bukhārī*, ed. ʿAbd al-Qādir Shaybat al-Ḥamd, 14 vols (Riyadh: ʿAbd al-Qādir Shaybat al-Ḥamd, 2001).

Al-ʿAynī, Badr al-Dīn, *ʿUmdat al-qārī sharḥ ṣaḥīḥ al-Bukhārī*, ed. Muḥammad Munīr ʿAbdah Aghā al-Dimashqī, 25 vols (Beirut: Idārat al-Ṭibāʿat al-Munīriyya, n. d.).

Al-ʿAynī, Badr al-Dīn, *Al-Bināya sharḥ al-hidāya*, ed. Amīn Ṣāliḥ Shaʿbān, 13 vols (Beirut: Dār al-Kutub al-ʿIlmiyya, 2000).

Al-Azraqī, Abū al-Walīd, *Akhbār makka wa-mā jāʾ fīhā min al-āthār*, ed. ʿAbd al-Malik Duhaysh (Mecca: Maktabat al-Asadī, 2003).

Al-Bābartī, Akmal al-Dīn, *Sharḥ al-ʿināya ʿalā al-hidāya*, 8 vols (Cairo: Būlāq, 1898–9).

Al-Bāqillānī, Abū Bakr, *Kitāb al-tamhīd*, ed. Richard J. McCarthy (Beirut: Al-Maktabat al-Sharqiyya, 1957).

Al-Bayāḍī, Kamāl al-Dīn, *Ishārāt al-marām min ʿibārāt al-imām Abī Ḥanīfa al-Nuʿmān fī uṣūl al-dīn*, ed. Aḥmad Farīd al-Mazīdī (Beirut: Dār al-Kutub al-ʿIlmiyya, 2007).

Al-Bayḍāwī, ʿAbd Allāh b. ʿUmar, *Anwār al-tanzīl wa-asrār al-taʾwīl*, ed. Maḥmūd Muṣṭafā al-Ḥalabī, 2 vols (Cairo: Muṣṭafā al-Bābī al-Ḥalabī wa-Awlāduhu, 1968).

Al-Bayhaqī, Aḥmad b. al-Ḥusayn, *Al-Sunan al-kubrā*, ed. Muḥammad ʿAbd al-Qādir ʿAṭā, 11 vols (Beirut: Dār al-Kutub al-ʿIlmiyya, 2003).

Al-Bazdawī, Abū al-Yusr, *Uṣūl al-dīn*, ed. Hans Peter Linss (Cairo: Al-Maktaba al-Azhariyya li-l-Turāth, 2003).

Al-Bazdawī, ʿAlī b. Muḥammad, *Kanz al-wuṣūl ilā maʿrifat al-uṣūl*, ed. Sāʾid Bakdāsh (Beirut: Dār al-Bashāʾir al-Islāmiyya, and Medina: Dār al-Sirāj, 2014).

Al-Bukhārī, ʿAbd al-ʿAzīz, *Kashf al-asrār ʿan uṣūl fakhr al-islām al-Bazdawī*, eds Aḥmad Khalūṣī, and Muṣṭafā Darwīsh, 4 vols (Durr Saʿāda, 1891).

Al-Bukhārī, Muḥammad b. Ismāʿīl, *Ṣaḥīḥ al-Bukhārī*, 3 vols (Vaduz: Thesaurus Islamicus Foundation, 2000).

Al-Dabūsī, Abū Zayd and Abū al-Ḥasan al-Karkhī, *Taʾsīs al-naẓar wa-yalīhi risālat al-imām Abī al-Ḥasan al-Karkhī fī al-uṣūl*, ed. Muṣṭafā Muḥammad al-Qabbānī (Beirut: Dār Ibn Zaydūn, n. d.).

Al-Fārābī, Abū Naṣr, *Kitāb ārāʾ ahl al-madīnat al-fāḍila*, ed. Albīr Naṣrī Nādir (Beirut: Dār al-Mashriq, 2002).

Al-Ghazālī, Abū Ḥāmid, *Al-Mustaṣfā min ʿilm al-uṣūl*, ed. Faraj Allāh Zakī al-Kurdī, 2 vols (Cairo: Būlāq, 1904).

Al-Ḥalabī, Aḥmad b. Yūsuf, *Al-Durr al-maṣūn fī ʿulūm al-kitāb al-maknūn*, ed. Aḥmad Muḥammad al-Kharāṭ, 11 vols (Damascus: Dār al-Qalam, 1985).

Al-Ḥalabī, Nūr al-Dīn, *Al-Sīrat al-Ḥalabiyya*, ed. ʿAbd Allāh Muḥammad al-Khalīlī, 3 vols (Beirut: Dār al-Kutub al-ʿIlmiyya, 2008).

Al-Hamdānī, al-Ḥasan b. Aḥmad, *Ṣifat jazīrat al-ʿarab*, ed. Muḥammad b. ʿAlī al-Akwaʿ al-Ḥawālī (Sana'a: Maktabat al-Irshād, 1990).

Al-Ḥanbalī, Ibn Rajab, *Sharḥ ʿilal al-Tirmidhī*, ed. Nūr al-Dīn ʿItr, 2 vols (Damascus: Dār al-Malāḥ li-l-Ṭibāʿa wa-l-Nashr, 2000).

Ibn ʿAbd Rabbih, Aḥmad, *Al-ʿIqd al-farīd*, ed. Mufīd Muḥammad Qumayḥa, 9 vols (Beirut: Dār al-Kutub al-ʿIlmiyya, 1983).

Ibn ʿĀbidīn, Muḥammad Amīn, *Radd al-muḥtār ʿalā al-durr al-mukhtār sharḥ tanwīr al-abṣār*, eds ʿĀdil Aḥmad ʿAbd al-Mawjūd, and ʿAlī Muḥammad Muʿawwiḍ, 14 vols (Riyadh: Dār ʿĀlam al-Kutub, 2003).

Ibn al-ʿArabī, Muḥammad b. ʿAbd Allāh, *Aḥkām al-qurʾān*, ed. ʿAlī Muḥammad al-Bajāwī, 4 vols (Beirut: Dār al-Maʿrifa, 1987).

Ibn Ḥabīb, Muḥammad, *Kitāb al-munammaq fī akhbār Quraysh*, ed. Khūrshīd Aḥmad Fārūq (Beirut: ʿĀlam al-Kutub, 1985).

Ibn Ḥanbal, Aḥmad, *Musnad*, ed. Shuʿayb Arnāʾūṭ, 50 vols (Beirut: Muʾassasat al-Risāla, 1999).

Ibn Hishām, ʿAbd al-Malik. *Al-Sīrat al-nabawiyya*. 4 vols (Cairo: Dār al-Fikr li-l-Turāth, 2004).

Ibn Juzayy, Muḥammad b. Aḥmad, *Al-Tashīl li-ʿulūm al-tanzīl*, ed. Abū Bakr b. ʿAbd Allāh Saʿdāwī (Sharjah: Al-Muntadā al-Islāmī, 2012).
Ibn Khaldūn, ʿAbd al-Raḥmān, *Muqaddimat Ibn Khaldūn*, ed. Majdī Fatḥī al-Sayyid (Cairo: Dār al-Tawfīqiyya li-l-Turāth, 2010).
Ibn Mājah, Muḥammad b. Yazīd, *Sunan Ibn Mājah* (Vaduz: Thesaurus Islamicus Foundation, 2000).
Ibn Manẓūr, Muḥammad b. Mukarram, *Lisān al-ʿarab*, 6 vols (Cairo: Dār al-Maʿārif, 1981).
Ibn al-Mundhir, Abū Bakr, *Al-Ishrāf ʿalā madhāhib al-ulamāʾ*, ed. Abū Ḥammād Ṣaghīr Aḥmad al-Anṣārī, 10 vols (Ras al-Khaimah: Maktaba Makkat al-Thaqāfiyya, 2004–5).
Ibn Nadīm, Muḥammad, *Kitāb al-fihrist li-l-Nadīm*, ed. Tajaddud ibn ʿAlī (Tehran: n. p., 1971).
Ibn Taymiyya, Aḥmad b. ʻAbd al-Ḥalīm, *Muqaddima fī uṣūl al-tafsīr*, ed. ʿAdnān Zarzūr (Beirut: Mu'assasat al-Risāla, 1972).
Ibn Taymiyya, Aḥmad b. ʿAbd al-Ḥalīm, *Al-Siyāsa al-sharʿiyya fī iṣlāḥ al-rāʿī wa-l-raʿiyya*, ed. Lajna Iḥyāʾ al-Turāth al-ʿArabī fī Dār al-Āfāq al-Jadīda (Beirut: Dār al-Āfāq al-Jadīda, 1983).
Al-Iṣfahānī, al-Rāghib, *Mufradāt alfāẓ al-qurʾān*, ed. Abū ʿAbd Allāh Muṣṭafā b. al-ʿAdawī (Cairo: Maktaba Fayyāḍ, 2009).
Al-Iṣfahānī, al-Rāghib, *Al-Mufradāt fī gharīb al-qurʾān*, 2 vols (Riyadh: Maktaba Nizār Muṣṭafā al-Bāz, n. d.).
Al-Jāḥiẓ, ʿUmar b. Baḥr, *Naẓm al-qurʾān*, ed. Saʿd ʿAbd al-ʿAẓīm Muḥammad (Cairo: Maktabat al-Zahrāʾ, 1995).
Al-Jamal, Sulaymān, *Al-Futūḥāt al-ilahiyya bi-tawḍīḥ tafsīr al-jalālayn li-l-daqāʾiq al-khafiyya*, 4 vols (Cairo: Maṭbaʿat al-ʿĀmirat al-Sharafiyya, 1886).
Al-Jaṣṣāṣ, Aḥmad b. ʿAlī, *Aḥkām al-qurʾān*, ed. Muḥammad al-Ṣādiq Qamḥāwī, 5 vols (Beirut: Dār Iḥyāʾ al-Turāth al-ʿArabī, 1992).
Al-Jaṣṣāṣ, Aḥmad b. ʿAlī, *Al-Fuṣūl fī al-uṣūl*, ed. ʿUjayl Jāsim al-Nashamī, 4 vols (Kuwait: Wizārat al-Awqāf wa-l-Shuʾūn al-Islāmiyya, 1994).
Al-Juwaynī, Abū al-Maʿālī, *Al-Shāmil fī uṣūl al-dīn*, ed. ʿAlī Sāmī al-Nashshār (Alexandria: Al-Manshūʾat al-Maʿārif, 1969).
Al-Juwaynī, Abū al-Maʿālī, *Al-Burhān fī uṣūl al-fiqh*, ed. ʿAbd al-ʿAẓīm Maḥmūd al-Dīb, 2 vols (Cairo: Dār al-Anṣār, 1979).
Al-Juwaynī, Abū al-Maʿālī, *Al-Ghiyāthī*, ed. ʿAbd al-ʿAẓīm Maḥmūd al-Dīb (Beirut: Dār al-Minhāj, 2011).
Al-Kāsānī, Abū Bakr b. Masʿūd, *Badāʾiʿ al-ṣanāʾiʿ fī tartīb al-sharāʾiʿ*, ed. ʿĀdil Aḥmad ʿAbd al-Mawjūd and ʿAlī Muḥammad Muʿawwiḍ, 10 vols (Beirut: Dār al-Kutub al-ʿIlmiyya, 2003).
Al-Khurāsānī, Abū al-Ghānim, *Al-Mudawwana al-kubrā*, ed. Muṣṭafā b. Ṣāliḥ Bājū, 3 vols (Muscat: Wizārat al-Turāth al-Qawmī wa-l-Thaqāfa, 2007).
Mālik b. Anas, *Al-Muwaṭṭaʾ* (Vaduz: Thesaurus Islamicus Foundation, 2000).

Al-Marghīnānī, Burhān al-Dīn, *Al-Hidāya*, ed. Naʿīm Ashraf Nūr Aḥmad, 8 vols (Karachi: Idārat al-Qurʾān wa-l-ʿUlūm al-Islāmiyya, 1996).
Al-Māturīdī, Abū Manṣūr, *Kitāb al-tawḥīd*, eds Bekir Topaloğlu, and Muḥammad Aruçi (Istanbul: Maktabat al-Irshād, 2006).
Al-Māturīdī, Abū Manṣūr, *Taʾwīlāt al-qurʾān*, eds Ertuğrul Boynukalin, and Bekir Topaloğlu, 18 vols (Istanbul: Dār al-Mīzān, 2006).
Al-Māwardī, ʿAlī b. Muḥammad, *Al-Aḥkām al-sultāniyya wa-l-walāyāt al-dīniyya*, ed. Aḥmad Mubārak al-Baghdādī (Kuwait: Maktaba Dār Ibn Qutayba, 1989).
Al-Mawṣalī, ʿAbd Allāh b. Maḥmūd, *Kitāb al-ikhtiyār li-taʿlīl al-mukhtār*, ed. Khālid ʿAbd al-Raḥmān al-ʿAkk, 5 vols (Beirut: Dār al-Maʿrifa, 2011).
Al-Mizzī, Jamāl al-Dīn, *Tahdhīb al-kamāl fī asmāʾ al-rijāl*, ed. Bashār ʿAwwād Maʿrūf, 35 vols (Beirut: Al-Muʾassasat al-Risāla, 1982).
Al-Mizzī, Jamāl al-Dīn, *Tuḥfat al-ashrāf bi-maʿrifat al-aṭrāf*, ed. Bashār ʿAwwād Maʿrūf, 13 vols (Beirut: Dār al-Gharb al-Islāmī, 1999).
Muqātil b. Sulaymān, *Tafsīr Muqātil ibn Sulaymān*, ed. ʿAbd Allāh Maḥmūd Shihātah, 5 vols (Beirut: Muʾassasat al-Tārīkh al-ʿArabī, 2002).
Muslim b. al-Ḥajjāj, *Ṣaḥīḥ Muslim*, 2 vols (Vaduz: Thesaurus Islamicus Foundation, 2000).
Al-Nasafī, Abū al-Barakāt, *Al-Manār fī uṣūl al-fiqh* (Durr Saʿāda, 1898).
Al-Nasafī, Abū al-Barakāt, *Madārik al-tanzīl wa-ḥaqāʾiq al-taʾwīl*, ed. ʿAbd al-Majīd Ṭamʿa Ḥalabī (Beirut: Dār al-Maʿrifa, 2008).
Al-Nasafī, Abū al-Barakāt, *Sharḥ al-ʿumda fī ʿaqīdat ahl al-sunna wa-l-jamāʿa*, ed. ʿAbd Allāh Muḥammad ʿAbd Allāh Ismāʿīl (Cairo: Al-Maktaba al-Azhariyya li-l-Turāth, 2011).
Al-Nasafī, Abū al-Muʿīn, *Tabṣirat al-adilla fī uṣūl al-dīn*, ed. Muḥammad Alanūr Ḥāmid ʿĪsā (Cairo: Al-Maktaba al-Azhariyya li-l-Turāth, 2011).
Al-Nasāʾī, Aḥmad b. Shuʿayb, *Sunan al-Nasāʾī*, 2 vols (Vaduz: Thesaurus Islamicus Foundation, 2000).
Al-Naḥḥās, Aḥmad b. Muḥammad, *Al-Nāsikh wa-l-mansūkh*, ed. Sulaymān b. Ibrāhīm al-Lāḥim, 3 vols (Beirut: Muʾassasat al-Risāla, 1991).
Al-Naḥḥās, Aḥmad b. Muḥammad, *Iʿrāb al-qurʾān*, ed. Khālid al-ʿAlī (Beirut: ʿĀlam al-Kutub, 2008).
Al-Qarāfī, Shihāb al-Dīn, *Sharḥ tanqīh al-fuṣūl fī ikhtiṣār al-maḥṣūl fī al-uṣūl*, ed. Nājī Suwayd (Beirut: Al-Maktabat al-ʿAṣriyya, 2011).
Al-Qazwīnī, Jalāl al-Dīn, *Al-Talkhīṣ fī ʿulūm al-balāgha*, ed. ʿAbd al-Raḥmān al-Barqūqī (Beirut: Dār al-Kitāb al-ʻArabī, 1932).
Al-Qurṭubī, Muḥammad b. Aḥmad, *Al-Jāmiʿ li-aḥkām al-qurʾān*, ed. ʿAbd Allāh b. ʿAbd al-Muḥsin al-Turkī, 24 vols (Beirut: Muʾassasat al-Risāla, 2006).
Al-Rāzī, Fakhr al-Dīn, *Al-Tafsīr al-kabīr*, ed. ʾAbd al-Raḥmān Muḥammad, 32 vols (Cairo: Al-Maṭbaʿat al-Bahiyyat al-Miṣriyya, 1938).
Al-Rāzī, Fakhr al-Dīn, *Muḥaṣṣal afkār al-mutaqaddimīn wa-l-mutaʾakhirīn min ʿulamāʾ wa-l-ḥukamāʾ wa-l-mutakallimīn*, ed. Ṭāhā ʿAbd al-Ruʾūf Saʿd (Cairo: Maktabat al-Kulliyāt al-Azhariyya, n.d.).

Al-Rāzī, ʿAbd al-Qādir, *Mukhtār al-ṣiḥāḥ* (Beirut: Maktaba Libnān Nāshirūn, 2007).

Al-Samarqandī, Abū Muqātil, *Al-ʿĀlim wa-l-mutaʿallim*, ed. Muḥammad Zāhid al-Kawtharī (Cairo: Maṭbaʿat al-Anwār, 1949).

Al-Samarqandī, ʿAlāʾ al-Dīn, *Mīzān al-uṣūl fī natāʾij al-ʿuqūl*, ed. ʿAbd al-Malik ʿAbd al-Raḥmān al-Saʿdī, 2 vols (Mecca: Jāmiʿat Umm al-Qurā, 1984).

Al-Samhūdī, Nūr al-Dīn, *Wafāʾ al-wafā bi-akhbār dār al-Muṣṭafā*, ed. Khālid ʿAbd al-Ghanī Maḥfūẓ, 4 vols (Beirut: Dār al-Kutub al-ʿIlmiyya, 2006).

Al-Sarakhsī, Shams al-Dīn, *Uṣūl al-Sarakhsī*, ed. Abū al-Wafāʾ al-Afghānī, 2 vols (Beirut: Dār al-Kutub al-ʿIlmiyya, 1993).

Al-Shāfiʿī, Muḥammad b. Idrīs, *Al-Risāla*, ed. Aḥmad Muḥammad Shākir (Cairo: Al-Bābī al-Ḥalabī, 1940).

Al-Shāfiʿī, Muḥammad b. Idrīs, *Aḥkām al-qurʾān*, ed. ʿAbd al-Ghanī ʿAbd al-Khāliq, 2 vols (Cairo: Maktabat al-Khānjī, 1994).

Shāh Walī Allāh al-Dahlawī, *Al-Fawz al-kabīr fī uṣūl al-tafsīr*, ed. Sulaymān al-Ḥusaynī al-Nadwī (Beirut: Dār al-Bashāʾir al-Islāmiyya, 2005).

Al-Shāshī, Niẓām al-Dīn, *Uṣūl al-Shāshī*, ed. Mohammad Akram al-Nadwī (Beirut: Dār al-Gharb al-Islāmī, 2000).

Al-Shāṭibī, Ibrāhīm b. Mūsā, *Al-Muwāfaqāt fī uṣūl al-sharīʿa*, ed. ʿAbd Allāḥ Drāz, 4 vols (Cairo: Dār al-Ḥadīth, 2005).

Al-Shaybānī, Muḥammad b. al-Ḥasan, *Muwaṭṭaʾ al-imām Mālik*, ed. ʿAbd al-Wahhāb ʿAbd al-Laṭīf (Cairo: Wizārat al-Awqāf al-Majlis al-Aʿlā li-l-Shuʾūn al-Islāmiyya, 1994).

Al-Shaybānī, Muḥammad b. al-Ḥasan, *Kitāb al-āthār*, ed. Khālid al-ʿAwwād, 2 vols (Kuwait: Dār al-Nawādir, 2008).

Al-Shaybānī, Muḥammad b. al-Ḥasan, *Al-Aṣl*, ed. Muḥammad Boynukalin, 12 vols (Doha: Wizārat al-Awqāf wa-l-Shuʾūn al-Islāmiyya, 2012).

Shaykhzāde, ʿAbd al-Raḥmān, *Kitāb naẓm al-farāʾid* (Cairo: Al-Maṭbaʿat al-Adabiyya, 1899).

Al-Suyūṭī, Jalāl al-Dīn and Jalāl al-Dīn al-Maḥallī, *Al-Qurʾān al-karīm wa-bi-hāmishihi tafsīr al-imāmayn al-Jalīlayn*, ed. ʿAbd al-Qādir al-Arnāʾūṭ (Damascus: Dār Ibn Kathīr, 1987).

Al-Suyūṭī, Jalāl al-Dīn, *Al-Itqān fī al-ulūm al-qurʾān*, ed. Aḥmad b. ʿAlī, 4 vols (Cairo: Dār al-Ḥadīth, 2004).

Al-Suyūṭī, Jalāl al-Dīn, *Lubāb al-nuqūl fi asbāb al-nuzūl* (Riyadh: Maktaba Nizār Muṣṭafā al-Bāz, 2004).

Al-Ṭabarī, Muḥammad b. Jarīr, *Tārīkh al-Ṭabarī*, ed. Muḥammad Abū al-Faḍl Ibrāhīm, 11 vols (Cairo: Dār al-Maʿārif, 1967).

Al-Ṭabarī, Muḥammad b. Jarīr, *Tafsīr al-Ṭabarī: jāmiʿ al-bayān ʿan taʾwīl āy al-qurʾān*, ed. ʿAbd Allāh b. ʿAbd al-Muḥsin al-Turkī, 26 vols (Cairo: Dār Hajr, 2001).

Al-Ṭaḥāwī, Abū Jaʿfar, *Sharḥ mushkil al-āthār*, ed. Shuʿayb Arnāʾūṭ, 16 vols (Beirut: Muʾassasat al-Risāla, 1994).

Al-Ṭaḥāwī, Abū Jaʿfar, *Aḥkām al-qurʾān al-karīm*, ed. Saʿd al-Dīn Awnāl, 2 vols (Istanbul: Markaz al-Buḥūth al-Islāmiyya al-Tābiʿ li-Waqf al-Diyānat al-Turkī, 1998).

Al-Ṭaḥāwī, Abū Jaʿfar, *Matn al-ʿaqīdat al-Ṭaḥāwiyya*, ed. Iqbāl Aʿẓami (Leicester: UK Islamic Academy, 2012).

Al-Ṭāʾī, Abū Tāmmām, *Dīwan al-Ḥimāsa*, ed. Aḥmad Ḥasan Basaj (Beirut: Dār al-Kutub al-ʿIlmiyya, 1998).

Al-Thaʿlabī, Abū Isḥāq, *Al-Kashf wa-l-bayān*, eds ʿAlī b. ʿĀshūr Abū Muḥammad and Naẓīr al-Sāʿidī, 10 vols (Beirut: Dār Iḥyāʾ al-Turāth al-ʿArabī, 2002).

Al-Tirmidhī, Muḥammad b. Abū ʿĪsa, *Sunan al-Tirmidhī*, 2 vols (Vaduz: Thesaurus Islamicus Foundation, 2000).

Al-Ṭūfī, Najm al-Dīn, *Darʾ al-qawl al-qabīḥ bi-l-taḥsīn wa-l-taqbīḥ*, ed. Ayman Shihadeh (Riyadh: Markaz al-Malik Fayṣal li-l-Buḥūth wa-l-Dirāsāt al-Islāmiyya, 2005).

Al-Ṭūsī, Abū Jaʿfar, *Al-Tibyān fī tafsīr al-qurʾān*, ed. Aḥmad Ḥabīb Qaṣīr al-ʿĀmilī, 10 vols (Beirut: Dār Iḥyāʾ al-Turāth al-ʿArabī, 1988–9).

Al-Zabīdī, Muḥammad al-Murtaḍā, *Tāj al-ʿarūs*, ed. ʿAbd al-Sattār Aḥmad Farāj, 40 vols (Kuwait: Maṭbaʿat Ḥakūmat al-Kuwayt, 1965).

Al-Zamakhsharī, Maḥmūd b. ʿUmar, *Al-Kashshāf ʿan ḥaqāʾiq al-tanzīl wa-ʿuyūn al-aqāwīl fī wujūh al-taʾwīl*, ed. Khalīl Maʾmūn Shīḥā (Beirut: Dār al-Maʿrifa, 2009).

Al-Zarkashī, Badr al-Dīn, *Al-Baḥr al-muḥīṭ fī uṣūl al-fiqh*, ed. ʿAbd al-Qādir ʿAbd Allāh al-ʿĀnī, 6 vols (Kuwait: Wizārat al-Awqāf wa-l-Shuʾūn al-Islāmiyya, 1992).

Al-Zarkashī, Badr al-Dīn, *Al-Burhān fī ʿulūm al-qurʾān*, ed. Abū al-Faḍl Dimyāṭī (Cairo: Dār al-Ḥadīth, 2006).

Zayd b. ʿAlī, *Al-Ṣafwa*, ed. Nājī Ḥasan (Najaf: Maṭbaʿat al-Ādāb, n. d.).

II. Secondary sources

ʿAbd al-Bāqī, Muḥammad Fuʾād, *Al-Muʿjam al-mufahras li-alfāẓ al-qurʾān al-karīm* (Cairo: Dār al-Ḥadīth, 1996).

Abdel Haleem, M. A. S., 'Grammatical Shift for Rhetorical Purposes: "*Iltifāt*" and Related Features in the Qur'ān', *Bulletin of the School of Oriental and African Studies, University of London*, 55/3 (1992), pp. 407–32.

Abdel Haleem, M. A. S., 'Early *Kalām*', in Seyyed Hossein Nasr and Oliver Leaman (eds), *History of Islamic Philosophy Vol 1* (Tehran: Arayeh Cultural Institute, 1996), pp. 71–88.

Abdel Haleem, M. A. S., 'The Qur'anic Employment of the Story of Noah', *Journal of Qurʾanic Studies*, 8/1 (2006), pp. 38–57.

Abdel Haleem, M. A. S., 'Qur'anic "*jihād*": A Linguistic and Contextual Analysis', *Journal of Qurʾanic Studies*, 12 (2010), pp. 147–66.

Abdel Haleem, M. A. S., *The Qurʾan: English Translation and Parallel Arabic Text* (Oxford: Oxford University Press, 2010).

Abdel Haleem, M. A. S., 'Euphemism in the Qur'an: A Case Study of Marital Relations as Depicted in Q. 2:222–3', *Journal of Qur'anic Studies*, 13/1 (2011), pp. 125–31.

Abdel Haleem, M. A. S., *Understanding the Qur'an: Themes and Style* (London: I. B. Tauris, 2011).

Abdel Haleem, M. A. S., 'The *Jizya* Verse (Q. 9:29): Tax Enforcement on Non-Muslims in the First Muslim State', *Journal of Qur'anic Studies*, 14/2 (2012), pp. 72–89.

Abdesselem, Ahmed, *Dirāsāt fī muṣṭalaḥ al-siyāsa ʿinda al-ʿarab* (Tunis: Al-Sharikat al-Tūnisiyya li-l-Tawzīʿ, 1978).

Abdul-Raof, Hussein, *Arabic Rhetoric: A Pragmatic Analysis* (London: Routledge, 2006).

Abū Zahra, Muḥammad, *Falsafat al-ʿuqūba fī al-fiqh al-islāmī* (Cairo: Maʿhad al-Dirāsāt al-ʿArabiyyat al-ʿĀliya, 1963).

Abū Zahra, Muḥammad, *Al-Aqīda al-islāmiyya ka-mā jāʾa bihā al-qurʾān al-karīm* (Cairo: Majmaʿ al-Buḥūth al-Islāmiyya, 1969).

Ahmad, Barakat, *Muḥammad and the Jews: A Re-examination* (Delhi: Vikas Publishing House, 1979).

ʿAlī, ʿAbdullāh Yūsuf, *The Holy Qur-ān: Arabic Text with an English Translation and Commentary*, 3 vols (Lahore: Shaikh Muhammad Ashraf, 1937).

ʿAlī, Jawād, *Al-Mufaṣṣal fī tārīkh al-ʿarab qabl al-islām*, 10 vols (Baghdad: Jāmiʿat Baghdad, 1993).

Ali, Kecia, *Sexual Ethics and Islam: Feminist Reflections on Qur'an, Hadith and Jurisprudence* (Oxford: Oneworld, 2006).

Ali, Ahmed, *Al-Qur'an: A Contemporary Translation* (Princeton: Princeton University Press, 1988).

Ali, Muhammad Mansur, *Al-Tirmidhī and the Role of the* Isnād *in his* Sunan, PhD thesis (Manchester: University of Manchester, 2009).

Ali, M. M. Y., *Medieval Islamic Pragmatics: Sunni Legal Theorists' Models of Textual Communication* (Richmond, Surrey: Curzon, 2000).

Anthony, Sean W, 'Crime and Punishment in Early Medina: The Origins of a *Maghāzī*-Tradition', in Harald Motzki, Nicolet Boekhoff-van der Voort, and Sean W. Anthony (eds), *Analysing Muslim Traditions: Studies in Legal, Exegetical and* Maghāzī Ḥadīth (Leiden: Brill, 2009), pp. 385–465.

Aquinas, Thomas, *The* 'Summa Theologica' *of St. Thomas Aquinas*, trans. Fathers of the English Dominican Province, 21 vols (London: R. & T. Washbourne, 1911–25).

Aristotle, *The Nicomachean Ethics*, trans. Terence Irwin (Indiapolis: Hackett Publishing Company, 1999).

Asad, Muhammad, *The Principles of State and Government in Islam* (Berkeley and Los Angeles: University of California Press, 1961).

Asad, Muhammad, *The Message of the Quran* (Gibraltar: Dar al-Andalus, 1984).

Al-Attas, Syed Muhammad Naquib, *Islām and Secularism* (Kuala Lumpur: International Institute of Islamic Thought and Civilization, 1993).

Al-Attas, Syed Muhammad Naquib, *Prolegomena to the Metaphysics of Islām* (Kuala Lumpur: International Institute of Islamic Thought and Civilization, 1995).

Al-Azmeh, Aziz, *The Emergence of Islam in Late Antiquity: Allāh and his People* (Cambridge: Cambridge University Press, 2014).

Auda, Jasser, *Maqāṣid al-Sharīʿah as Philosophy of Islamic Law: A Systems Approach* (London: The International Institute of Islamic Thought, 2008).

Audi, Robert (ed.), *The Cambridge Dictionary of Philosophy, Second Edition* (Cambridge: Cambridge University Press, 1999).

Avery-Peck, Alan J., 'Charity in Judaism', in Jacob Neusner, Alan J. Avery-Peck, and William Scott Green (eds), *The Encyclopaedia of Judaism, Second Edition*, 4 vols (Leiden: Brill, 2005).

Bacon, John, *Universals and Property Instances: The Alphabet of Being* (Oxford: Blackwell, 1995).

Badawī, Aḥmad Aḥmad, *Usus al-naqd al-adabī ʿinda al-ʿarab* (Cairo: Dār Nahṣat Miṣr li-l-Ṭibaʿa wa-l-Nashr, 1979).

Badawi, El-Said and M. A. S. Abdel Haleem, *Arabic-English Dictionary of Qur'anic Usage* (Leiden: Brill, 2008).

Al-Bārbartī, Muḥammad b. Muḥammad, *Sharḥ al-talkhīṣ* (Tripoli: Al-Munshaʾat al-ʿĀmma li-l-Nashr wa-l-Tawzīʿ wa-l-Iʿlān, 1983).

Barlas, Asma, *"Believing Women" in Islam: Unreading Patriarchal Interpretations of the Qur'an* (Austin: University of Texas Press, 2002).

Barnhart, Robert K. (ed.), *Chambers Dictionary of Etymology* (London: Chambers, 1988).

Bauer, Karen, *Gender Hierarchy in the Qur'ān: Medieval Interpretations, Modern Responses* (Cambridge: Cambridge University Press, 2015).

Bedir, Murteza, 'An Early Response to Shāfiʿī: ʿĪsā b. Abān on the Prophetic Report (*Khabar*)', *Islamic Law and Society*, 9/3 (2002), pp. 285–311.

Berg, Herbert, *The Development of Exegesis in Early Islam: The Authenticity of Muslim Literature from the Formative Period* (Richmond: Curzon, 2000).

Berg, Herbert, 'Competing Paradigms in the Study of Islamic Origins: Qurʾān 15:89–91 and the Value of *Isnād*s', in Herbert Berg (ed.), *Method and Theory in the Study of Islamic Origins* (Leiden: Brill, 2003), pp. 259–90.

Bilfaqīh, ʿAlawī b. Muḥammad and Muḥammad Karīm Rājiḥ, *Al-Qirāʾāt al-ʿashr al-mutawātira min ṭarīqay al-Shāṭibiyya wa-l-Durra* (Medina and Tarim: Dār al-Muhājir, 1994).

Black, Antony, *The History of Islamic Political Thought: From the Prophet to the Present* (Edinburgh: Edinburgh University Press, 2001).

Blackburn, S. (ed.), *The Oxford Dictionary of Philosophy* (Oxford: Oxford University Press, 2008).

Blois, François de, 'Sabians', in Jane Dammen McAuliffe (ed.), *Encyclopaedia of the Qur'ān,* 6 vols (Leiden: Brill, 2001–6).

Bloom, Allan (trans.), *The Republic of Plato* (New York: Basic Books, 1991).

Bonner, Michael, 'Poverty and Economics in the Qur'an', *The Journal of Interdisciplinary History*, 35/3 (2005), pp. 391–406.

Bonner, Michael, 'The Arabian Silent Trade: Profit and Nobility in the "Markets of the Arabs"', in Roxani Eleni Margariti, Adam Sabra, and Petra M. Sijpesteijn (eds), *Histories of the Middle East*: *Studies in Middle Eastern Society, Economy and Law in Honor of A. L. Udovitch* (Leiden: Brill, 2010), pp. 23–52.

Bosworth, C. E., 'Buʿāth', in P. Bearman, Th. Bianquis, C. E. Bosworth, E. Van Donzel, and W. P. Heinrichs (eds), *The Encyclopaedia of Islam, New Edition,* 12 vols (Leiden: Brill, 1986–2004).

Boullata, I. J., 'Rhetorical Interpretation of the Qur'an: *iʿjāz* and Related Topics', in A. Rippin (ed.), *Approaches to the History of the Interpretation of the Qur'ān* (Oxford: Clarendon Press, 1988), pp. 139–57.

Bowersock, G. W., *Roman Arabia* (Cambridge, MA: Harvard University Press, 1983).

Bowersock, G. W., *The Crucible of Islam* (Cambridge, MA: Harvard University Press, 2017).

Bravmann, M. M., *The Spiritual Background of Early Islam* (Leiden: Brill, 1972).

Brown, Francis (ed.), *A Hebrew and English Lexicon of the Old Testament* (Oxford: Oxford University Press, 1939).

Brown, Jonathan A. C., *The Canonization of al-Bukhārī and Muslim: The Formation and Function of the Sunnī Ḥadīth Canon* (Leiden: Brill, 2007).

Brown, Jonathan A. C., 'How We Know Early Ḥadīth Critics Did *Matn* Criticism and Why It's So Hard to Find', *Islamic Law and Society*, 15 (2008), pp. 143–84.

Brown, Jonathan A. C., 'Did the Prophet Say It or Not? The Literal, Historical, and Effective Truth of *Ḥadīth*s in Early Sunnism', *Journal of the American Oriental Society*, 129/2 (2009), pp. 259–85.

Brown, Jonathan A. C., *Hadith: Muḥammad's Legacy in the Medieval and Modern World* (Oxford: Oneworld, 2009).

Brown, Jonathan A. C. *Misquoting Muḥammad: The Challenge and Choices of Interpreting the Prophet's Legacy* (London: Oneworld, 2014).

Brunschvig, R., 'ʿAbd', in P. Bearman, Th. Bianquis, C. E. Bosworth, E. Van Donzel, and W. P. Heinrichs (eds), *The Encyclopaedia of Islam, New Edition*, 12 vols (Leiden: Brill, 1986–2004).

Buchholz, Stephan, 'Marriage', in Hubert Cancik, Helmuth Schneider, and Manfred Landfester (eds), *Brill's New Pauly*, 22 vols (Leiden: Brill, 2011).

Bukharin, Mikhail D., 'Mecca on the Caravan Routes in Pre-Islamic Antiquity', in Nicolai Sinai, Angelika Neuwirth, and Michael Marx (eds), *The Qur'ān in Context* (Leiden: Brill, 2010), pp. 115–34.

Burrell, David B., 'A Philosophical-Theologian's Journey', in Christian W. Troll, and C. T. R. Hewer (eds), *Christian Lives Given to the Study of Islam* (New York: Fordham University Press, 2012), pp. 53–62.

Al-Būṭī, Muḥammad Saʿīd Ramaḍan, *Fiqh al-sīrat al-nabawwiya* (Damascus: Dār al-Fikr, 1991).

Calder, Norman, 'History and Nostalgia: Reflections on John Wansbrough's *The Sectarian Milieu*', *Method & Theory in the Study of Religion*, 9/1 (1997), pp. 47–73.

Cerić, Mustafa, *Roots of Synthetic Theology in Islam: A Study of the Theology of Abū Manṣūr al-Māturīdī (d. 333/944)* (Kuala Lumpur: International Institute of Islamic Thought and Civilization, 1995).

Chaudhry, Ayesha S., '"I Wanted One Thing and God Wanted Another …": The Dilemma of the Prophetic Example and the Qur'anic Injunction on Wife-Beating', *Journal of Religious Ethics*, 39/3 (2001), pp. 416–39.

Chaudhry, Ayesha S., *Domestic Violence and the Islamic Tradition* (Oxford: Oxford University Press, 2013).

Choudhury, Masudul Alam, 'Usury', in Jane Dammen McAuliffe (ed.), *Encyclopaedia of the Qur'ān*, 6 vols (Leiden: Brill, 2001–6).

Cilardo, Agostino, *The Qur'anic Term Kalāla* (Edinburgh: Edinburgh University Press, 2005).

Cornell, Vincent J., 'In the Shadow of Deuteronomy: Approaches to Interest and Usury in Judaism and Christianity', in Abdulkader S. Thomas (ed.), *Interest in Islamic Economics: Understanding Riba* (London: Routledge, 2010), pp. 13–25.

Cragg, Kenneth, *The Event of the Qur'an: Islam in Its Scripture* (London: Allen and Unwin, 1971).

Cragg, Kenneth, *A Certain Sympathy of Scriptures: Biblical and Qur'anic* (Brighton: Sussex Academic Press, 2005).

Crone, Patricia, and Martin Hinds, *God's Caliph: Religious Authority in the First Centuries of Islam* (Cambridge: Cambridge University Press, 1986).

Crone, Patricia, *Roman, Provincial and Islamic Law* (Cambridge: Cambridge University Press, 1987).

Crone, Patricia, 'Two Legal Problems Bearing on the Early History of the Qurʾān', *Jerusalem Studies in Arabic and Islam*, 18 (1994), pp. 1–37.

Crowe, Michael Bertram, *The Changing Profile of the Natural Law* (The Hague: Martinus Nijhoff, 1977).

Cuypers, Michel, *The Banquet: A Reading of the Fifth Sura of the Qur'an* (Miami: Convivium, 2009).

Cuypers, Michel, *The Composition of the Qur'an: Rhetorical Analysis* (London: Bloomsbury, 2015).

Daiber, Hans, *The Islamic Concept of Belief in the 4th/10th Century: Abū l-Lait as-Samarqandī's Commentary on Abū Ḥanīfa (died 150/767) al-Fiqh al-absaṭ* (Tokyo: Institute for the Study of Languages and Cultures of Asia and Africa, 1995).

Danby, Herbert (trans.), *Tractate Sanhedrin Mishnah and Tosefta* (London: Society for Promoting Christian Knowledge, 1919).

Dāwūd, Muḥammad Muḥammad, *Muʿjam al-furūq al-dalāliyya fī al-qurʾān al-karīm* (Cairo: Dār Gharīb, 2008).

Ḍayf, Shawqī (ed.), *Al-Muʿjam al-wasīṭ* (Cairo: Maktabat al-Shurūq al-Dawliyya, 2008).
Denny, Frederick M., 'Ethics and the Qurʾān: Community and World View', in Richard G. Hovannisian (ed.), *Ethics in Islam* (Malibu, CA: Undena Publications, 1985), pp. 103–21.
Dhanani, Alnoor, 'Al-Māturīdī and al-Nasafī on Atomism and the Ṭabāʾiʿ', in Büyük Türk Bilgini Imām Māturidi ve Māturidilik: Milletlerarasi tartismall ilmi toplanti, 22–24 Mayis 2009 Istanbul (Istanbul: IFAU, 2012), pp. 65–76.
Donaldson, D. M., *Studies in Muslim Ethics* (London: SPCK, 1953).
Donner, Fred M., *Narratives of Islamic Origins: The Beginning of Islamic Historical Writing* (Princeton: Darwin Press, 1998).
Donner, Fred M., 'The Qur'an in Recent Scholarship: Challenges and Desiderata', in Gabriel Said Reynolds (ed.), *The Qur'an in Its Historical Context* (London: Routledge, 2008), pp. 29–50.
Donner, Fred M., *Muhammad and the Believers: At the Origins of Islam* (Cambridge, MA: Harvard University Press, 2010).
Dorroll, Philip, 'The Universe in Flux: Reconsidering Abū Manṣūr al-Māturīdī's Metaphysics and Epistemology', *Journal of Islamic Studies*, 27/2 (2016), pp. 119–35.
Draz, M. A., *The Moral World of the Qur'an*, trans. Danielle Robinson, and Rebecca Masterton (London: I. B. Tauris, 2004).
Ehring, Douglas, *Tropes: Properties, Objects, and Mental Causation* (Oxford: Oxford University Press, 2011).
El-Awa, Salwá Muḥammad, *Textual Relations in Qur'an: Relevance, Coherence and Structure* (London: Routledge, 2005).
El Shamsy, Ahmed, 'The Wisdom of God's Law: Two Theories', in A. Kevin Reinhart, and Robert Gleave (eds), *Islamic Law in Theory: Studies on Jurisprudence in Honor of Bernard Weiss* (Leiden: Brill, 2014), pp. 10–37.
Emon, Anver M., *Islamic Natural Law Theories* (Oxford: Oxford University Press, 2010).
Ernst, Carl W., 'Muḥammad as the Pole of Existence', in Jonathan E. Brockopp (ed.), *The Cambridge Companion to Muḥammad* (Cambridge: Cambridge University Press, 2010), pp. 123–38.
Esack, Farid, 'Qur'anic Hermeneutics: Problems and Prospects', in Mustafa Akram Ali Shah (ed.), *Tafsir: Interpreting the Qurʾan*, vol. 4 (Abingdon: Routledge, 2012), pp. 379–402.
Fakhry, Majid, *Ethical Theories in Islam* (Leiden: Brill, 1994).
Al-Farāhī, Ḥamīd al-Dīn, *Dalāʾil al-niẓām*, ed. Badr al-Dīn al-Iṣlāḥī (Sarai Mir: Al-Dāʾirat al-Ḥamīdiyya, 1969).
Al-Farāhī, Ḥamīd al-Dīn, *Asālīb al-qurʾān* (Sarai Mir: Al-Dāʾirat al-Ḥamīdiyya, 1970).
Al-Farāhī, Ḥamīd al-Dīn, *Mufradāt al-qurʾān* (Beirut: Dār al-Gharb al-Islāmī, 2002).

Al-Farāhī, Ḥamīd al-Dīn, *Rasāʾil fī ʿulūm al-qurʾān al-majmūʿat al-thāniya* (Sarai Mir: Al-Dāʾirat al-Hamīdiyya, 2011).

Farès, B., and eds., 'Murūʾa', in P. Bearman, Th. Bianquis, C. E. Bosworth, E. Van Donzel, and W. P. Heinrichs (eds), *The Encyclopaedia of Islam, New Edition*, 12 vols (Leiden: Brill, 1986–2004).

Fiey, J. M., 'Naṣārā', in P. Bearman, Th. Bianquis, C. E. Bosworth, E. Van Donzel, and W. P. Heinrichs (eds), *The Encyclopaedia of Islam, New Edition*, 12 vols (Leiden: Brill, 1986–2004).

Finster, Barbara, 'Arabia in Late Antiquity: An Outline of the Cultural Situation in the Peninsula at the Time of Muḥammad,' in Nicolai Sinai, Angelika Neuwirth, and Michael Marx (eds), *The Qurʾān in Context* (Leiden: Brill, 2010).

Firestone, Reuvan, 'Disparity and Resolution in the Qurʾānic Teachings on War: A Reevaluation of a Traditional Problem', *Journal of Near Eastern Studies*, 56/1 (1997), pp. 1 –19.

Foucault, Michel, *Discipline and Punish: The Birth of the Prison*, trans. Alan Sheridan (Harmondsworth: Penguin Books, 1991).

Frank, Richard M., '*Al-Maʿnā*: Some Reflections on the Technical Meanings of the Term in the Kalām and Its Use in the Physics of Muʿammar', *Journal of the American Oriental Society*, 87/3 (1967), pp. 248–59.

Frank, Richard M., 'Notes and Remarks on the Ṭabāʾiʿ in the Teaching of al-Māturīdī', in P. Salmon (ed.), *Mélanges d'Islamologie* (Leiden: Brill, 1974).

Frank, Richard M., '*Kalām* and Philosophy: A Perspective from one Problem', in Parviz Morewedge (ed.), *Islamic Philosophical Theology* (Albany: State University of New York Press, 1979), pp. 71–95.

Frank, Richard M., 'Moral Obligation in Classical Muslim Theology', *Journal of Religious Ethics*, 11 (1983), pp. 204–23.

Frank, Richard M., 'Can God Do What Is Wrong?', in Tamar Rudavsky (ed.), *Divine Omniscience and Omnipotence in Medieval Philosophy* (Dordrecht: Springer-Science+Business Media, 1985), pp. 69–79.

Frank, Richard M., 'Currents and Countercurrents', in Peter G. Riddell, and Tony Street (eds), *Islam: Essays in Scripture, Thought and Society: A Festschrift in Honour of Anthony H. Johns* (Leiden: Brill, 1997).

Fück, J.W., 'Fidjār', in P. Bearman, Th. Bianquis, C. E. Bosworth, E. Van Donzel, and W. P. Heinrichs (eds), *The Encyclopaedia of Islam, New Edition*, 12 vols (Leiden: Brill, 1986–2004).

Gadamer, Hans-Georg, *Truth and Method*, trans Joel Weinsheimer, and Donald G. Marshall (London: Bloomsbury, 2013).

Galli, Ahmad Mohmed Ahmad, 'Some Aspects of al-Māturīdī's Commentary on the Qur'ān', *Islamic Studies*, 21/1 (1982), pp. 3–21.

Gardet, L., 'Al-Djubbāʾī', in P. Bearman, Th. Bianquis, C. E. Bosworth, E. Van Donzel, and W. P. Heinrichs (eds), *The Encyclopaedia of Islam, New Edition*, 12 vols (Leiden: Brill, 1986–2004).

Garner, Richard T., and Bernard Rosen, *Moral Philosophy: A Systematic Introduction to Normative Ethics and Meta-ethics* (New York: Macmillan, 1967).

Gericke, J. D., 'Platonic Justice for the New Millenium?', *Phronimon*, 2/1 (2000), pp. 129–43.

Germann, Nadja, 'Al-Farabi's Philosophy of Society and Religion', in Edward N. Zalta (ed.), *The Stanford Encyclopedia of Philosophy* (Fall 2016 Edition), <https://plato.stanford.edu/archives/fall2016/entries/al-farabi-soc-rel/>.

Gerson, Lloyd, 'Plotinus', in Edward N. Zalta (ed.), *The Stanford Encyclopedia of Philosophy* (Summer 2014 Edition), <http://plato.stanford.edu/archives/sum2014/entries/plotinus/>.

Ghānim, Muḥammad Sulaymān, *Al-Qurʾān wa-l-iqtiṣād al-siyāsī* (Beirut: Dār al-Fārābī, 1999).

Al-Ghazālī, Abū Ḥāmid, *The Remembrance of Death and the Afterlife*, trans. T. J. Winter (Cambridge: The Islamic Texts Society, 1989).

Al-Ghazālī, Muḥammad, *Nahw tafsīr mawḍūʿī li-suwar al-qurʾān al-karīm* (Cairo: Dār al-Shurūq, 2010).

Giladi, Avner, 'Family', in Jane Dammen McAuliffe (ed.), *Encyclopaedia of the Qurʾān*, 6 vols (Leiden: Brill, 2001–6).

Giladi, Avner, 'Parents', in Jane Dammen McAuliffe (ed.), *Encyclopaedia of the Qurʾān*, 6 vols (Leiden: Brill, 2001–6).

Gimaret, D., 'Muʿtazila', in P. Bearman, Th. Bianquis, C. E. Bosworth, E. Van Donzel, and W. P. Heinrichs (eds.), *The Encyclopaedia of Islam, New Edition*, 12 vols (Leiden: Brill, 1986–2004).

Goldziher, Ignaz, *Muslim Studies*, trans C. R. Barber, and S. M. Stern, 2 vols (Albany: State University of New York Press, 1971).

Gomaa, ʿAlī, *Al-Bayān li-mā yashghal al-adhhān* (Cairo: Dār al-Muqaṭṭam, 2009).

Gomaa, ʿAlī, *Wa-qāla al-imām* (Cairo: Al-Wābil al-Ṣayyib li-l-Intāj wa-l-Tawzīʿ wa-l-Nashr, 2010).

Griffith, Sidney, 'Christians and Christianity', in Jane Dammen McAuliffe (ed.), *Encyclopaedia of the Qurʾān*, 6 vols (Leiden: Brill, 2001–6).

Gül, Ali Rıza. 'Ribā (Usury) Prohibition in the Qur'ān in Terms of its Historical Context,' *Journal of Religious Culture*, 116 (2008), pp. 1–17.

Al-Ḥaddād, ʿAbd Allāh b. ʿAlawī, *Worship*, trans. Abdul Aziz Ahmed (Glasgow: Kitaba, 2011).

Hallaq, Wael B., 'Was al-Shafiʿi the Master Architect of Islamic Jurisprudence?' *International Journal of Middle East Studies*, 25/4 (1993), pp. 587–605.

Hallaq, Wael B., *A History of Islamic Legal Theories: An Introduction to Sunnī* Uṣūl al-Fiqh (Cambridge: Cambridge University Press, 1997).

Hallaq, Wael B., 'The Authenticity of Prophetic Hadith: A Pseudo-problem', *Studia Islamica*, 89 (1999), pp. 75–90.

Hallaq, Wael B., 'Groundwork of the Moral Law: A New Look at the Qurʾān and the Genesis of Sharīʿa', *Islamic Law and Society*, 16 (2009), pp. 239–79.

Hallaq, Wael B., 'Qur'ānic Constitutionalism and Moral Governmentality: Further Notes on the Founding Principles of Islamic Society and Polity', *Comparative Islamic Studies*, 8/1–2 (2012), pp. 1–51.

Hallaq, Wael B., *The Impossible State: Islam, Politics, and Modernity's Moral Predicament* (New York: Columbia University Press, 2013).

Hamid, Eltigani Abdelgadir, *The Qur'an & Politics: A Study of the Origins of Political Thought in the Makkan Qur'an*, trans. Abdul-Wahid Lu'lu'a (London: The International Institute of Islamic Thought, 2004).

Hanafi, Hassan, 'Method of Thematic Interpretation of the Qur'an', in Stefan Wild (ed.), *The Qur'an as Text* (Leiden: Brill, 1996), pp. 195–211.

Harvey, Ramon, 'The Preferences of al-Kisāʾī (d. 189/815): Grammar and Meaning in a Canonical Reading of the Qur'an', *International Journal for the Semiotics of Law*, 29/2 (2016), pp. 313–32.

Harvey, Ramon, 'The Legal Epistemology of Qur'anic Variants: The Readings of Ibn Masʿūd in Kufan *fiqh* and the Ḥanafī *madhhab*', *Journal of Qur'anic Studies*, 19/1 (2017), pp. 72–101.

Al-Ḥaṣkafī, Muḥammad ʿAlāʾ al-Dīn, *The Durr-ul-Mukhtar*, trans. B. M. Dayal (New Delhi: Kitab Bhavan, 1992).

Hawting, G. R., *The Idea of Idolatry and the Emergence of Islam: From Polemic to History* (Cambridge: Cambridge University Press, 1999).

Hawting, G. R., 'The "Sacred Offices" of Mecca from Jahiliyya to Islam', in F. E. Peters (ed.), *The Arabs and Arabia on the Eve of Islam* (Brookfield: Ashgate, 1999).

Heck, Gene. '"Arabia without Spices": An Alternate Hypothesis', *Journal of the American Oriental Society*, 123/3 (2006), pp. 547–76.

Heidegger, M., *An Introduction to Metaphysics* (New Haven: Yale University Press, 1959)

Hidayatullah, Aysha A., *Feminist Edges of the Qur'an* (Oxford: Oxford University Press, 2014).

Al-Hilālī, Muḥammad Taqī-ud-Dīn and Muḥammad Muhsin Khan, *Translation of the Meanings of the Noble Qur'an in the English Language* (Medina: King Fahd Complex for the Printing of the Holy Qur'an, 1998).

Hinds, M., 'Miḥna', in P. Bearman, Th. Bianquis, C. E. Bosworth, E. Van Donzel, and W. P. Heinrichs (eds), *The Encyclopaedia of Islam, New Edition*, 12 vols (Leiden: Brill, 1986–2004).

Hourani, George F., *Reason and Tradition in Islamic Ethics* (Cambridge: Cambridge University Press, 1985).

Hoyland, Robert G., *Arabia and the Arabs* (London: Routledge, 2001).

Ibn ʿĀshūr, Muḥammad, *Tafsīr al-taḥrīr wa-l-tanwīr*, 30 vols (Tunis: Dār al-Tūnisiyya li-l-Nashr, 1984).

Ibn ʿĀshūr, Muḥammad, *Al-Tafsīr wa-rijāluhu* (Tunis: Dār al-Sālām li-l-Ṭibāʿa wa-l-Nashr wa-l-Tawzīʿ wa-l-Tarjama, 2008).

Ibrahim, Mahmood, *Merchant Capital and Islam* (Austin: University of Texas Press, 1990).

Iser, Wolfgang, 'The Reading Process: A Phenomenological Approach', *New Literary History*, 3/2 (1972), pp. 279–99.

Iṣlāḥī, Amīn Aḥsan, *Tadabbur-e-Qur'ān*, trans. Mohammad Saleem Kayani, vol. 1 (Kuala Lumpur: Islamic Book Trust, 2007).

Al-ʿIwaḍī, Rifʿat al-Sayyid, '*Iʿjāz al-qurʾān al-karīm fī āyāt qiṣṣat Shuʿayb ʿalayhi al-salām*', *Majmaʿ al-Buḥūth al-Islāmiyya* (2003), pp. 175–204.

Izutsu, Toshihiko, *The Structure of the Ethical Terms in the Koran* (Tokyo: Keio University, 1959).

Izutsu, Toshihiko, *Ethico-Religious Concepts in the Qur'an* (Montreal: McGill-Queen's University Press, 2002).

Jackson, Sherman A., 'Fiction and Formalism: Toward a Functional Analysis of *Uṣūl al-Fiqh*', in Bernard G. Weiss (ed.), *Studies in Islamic Legal Theory* (Leiden: Brill, 2002).

Jackson, Sherman A., *Islam and the Problem of Black Suffering* (Oxford: Oxford University Press, 2009).

Al-Jārim, ʿAlī, and Muṣṭafā Amīn, *Al-Balāghat al-wāḍiḥa* (Cairo: Dār al-Maʿārif, 1999).

Jeffery, Arthur (ed.), *Materials for the History of the Text of the Qurʾān: The Old Codices* (Leiden: Brill, 1937).

Jeffery, Arthur, *The Foreign Vocabulary of the Qur'ān* (Baroda: Oriental Institute, 1938).

Jenssen, Herbjørn, *The Subtleties and Secrets of the Arabic Language: Preliminary Investigations into Al-Qazwīnī's* Talkhīṣ Al-Miftāḥ (Bergen: Centre for Middle Eastern and Islamic Studies, 1998).

Johns, A. H., 'A Humanistic Approach to *Iʿjaz* in the Qur'an: The Transfiguration of Language', *Journal of Qur'anic Studies*, 13/1 (2011), pp. 79–99.

Johns, A. H., 'Shuʿayb, Orator of the Prophets: Reflections on Qur'anic Narrative', *Journal of Qur'anic Studies*, 13/2 (2011), pp. 136–48.

Johns, A. H., 'Solomon and the Horses: The Theology and Exegesis of a Koranic Story, Sura 38 (*Ṣād*): 30–33', in Mustafa Akram Ali Shah (ed.), *Tafsir: Interpreting the Qur'an*, vol. 4 (Abingdon, Oxon: Routledge, 2012), pp. 3–26.

Jones, A. 'The Language of the Qur'an', *The Arabist. Budapest Studies in Arabic Proceedings of the Colloquium on Arabic Lexicology and Lexicography*, 6/7 (1993), pp. 29–48.

Jones, J. M. B., 'The Chronology of the Maghāzī', in Uri Rubin (ed.), *The Life of Muḥammad* (Aldershot: Ashgate, 1998), pp. 193–298.

Juynboll, G. H. A., *Muslim Tradition: Studies in Chronology, Provenance and Authorship of Early* Ḥadīth (Cambridge: Cambridge University Press, 1983).

Kamali, Mohammad Hashim, *Punishment in Islamic Law: An Enquiry into the Hudud Bill of Kelantan* (Kuala Lumpur: Institut Kajian Dasar, 1995).

Kamali, Mohammad Hashim, *Principles of Islamic Jurisprudence* (Cambridge: Islamic Texts Society, 2003).

Kamali, Mohammad Hashim, *Freedom, Equality and Justice in Islam* (Cambridge: Islamic Texts Society, 2010).

Al-Kāndahlawī, Muḥammad Zakariyyā, *Awjaz al-masālik ilā muwaṭṭa' Mālik*, ed. Taqī al-Dīn al-Nadwī, 17 vols (Damascus: Dār al-Qalam, 2003).

Kelsay, John, 'Divine Command Ethics in Early Islam: Al-Shāfiʿī and the Problem of Guidance', *The Journal of Religious Ethics*, 22/1 (1994), pp. 101–26.

Kelsay, John, *Arguing the Just War in Islam* (Cambridge, MA: Harvard University Press, 2007).

Kennedy, Philip F. (ed.), *On Fiction and* Adab *in Medieval Arabic Literature* (Wiesbaden: Harrassowitz Verlag, 2005).

Khadduri, Majid, *War and Peace in the Law of Islam* (Baltimore: Johns Hopkins University Press, 1955).

Khadduri, Majid, *The Islamic Law of Nations: Shaybānī's Siyar* (Baltimore: Johns Hopkins University Press, 1966).

Khadduri, Majid, *The Islamic Conception of Justice* (Baltimore: Johns Hopkins University Press, 1984).

Al-Khālidī, Ṣalāḥ ʿAbd al-Fattāḥ, *Al-Tafsīr al-mawḍūʿī bayna al-naẓiriyya wa-l-taṭbīq* (Amman: Dār al-Nafā'is, 1997).

Khan, Qamaruddin, *Political Concepts in the Qur'an* (Karachi: Institute of Islamic Studies, 1973).

Kister, M. J., 'Mecca and Tamīm (Aspects of their Relations)', *Journal of the Economic and Social History of the Orient*, 8 (1965), pp. 113–63.

Kister, M. J., 'The Market of the Prophet', *Journal of the Economic and Social History of the Orient*, 8 (1965), pp. 272–6.

Kister, M. J., 'Al-Ḥīra: Some Notes on Its Relations with Arabia', *Arabica*, 15 (1968), pp. 143–69.

Kister, M. J., 'Some Reports Concerning Mecca from Jāhiliyya to Islam', *Journal of the Economic and Social History of the Orient*, 15 (1972), pp. 61–93.

Kister, M. J., 'Mecca and the Tribes of Arabia: Some Notes on Their Relations', in M. Sharon (ed.), *Studies in Islamic History and Civilization in Honour of Professor David Ayalon* (Leiden: Brill, 1986).

Kister, M. J., 'Khuzāʿa', in P. Bearman, Th. Bianquis, C. E. Bosworth, E. Van Donzel, and W. P. Heinrichs (eds), *The Encyclopaedia of Islam, New Edition*, 12 vols (Leiden: Brill, 1986–2004).

Klein, Ralph W., 'Call, Covenant, and Community: The Story of Abraham and Sarah', *Currents in Theology and Mission*, 15 (1988), pp. 120–7.

Kurt, Erkan M., *Creation: The Principle of Nature in Islamic Metaphysics* (New York: Blue Dome Press, 2012).

Lace, O. Jessie, *Understanding the Old Testament* (Cambridge: Cambridge University Press, 1972).

Lane, E. W., *Arabic–English Lexicon*, 2 vols (Cambridge: Islamic Texts Society, 2003).

Lecker, Michael, 'Muḥammad at Medina: A Geographical Approach', *Jerusalem Studies in Arabic and Islam*, 6 (1985), pp. 29–62.

Lecker, Michael, *Muslims, Jews and Pagans: Studies on Early Islamic Medina* (Leiden: Brill, 1995).

Lecker, Michael, 'Wāqidī's Account of the Status of the Jews of Medina: A Study of a Combined Report', *Journal of Near Eastern Studies*, 54 (1995), pp. 15–32.

Lecker, Michael, 'Did Muḥammad Conclude Treaties with the Jewish Tribes Naḍīr, Qurayẓa and Qaynuqāʿ?', in Uri Rubin, and David J. Wasserstein (eds) *Israel Oriental Studies XVII: Dhimmis and Others: Jews and Christians and the World of Classical Islam* (Tel-Aviv: Eisenbrauns, 1997).

Lecker, Michael, 'Zayd B. Thābit, "A Jew with Two Sidelocks": Judaism and Literacy in Pre-Islamic Medina (Yathrib)', *Journal of Near Eastern Studies*, 56/4 (1997), pp. 259–73.

Lecker, Michael, 'The Levying of Taxes for the Sassanians in Pre-Islamic Medina (Yathrib)', *Jerusalem Studies in Arabic and Islam*, 27 (2002), pp. 109–26.

Lecker, Michael, 'King Ibn Ubayy and the Quṣṣāṣ', in Herbert Berg (ed.), *Methods and Theories in the Study of Islamic Origins* (Leiden: Brill, 2003), pp. 29–71.

Lecker, Michael, *The 'Constitution of Medina' Muḥammad's First Legal Document* (Princeton: The Darwin Press, 2004).

Lecker, Michael, *People, Tribes and Society in Arabia around the Time of Muḥammad* (Aldershot: Ashgate, 2005).

Lecker, Michael, 'Glimpses of Muḥammad's Medinan Decade', in Jonathan E. Brockopp (ed.), *The Cambridge Companion to Muḥammad* (Cambridge: Cambridge University Press, 2010).

Lecker, Michael, 'On the Markets of Medina (Yathrib) in Pre-Islamic and Early Islamic Times', in Amer al-Roubaie, and Shafiq Alvi (eds), *Islamic Banking and Finance: Critical Concepts in Economics* (London: Routledge, 2010), pp. 185–96.

Liebesny, Herbert J., *The Law of the Near and Middle East: Readings, Cases and Materials* (Albany: State University of New York Press, 1975).

Lizzini, Olga, 'Ibn Sina's Metaphysics', in Edward N. Zalta (ed.), *The Stanford Encyclopedia of Philosophy* (Fall 2016 Edition), <https://plato.stanford.edu/archives/fall2016/entries/ibn-sina-metaphysics/>.

Locate, Samia, *Makkan and Madinan Revelations: A Comparative Study* (München: Lincom, 2009).

Lowry, Joseph E., 'Early Islamic Exegesis as Legal Theory: How Qur'ānic Wisdom (*Ḥikma*) Became the Sunna of the Prophet', in Natalie B. Dohrmann, and David Stern (eds), *Jewish Biblical Interpretation and Cultural Exchange: Comparative Exegesis in Context* (Philadelphia: University of Pennsylvania Press, 2013), pp. 139–60.

Lüling, Günter, *Über den Ur-Qur'an: Ansätze zur Rekonstruktion vorislamischer christlicher Strophenlieder im Qur'an* (Erlangen: Lüling, 1974).

Lüling, Günter, *A Challenge to Islam for Reformation: The Rediscovery and Reliable Reconstruction of a Comprehensive Pre-Islamic Christian Hymnal Hidden in the Koran under Earliest Islamic Reinterpretations* (New Delhi: Motilal Banarsidass Publishers 2003).

Lumbard, Joseph E. B., 'Covenant and Covenants in the Qur'an', *Journal of Qur'anic Studies*, 17/2 (2015), pp. 1–23.

Luxenberg, Christoph, *Die Syro-Aramäische Lesart des Koran: Ein Beitrag zur Entschlüsselung der Koransprache* (Berlin: Verlag Hans Schiler, 2000).

McGinnis, Jon, 'Arabic and Islamic Natural Philosophy and Natural Science', in Edward N. Zalta (ed.), *The Stanford Encyclopedia of Philosophy* (Fall 2015 Edition), <https://plato.stanford.edu/archives/fall2015/entries/arabic-islamic-natural/>.

MacIntyre, Alasdair, *Whose Justice? Which Rationality?* (London: Duckworth, 1988).

MacIntyre, Alasdair, 'A Partial Response to My Critics', in John P. Horton, and Susan Mendus (eds), *After MacIntyre: Critical Perspectives on the Work of Alasdair MacIntyre* (Notre Dame: University of Notre Dame Press, 1994), pp. 283–303.

MacIntyre, Alasdair, *The Tasks of Philosophy* (Cambridge: Cambridge University Press, 2006).

MacIntyre, Alasdair, *After Virtue: A Study in Moral Theory*, 3rd edn (Notre Dame: University of Notre Dame Press, 2007).

Madelung, Wilferd, *The Succession to Muḥammad: A Study of the Early Caliphate* (Cambridge: Cambridge University Press, 1997).

Madelung, Wilferd, 'al-Māturīdī', in P. Bearman, Th. Bianquis, C. E. Bosworth, E. Van Donzel, and W. P. Heinrichs (eds), *The Encyclopaedia of Islam, New Edition*, 12 vols (Leiden: Brill, 1986–2004).

Madigan, Daniel A., *The Qur'ān's Self-Image: Writing and Authority in Islam's Scripture* (Princeton: Princeton University Press, 2001).

Maḥmūd, Muḥammad Aḥmad, *Dirāsāt fī al-tafsīr al-mawḍūʿī* (Cairo: Jāmiʿat al-Azhar, 2004).

Maḥmūd, ʿAbd Al-Ḥalīm, *Fatāwā* (Cairo: Dār al-Maʿārif, 1979).

Maine, Henry Sumner, *Ancient Law: Its Connection with the Early History of Society and its Relation to Modern Ideas* (London: John Murray, 1908).

Mair, Lucy, *Primitive Government* (London: Penguin Books, 1966).

Al-Matroudi, ʿAbd al-Ḥakīm, '*Al-Qarīna wa-l-ḥīla fī sūrah Yūsuf*', *Journal of Qur'anic Studies*, 9/1 (2007), pp. 199–235.

Meeker, Michael E., *Literature and Violence in North Arabia* (Cambridge: Cambridge University Press, 1979).

Al-Mehri, A. B. (ed.), *The Qur'ān with Sūrah Introductions and Appendices: Saheeh International Translation* (Birmingham: Maktabah Booksellers and Publishers, 2010).

Miller, Caleb, 'Realism, Antirealism, and Common Sense', in William P. Alston (ed.), *Realism & Antirealism* (Ithaca: Cornell University Press, 2002), pp. 13–25.

Milton, John, *Paradise Lost* (Oxford: Oxford University Press, 2004).

Mir, Mustansir, *Coherence in the Qur'an: A Study of Islahi's Concept of Nazm in Tadabbur-I Qur'an* (Indianapolis: American Trust Publications, 1986).

Mir, Mustansir, 'The Sūra as a Unity: A Twentieth Century Development in Qur'ān Exegesis', in G. R. Hawting, and Abdul-Kader A. Shareef (eds), *Approaches to the Qur'an* (London: Routledge, 1993), pp. 211–24.

Mir, Mustansir, *Understanding the Islamic Scripture: A Study of Selected Passages from the Qur'ān* (New York; London: Pearson Longman, 2008).

Al-Misrī, Aḥmad b. Naqīb, *Reliance of the Traveller: A Classical Manual of Islamic Sacred Law*, trans. Nuh Ha Mim Keller (Beltsville, MD: Amana Publications, 1994).

Motzki, Harald, 'Introduction', in Harald Motzki (ed.), *The Biography of Muḥammad: The Issue of the Sources* (Leiden: Brill, 2000), pp. xi–xvi.

Motzki, Harald, 'The Murder of Ibn Abī l-Huqayq', in Harald Motzki (ed.), *The Biography of Muḥammad: The Issue of the Sources* (Leiden: Brill, 2000).

Motzki, Harald, 'The Question of the Authenticity of Muslim Traditions Reconsidered: A Review Article', in Herbert Berg (ed.), *Method and Theory in the Study of Islamic Origins* (Leiden: Brill, 2003), pp. 170–239.

Motzki, Harald, 'Dating Muslim Traditions: A Survey', *Arabica*, 52/2 (2005), pp. 204–53.

Motzki, Harald, '*Al-Radd ʿalā l-Radd*: Concerning the Method of *Ḥadīth* Analysis', in Harald Motzki, Nicolet Boekhoff-van der Voort, and Sean W. Anthony (eds), *Analysing Muslim Traditions: Studies in Legal, Exegetical and* Maghāzī Ḥadīth (Leiden: Brill, 2009), pp. 209–29.

Motzki, Harald, 'The Origins of Muslim Exegesis. A Debate', in Harald Motzki, Nicolet Boekhoff-van der Voort, and Sean W. Anthony (eds), *Analysing Muslim Traditions: Studies in Legal, Exegetical and* Maghāzī Ḥadīth (Leiden: Brill, 2009), pp. 231–303.

Motzki, Harald, 'Whither *Ḥadīth* Studies?', in Harald Motzki, Nicolet Boekhoff-van der Voort, and Sean W. Anthony (eds), *Analysing Muslim Traditions: Studies in Legal, Exegetical and* Maghāzī Ḥadīth (Leiden: Brill, 2009), pp. 47–124.

Munt, Harry, *The Holy City of Medina: Sacred Space in Early Islamic Arabia* (Cambridge: Cambridge University Press, 2014).

Munt, Harry, '"No Two Religions": Non-Muslims in the Early Islamic Ḥijāz', *Bulletin of the School of Oriental and African Studies*, 78/2 (2015), pp. 249–69.

Nader, A. N., 'al-Balkhī', in P. Bearman, Th. Bianquis, C. E. Bosworth, E. Van Donzel, and W. P. Heinrichs (eds), *The Encyclopaedia of Islam, New Edition*, 12 vols (Leiden: Brill, 1986–2004).

Na'im, Abdullahi Ahmed, *Toward an Islamic Reformation: Civil Liberties, Human Rights, and International Law* (New York: Syracuse University Press, 1990).

Nasr, Seyyed Hossein, *Religion and the Order of Nature* (Oxford: Oxford University Press, 1996).

Nebes, Norbert, 'The Martyrs of Najrān and the End of the Ḥimyar: On the Political History of South Arabia in the Early Sixth Century', in Nicolai Sinai, Angelika Neuwirth, and Michael Marx (eds), *The Qur'ān in Context* (Leiden: Brill, 2010), pp. 27–59.

Neusner, Jacob, 'Midrash and the Oral Torah: What Did the Rabbinic Sages Mean by "the Oral Torah"?', in Jacob Neusner, Alan J. Avery-Peck, and William Scott Green (eds), *The Encyclopaedia of Judaism, Second Edition*, 4 vols (Leiden: Brill, 2005).

Neuwirth, Angelika, 'Structure and the Emergence of Community', in Andrew Rippin (ed.), *The Blackwell Companion to the Qur'an* (Oxford: Blackwell, 2005), pp. 140–58.

Neuwirth, Angelika, *Scripture, Poetry and the Making of Community: Reading the Qur'an as a Literary Text* (Oxford: Oxford University Press, in association with the Institute of Ismaili Studies, 2014).

Newby, Gordon Darnell, *A History of the Jews of Arabia: From Ancient Times to their Eclipse under Islam* (Columbia, SC: University of South Carolina Press, 1988).

Nicholson, Reynold A., *A Literary History of the Arabs* (London: T. Fisher Unwin, 1907).

Nöldeke, Theodor, *Geschichte des Qorāns*, ed. Friedrich Schwally, 2nd edn, 2 vols (Leipzig: Dieterich'sche Verlagsbuchhandlung, 1909).

Nuʿmānī, Shiblī, *Sīrat al-nabī*, trans. Fazlur Rahman, vol. 1 (Karachi: Pakistan Historical Society, 1970).

Nyazee, Imran Ahsan Khan, *Islamic Jurisprudence* (Islamabad: International Institute of Islamic Thought, 2000).

O'Shaughnessy, Thomas J., 'Creation with Wisdom and with the Word in the Qur'ān', *Journal of the American Oriental Society*, 91/2 (1971), pp. 208–21.

Owens, Jonathan (ed.), *The Oxford Handbook of Arabic Linguistics* (Oxford: Oxford University Press, 2013).

Pangle, Thomas L., and Timothy W. Burns, *The Key Texts of Political Philosophy: An Introduction* (Cambridge: Cambridge University Press, 2015).

Pavlovitch, Pavel, *The Formation of the Islamic Understanding of* Kalāla *in the Second Century AH (718–816 CE)* (Leiden: Brill, 2016).

Pessagno, J. Meric, 'The Uses of Evil in Maturidian Thought', *Studia Islamica*, 60 (1984), pp. 59–82.

Petráček, K., 'Durayd b. al-Ṣimma', in P. Bearman, Th. Bianquis, C. E. Bosworth, E. Van Donzel, and W. P. Heinrichs (eds), *The Encyclopaedia of Islam, New Edition*, 12 vols (Leiden: Brill, 1986–2004).

Powers, David S., *The Formation of the Islamic Law of Inheritance* (Princeton: Princeton University Press, 1979).

Powers, David S., 'On the Abrogation of the Bequest Verses', *Arabica*, 29/3 (1982), pp. 246–95.

Powers, David S., 'The Exegetical Genre *nāsikh al-Qur'ān wa mansūkhuhu*', in Andrew Rippin (ed.), *Approaches to the History of the Interpretation of the Qur'an* (Oxford: Oxford University Press, 1988).

Powers, David S., *Muḥammad is Not the Father of Any of Your Men* (Philadelphia: University of Pennsylvania Press, 2009).

Qadhi, Yasir, *An Introduction to the Sciences of the Qur'aan* (Birmingham: Al-Hidaayah Publishers, 1999).
Al-Qāḍī, Wadād, 'The Term "Khalīfa" in Early Exegetical Literature', *Die Welt des Islams*, 28/1 (1988), pp. 392–411.
Al-Qāḍī, Wadād, 'The Primordial Covenant and Human History in the Qur'ān', *Proceedings of the American Philosophical Society*, 147/4 (2003), pp. 332–8.
Al-Qaraḍāwī, Yūsuf, *Fiqh al-zakāt*, 2 vols (Damascus: Muʾassasat al-Risāla, 1973).
Al-Qaraḍāwī, Yūsuf, *Fiqh al-jihād*, 2 vols (Cairo: Maktaba Wahba, 2009).
Qaṭṭān, Mannāʿ, *Mabāḥith fī 'ulūm al-qur'ān* (Manshūrāt al-ʿAṣr al-Ḥadīth, 1971).
Quṭb, Sayyid, *Fī ẓilāl al-qurʾān*, 6 vols (Cairo: Dār al-Shurūq, 1992).
Quṭb, Sayyid, *Social Justice in Islam*, trans John B. Hardine, and Hamid Algar (Oneonta, NY: Islamic Publications International, 2000).
Rahbar, Daud, *God of Justice: A Study in the Ethical Doctrine of the Qur'an* (Leiden: Brill, 1960).
Rahman, Fazlur, 'Riba and Interest', *Islamic Studies*, 3/1 (1964), pp. 1–43.
Rahman, Fazlur, 'The Concept of Ḥadd in Islamic Law', *Islamic Studies*, 4/3 (1965), pp. 237–51.
Rahman, Fazlur, *Islam and Modernity: Transformation of an Intellectual Tradition* (Chicago: The University of Chicago Press, 1984).
Rahman, Fazlur, *Major Themes of the Qur'an* (Minneapolis: Bibliotheca Islamica, 1989).
Ramadan, Tariq, *Radical Reform: Islamic Ethics and Liberation* (Oxford: Oxford University Press, 2009).
Al-Raysūnī, Aḥmad, *Imām Al-Shāṭibī's Theory of the Higher Objectives and Intents of Islamic Law*, trans. Nancy Roberts (London: International Institute of Islamic Thought, 2005).
Reinhart, A. Kevin, 'Islamic Law as Islamic Ethics', *The Journal of Religious Ethics*, 11/2 (1983), pp. 186–203.
Reinhart, A. Kevin, *Before Revelation: The Boundaries of Muslim Moral Thought* (Albany: State University of New York Press, 1995).
Reinhart, A. Kevin, '"Like the Difference between Heaven and Earth:" Ḥanafī and Shāfiʿī Discussions of *Farḍ* and *Wājib* in Theology and Uṣūl', in Bernard G. Weiss (ed.), *Studies in Islamic Legal Theory* (Leiden: Brill, 2002), pp. 205–34.
Reinhart, A. Kevin, 'Jurisprudence', in Andrew Rippin (ed.), *The Blackwell Companion to the Qur'an* (Oxford: Blackwell, 2005), pp. 434–49.
Reinhart, A. Kevin, 'Ethics and the Qurʾān', in Jane Dammen McAuliffe (ed.), *Encyclopaedia of the Qurʾān*, 6 vols (Leiden: Brill, 2001–6).
Reinhart, A. Kevin, 'Juynbolliana, Gradualism, the Big Bang, and *Ḥadīth* Study in the Twenty-First Century', *Journal of the American Oriental Society*, 130/3 (2010), pp. 413–44.
Retsö, Jan, *The Arabs in Antiquity: Their History from the Assyrians to the Umayyads* (London: RoutledgeCurzon, 2002).

Riḍā, Muḥammad Rashīd, *Tafsīr al-manār*, 12 vols (Cairo: Dār al-Manār, 1948).

Rippin, A., 'Al-Zarkashī and al-Suyūṭī on the "Occasion of Revelation" Material', *Islamic Culture*, 59 (1985), pp. 243–58.

Rippin, A., 'The Exegetical Genre *asbāb al-nuzūl*: A Bibliographical and Terminological Survey', *Bulletin of the School of Oriental and African Studies*, 48 (1985), pp. 1–15.

Rippin, A., 'The Function of *asbāb al-nuzūl* in Qurʾānic Exegesis', *Bulletin of the School of Oriental and African Studies*, 51 (1988), pp. 1–20.

Robinson, Neal, *Discovering the Qur'an: A Contemporary Approach to a Veiled Text* (London: SCM Press, 1996).

Rosen, Lawrence, *The Justice of Islam* (Oxford: Oxford University Press, 2000).

Rosenthal, Erwin I. J., *Political Thought in Medieval Islam: An Introductory Outline* (Cambridge: Cambridge University Press, 1985).

Rosenthal, Franz, *Knowledge Triumphant* (Leiden: Brill, 1970).

Rubin, Uri, *The Eye of the Beholder: The Life of Muḥammad as Viewed by the Early Muslims* (Princeton: Darwin Press, 1997).

Rudolph, Ulrich, *Al-Māturīdī and the Development of Sunnī Theology in Samarqand*, trans. Rodrigo Adem (Leiden: Brill, 2015).

Al-Ṣabbāḥ, Ṣubḥī, *Mabāḥith fī uṣūl al-qurʾān* (Beirut: Dār al-ʿIlm li-l-Malāyīn, 1964).

Sadeghi, Behnam, 'The Chronology of the Qurʾān: A Stylometric Research Program', *Arabica*, 58 (2011), pp. 210–99.

Sadeghi, Behnam and Uwe Bergmann, 'The Codex of a Companion of the Prophet and the Qurʾān of the Prophet', *Arabica*, 57 (2010), pp. 343–436.

Saeed, Abdullah, *Interpreting the Qur'an: Towards a Contemporary Approach* (New York: Routledge, 2005).

Saeed, Abdullah, 'Fazlur Rahman: A Framework for Interpreting the Ethico-Legal Content of the Qur'an', in Suha Taji-Farouki (ed.), *Modern Muslim Intellectuals and the Qur'an* (Oxford: Oxford University Press, 2006), pp. 37–66.

Saleh, Walid A., 'The Etymological Fallacy and Qur'anic Studies: Muḥammad, Paradise and Late Antiquity', in Nicolai Sinai, Angelika Neuwirth, and Michael Marx (eds), *The Qur'ān in Context* (Leiden: Brill, 2010), pp. 649–98.

Saleh, Walid A., and Kevin Casey, 'An Islamic Diatessaron: Al-Biqāʿī's Harmony of the Four Gospels', in Sara Binay, and Stefan Leder (eds), *Translating the Bible into Arabic: Historical, Text-Critical, and Literary Aspects* (Würzburg: Ergon, 2012), pp. 85–116.

Schaffer, Jonathan, 'The Individuation of Tropes', *Australasian Journal of Philosophy*, 79/2 (2001), pp. 247–57.

Scherman, N. (ed.), *Tanach: The Stone Edition* (New York: Mesorah Publications, 1996).

Schleiermacher, Friedrich, *Hermeneutics and Criticism: And Other Writings*, trans. and ed. Andrew Bowie (Cambridge: Cambridge University Press, 1998).

Schöck, Cornelia, 'Jahm b. Ṣafwān (d. 128/745–6) and the "Jahmiyya" and Ḍirār b. ʿAmr (d. 200/815)', in Sabine Schmidtke (ed.), *The Oxford Handbook of Islamic Theology* (Oxford: Oxford University Press, 2016), pp. 55–80.

Schoeler, Gregor, *The Oral and Written in Early Islam*, trans. Uwe Vagelpohl, ed. James E. Montgomery (London: Routledge, 2006).

Schoeler, Gregor. *The Biography of Muḥammad: Nature and Authenticity*, trans. Uwe Vagelpohl (London: Routledge, 2011).

Serjeant, R. B., 'Meccan Trade and the Rise of Islam: Misconceptions and Flawed Polemics', *Journal of the American Oriental Society*, 110/3 (1990), pp. 472–86.

Shāh Walī Allāh al-Dahlawī, *The Conclusive Argument from God: Shah Walī Allāh of Delhi's Ḥujjat Allāh Al-Bāligha*, trans. Marcia K. Hermansen (Leiden: Brill, 1996).

Shahid, Irfan, 'Ghassān', in P. Bearman, Th. Bianquis, C. E. Bosworth, E. Van Donzel, and W. P. Heinrichs (eds), *The Encyclopaedia of Islam, New Edition*, 12 vols (Leiden: Brill, 1986–2004).

Shahid, Irfan, 'Lakhmids', in P. Bearman, Th. Bianquis, C. E. Bosworth, E. Van Donzel, and W. P. Heinrichs (eds), *The Encyclopaedia of Islam, New Edition*, 12 vols (Leiden: Brill, 1986–2004).

Shahid, Irfan, 'ʿUkāẓ', in P. Bearman, Th. Bianquis, C. E. Bosworth, E. Van Donzel, and W. P. Heinrichs (eds), *The Encyclopaedia of Islam, New Edition*, 12 vols (Leiden: Brill, 1986–2004).

Shahid, Irfan, *Byzantium and the Arabs in the Fifth Century* (Washington, DC: Dumbarton Oaks Research Library and Collection, 1989).

Al-Shamma, S. H., *The Ethical System Underlying the Qur'an: A Study of Certain Negative and Positive Notions* (Tübingen: Hopfer Verlag, 1959).

Shehaby, Nabil, 'ʿIlla and Qiyās in Early Islamic Law', *Journal of the American Oriental Society*, 102/1 (1982), pp. 27–46.

Sherif, Mohamed Ahmed, *Ghazali's Theory of Virtue* (Albany: State University of New York Press, 1975).

Shihadeh, Ayman, *The Teleological Ethics of Fakhr al-Dīn al-Rāzī* (Leiden: Brill, 2006).

Shihadeh, Ayman, 'Theories of Ethical Value in Kalām: A New Interpretation', in Sabine Schmidtke (ed.), *The Oxford Handbook of Islamic Theology* (Oxford: Oxford University Press, 2016), pp. 384–407.

Al-Shinqīṭī, Muḥammad al-Amīn, *Aḍwāʾ al-bayān fī īḍāḥ al-qurʾān bi-l-qurʾān* (Beirut: Dār al-Kutub al-ʿIlmiyya, 2006).

Al-Sibāʿī, Muṣṭafā, *Al-Sunna wa-makānatuhā fī tashrīʿ al-islāmī* (Cairo: Dār al-Warrāq, 1949).

Sinai, Nicolai, 'When Did the Consonantal Skeleton of the Qur'an Reach Closure? Part I', *Bulletin of the School of Oriental and African Studies,* 77/2 (2014), pp. 273–92.

Sinai, Nicolai, 'When Did the Consonantal Skeleton of the Qur'an Reach Closure? Part II', *Bulletin of the School of Oriental and African Studies,* 77/3 (2014), pp. 509–21.

Sinai, Nicolai, and Angelika Neuwirth, 'Introduction', in Nicolai Sinai, Angelika Neuwirth, and Michael Marx (eds), *The Qur'ān in Context* (Leiden: Brill, 2010), pp. 1–24.

Smirnov, A., 'Understanding Justice in an Islamic Context: Some Points of Contrast with Western Theories', *Philosophy East and West*, 46/3 (1996), pp. 337–50.

Smith, William Cantwell, 'The True Meaning of Scripture: An Empirical Historian's Nonreductionist Interpretation of the Qur'an', *International Journal of Middle East Studies*, 11/4 (1980), pp. 487–505.

Sorabji, Richard, *Matter, Space and Motion: Theories in Antiquity and their Sequel* (London: Duckworth, 1988).

Sosevsky, Moshe Ch., *Samuel II: A New English Translation of the Text and Rashi, with a Commentary Digest* (New York: The Judaica Press, 1981).

Stefanidis, Emmanuelle, 'The Qur'an Made Linear: A Study of the *Geschichte des Qorāns*' Chronological Reordering', *Journal of Qur'anic Studies*, 10/2 (2008), pp. 1–22.

Stenton, F. M., *Anglo-Saxon England* (Oxford: Oxford University Press, 1997).

Stetkevych, Suzanne Pinckney, *The Poetics of Islamic Legitimacy: Myth, Gender and Ceremony in the Classical Arabic Ode* (Bloomington: Indiana University Press, 2002).

Stevenson, Angus (ed.), *Shorter Oxford English Dictionary*, 2 vols (Oxford: Oxford University Press, 2007).

Surty, Muḥammad Ibrahim H. I., *Studies on the Islamic Judicial System* (Birmingham: QAF Qur'ānic Arabic Foundation, 2012).

Taylor, Charles, 'Justice after Virtue', in John P. Horton, and Susan Mendus (eds), *After MacIntyre: Critical Perspectives on the Work of Alasdair MacIntyre* (Notre Dame: University of Notre Dame Press, 1994).

Thiele, Jan, 'Abū Hāshim al-Jubbāʾī's (d. 321/933) Theory of "States" (aḥwāl) and its Adaption by Ashʿarite Theologians', in Sabine Schmidtke (ed.), *The Oxford Handbook of Islamic Theology* (Oxford: Oxford University Press, 2016), pp. 364–83.

Torchia, N. Joseph, Creatio ex nihilo *and the Theology of St. Augustine* (New York: Peter Lang, 1999).

Usmani, Muḥammad Taqi, *The Historic Judgement on Interest* (Karachi: Maktaba Maʿariful Qurʾan, 2007).

Vajda, G., 'ʿAmālīḳ', in P. Bearman, Th. Bianquis, C. E. Bosworth, E. Van Donzel, and W. P. Heinrichs (eds), *The Encyclopaedia of Islam, New Edition*, 12 vols (Leiden: Brill, 1986–2004).

van Roojen, Mark, 'Moral Cognitivism vs. Non-Cognitivism', in Edward N. Zalta (ed.), *The Stanford Encyclopedia of Philosophy* (Winter 2016 Edition), <https://plato.stanford.edu/archives/win2016/entries/moral-cognitivism/>.

Vasalou, Sophia, *Moral Agents and their Deserts: The Character of Muʿtazilite Ethics* (Princeton: Princeton University Press, 2008).
Vasalou, Sophia, *Ibn Taymiyya's Theological Ethics* (Oxford: Oxford University Press, 2016).
Vishanoff, David R., *The Formation of Islamic Hermeneutics: How Sunni Legal Theorists Imagined a Revealed Law* (New Haven: American Oriental Society, 2011).
Wadud, Amina, *Qur'an and Woman: Rereading the Sacred Text from a Woman's Perspective* (Oxford: Oxford University Press, 1999).
Al-Wāḥidī, ʿAlī b. Aḥmad, *Reasons & Occasions of the Revelation of the Holy Quran*, trans. Adnan Salloum (Beirut: Dār al-Kutub al-ʿIlmiyya, 2004).
Wansbrough, John, 'Res Ipsa Loquitur: History and Mimesis', in Herbert Berg (ed.), *Method and Theory in the Study of Islamic Origins* (Leiden: Brill, 2003), pp. 3–19.
Wansbrough, John, *Quranic Studies: Sources and Methods of Scriptural Interpretation*, ed. Andrew Rippin (New York: Prometheus Books, 2004).
Ward, Keith, *Religion and Creation* (Oxford: Oxford University Press, 1996).
Watt, W. Montgomery, *Muḥammad at Mecca* (Oxford: Clarendon Press, 1953).
Watt, W. Montgomery, *Muḥammad at Medina* (Oxford: Clarendon Press, 1956).
Watt, W. Montgomery, 'Hawāzin', in P. Bearman, Th. Bianquis, C. E. Bosworth, E. Van Donzel, and W. P. Heinrichs (eds), *The Encyclopaedia of Islam, New Edition*, 12 vols (Leiden: Brill, 1986–2004).
Watt, W. Montgomery, 'Kaʿb b. Ashraf', in P. Bearman, Th. Bianquis, C. E. Bosworth, E. Van Donzel, and W. P. Heinrichs (eds), *The Encyclopaedia of Islam, New Edition*, 12 vols (Leiden: Brill, 1986–2004).
Weiss, Bernard G., *The Search for God's Law: Islamic Jurisprudence in the Writings of Sayf al-Dīn al-Āmidī* (Salt Lake City: University of Utah Press, 1992).
Wildberg, Christian, 'John Philoponus', in Edward N. Zalta (ed.), *The Stanford Encyclopedia of Philosophy* (Spring 2016 Edition), <https://plato.stanford.edu/archives/spr2016/entries/philoponus/>.
Winter, Tim, 'The Last Trump Card: Islam and the Supersession of Other Faiths', *Studies in Interreligious Dialogue*, 9/2 (1999), pp. 133–55.
Wirtzum, Joseph, 'Q 4:24 Revisited', *Islamic Law and Society*, 16/1 (2009), pp. 1–33.
Wolf, Eric R., 'The Social Organization of Mecca and the Origins of Islam', *Southwestern Journal of Anthropology*, 7/4 (1951), pp. 329–56.
Wolterstorff, Nicholas, *Justice: Rights and Wrongs* (Princeton: Princeton University Press, 2010).
Zahniser, A. H. Mathias, 'Major Transitions and Thematic Borders in Two Long Sūras: Al-Baqara and Al-Nisāʾ', in Issa J. Boullata (ed.), *Literary Structures of Religious Meaning in the Qur'an* (Richmond: Curzon, 2000), pp. 26–55.
Zalaṭ, Al-Qaṣṣabī, *Mabāḥith fī ʿulūm al-qur'ān* (Cairo: Dār al-Qalam, 1987).
Zalaṭ, Al-Qaṣṣabī, *Tafsīr āyāt al-aḥkām*, 4 vols (Cairo: Dār al-Qalam, 1987).

Zaman, Muhammad Qasim, *Modern Islamic Thought in a Radical Age: Religious Authority and Internal Criticism* (Cambridge: Cambridge University Press, 2012).

Zaydān, Ṣalāḥ, *Al-Ḥukm al-sharʿī al-taklīfī* (Cairo: Dār al-Ṣaḥwa li-l-Nashr wa-l-Tawzīʿ, 1998).

Zebiri, Katherine Patricia, *Maḥmūd Shaltūt and Islamic Modernism* (Oxford: Clarendon Press, 1993).

Zellentin, Holger, *The Qur'an's Legal Culture* (Tübingen: Mohr Siebeck, 2013).

Al-Zuhaylī, Wahba, *Uṣūl al-fiqh al-islāmī*, 2 vols (Damascus: Dār al-Fikr, 1986).

Al-Zuhaylī, Wahba, 'The Juridical Meaning of Riba', in Abdulkader S. Thomas (ed.), *Interest in Islamic Economics: Understanding Riba* (London: Routledge, 2010), pp. 26–54.

Al-Zurqānī, Muḥammad, *Manāhil al-ʿirfān fī ʿulūm al-qurʾān*, 2 vols (Cairo: ʿĪsa al-Bābī al-Ḥalabī wa-Sharakāhu, 1954).

Zysow, Aron, 'Muʿtazilism and Māturīdism in Ḥanafī Legal Theory', in Bernard G. Weiss (ed.), *Studies in Islamic Legal Theory* (Leiden: Brill, 2002), pp. 233–65.

Zysow, Aron, *The Economy of Certainty: An Introduction to the Typology of Islamic Legal Theory* (Atlanta: Lockwood Press, 2013).

Index of Qur'anic Verses

Index of Biblical Verses

General Index

Black, Antony, 210n2
Blackburn, S., 219n1
blinding, 179
Blois, François de, 214n12
blood feuds, 77; *see also* retaliation
blood money (*diya*), 77, 173–4, 175, 176
bondage, those in (*fī al-riqāb*), 134, 136, 137–40; *see also* bondswomen; captives; indentured slaves; slavery
bondswomen (*mā malakat aymānukum*),74, 139–40, 144–5, 163, 187; *see also* indentured slaves; slavery
Bonner, Michael, 72, 219n23
booty, 110, 134–5
Bosworth, C. E., 208n42
Boullata, I. J., 197n49
Bowersock, G. W., 207n7, 208n48, 209n67
Bravmann, M. M., 210n130
bribery, 124
brigandage (*ḥirāba*), 77, 174, 178–80, 182, 217n14
brotherhood, 16, 148, 161
Brown, Jonathan, 55, 58, 150, 205n76–7, 206n82, 221n71, 224n21
Brunschvig, R., 209n99
Buʿāth, Battle of, 69
Buchholz, Stephan, 220n5
al-Bukhārī, Muḥammad b. Ismāʿīl, 56, 57, 116, 161, 179, 196n10, 202n112, 206n113, 206n116, 207n130, 208n23, 209n75, 209n77–8, 209n92, 209n96–8, 210n105, 212n53, 212n57, 213n6, 215n11, 215n15, 215n19, 215n26, 215n28, 216n53, 216n57, 216n59, 218n59, 218n19, 219n29, 220n20, 220n23, 221n63–4, 221n73, 222n10–11, 222n18–19, 223n35, 223n38, 224n24, 225n5, 225n7, 225n36
Bukharin, Mikhail D., 208n53, 214n14
bundle theory, 34
Burrell, David, 197n36
al-Būṭī, Muḥammad Saʿīd Ramaḍan, 214n27, 224n45, 224n1
Byzantine empire, 65, 66, 70, 71, 216n42

Cain, 174–5
Calder, Norman, 206n96
camels, 65, 66, 70, 77, 179
capital punishment, 78, 109–10, 172–6, 178, 179
captives, 133, 134, 145
Casey, Kevin, 206n97
causation, 34, 41, 59–62, 174
cause (*sabab*), 41, 59–61, 95
Cerić, Mustafa, 199n14, 200n44, 200n57, 201n61, 202n119
chains of authority (*isnāds*), 53–8, 61, 64
charity *see* alms
chaste women (*muḥṣināt*), 187, 188–90
chastity, 138, 140, 143, 144–5, 147, 182, 187, 188–90
Chaudhry, Ayesha S., 220n32, 221n67, 221n71, 221n74
child-killing, 181
child-rearing *see* parenting
Children of Adam, 10–11
Children of Israel, 15, 48, 81, 85–94, 100, 133, 174, 179; *see also* Jews
chivalric virtue (*murūʾa*), 75, 132
Choudhury, M. A., 218n57
Christians, 27, 100–1, 103, 104, 113, 115, 116, 174; *see also* Bible; Scriptuaries
Cilardo, Agostino, 223n42
clans (*ʿashīra*), 65
clients (*mawālī*), 65
collective punishment, 109–10, 179
community (*umma*), 16, 84, 192
compensation, 77, 134, 137, 139, 171–2, 173–4, 177, 185, 193
compensatory divorce (*khulʿa*), 149, 150, 155
concubines, 144–5; *see also* bondswomen
Conquest of Mecca, 68, 95, 104, 105–6, 130, 181
conjunction (*waṣl*), 49, 50
consultation (*shūrā*), 92
contextual semantics (*ʿilm al-maʿānī*), 48, 49
continuous mass transmission (*tawātur*), 54, 61
contracts, 125–7, 143–6
contrary implicature (*mafhūm al-mukhālafa*), 62
Cornell, Vincent J., 218n58
corrective justice, 43, 74–8, 169–90, 191, 193
corruption (*fasād*), 9, 20, 84–5, 89, 123–4, 129, 13, 161, 175
council of chiefs (*malaʾ*), 66, 86, 89
covenant *see* primordial covenant (*mīthāq*), 10–13
Covenant of Medina, 102–4, 109
crafts, 70, 72–3
Cragg, Kenneth, 197n52, 205n57
creation, 27–35
  from existing material (*takhlīq*), 30
creativity, *ex nihilo* (*takwīn*), 27–30, 33
crimes
  accidental killing, 177
  aggression (*baghy*), 178, 182
  alcohol, drinking of (*sharb*), 40, 182
  apostasy, 40, 179, 182
  bribery, 124
  brigandage (*ḥirāba*), 77, 174, 178–80, 182
  child-killing, 181
  fornication (*zinā*), 40, 78, 126, 128, 181, 185–90
  idolatry, 76, 96, 105, 110–11
  lewd acts (*fāḥisha*), 155, 156, 185–6
  murder (*qatl*), 40, 76–7, 104, 172–7, 179, 181, 182
  private crimes (*ḥudūd*), 177, 181–90, 193
  prostitution, 140
  public crimes, 171–80, 193
  punishments for *see* punishment
  shirk (worship of another besides God), 20, 25
  slander (*qadhf*), 181, 188–90
  thievery (*sariqa*), 40, 77, 174, 179, 181, 182–5
  usury (*ribā*), 72, 121, 124, 125–6, 127–31, 193
  see also transgression; wrongdoing
Crone, Patricia, 138, 209n102–3, 211n14
Crowe, Michael Bertram, 200n29
crucifixion, 178, 179
customarily recognised (*maʿrūf*), 143–4, 155–6, 158
Cuypers, Michel, 138, 204n40, 223n16

al-Dabūsī, Abū Zayd, 203n137
Daiber, Hans, 197n34
Danby, Herbert, 224n22
Dār al-Nadwa, Mecca, 66, 76
David, Prophet 86–90, 93, 94
Dāwūd, Muḥammad, 20

qirā'āt (variant readings), 5, 53, 167–8
qiṣāṣ (retaliation), 76–7, 151, 168, 173–7, 182
qisṭ (societal justice), 3, 17, 19–22, 42–3, 103, 127, 185, 191–4
qiyāda (allowing mounts permission to travel), 66, 67–8, 71
qiyās (analogy), 60, 62
qiyās al-ghā'ib 'alā al-shāhid (the hidden is analogous to the manifest), 27–8
Queen of Sheba, 87, 92
Qur'an
 abrogation of (*naskh*), 41, 58–9, 102, 107, 145, 157, 166, 167, 183, 187, 194
 on alms, 132–41
 androcentrism of, 152–3
 on corrective justice, 169–90
 disciplines of (*'ulūm al-qur'ān*), 44, 48
 distinction between absolute meaning and human understanding, 3–4
 ethical structure of, 2–3, 194
 ethical theories about, 1–2
 exegesis *see tafsīr*
 extraction of *ḥikma*s, 44, 52, 61–3
 forms of address (*mukhāṭaba*), 48–9, 84, 95, 96, 111, 153, 174
 hermeneutic analysis, 44–63
 on inheritance, 159–68
 intra-textuality, 44, 45–6
 on legitimacy, 81–95
 on loyalty, 95–8
 manuscript sources, 53–4
 on marriage, 142–58
 Meccan verses, 84, 86–7, 90, 100–2, 121–4, 128–9, 131, 132–4, 143, 147–8, 159–60, 172–3, 178, 182, 185, 188, 193–4
 Medinan verses, 84, 86–7, 89–90, 95–7, 100–4, 108–13, 122, 124–5, 127, 129–31, 133–6, 149, 159–64, 172–3, 178, 181, 185–6, 188, 193–4
 non-linear nature of, 9
 occasions of revelation (*asbāb al-nuzūl*), 58, 59–61, 96, 130, 140, 149, 173
 on peace, 99–106
 on politics, 81–98
 polysemy (*wujūh al-qur'ān*), 46, 198n89
 prohibition of *ribā*, 127–31
 semantics, 44, 46–7
 socio-historical context, 44, 53–61
 'sura-as-a-unity' thesis, 51
 syntax-pragmatics (*naẓm*), 44, 47–50, 60, 62, 123, 150–2, 162, 173, 174
 textual structure (*niẓām*), 44, 50–2, 60–1, 84–5, 114, 125, 138, 149, 163, 174, 188
 on trade, 121–7
 translation of, 5
 variant readings of (*qirā'āt*), 5, 53, 167–8
 on war, 107–17
 see also Index of Qur'anic Verses
Quraysh tribe, 65–8, 70–2, 75–6, 86, 94–5, 100, 102, 105–6, 108, 109, 121–2
al-Qurṭubī, Muḥammad b. Aḥmad, 93, 126, 128–9, 157, 213n94, 213n100, 213n102, 213n107, 214n26, 214n42, 216n33, 216n35, 217n31, 217n34, 218n5, 219n29, 219n31, 220n42, 222n13, 223n37, 223n12–13, 225n3
Quṣayy b. Kilāb b. Murra, 65–6
al-Qushayrī, Abū Naṣr, 93
Quṭb, Sayyid, 51, 108, 198n100, 205n42, 216n2, 219n24, 222n1

Rahbar, Daud, 24
raḥma (mercy), 10, 13, 25, 30, 143, 193, 196n10; *see also* forgiveness
Rahman, Fazlur, 2, 3, 129, 217n44, 218n48, 225n6
al-Rā'ī, 134
raids (*ghazw*), 70, 72, 77; *see also* war
Ramadan, Tariq, 203n125, 203n151
Rashi, 88
rational theology (*kalām*), 26–38; *see also* theology
rationally grounded polities (*siyāsa 'aqliyya*), 82
al-Raysūnī, Aḥmad, 203n141, 203n143, 203n152
al-Rāzī, Fakhr al-Dīn, 29, 36, 47, 50, 88–9, 125, 126, 130, 140, 164, 196n22, 196n26, 198n79, 198n92, 211n15, 212n59, 212n67–70, 212n72, 215n25, 215n30, 216n4, 217n8, 217n40, 220n39, 222n14, 223n13, 224n33, 225n11
reason (*'aql*), 37–8, 40
recommended (*mandūb*) actions, 39
rectification (*iṣlāḥ*), 9, 89, 123–4, 161
Reinhart, A. Kevin, 15, 38, 196n30, 197n33, 201n69, 201n84–5, 202n89, 202n117, 202n123–5, 203n127, 203n129–31, 205n55, 205n60, 206n86, 207n128
relatives, 133, 135
religion (*dīn*), 11, 22, 40
religious freedom, 107, 108, 117, 192
religiously grounded polities (*siyāsa dīniyya*), 82
remarriage, 145, 146, 149, 153, 156, 157
repentance, 11, 13, 25, 91–2, 171, 177, 179–80, 182, 184–6, 188–9, 193
reputation, 147, 182, 188–9
restriction, grammatical (*qaṣr*), 49, 173, 183
retaliation (*qiṣāṣ*), 76–7, 151, 168, 173–7, 182
Retsö, Jan, 207n8
revelation, 13, 14–15, 17–19, 22–3, 36–8, 39, 83, 191; *see also* Qur'an
 occasions of (*asbāb al-nuzūl*), 58, 59–61, 96, 130, 140, 149, 173
revocation, of alliances or treaties (*barā'*), 104, 105, 107, 109–13
reward, 24–5, 35, 36
rhetoric (*balāgha*), 48
ribā (usury), 72, 121, 124, 125–6, 127–31, 193
 ribā al-faḍl (uneven exchange), 127–8
 ribā al-nasī'a (loan interest), 127
Riḍā, Rashīd, 130
rifāda (hosting with food), 66, 67
right (*ḥaqq*), 133, 173, 175, 177, 178, 180, 181–2
Rippin, Andrew, 60, 205n51, 206n106, 206n109–10
Robinson, Neal, 204n40
Rosen, Bernard, 201n82
Rosen, Lawrence, 128
Rosenthal, Irwin I. J., 210n3, 211n9
Rozenthal, Franz, 199n13